D0202718

SEPTEMBER 11 IN
POPULAR CULTURE

SEPTEMBER 11

— IN —

POPULAR CULTURE

A GUIDE

Sara E. Quay and Amy M. Damico, Editors

 GREENWOOD

AN IMPRINT OF ABC-CLIO, LLC
Santa Barbara, California • Denver, Colorado • Oxford, England

Library of Congress Cataloging-in-Publication Data

September 11 in popular culture : a guide / Sara E. Quay and Amy M. Damico, editors.
    p. cm.
  Includes bibliographical references and index.
    ISBN 978–0–313–35505–9 (hbk. : alk. paper) — ISBN 978–0–313–35506–6 (ebook)
1. September 11 Terrorist Attacks, 2001—Influence. 2. September 11 Terrorist Attacks, 2001, in mass media.
I. Quay, Sara E. II. Damico, Amy M.
HV6432.7.S455   2010
973.931—dc22   2010019889

ISBN: 978–0–313–35505–9
EISBN: 978–0–313–35506–6

14 13 12 11 10   1 2 3 4 5

This book is also available on the World Wide Web as an eBook.
Visit www.abc-clio.com for details.

Greenwood
An Imprint of ABC-CLIO, LLC

ABC-CLIO, LLC
130 Cremona Drive, P.O. Box 1911
Santa Barbara, California 93116-1911

This book is printed on acid-free paper ∞

Manufactured in the United States of America

FOR OUR STUDENTS

Contents

Photo Essay Follows Page 172

Acknowledgments

We could not have completed this work without the support of a number of people and organizations. Endicott College offered generous professional resources for our early research, helping us visit Ground Zero, attend conferences, and collect materials. Endicott and its administration also provided us with the freedom to teach the subject of 9/11 in our courses, providing additional testing ground for ideas that are present in the book. Dr. Cynthia Ricciardi gave us a foundation for the book by collecting the most current sources on each of the book's chapters. We relied on her research throughout the writing process. Debby Adams helped us launch the project, and George Butler oversaw its completion. Finally, our contributors deepened our understanding of the relationship between 9/11 and popular culture through their rich perspectives on the topic.

On a personal note, Sara is grateful for Amy's gracious intellect and friendship—and for many early mornings of walking and talking through the book. Jenn Vaughan offered friendly encouragement and delicious meals that helped ease long days of writing. Finally, Charlie Van Eman brought big energy to the final months of the project—and that made all the difference.

Amy would like to acknowledge the continual support and encouragement of her family, especially her husband, Glen Zoladz, who always listened to her process ideas, joined her in reviewing much of the media discussed in the book, and helped make the project doable by way of his support, parenting, and partnership. The idea for this book was Sara's, and Amy would like to acknowledge her vision, talent, and insight that guided us through the process of working on such an engaging and interesting project.

Introduction

September 11, 2001, changed the landscape of American culture. Security lines at airport checkpoints, a national terror alert system, and years of war in Iraq and Afghanistan are visible changes to American life that can be directly traced to the events of that day. More poignantly, memorial sites in New York City, at the Pentagon, and outside Shanksville, Pennsylvania, remind visitors from around the world that life before and after September 11 is forever marked by senseless loss of life that will impact children, loved ones, and an entire nation for generations to come.

While such changes are worth studying in their own right, other shifts in American life since 9/11 have also been powerful and long lasting. Virtually all areas of popular culture—those well-known, widely recognized books, TV shows, movies, songs, and visual images so central to twenty-first-century America—were deeply affected by the 9/11 attacks. A close examination of the relationship between September 11 and popular culture can reveal much about how the attacks were processed by ordinary people, how they have gradually become integrated into everyday life, places in which that integration has been resisted or slow to occur, and, finally, how popular culture has changed in the years since that tragic fall day.

September 11 in Popular Culture: A Guide offers readers a chance to look closely at seven different areas of American life after September 11: everyday life, books, news and information, television, film, music, and visual culture. A chapter is devoted to each of these topics, and each chapter includes two parts. The chapter introductions trace the way each particular area of popular culture responded to the attacks, both in the immediate aftermath and over time. In many cases, this evolution followed a similar path from grassroots reactions and industry-based responses, to the gradual production of books, films, TV shows, songs, and art about September 11. Most recently, September 11 has appeared in popular culture as a plot point or backdrop to other events or narratives suggesting that the event has become integrated into the way America thinks about itself. The second section of each chapter, Spotlight Essays, focuses more in depth on specific examples of the chapter's topic. For example, in Chapter 3, "Books," the Spotlight Essay section gives readers in-depth essays on a range of 9/11-related books, including novels, memorial texts, comic books, and graphic novels. These essays are meant to offer a variety of perspectives not only on how September 11 has been represented in popular culture, but on the ways popular culture has changed as a result of the attacks.

Chapter 1, "Everyday Life," examines the immediate response Americans had to the attacks, including the trend toward nesting, increased attendance at religious services, decreased attendance at entertainment venues, the flying of flags, newly identified heroes, and expressions of grief. The ways Americans dealt with the first holidays after September 11, including Halloween, Thanksgiving, Christmas, and Hanukkah, as well as New Year's Eve and the first anniversary of the attacks are also discussed. Other topics include children and schools, volunteerism and philanthropy, as well as the birth of 9/11 memorials, in particular the way Ground Zero has become a site that symbolizes the attacks. Spotlight essays in Chapter 1 offer readers a glimpse into aspects of American daily activities that changed as a result of September 11, for example humor, sports, use of the Internet, interest in comfort food, purchasing patriotic products, along with attitudes toward travel, hate crimes, and the quick appearance of urban legends.

Chapter 2, "News and Information," traces the media's coverage of September 11 from the moment the attacks occurred until the return to regularly scheduled programming days, and in some instances weeks, later. The chapter discusses a range of news and information outlets that stepped into action as soon as the attacks took place, including broadcast news, newspapers, the Internet, talk shows, news programs, the *New York Times'* Pulitzer Prize winning "A Nation Challenged," as well as the Sunday comics. The Spotlight Essays in Chapter 2 offer more focused attention on specific aspects of 9/11 coverage, including newspaper headlines, editorial cartoons, news photography, magazines, speeches made by President George W. Bush, and the controversial 9/11 Truth movement.

Chapter 3, "Books," considers the evolution of writing about 9/11, which began with poems written and left at Ground Zero within hours of the attacks. The chapter explores the early collections of writings directly about September 11 and memorial books such as *One Nation: America Remembers September 11, 2001, Portraits of 9/11/01: The Collected "Portraits of Grief,"* and *September 11, 2001: A Record of Tragedy, Heroism and Hope.* Informational books such as *102 Minutes* and comic books like *Spider-Man #36*, also known as *The Black Issue,* are also examined, in addition to plays such as *The Guys* and, finally, full-length novels. The Spotlight Essays in Chapter 3 provide closer analysis of a range of 9/11-related writings, including *The 9/11 Commission Report* and its graphic novel adaptation, Art Spiegelman's *In the Shadow of No Towers*, children's literature, Don DeLillo's *Falling Man*, Jonathan Safran Foer's *Extremely Loud and Incredibly Close*, and Frédéric Beigbeder's *Windows on the World.*

Chapter 4, "Television," traces the role TV played in capturing the September 11 attacks, as well as 9/11-based programming produced specifically for TV that appeared in the aftermath. Initial changes in programming—including late-night comedy and previously scheduled shows containing violence—as well as celebrity fundraising events are explored. The chapter examines changes to shows like *Third Watch* and special episodes of nighttime dramas such as *The West Wing*, as well as the release of documentaries and miniseries such as *Inside 9/11* and *DC 9/11: Time of Crisis*. Particular attention is paid to trends in post-9/11 television, including the rise of "militainment" and counterterrorism TV programming. The Spotlight Essay section of Chapter 4 focuses on specific aspects of 9/11 television, including popular shows already running when 9/11 occurred—such as *24, The Unit*, and *Sex and the City*—as well as post-9/11 programs such as *Rescue Me, Dexter, Generation Kill*, and *Lost*, which reflect post-9/11 cultural concerns.

Chapter 5, "Film," looks at the film industry's response to September 11, beginning with changes in scheduled release dates and deletion of scenes with buildings under attack. The chapter addresses the role that New York City, and the Twin Towers, has played in film history and looks at the post-9/11 connection between Hollywood and Washington officials. Early filmic responses like *7 Days in September, 9/11*, and *The First 24 Hours* are discussed as are fictionalized stories of the attacks in movies such as *United 93* and *World Trade Center*. Particular attention is paid to the post-9/11 increase in films about terrorism and the Global War on Terror. The Spotlight Essays provide readers with more focused exploration of specific films, including *Black Hawk Down*; *Kingdom of Heaven*; conspiracy films, *Loose Change* and *Zeitgeist*; *The Quiet American*; *United 93*; and Oliver Stone's *World Trade Center*.

Chapter 6, "Music," considers the songs and albums that arose in response to September 11. The chapter begins with a look at the music industry's initial reactions—removing particular songs from playlists, hosting benefit concerts, and changing song titles and artwork—and then moves on to a discussion of songs released after the attacks, for example, Dolly Parton's "Halos and Horns," Neil Young's "Let's Roll," Michael Jackson's "What More Can I Give," and Alan Jackson's "Where Were You When the World Stopped Turning/Do You Remember." Music composed to mark the anniversary of the attacks, such as "Around the World Requiem," the post-9/11 popularity of music videos like Ryan Adams's "New York New York," and the music world's reaction to the post-9/11 war on terrorism is also discussed. In the Spotlight Essays section a range of 9/11 music is explored in depth, including Christian Rock, Ani DiFranco's "Self Evident," William Basinski's *The Disintegration Loops I–IV*, Cassetteboy's "Fly Me to New York," and John Adams's *On the Transmigration of Souls*.

Finally, Chapter 7, "Visual Culture," examines the visual responses to September 11, beginning with the spontaneous memorials and posters of the missing at Ground Zero and the other crash sites immediately after the attacks. Grassroots exhibits such as *Here is New York*, the *September 11 Photo Project*, and *Reactions* at Exit Art are discussed as are individual exhibits and permanent collections such as *Witness and Response: September 11 Acquisitions at the Library of Congress* and *September 11: Bearing Witness to History* at the Smithsonian Institution. Memorial objects, including the "Heroes" U.S. Postal Stamp, "The Sphere," "Tumbling Woman," and "FDNY Memorial Wall," are examined along with the memorials that mark each of the three crash sites. The Spotlight Essays focus more in depth on art at the World Trade Center, spontaneous memorials, the Twin Towers as visual icons, "Falling Man," the impact of the USA Patriot Act on visual artists, postcards, photographs, and the Ground Zero memorial.

September 11 in Popular Culture: A Guide can be read in a variety of ways. Readers interested in a particular genre of popular culture can focus on the chapter specifically written on the topic. Those who want to understand the overall responses and shifts in popular culture after 9/11 can read the introductory sections of each chapter. For readers interested in a particular book, TV program, film, song, or work of art, the Spotlight Essays focus in more deeply on specific pop-culture media. Some subjects, such as the photo "Falling Man" or the topic of firefighters, are addressed in more than one chapter.

There are two appendices included in this book: "Selected 9/11 Books, TV Shows, Films, Music, and Visual Arts," which provides a quick reference to key September 11 media; and "Further Reading," a selected list of books, articles, and websites that are useful for readers interested in learning more about specific topics.

As September 11, 2001, becomes a date further and further removed from current history, the events that took place that day will begin to fade from memory, leaving the official memorials and museums as the lasting repositories of how the attacks impacted Americans, the nation, and the world. Popular culture offers a less centralized, but no less rich, resource through which the immediate reactions, careful responses, gradual shifts, and ultimate transformations of ordinary Americans, and the country they live in, can be traced and understood.

SARA E. QUAY, PHD
AMY M. DAMICO, PHD
ENDICOTT COLLEGE

Chapter 1

EVERYDAY LIFE

INTRODUCTION: EVERYDAY LIFE AND SEPTEMBER 11, 2001

In the days, weeks, and months after the September 11 attacks, U.S. culture entered a period of transition. Life as it had been prior to 9/11 seemed, at least momentarily, no longer possible to ordinary Americans. As one man reflected soon after the attacks, "We're living through an eclipse of normality, a twilight landscape. The sun isn't quite right. It's a little darker than it should be when you look at it" (Gibbs, 2001, p. 30). Uncertain how to respond to such dramatic acts of terrorism on their own shores, and unsure what the recovery process would look like, Americans turned to what was familiar: the comforts of home, the love of family, the support of religion, and the escapism of shopping. At the same time, changes in U.S. life were visible everywhere. From new restrictions and regulations around national security, to widespread expressions of patriotism, daily life in the aftermath of 9/11 had a distinct character that registered the country's anxieties, grief, and resilient hope for the future.

Patriotism

One of the most visible shifts in everyday life after September 11 was the prevalent display of patriotism. In responding to the devastation of the attacks, the fear of what might happen next, and the uncertainty about how the country might react, Americans began to noticeably exhibit their support for, and belief in, the United States. The U.S. flag, perhaps the most obvious example of U.S. patriotism, appeared everywhere. Indeed, Old Glory took on renewed significance as Americans sought ways to express their love of country, feelings of unity, and longing to heal in the face of the tragedy. On September 11 alone, Walmart sold 116,00 U.S. flags, compared to only 6,400 sold on the same day a year earlier ("Remains of the Day," 2002). By the end of September orders for flags had increased 10-fold, and U.S. flag makers expressed pride in their ability to contribute to the national outpouring of support for the victims and the country (Bland, 2001; Johnson, 2001).

Flags of all shapes, sizes, and mediums were flown and displayed. Traditional fabric flags were hung from buildings around the Twin Towers and at the Pentagon, draped over bodies recovered at Ground Zero, held by mourners during candlelight vigils, flown from the back of pickup trucks, and hawked by street vendors. The flag's image was fashioned into safety-pin jewelry, tattoos, and T-shirts. Digitized flags could be seen waving at the bottom of TV screens, while news programs, which were on the air constantly during and after the attacks, used flag imagery as a backdrop to their broadcasts. In a slight variation on the trend, the U.S. Navy flew the historic "Don't Tread on Me" version of the flag to represent a resilient attitude in the face of adversity ("Remains of the Day," 2002).

Other variations on the flag included Honor and Hero flags that encouraged Americans to "Always Remember" those who were lost. Available either as a cloth flag that could be flown or as a poster version that could be framed, the Flag of Honor listed every name of those who died on September 11 in the attacks. The Flag of Heroes listed the names of the emergency workers who lost their lives in the line of duty. Honor and Hero flags were given to families of those who were lost on or as a result of September 11. They were also hung in restaurants and businesses across the country (http://www.flagofhonorfund.org).

Additional expressions of patriotic spirit were apparent in the creation of items like 9/11 bumper stickers that included messages such as "9/11: Never Again." Greeting card companies created cards that could be either sent to those who had lost loved ones or given simply to inspire people to believe in the country and its ability to recover. Advertisements emphasized U.S.-made products and encouraged consumers to "buy American." In fact, in the weeks after the attacks patriotism was often linked to shopping, as then President George W. Bush suggested in his 8:30 p.m., September 11 speech in which he assured the people of the United States that the nation was still "open for business" (Bush, 2001, para. 9).

Another example of post-9/11 patriotism was the 9/11 Ribbon, sometimes called the "loyalty ribbon," which appeared within days of the attacks. The first ribbon, attributed to graphic artist Robert M. "Bob" West, was posted on the Internet as an animated image of red, white, and blue ribbon tied around a flickering candle and marked with the tragic date. The image was downloaded, reproduced, and eventually transformed into different variations including cloth-loop ribbons and metal pins sometimes embellished with images of the Twin Towers or the date (http://www.candleandribbon.org).

Hearth and Home

In addition to externally exhibiting their patriotism, Americans also turned inward, reflecting on their values, lifestyles, and relationships. Stories in the media shone light on the fact that daily life had been dramatically changed without warning on September 11. In response, many people decided that they should live life to the fullest in case another tragedy like 9/11 struck. Doing so meant taking a second look at their current lives and assessing what was important to their personal happiness.

One of the most common responses was a renewed interest in hearth and home. Known as "cocooning" or "nesting," this trend emphasized home life and time spent with family. The most obvious manifestation of cocooning could be seen in the sales of specific home and home-related items, which increased in the weeks and months after 9/11. Home furnishings, for example, were purchased in large numbers in the months after the attacks. Popular stores such as Pottery Barn reported increased sales in upholstered furniture, while Martha Stewart's home goods sales—both in her catalog and online—also showed growth after September 11. Earnings at do-it-yourself stores also saw increases. Home Depot, for example, reported record sales in the quarter after the attacks (McGuigan, 2001). Home magazines, also called "shelter magazines," similarly rose in popularity after the attacks with more than 40 new titles appearing on stands in 2002 (Lloyd, 2004).

Other evidence of the nesting trend was also apparent. DVD rentals—which increased by some accounts as much as 10 percent—reflected the nation's desire to stay close to home rather than venture out for entertainment (Sporich, 2001). Baking goods supplies and cookbooks for foods such as soup also saw greater sales numbers as people sought comfort in the familiar acts of cooking and baking (Streisand, 2001). Comfort foods in general—such as macaroni and cheese, stews, and other nourishing hearty meals—found renewed popularity at dinner tables across the country. Americans also became more interested in doing crafts and hobbies after September 11. According to the National Needleworkers Association, yarn sales grew by 40 percent a year after September 11. Sewing machines and craft sales increased as well (Gibbs, 2001; "Knit 1, Purl 2," 2008).

A renewed focus on relationships was another characteristic of the cocooning trend; however, the expression of this characteristic took many forms. After the attacks, many Americans felt more connected to other people and their communities. Spontaneous gatherings sprang up across the country, from the crash sites where vigils were held in honor of victims, to small towns and large cities where people felt drawn to interact with others during the time of crisis. People reported they felt closer to their neighbors, were more likely to greet strangers on the street, and experienced a general increased sense of humanity in the period directly after the attacks. While these feelings dissipated as life returned to normal, many still associate the terrible events of 9/11 with memories of kindness among strangers and support within communities. As one witness recalled, "Immediately, people started to connect, to comfort each other, to help each other" ("Richard Cohen," 2009).

Some Americans reprioritized the importance of family and friends in their lives, making a conscious choice to spend more time with both. Reconsideration of long-time grudges or broken relationships led some Americans to make amends with old friends or relatives. Romance became a significant focus for many people as well. Seeking out long-term relationships through dating services and personal ads became commonplace as Americans made an effort to reach out and connect after the fear and isolation felt during and after the attacks. Some people—both couples and individuals—who had long debated whether or not to have a child chose to do so soon after 9/11 leading to predictions that the number of babies born nine months after the attacks—June 2002— would show a spike over the usual number of births counted at that time of year (Gibbs, 2001; Kelly, 2001).

In contrast to the impulse to nest after 9/11, some Americans chose to throw caution to the wind and pursue long-delayed dreams. Unrewarding jobs were left behind, unhappy relationships were broken off, and personal goals were emphasized. Planning for the future became the focus for large numbers of Americans, leading them to get their finances in order, draw up a will, name a power-of-attorney, or purchase life and/or disability insurance (Lim, Perry, Slania, & Sharpe, 2001).

Religion and Philanthropy

Many Americans turned to religion as a way to cope with the events of September 11. Churches, mosques, and synagogues reported a surge in the number of worshippers whose interest ranged from attending organized services to simply finding a sacred place to pray. A *Time*/CNN poll (2001) reported that 57 percent of the people surveyed said they had "thought more about the spiritual part" of their life since the attacks. Attendance at religious services was not the only way Americans expressed their revival of faith. In the days after the attacks Bible sales increased 42 percent over the same time period the prior year, and Christian crosses were popular items at jewelers like Zales (Gibbs, 2001, p. 38).

Going hand-in-hand with the increased attendance at religious services, a spirit of volunteerism and philanthropy marked post-9/11 life. From money to time, Americans gave of their resources and themselves to support 9/11 victims, survivors, and the recovery effort. One poll determined that 7 out of 10 Americans gave money or material goods after the attacks and that by October 22, just six weeks later, the total funds raised in response to September 11—$934 million—was the largest in the nation's history of financial aid (Cannon, Shapiro, & Perry, 2001, para. 3). From popular musicians like Mick Jagger and Paul McCartney, who were featured in a benefit concert, to high-profile politicians such as former President Bill Clinton and former Senator Bob Dole, who raised scholarship money for children who lost a parent in the attacks, there was no lack of effort or generosity. Proceeds of many books about 9/11, as well as memorial objects, were donated to charities set up specifically to help the families of victims and other relief efforts.

Donations of money and goods were not the only forms of philanthropy that took place after September 11. People from all over the world volunteered their time, especially at Ground Zero, during the recovery effort. From donating blood to serving food at Ground Zero, Americans gave their time and energy wherever they were needed. For example, standing across the street from the Twin Towers, St. Paul's Chapel was a central site of volunteer efforts. The chapel, which withstood the attacks with little damage to its structure, sheltered relief workers providing them with a place to eat, sleep, and pray throughout the darkest days after the attacks.

Volunteers showed up in droves to serve food, give massages, donate blankets and clothes, or offer counseling to those engaged in the grim recovery process. St. Paul's played such an important role in the recovery efforts that it gradually became a destination for visitors to Ground Zero, drawing by one account 35,000 visitors a year and becoming a stop on bus and walking tours of lower Manhattan (Miller & Eady, 2007).

Holidays

The first post-9/11 holidays gave Americans the chance to reflect on, and respond to, the changes the attacks had rendered on the country. Halloween's usual emphasis on ghosts and goblins was tempered by awareness of the lives lost on September 11. Thanksgiving offered people a chance to gather together in the face of tragedy, while New Year's Eve gave symbolic closure to the difficult year.

9/11 AND APOCALYPTIC THINKING

While the word "apocalypse" has often been used to describe a revealing of divine purpose, for some Americans September 11, 2001, was an expression of a particular definition of the word. *Premillennial apocalypticism* is a belief expressed by some leaders within evangelical and fundamentalist Christianity. This position claims that the world is "wrecked" and will continue to decline until the End of Days (Balmer, 2006, p. 147). More specifically, according to Preston Shires (2007) it is believed that Americans will play a role in the unfolding of such biblical prophecy. Hailing from this perspective, after 9/11 some prominent Christian conservatives referred to the terrorist attacks as either evidence of God's judgment or the approaching End of Days. For example, during an appearance on network television, Anne Graham Lotz, daughter of evangelist Billy Graham, suggested that the attacks on 9/11 were a result of secularization within the public school system. The result was the removal of God's protection (Lotz, 2006). In another interpretation, Jerry Falwell claimed the attacks were caused by people with alternative lifestyles, including gays and lesbians (Applebome, 2007, p. 1). Fictional works about the End of Days including the *Left Behind* series, authored by Tim LaHaye and Jerry B. Jenkins (1995–2007), were popular after 9/11 in part because they reflected such apocalyptic narratives.

—*Shawn David Young*

References

Applebome, P. (2007, May 15). Jerry Falwell, leading religious conservative, dies. *The New York Times*, pp. 1–3.

Balmer, R. (2006). *Thy kingdom come: An evangelical's lament: How the religious right distorts the faith and threatens America*. New York: Basic Books.

LaHaye, T., & Jenkins, J. B. (1995–2007). Book series: *Left behind*. Carol Stream: Tyndale House.

Lotz, A. G. (2006, September/October). A morning to remember. *Today's Christian* [online]. Retrieved from http://www.christianitytoday.com

Shires, P. (2007). *Hippies of the religious right*. Waco: Baylor University Press.

Arriving just six weeks after the attacks, Halloween was the first major holiday in the post-9/11 world. For a country still gripped by images of death and destruction, fear of terrorism, and anxiety about strangers, the traditional Halloween activities seemed inappropriate if not plain offensive. Costumes usually advertised as appropriate for Halloween—those celebrating blood and gore, bones and ghosts—seemed too closely associated with the real events of September 11. Annual Halloween events, such as Universal Studios Horror Nights with its Bloodbath Underground, sounded out-of-step with the televised attacks and their aftermath. Yet Halloween also offered Americans a chance to participate in a quintessential American holiday, one in which front doors were opened to strangers, and neighbors greeted each other on the street after dark (Gibbs, 2001).

In light of these concerns, across the nation, Halloween 2001 took on a unique look. The most popular costumes of the season reflected a patriotic spirit: firefighters, police officers, soldiers, Uncle Sam, and the Statue of Liberty were best sellers. Especially popular were masks of U.S. leaders such as Bill Clinton, George W. Bush, and—in specific reference to his role in the response to 9/11—Rudy Giuliani. Store displays featured red, white, and blue rather than the more traditional orange and black. Many of the large-scale trick-or-treating events at malls were cancelled because of security concerns and a reluctance by many people to venture out into those and other public spaces. In contrast, small-town and neighborhood events flourished. Events that a year earlier would have seemed entirely appropriate in their Halloween-themed emphasis on death and gore were renamed or reshaped out of respect for the real death and destruction that had occurred just a month earlier (Corliss, Bruce, Philadelphia, & Ressner, 2001; Gibbs, 2001; Jabs, 2001).

In contrast to Halloween's customs, which were altered in response to post-9/11 sentiment, Thanksgiving's traditions seemed to reflect exactly the mood of American culture. The literal meaning of the holiday—to give thanks—captured the sense of gratitude Americans felt for their nation and their lives, for the lives of the 9/11 victims, and for the heroism of those who aided in the recovery. Connecting with family and friends, as is typical on Thanksgiving Day, registered the post-9/11 surge in caring and outreach to others. Americans made extra efforts to gather together for the 2001 Thanksgiving holiday. A *Time* magazine poll found that approximately three-fourths of those surveyed believed they were "more appreciative" on Thanksgiving 2001 than they had been in the past (Gibbs, 2001, p. 38).

The comforts of home and food, already the focus of a culture reeling from the shock of terrorist attacks, were especially reassuring. The Butterball Turkey Talk-Line reported that callers were interested in cooking larger turkeys in 2001; the Food Network saw a 25 percent increase in ratings; and department stores reported greater sales of overstuffed, comfortable furniture (Adler, 2001). *Time* magazine's Thanksgiving 2001 cover captured the basis of the nation's sentiments in its simple image: a U.S. flag planted firmly in a pumpkin pie. A sense of returning to essential American values pervaded the Thanksgiving season.

The winter holidays of 2001, specifically Hanukkah and Christmas, were also marked by cultural shifts after 9/11. Hanukkah, or the Festival of Lights, which fell

between December 9 and December 16 that year, gave Jewish Americans the opportunity to pause for reflection. Some synagogues found ways to tie the holiday to the
remembrance and recognition of those who died or worked in the recovery effort.
For example, the National Jewish Center for Learning and Leadership in New York
City dedicated "each night of Hanukkah to an act of heroism" to recognize a wide
range of 9/11 heroes, including firefighters, doctors, government officials, and service
men and women (Brenner, 2001, para. 6).

Christmas's emphasis on shopping as an expression of patriotism was apparent
during the holiday season. Increased sales ranged across the spectrum of gifts. Religious items such as Bibles and crosses were popular, as were gifts that supported the
country's nesting trend such as DVD players, an item that increased 50 percent in
sales from the year before. Classic children's toys—rescue heroes, G.I. Joe, and
Shrinky Dinks—found their way into homes across the country reflecting nostalgia
for the "simpler times" of the past (Song & van Dyk, 2001). Traditional red and green
Christmas cards were supplemented by Hallmark's best-selling cards sporting patriotic
greetings in red, white, and blue. Despite a recession, Americans shopped during the
holidays. However, more did so from the comfort of their own home: Online sales
during the first week of the Christmas shopping season increased 43 percent over
the prior year (Song & van Dyk, 2001).

Other holidays were also marked by the post-9/11 climate. On New Year's Eve, for
example, there was high security at public celebrations such as the traditional Times
Square countdown and ball drop. Backpacks and bags were examined at numerous
checkpoints, and 7,000 police officers were on duty. Despite the new restrictions
around gathering in public spaces, large numbers of revelers came out for the celebration registering a patriotic spirit and belief in the future. New Year's Eve in Times
Square was not only about celebration, however. In 2001, the crystal ball that drops
every year at midnight was inscribed with the names of Americans who had been lost
in the 9/11 attacks, as well as the names of other countries who had lost citizens
(Suarez, 2002).

Similar celebrations—and the accompanying security—were apparent in cities across
the country. In Boston, Massachusetts, the National Guard was called on to support the
regular police force, and in Washington, D.C., metal detectors were used at 24 different
checkpoints to ensure the crowd's safety. Given these circumstances, it is not surprising
that many Americans chose to stay home and celebrate quietly reflecting on the events
of 2001 and looking forward to better times ahead (Edwards, 2001).

Another significant holiday was July 4, 2002, the first Independence Day after the
attacks. The Fourth of July was marked by both high security and patriotic celebrations. No-fly zones were enforced over national monuments and major cities such as
New York and Washington, D.C., while across the country increased police presence
and security checkpoints were apparent at public gathering places such as the National
Mall and the Boston Esplanade. Bags, backpacks, and coolers were searched, and there
were long lines at popular tourist spots (Suarez, 2002).

Finally, the one-year anniversary of September 11 was significant on many levels and
was commemorated in a variety of ways. In San Francisco, a five-mile banner made of

THE NEW YORK CITY MARATHON

The annual New York City Marathon held special significance in 2001. Scheduled for November 4, almost two months after September 11, the 26.2-mile race through the streets of New York was the first major event sponsored by the city since the attacks. Despite widespread fears about traveling and public gatherings, few runners cancelled their plans to run in the race, and by some counts even more participants asked to join in after the attacks. More than two million spectators lined the streets to cheer on the runners, symbolizing the patriotic spirit of renewal that the city needed. For some runners, the marathon was not just an event but an act of remembrance. Relatives of those who died on United Flight 93 ran in the race with T-shirts that read "Flight 93 Family Runners: They Never Gave Up and Neither Will We." On the backs of each shirt the names of those who died were listed (DeBaise, 2001; Lieber, 2002; http://www.nycmarathon.org).

—*Sara E. Quay*

References

DeBaise, C. (2001, October 5). Race for life: New Yorkers see marathon as one way to bolster the city's psyche. *The Wall Street Journal*, p. A6.
Lieber, J. (2002, September 10). Marathon a mission. *USA Today*. Retrieved from http://www.usatoday.com

3,000 U.S. flags was displayed, while in Cincinnati, Ohio, a memorial to firefighters was marked with 343 pairs of empty boots ("Marking the Anniversary," 2002). Visions of the Future, a program sponsored by Bloomingdale's department store, featured murals created by children that were displayed at Bloomingdale's stores across the country (Bovino, 2002).

Individual Americans also chose ways to recognize the first anniversary of the attacks. This is not surprising given the fact that 30 percent of adults ages 18 and older said they thought about the attacks every day, while 35 percent said they thought about it several times a week. In terms of how they planned to spend the first anniversary date, 80 percent said they were going to fly the U.S. flag, 77 percent were going to "pray by myself," 32 percent planned to attend a memorial service," and 68 percent said they were going to watch a program about 9/11 on television ("What We Think," 2002).

Entertainment

While initial responses to the 9/11 attacks left Americans glued to news programs and focused on the events as they unfolded, eventually people sought entertainment in a variety of forms. Doing so was not as simple as it had been prior to September 11, however.

From television programs and movies, to theater and sports, popular forms of entertainment also reflected 9/11 and its aftermath.

TV programming in the immediate aftermath of 9/11 focused exclusively on coverage of the attacks. Capturing the events live during regularly scheduled shows, the TV and cable networks worked together to provide viewers with correct and up-to-date information. Within a week, many viewers had fatigued of the intense coverage of the attacks and their aftermath, and networks sought to return to regularly scheduled programming. Not all was as it had been prior to September 11, however. Shows that seemed inappropriate in light of the attacks were edited or held from release. Televised benefits, hosted by Hollywood stars and TV personalities, aired to raise money for the families of victims. Over time, television content reflected the post-9/11 world in its entertainment and informational programming. Yet in the early days of fall 2001, viewers found entertainment, as well as reassurance, in much of post-9/11 TV (see Chapter 4, Television).

Movie theaters followed a similar path, holding off on releasing films with excessive violence or destruction, altering scenes and plots deemed too evocative of the attacks, and promoting positive images of Americans and the United States. As time went by, however, movies reclaimed their place as a popular form of entertainment and provided viewers much needed relief from daily realities. *Harry Potter and the Sorcerer's Stone* (2001), *Lord of the Rings: The Fellowship of the Ring* (2001), and *Zoolander* (2001) were especially welcome movies in the weeks and months following 9/11 (see Chapter 5, Film).

Not surprisingly, interest in dramatic performances—Broadway or otherwise—in the weeks after September 11 waned significantly, and musicals like Stephen Sondheim's *Assassins*—slated to open in 2001—were held back due to subject matter deemed inappropriate in light of the attacks. Indeed, Broadway theaters were shut down until September 13. When they reopened, the marquees were only partially lit reflecting the sentiments of a country in mourning. However, as Americans grew weary from the unrelenting news and information about the attacks, including regular reports on the recovery process at Ground Zero, the unfolding details of how the attacks were planned and carried out, and the initiation of the War on Terror, entertainment returned to a central place in American life. Specific types of entertainment were most popular. By the end of October, for example, ticket sales for such Broadway shows as *The Lion King, The Rocky Horror Picture Show,* and *The Producers* was underway. It was the popular musical *Mamma Mia!*—known for its catchy Abba tunes and optimistic, sunny plot—that captured audiences' attention the most. The show opened to record advance-ticket sales offering a "feel-good remedy" to the dark days of September (Zoglin & Goehner, 2001).

While theaters gave Americans an escape from harsh post-9/11 realties, plays written and performed specifically in response to the attacks provided some of the earliest examples of how American theater would represent the events. Anne Nelson's *The Guys* (2001), Charles Evered's *Adopt a Sailor* (2002), Neil LaBute's *Mercy Seat* (2002), Theresa Rebeck's *Omnium Gatherum* (2003), and Craig Wright's *Recent Tragic Events* (2003) all took September 11 as their subject. In doing so such

THE DRAG AND BURLESQUE SCENE AFTER 9/11

Many artists responded prolifically to the attacks of September 11, 2001, and the New York City drag and burlesque scene was no exception. This shift is perhaps nowhere more apparent than in the work of Taylor Mac, an actor/playwright/theater artist/drag queen. One of Mac's first works to address post-9/11 United States was written before his turn to drag in 2004. *Okay* focused on high school students at a prom and their diverse problems. One of the monologues in the play elaborates on the political and commercial exploitation of 9/11 and was later rewritten into a song and added to Mac's one-person show, *The Face of Liberalism*. Ukulele in hand, his face painted to depict a U.S. flag edged with thumb tacks, Mac turns his face into a mask of war and confronts his American audience, urging them to become aware of the exploitation of the 9/11 attacks to justify the war in Iraq.

Other artists have also joined in this post-9/11 shift toward the address of government politics in drag and burlesque. During the Republican National Convention in 2004, Mac created and curated *Live Patriot Acts: Patriots Gone Wiiiild!*, a political vaudeville with acts by many New York City burlesque and drag performers, including a striptease by James "Tigger!" Ferguson as George W. Bush. In 2007 the event was turned into a series with the follow-up performance, *Live Patriot Acts 2: An Alien Nation—An Immigration Odyssey*, starring amongst others, Scotty the Blue Bunny lolloping on stage disguised as an unattended bag and nominating a spectator ambassador to keep people from visiting the United States.

Although the format of U.S. burlesque shows—a juicy combination of entertainment, satire, and striptease—as well as the format of the drag show—characterized by the emphasis of the personal as political—might not be obvious choices when looking to express feeling about a national tragedy, their characteristic snide pastiche blends well with scathing critiques of post-9/11 U.S. policies.

—*Anneka Esch-van Kan and Elizabeth Bojsza*

References

Criscuolo, Michael. (2007, February). An interview with Taylor Mac. Retrieved from http://www.nytesmallpress.com/pp07int_mac.php
Mac, Taylor. (n.d.). *Artist statement*. Retrieved from http://taylormac.net
Mac, Taylor. (n.d.). *The face of liberalism*. Retrieved from http://taylormac.net/TaylorMac.net
Mac, Taylor. (2007). Red tide blooming. In Martin Denton (Ed.), *NYTE's plays and playwrights 2007* (pp. 2–36). New York: NY Publications.

performances gave theater goers a mirror through which to look at and reflect on the impact 9/11 had had on American life (see Chapter 3, Books).

Other popular forms of entertainment also underwent changes after the attacks. Humor—from online satiric Web sites to late-night comedy—went on hiatus in the aftermath of the attacks. Sport teams debated whether or not it was appropriate to play scheduled games while the country was in mourning. When games were played a week later, it was with a patriotic spirit that seemed to reflect the nation's belief in its ability to overcome adversity and, literally, win the war that had been waged against it.

AMERICAN LIFE AS OF NOVEMBER 2001: SOME STATISTICS (GIBBS, 2001)

Peace Corps applications in San Francisco jumped 72 percent.

Visitors to *Resolve: The National Infertility Association* Web site increased 50 percent.

Teenagers' attendance at Spirit Rock, a Northern California center for Buddhist meditation, increased 30 percent.

Bible sales at the American Bible Society were 42 percent higher than the year before. Beer sales were up by 7 percent.

The National Security Association (NSA) received more than 19,000 resumes in the eight weeks following the attacks, more than four times the typical number.

Habitat for Humanity saw a 20 percent jump in volunteers in the Northeast region of the country.

—*Compiled by Sara E. Quay*

Reference

Gibbs, N. (2001, November 19). We gather together. *Time, 158*(22), 28–41.

Stands filled with fans who flew flags, dressed in red, white, and blue, and sang the national anthem, and the "Star-Spangled Banner" created a communal spirit much needed and embraced. Music, too, responded to September 11. Songs like Ryan Adams' 2001 "New York, New York"—released prior to the attacks with a music video featuring the Twin Towers as the backdrop—became instant hits while musicians as diverse as Paul McCartney, Alan Jackson, and Toby Keith wrote new songs that reflected the significance of the events (see Chapter 6, Music).

Travel and Security

One of the most immediate and long-lasting changes to life after September 11 involved travel and security. On the day of the attacks, the Federal Aviation Association (FAA) closed airspace across the country for several days, leaving the skies empty and quiet in the aftermath. Flights scheduled to land in the United States were diverted to Mexico and Canada, leaving passengers temporarily stranded or forced to find their own way to their destination. When air travel resumed on September 13, airport security was at an all-time high with new policies and procedures in place. Sky marshals were assigned to travel undercover on planes, especially those flying in and out of major U.S. cities. Armed guards were on duty at many airports for weeks after the attacks. Most significant for travelers, however, were the newly enforced security guidelines. Restrictions on what could and could not be carried onto planes meant that airport security checks took long periods of time, and travelers were forced to adjust to changes in carry-on luggage requirements. Generally people were patient and understanding about the need to make sure air travel was safe, adjusting to the changes with few complaints (Edwards, 2001).

In addition to airspace being shut down and heavily monitored, some public venues and tourist attractions were closed or evacuated on September 11 and afterwards. Closings included the Statue of Liberty and Ellis Island, a number of state capitols, national landmarks such as the Space Needle in Seattle, Washington, federal buildings throughout Washington, D.C., and the Washington Monument. While most reopened relatively quickly, the Statue of Liberty remained shut until the summer of 2009. At the Empire State Building, the New York Skyride attraction, in which visitors take a simulated tour of New York, was closed and reinvented to reflect post-9/11 concerns with dangerous travel (http://www.empirestatebuildingnewyork.com).

Other changes to the nation's security were apparent in creation of the Patriot Act, the Homeland Security Advisory System, and the Department of Homeland Security. The USA Patriot Act, popularly called simply the Patriot Act, was signed into law on October 26, 2001. In the name of protecting the United States from further terrorist attacks, the law gave the government unprecedented access to the records of everyday citizens, including e-mails, telephone calls, financial statements, and library records. These changes had implications for Americans long after 9/11, shifting the landscape of civil liberties indefinitely. While many Americans accepted the changes in order to feel more secure after the attacks, others resisted what was considered an invasion of privacy, pushing back in public ways against the new regulations.

Shortly after the attacks, then President Bush put into motion the establishment of the Department of Homeland Security (DHS), a government agency created to oversee the American homeland and protect the country against acts or threats of terror. In March 2002, a new Homeland Security Advisory System was released to the public consisting of color-coded levels of threats to the country. The threat levels—red being a severe risk of threat and blue being a low risk of threat—became familiar to Americans in the years after September 11. Associated with a new tendency toward national pride and protection, both the security alert system and the DHS helped popularize the term "homeland" as a post-9/11 reference to American soil and the need to keep it safe from external threats.

While new laws and agencies were created to protect the country, particular groups within the nation's borders faced intimidation and threats because of the color of their skin, their dress, or their clothing. Arab Americans and those practicing the Muslim faith were particular targets because they appeared to be of a similar background to the hijackers. In fact, between September 11 and September 13, 2001, the Council on American-Islamic Relations reported receiving "more than 300 reports of harassment and abuse . . . nearly half the number it received all" the previous year ("Hate Crime," 2002, para. 2). Local and national groups fought to educate Americans about the Islamic religion and to keep people safe regardless of their beliefs or appearance.

Another form of terrorism also haunted Americans in the months after September 11. In addition to concerns about attacks on buildings or forms of transport, biological weapons—specifically anthrax—frightened people across the country as cases of the weapons being delivered through the daily mail were reported in New York and Florida.

LOOKING "LIKE A TERRORIST" AFTER SEPTEMBER 11

In the years following 9/11, people who looked Middle Eastern in even the most super-ficial ways were often the focus of suspicion. Even politicians and celebrities were sub-ject to scrutiny if they happened to wear the "wrong" hairstyle or article of clothing. During a recess from Congress in 2007, for example, Republican Idaho representative Mike Simpson grew a beard, but reportedly shaved it off when his wife told him he "looked like a terrorist" (Rothstein, 2008). When David Letterman grew a beard during a writers strike the same year, a fan joked, "Is David . . . becoming a terrorist with all that hair?" urging him to get rid of it (Huff, 2008, p. 8). In May 2008, the popular donut-and-coffee chain, Dunkin' Donuts, was forced to pull an advertisement featur-ing Rachel Ray, host of the popular Food Network show "30 Minute Meals," because it showed Ray wearing a scarf that resembled a *kaffiyeh*. A blogger for www.feministe.us observed, "At this point, we're in the territory where any black and white scarf becomes suspect, whether worn around your head like Arafat or draped loosely around your neck. Extra Axis-of-Evil points if it has knotted tassels!" (Holly, 2008). In fact, blogs like www.jewlicious.com have observed that the retail chain Urban Outfitters used to sell *kaffiyehs* as "antiwar" scarves until criticism forced them to pull the garments out of the U.S. market. The chain continued to sell them in Europe as "desert scarves" (ck, 2007).

—*Heather Marie Akou*

References

ck. (2007, January 27). *Urban Outfitters bends to the will of the Jews on Keffiyeh* . . . [Web blog message]. Retrieved from http://www.jewlicious.com/?p=3065

Holly. (2008, May 24). *If you wear a black & white scarf, the terrorists win* [Web blog message]. Retrieved from http://www.feministe.us/blog/archives/2008/05/24/if-you-wear-a -black-white-scarf-the-terrorists-win/

Huff, R. (2008, January 8). Letterman shaves his beard. *Daily News.* Retrieved from http://www .NYDailyNews.com.

Rothstein, B. (2008, January 22). Memo to Rep. Simpson: Cut your hair. Retrieved from http:// thehill.com/in-the-know/rep.-franks-restricts-himself-to-the-no-sports-watching-diet -2008–01–22.html

Americans stocked up on drugs that could fight the effects of anthrax, such as the anti-biotic Cipro. Gas masks and in-home safe houses were topics of conversation around the water cooler as Americans planned ways to protect their homes by sealing rooms with duct tape and plastic (Comarow & Hobson, 2001).

Leaders and Heroes

Not surprisingly, as the events of September 11 unfolded Americans looked to leaders for reassurance and guidance. Occurring just nine months into his presidency, the attacks gave President George W. Bush a platform on which to shape his image. His approval rating quickly soared to 90 percent, a result of his speeches to the country, his visits to Ground Zero, and his expressions of outrage at the attacks (Cardwell, 2001).

Like Bush, New York City Mayor Rudolph Giuliani was also viewed as a hero in the immediate aftermath of the attacks. Named *Time* magazine's 2001 Person of the Year, Giuliani's presence at Ground Zero after the attacks reassured New Yorkers that they would be safe and that the city would recover. His proclamation that "We will rebuild. We're going to come out of this stronger than before, politically stronger, economically stronger. The skyline will be made whole again" was the positive message the city needed to hear (Cardwell, 2001, p. A1). When Giuliani left his office as mayor at the end of the year, he did so in a speech symbolically staged next to Ground Zero at St. Paul's Chapel, which promised a "soaring monumental" memorial where the Twin Towers once stood (Cardwell, 2001, p. A1).

OSAMA BIN LADEN: WANTED DEAD OR ALIVE

Americans' interpretation of the world after 9/11 was impacted by President Bush's use of the iconic cowboy to frame his foreign policy in simplistic terms of good versus evil. Long an icon in American culture, the cowboy's association with good and bad, righteous justice, protection of Edenic communities, and the eradication of a threat from a new frontier made the cowboy an ideal figure for the President to use in generating support for his post-9/11 foreign policy goals. A week after the attacks, for example, Bush evoked the cowboy when he claimed: "I want justice. There's an old poster out West, as I recall, that said, 'Wanted: Dead or Alive'" (Bush, 2001). When the press questioned the President about his reference, he recalled, "When I was a kid I remember that they used to put out there in the Old West, a wanted poster. It said 'Wanted Dead or Alive.' All I want and America wants him [Osama bin Laden] brought to justice" (Bush, 2001).

In response to the President's remarks, three New York newspapers printed headlines reading "Wanted: Dead or Alive," with a picture of bin Laden underneath the emblazoned words (Chetwynd, 2001, p. 1). The *New York Post* printed "a double page pullout 'Wanted: Dead or Alive' poster that could be seen pasted on shop windows and vehicles around the city, sometimes with the 'Alive' scratched out" (Chetwynd, 2001). T-shirts with the saying also proliferated in kiosks across the country (Stein, 2001). By employing the iconic cowboy, Bush drew upon a historical myth that resonated with most Americans. Popular culture took hold of the cowboy narrative that helped channel feelings of anger and revenge in the aftermath of September 11.

—*Ryan Malphurs*

References

Bush, G. W. (2001, September 17). *Guard and reserves "define spirit of America."* Retrieved from http://www.whitehouse.gov.

Chetwynd, P. (2001, September 19). Bush's cowboy talk nudges some U.S. papers down jingoistic path. *Agence France Presse.* Retrieved from http://www.lexisnexis.com

Stein, J. (2001, October 29). Shopping during wartime. *Time, 158*(19), 78.

Other heroes were also brought center stage as a result of 9/11. Firefighters, especially those of the New York City Fire Department (FDNY), were hailed for their bravery and held up as role models for children. A group of 9/11 widows, who came to be referred to as "the Jersey Girls," became unsuspecting heroes to many in their persistent effort to determine what actually happened on the day that took their husbands' lives. Kristen Breitweiser, Patty Casazza, Lorie Van Auken, and Mindy Kleinberg used a range of tactics—from garnering media attention to personal appeals—to pressure the government into examining the events that surrounded September 11. The result was the lengthy *9/11 Commission Report*, the official document about the 9/11 attacks. The Jersey Girls were criticized by some, including conservative writer Anne Coulter, for benefitting financially from their husbands' deaths. While such comments were controversial, and even offensive, they did not inhibit the Jersey Girls from pursuing their quest for the truth about September 11.

The Economy and Technology

The economic impact of September 11 was significant. The airline industry, in particular, was hit hard by the widespread fear of flying, high gas and oil prices, as well as shutdown airports that were slow to regain regular service. Security measures increased quickly, as airlines installed protective bars on the doors to airplane cockpits and President Bush announced "a 25% increase in National Guard troops, to a total of 9,000" stationed at the nation's airports (Cohen et al., 2001, para. 6). Despite these measures, holiday travel dropped significantly: 27 percent fewer Americans reported planning to travel for the 2001 holidays via trains, airplanes, or buses (Cohen et al., 2001). Indeed, in the months after 9/11 fear of flying led airlines to "cut flights 20% from pre-Sept. 11 levels" and even then planes flew "at just 65% of capacity, compared with an estimated 73% before the terror attacks" (Cohen et al., 2001, para. 2).

New York City was also gravely impacted. In addition to the loss of jobs and businesses around the World Trade Center (WTC) and lower Manhattan, fear about living in urban areas and working in high-rise buildings led to a transitional period in the economy of the city. Wall Street, shut down for four days, also suffered large losses on reopening. However, the recovery was relatively fast, in part because of the visual presence of political leaders and Hollywood stars who, along with visits to Ground Zero, rang the opening or closing bells on the Stock Exchange (Atkins, 2008; Martens, 2001).

Ordinary Americans felt the impact as well, spending less money out of fear and uncertainty of what the future held. Shopping malls, including the massive Mall of America, reported that shoppers visiting the mall decreased by 30 percent immediately after the attacks (Stein, 2001, para. 4). Fear of public spaces, as well as concern that national landmarks like the Mall of America would be the next sites of attack, left American malls with low sales for some time.

In contrast, some people gave in to their urge to splurge, feeling they should seize the day because the future felt so unpredictable (Gibbs, 2001). Advertising campaigns, combined with leaders' speeches promoting the relationship between shopping and patriotism, supported such behavior and reflected a widespread desire to bring American consumerism back from the brink. A subcategory of consumer products arose within this time period, focused on products related to the September 11 attacks. Around the attack sites, especially at Ground Zero, patriotic products, images, and souvenirs of the Twin Towers, and other September 11 memorabilia proliferated. Images of New York pre-September 11—with the Twin Towers standing watch over the city—became especially popular and were reproduced as framed photographs, postcards, T-shirts, and posters (Heller, 2005).

Technology also played an important role in the events of September 11. Cell phones recorded images of the events as they unfolded, and photos were quickly

---

AMERICAN CARS

Beginning September 20, 2001, the same day President Bush reiterated his call to participate in the U.S. economy, General Motors provided an outlet for patriotic consumption with a commercial that read:

> On September 11, the world as we knew to came to a halt. We sat glued to our televisions, watching events unfold that shook us to our very core. And, suddenly, the little things that had previously divided us became wholly insignificant. Now, it's time to move forward. (Garfield, 2001, p. 49)

Luckily for those in the market for a new car, "moving forward" meant 0 percent financing on every new GM car and truck. GM (and all other auto manufacturers) may well have offered such incentives as a result of slumping car sales throughout 2001, but the message of this advertising campaign was clear. It was patriotic to buy a car. Not just any car, an American car. Invoking a GM tagline, which coincidentally was eerily similar to the reported final words from Flight 93 that crashed in Pennsylvania, consumers were told to "Keep America Rolling." According to GM, an American's patriotic duty was to buy a GMC Suburban.

The Ford Motor Company quickly followed GM's lead. The maker of the nation's most popular sport utility vehicle, the Explorer, as well as the gas-guzzling Expedition and Excursion, offered its own moral imperative to purchase a vehicle. Ford offered to "do their part to move America forward" by offering interest-free financing on new vehicles. Yet, moving America forward did not necessarily mean moving American workers forward. In January 2002, just three months after these commercials began airing, Ford announced plans to close five plants, leaving 22,000 Americans out of work (Nicklaus, 2002).

—*Lori Bindig and M. Bosau*

References

Garfield, B. (2001, October 15). Patriot games. *Advertising Age, 72*(42), 1.
Nicklaus, D. (2002, January 16). Excess plant capacity forces Ford's hand. *St. Louis Post-Dispatch*, p. C1.

posted to Web sites. While news media tried to keep up with the constant, and constantly changing, information on 9/11, ordinary citizens turned to the Internet. In 2001 blogs and other social networking sites were not as widely used as they would become in the years after 9/11, yet when the attacks occurred electronic communication gave people an immediate way to share information—accurate or not—about what had happened and how they were feeling in the moment. Robert Andrews (2006) called September 11 "the birth of the blog" in his essay by the same name. In a similar way, Americans' perspectives on owning cell phones may have shifted after 9/11 from being seen as convenient accessories to necessary resources in case of an emergency. The fact that passengers on the hijacked airplanes, as well as workers trapped in the Twin Towers, were able to communicate for a final time with loved ones because they had cell phones made owning such devices seem like a prudent thing to do. Many of those calls were used to re-create the timelines of events or saved to memorial Web sites like National Public Radio's Sonic Memorial Project.

Children and Schools

Children were affected in specific ways by the events of September 11. Children in schools around the country had a wide range of experiences. Some schools turned on the television coverage of the attacks, and students were allowed or even encouraged to watch. Other schools dismissed students early to the care of their parents, passing the decision about what children should and should not know about the attacks to mothers and fathers.

Children also inspired acts of kindness in the city. For example, Sue Lucarelli, a teacher at the Churchill School in lower Manhattan, began a teddy bear campaign for children in New York City. On September 11, in an effort to comfort her young students, Lucarelli gave them teddy bears to hug. Soon all of the students in Lucarelli's school, as well as those in neighboring schools, wanted teddy bears. Quickly known as the Bear Lady, Lucarelli and members of the Community Reformed Church of Manhasset, distributed 58,000 teddy bears to young people throughout New York City (Lucarelli, 2004).

Art was another way that children dealt with the aftermath of September 11. Schools encouraged children to make art to express their anxieties, concerns, and sadness. Among the most recognized collections of children's art was the exhibit, *The Day Our World Changed: Children's Art of 9/11*, which opened at the Museum of the City of New York and was published in a book by the same name. Other children's artwork was collected in *Do Not Be Sad*, a collection of children's writing and drawings sent to the Engine 24 Ladder 5 FDNY firehouse. The children of Staten Island created art that was displayed in *Healing Hands from Hurting Hearts*, part of Freedom From Fear, a national mental health advocacy organization ("Children Use Art," 2002).

Books, pamphlets, and programs were also created to help children who were impacted by the attacks or to assist parents, teachers, and other community workers in talking with children about what had happened. For example, *Helping America*

VIDEO GAMES AFTER 9/11

In the aftermath of September 11, video games were faced with a particular visual dilemma: Would the images they typically include be inappropriate for a nation so deeply impacted by the attacks? Several companies withdrew their games from the shelves or temporarily held back release dates. Activision's "Spider-Man 2 Enter: Electro," for example, was delayed in its release because twin buildings suggestive of the Twin Towers appeared in game. The logo of Arush Entertainment's "Duke Nukem: Manhattan Project"—which included the World Trade Center—was removed from its Web site. Microsoft deleted images of the World Trade Center from its popular "PC Flight Simulator," a computer game in which players learn to fly airplanes. As one spokesperson stated, "We don't want to have any imagery in there that would upset anyone" ("Game Makers," para. 6). Despite such concerns, in 2003 "9–11 Survivor" was briefly available on the Internet. The game placed the player in the burning Twin Towers from which the player must try to escape. In 2008, a French company released "New York Defender." The object of the game is to prevent planes from hitting towers; players do so by shooting the planes down. Families of the 9/11 victims expressed outrage at the game's premise, despite the fact that the company said they just wanted to teach players a lesson about terrorism ("Families, Victims Outraged," 2008).

—*Sara E. Quay*

References

Families, victims outraged by 9/11 online game. (2008, January 2). *CBS*. Retrieved from http://wcbstv.com

Game makers blot out signs of WTC tragedy. (2001, September 19). *The Hollywod Reporter*. Retrieved from http://www.allbusiness.com

---

Cope (2001) was released soon after the attacks. Copies were given to families with young school-age children in preparation for the first anniversary of the attacks. The international aid agency, Mercy Corps, offered a collection of materials, including a free pamphlet titled *How Are We Now? Promoting Continued Healing for Our Children*, a curriculum titled "Becoming the World," and a trauma education program called "Comfort for Kids." Publisher Scholastic created a special online report for kids on its Scholastic New Zone called *9/11: Six Months Later*. Scholastic News and Junior Scholastic—news magazines for children in grades five through eight—also covered the six-month anniversary of the attacks, while AOL Time Warner Foundation offered schools a guide called *Reflect, Reach Out, Rebuild: Remembering 9/11*, which was created to help commemorate the first anniversary.

Memorials

Almost as quickly as the terrorist attacks took place, people gathered in public spaces around the country to remember those who were lost. Spontaneous memorials—public collections of flowers, mementos, notes, candles, and other expressions of sympathy—appeared almost immediately at the crash sites and in other places where individuals gathered together to mourn. As time went by, the number of items left at spontaneous memorials grew so large—especially at locations like Ground Zero— that more organized memorials sites were created. At Ground Zero, for example,

---

ST. PAUL'S CHAPEL: THE LITTLE CHAPEL THAT COULD

Standing near the Twin Towers, St. Paul's Chapel—a small church built in 1766—was an unlikely candidate to play a significant role in the aftermath of the attacks. Yet the church, despite being directly across from where both the North and the South Towers came crashing down, sustained little damage and opened its doors to rescue and recovery workers who ate and rested there for the next eight months. Volunteers arrived at the church in droves to cook, clothe, and care for the firefighters, police officers, and other personnel. As Arthur C. Benedict, a volunteer at St. Paul's, described it the chapel became

> a place of rest and refuge for firefighters, police, and others . . . involved in the massive search, rescue and recovery effort. Its pews became beds. Massage therapists and chiro-practors relieve the pain in their backs while others—and the peace of the place itself— help ease the hurt in their souls. And volunteers like ourselves serve food, make beds, haul supplies, and do whatever else we can to help out. (Benedict, 2001, para. 2)

Local restaurants donated food, and gradually letters, teddy bears, and other tokens of appreciation appeared at St. Paul's. Banners from people around the world were hung on the chapel walls. The church continued to serve the Ground Zero work-ers until May 31, 2002, the day after the Closing Ceremony at Ground Zero and on June 2, the St. Paul's Chapel closed in order to be cleaned and restored.

Registering its crucial role in, and inescapable connection with 9/11, on the first anniversary of the attacks the chapel opened an exhibit called *Out of the Dust: A Year of Ministry at Ground Zero*. Since then, St. Paul's has incorporated September 11 into its identity, offering the more than one million visitors to its walls a place to reflect, learn, and absorb the events of 9/11. Online exhibits and information, such as "Unwavering Spirit: Hope and Healing at Ground Zero" (2009) incorporate artifacts, community messages, and photographs of the church at different times after 9/11. A book containing images of St. Paul's after the attacks, *Light at Ground Zero* (Sanderson, 2004), was published to record the chapel's role in the recovery efforts. In addition, a children's book, *The Little Chapel That Stood* (2003) reminds readers of all ages that it is not size, but commitment, that can make a difference in challenging moments.

—Sara E. Quay

References

Benedict, A. C. (2001, November 22). Hope of recovery. *Philadelphia Inquirer*. Retrieved from http://www.philly.com

Greca, A. M. L., Evin, S. W., & Sevin, E. L. (2001). *Helping America Cope*. Coral Gables, FL: 7-Dippity, Inc.

Sanderson, K. (2004). *Light at Ground Zero: St. Paul's chapel after 9/11*. Baltimore: Square Halo Books.

Unwavering Spirit: Hope and Healing at Ground Zero. (2009). Exhibit at St. Paul's Chapel. Retrieved from http://www.stpaulschapel.org

St. Paul's Chapel became a place where mourners could leave flowers, tokens, and messages in honor of the dead. Similarly, viewing platforms at Ground Zero were created to contain and direct those who were determined to visit the wreckage. Hollywood stars and other celebrities—including then political leaders President George W. Bush and Mayor Rudolph Giuliani—paid their respects at Ground Zero soon after the attacks adding to national attention to the site.

As time went by, official memorials were established at all three crash sites. St. Paul's Chapel retained its function at Ground Zero as a place for visitors to see firsthand some of the relics from the recovery effort, including pews, beds, and messages from people around the world. The Tribute WTC Visitor Center, located near the Ground Zero construction area, opened in 2006. Created by the September 11th Families' Association, the Tribute Center gives visitors to Ground Zero the chance to learn more about "the September 11th community" (http://www.tributewtc.org). A firefighter memorial was also unveiled in 2006 at the fire station next to Ground Zero (http://www.fdnytenhouse.com). After complicated discussion and debate, the National September 11 Memorial and Museum at the World Trade Center was approved, and a location at which visitors could preview the future building was opened in August 2009 (http://www.national911memorial.org).

In Shanksville, Pennsylvania, the United 93 memorial, managed by the National Park Service, gives visitors the opportunity to remember those who died on the plane that crashed into the rural landscape. Like the memorial planned for Ground Zero, the United 93 memorial design has been selected, and after initial conflict over use and ownership of the land on which the memorial will be built, construction is slated to begin in 2010 (http://www.nps.gov). Finally, at the Pentagon a memorial to those who died aboard American Airlines Flight 77 was erected in 2007 (http://www.whs.mil/memorial/) (see Chapter 7, Visual Culture).

In addition to formal and informal memorials, other forms of remembering 9/11 and its victims also appeared after the attacks. Souvenirs of the Twin Towers, for example, were quickly available for purchase by street vendors around Ground Zero. Photographs, postcards, snow globes, coins, and T-shirts were among the many goods visitors could buy to commemorate the fallen buildings.

Conclusion

Everyday life was changed after September 11. From beliefs and values to actions and behaviors, Americans found themselves in a transitional period where the old rules did not necessarily hold. While each individual responded in his or her own way, general trends pervaded the country as ordinary citizens adjusted to an extraordinary time. Increased emphasis on family, friends, religion, and philanthropy were common as people sought comfort in the face of tragedy. At the same time, hate crimes increased, people became fearful of travelling, and ordinary events seemed dangerous to attend. Some activities were deemed more appropriate than others, and the entertainment

GROUND ZERO

While the attacks led to plane crashes in three distinct sites—lower Manhattan, Washington, D.C., and Shanksville, Pennsylvania—the place most clearly associated with September 11 is lower Manhattan, specifically where the Twin Towers formerly stood. The location was quickly given the name Ground Zero, a term that evokes a location in which violent change has taken place. First the focus of recovery efforts, Ground Zero has also come to stand for a sacred ground, a place to remember those who were lost on September 11.

Within days of the attacks, Ground Zero drew visitors from around the world who travelled to the site to mourn those who were killed, leave written messages and physical tokens at spontaneous shrines, help support the rescue workers, and simply experience the place where such dramatic events had taken place. Fences were quickly raised around Ground Zero to keep visitors from getting to close to the debris, while viewing platforms were erected at specific locales around the perimeter to give people a glimpse of the gaping space where the Twin Towers had once stood. Separate areas were created for families of victims to visit Ground Zero in privacy.

The recovery process began within days of September 11 and continued until May 30, 2002. During that time, the 17-acre site developed its own words, customs, and communication process. As Gary Suson (2005) documents in his description of "Ground Zero Lingo," bucket brigades, "the human chain of rescue workers who removed rubble from the hole by passing buckets of debris" from one person to the next, were implemented during the first weeks after the attacks. Ground Zero was also called "the pit," "the hole," and "the bathtub." The Salvation Army tent, a "huge white dome" where food and beds were available was called "the Bubble" or "the Tent." Phrases like "Ground Zero Time"—the way workers at Ground Zero tended to lose track of what time or day it was—and "Ground Zeroed Out"—when a person had been at Ground Zero too long and needed to take time off—were developed to express the experience of the recovery effort.

On May 30, a closing ceremony was organized to officially end the cleanup. Those working that day participated in the symbolic act of removing "The Last Piece of Steel" from the site, accompanied by a single drumbeat (Atkins, p. 70). Ground Zero has continued to attract visitors from around the world, becoming the focal point for numerous organized tours of lower Manhattan and an official destination in many guidebooks to New York City.

—*Sara E. Quay*

References

Cleanup operations at ground zero. (2008). In S. E. Atkins (Ed.), *The 9/11 Encyclopedia*. (Vol. 1). Westport, CT: Praeger Security International, 68–71.

Muschamp, H. (2001, December 22). With viewing platforms, a dignified approach to ground zero. *The New York Times*, p. B8.

Suson, G. (2005, June). *Ground Zero lingo*. Ground Zero Museum workshop. Retrieved from http://www.groundzeromuseumworkshop.com

industry made changes in programming and offerings in the aftermath of the attacks. Shopping, always an American pastime, became a recognized expression of patriotism and patriotic products filled store shelves and advertisements. Eventually, everyday life settled into a more regular, familiar, pattern. Yet life as Americans knew it prior to 9/11 would never be quite the same.

—*Sara E. Quay*

References

Adler, J. (2001, November 26). Rites of comfort: This Thanksgiving, Americans will gather, overeat, cuddle—and be especially grateful for what we've got. *Newsweek,* 66.

Andrews, R. (2006, September 11). 9/11: Birth of the blog. *Wired.* Retrieved from http://www.wired.com

Atkins, S. E. (Ed.) (2008). *The 9/11 encyclopedia* (Vol. 1). Westport, CT: Praeger Security International.

Bland, E. (2001, November 26). Frosty the flag waver. *Time, 158*(23), 25.

Bovino, A. (2002, August 18). In 9/11 art, children look back and ahead. *The New York Times.* Retrieved from www.nytimes.com

Brenner, D. S. (2001, November 30). Hanukkah 2001 transcends Judaism. *Jewish News of Greater Phoenix, 54*(12). Retrieved from http://www.jewishaz.com

Bush, G. W. (2001, September 11). Statement from the president in his address to the nation. Retrieved from http://georgewbush-whitehouse.archives.gov

Cannon, A., Shapiro, J., & Perry, J. (2001, October 22). A people involved. *U.S. News & World Report, 131*(17), 50.

Cardwell, D. (2001, December 28). In final address, Giuliani envisions soaring memorial; shrine at Ground Zero; he urges that plans for site need not be driven by need for economic development. *The New York Times,* p. A1.

Children use art to express and soothe feelings from 9-11; hundreds of Staten Island children lost parents, neighbors, friends. (2002, August 13). *PR Newswire.* Retrieved from http://www.highbeam.com

Cohen, A., Bradford, L., Donnelly, S., Thigpen, D., Thomas, C., & Underwood, J. (2001, November 19). Flying low. *Time, 158*(22), 68.

Comarow, A., & Hobson, K. (2001, October 22). Protecting yourself. *U.S. News & World Report, 131*(17), 46.

Corliss, R., Bruce, L., Philadelphia, D., & Ressner, J. (2001, October 29). Red, white and boo! *Time, 158*(19), 76.

Edwards, B. (2001, October 26). Profile: Airport security measures. *Morning Edition.* Retrieved from www.npr.org

Gibbs, N. (2001, November 19). We gather together. *Time, 158*(22), 28–41.

Hate crime reports up in wake of terrorist attacks. (2002, September 16). *CNNOnline.* Retrieved from http://www.cnn.com

Heller, D. (Ed.). (2005). *The selling of 9/11: How a national tragedy became a commodity.* New York: Palgrave Macmillan.

Jabs, C. (2001, October 29). A day for my kids to be scary, not scared: This Halloween, I'll draw the line at gore, but allow my children to look as monstrous as they want. *Newsweek, 138*(18), 14.

Johnson, D. (2001, September 24). Filling the demand. *Newsweek, 138*(13), 84.

Kelly, K. (2001, October 8). Looking for meaning in the ruins. *U.S. News & World Report, 131*(14), 52.

Knit 1, purl 2, point and click. (2008, July 21). *Marketplace.* Retrieved from http://marketplace.publicradio.org

Lim, P., Perry, J., Slania, J., & Sharpe, R. (2001, December 10). A plan for all seasons. *U.S. News & World Report, 131*(24), 40.

Lloyd, C. (2004, March 23). Shelter-shocked: Is the proliferation of home magazines about post-9/11 nesting or the need to fetishize our big mortgages? *San Francisco Chronicle* [online]. Retrieved from http://sfgate.com

Lucarelli, S. (2004). *T. bear's hugs across America.* Escondido, CA: Old Castle.

Marking the anniversary. (2002, September 11). *Time, 160*(11). Retrieved from http://www.time.com

Martens, E. (2001, December 10). Dow soars. Thanks, Tyra. *Time, 158*(25), 27.

McGuigan, C. (2001, November 26). Nesting instincts: Despite the economy, we want comfy new things where we live. *Newsweek, 138*(22), 72.

Miller, L., & Eady, A. (2007, July 2). Shrine. *Newsweek, 150*(2), 14.

Remains of the day. (2002, September 9). *Time, 160*(11), 45.

Richard Cohen still wants revenge for 9/11. (2009, September 11). (Interview). *Talk of the Nation.* Retrieved from http://www.npr.org

Song, S., & van Dyk, D. (2001, December 3). Christmas present. *Time, 158*(24), 20.

Sporich, B. (2001, September 18). Video surge in wake of terror. *Hollywood Reporter—International Edition, 370*(4), 5.

Stein, J. (2001, October 29). Shopping during wartime. *Time, 158*(19), 78.

Streisand, B. (2001, November 10). The comfort zone. *U.S. News & World Report, 131*(21), 39.

Suarez, R. (2002, July 4). Securing the fourth. *Online News Hour.* Retrieved from http://www.pbs.org/newshour

What we think. (2002, September 11). *Time, 160*(11), 18.

Zoglin, R., & Goehner, A. (2001, October 29). The feel-good remedy. *Time, 158*(19), 84.

SPOTLIGHT ESSAY/EVERYDAY LIFE: ADVERTISING

When it became clear that the United States was being attacked on September 11, 2001, the nation's media outlets began covering the situation without commercial breaks. Some radio stations resumed commercial interruptions in the evening or the next day while television broadcasts remained ad free until September 15 when commercials began to reappear (Aberman, 2001). In the weeks following September 11, advertisements by companies such as AT&T, Miller beer, American Express, the National Restaurant Association, Ford, General Motors (GM), and Cotton, Inc. used patriotic themes, depicted U.S. flags, and turned to red, white, and blue color schemes. Companies also developed patriotic-themed products, such as Breathe Right's Stars and Stripes strips, and hung flags in their store windows, as was the case with Ralph Lauren (Campbell, 2003). Other ad campaigns, such as those containing tasteless humor or insensitive copy, were withdrawn from circulation. For example, after September 11 Coca-Cola pulled an ad featuring the slogan "Life tastes good," while American Trans Air withdrew its offbeat campaign featuring a print ad with the line: "If there's going to be a war, we'll fight it out on our own turf" (Aberman, 2001).

Given concerns regarding what impact the terrorist attacks would have on the economy, Americans were urged to continue their spending. Some ad campaigns even centered on the theme that consuming goods and services was important for the nation and would assist the country in returning to "normal." San Francisco Mayor Willie Brown Jr. and the San Francisco Chamber of Commerce launched the "America: Open for Business Campaign" in November of 2001. The campaign spread across the country and Mayor Brown said the campaign was designed to "let the world know that this city, and this nation, will rise from the ashes of this national tragedy and get this economy moving again" (Brown, 2001, para. 1).

It was not as easy, however, for companies to market travel and tourism, particularly airline travel. Here, themes of perseverance in times of trauma were integrated into ad campaigns. For example, the Travel Industry Association of America crafted a print ad that stated travelling was a "cherished right," it was "safe and secure," and that "nobody can take that away from us. Not now. Not ever" (Magenheim, 2001, p. 4). The Association's television ad featured excerpts from President Bush's speech calling for a return to normalcy (Millard, 2001). The airlines themselves, faced with the difficult challenge of promoting their services when the country was fearful of flying, also crafted advertisements that took nationalism and freedom as its main themes. United Airlines created a commercial that aired in the weeks after September 11 where pilots and flight attendants reflected on their love of flying. Titled "We Are United," United employees stated their longevity with the company, the enjoyment of the "freedom of flying," and stated "we're not going to let anyone take that away from us. We're Americans and this is not going to beat us down" (United Airlines, 2001). Similarly, American Airlines declared in their commercial spot that they were "proud to bear the name American" ("American Airlines Post 9/11 Commercial," 2001).

The American automotive industry also referred to the terrorist attacks' potential impact on the economy in their post-9/11 advertising campaigns. General Motors launched a campaign at the end of September called "Keep America Rolling," and Ford debuted a campaign titled "Ford Drives America." Both companies offered interest-free financing and suggested that buying a car would be good for the country. General Motors was the first to launch the campaign, and the interest-free incentive (an average savings of $3,600 per car) worked to increase their sales, prompting Ford to follow suit (Meredith, 2001). In their commercial, General Motors refers to the American Dream and refuses "to let anyone take it away," while another commercial encourages viewers to experience "the simple joy of buying a new car" (General Motors, 2001). In its commercial, Ford stated "In light of these challenging times, we at Ford want to do our part in moving America forward" (Campbell, 2003, p. 52).

Other advertising campaigns referenced September 11 in a more somber way. In November 2001, the *New York Times* began its own print ad campaign that featured altered images of well-known Norman Rockwell paintings. Between November 2 and December 1, 2001, the *New York Times* campaign displayed five altered Rockwell paintings: The newspaper in the original painting was replaced with an image of the *New York Times* displaying a current headline (Frascina, 2003). At the Superbowl in January 2002, Anheuser-Busch aired a 60-second Budweiser beer commercial featuring the iconic Clydesdale horses walking through rural countryside, then through a small town, and finally over the Brooklyn Bridge to halt before a view of the New York City skyline, now absent the Twin Towers. A close-up of one of the horses' teary eyes is seen, and the group of animals kneel down together before the screen fades to black. The commercial aired only once on broadcast television but is available for viewing on many Internet Web sites and frequently appears on top advertising lists (see for example, Horovitz, 2008). In 2003, the Port Authority of New York and New Jersey commissioned a print ad to commemorate September 11 that ran in the *New York Times*, the *New Yorker*, and various other New York publications. The ad's image shows two towers being drawn on a chalkboard by a young boy. The copy reads: "Generations will remember. Honoring the past. Envisioning the future. Rebuilding together" (Sampey, 2003).

The advertising industry monitored consumer responses to advertising and ad campaigns after September 11 in order to best craft messages to which the nation in mourning would be receptive. After nonstop media coverage of the attacks, consumers reported the return of advertising a relief (Aberman, 2001), and as more patriotic-themed ads made their way into the culture, the industry tracking polls noted that integration of patriotic themes was well received provided ads were not exploiting the tragedy or too saturated with nationalism (Campbell, 2003). Over the year, polls indicated that the most popular ads were light and funny whereas ads that were unkind or tasteless were viewed unfavorably (Howard, 2002). As the one-year anniversary drew near, many companies, including Pepsi, Coke, GM, Sears, Target, and Nissan made the decision not to advertise on that day, while a few, including Nextel, underwrote September 11-themed programs (Gaffney, 2002).

—*Amy M. Damico*

References

Aberman, S. (2001, October 24). Judging the mood of a nation. *PBS NewsHour Extra*. Retrieved June 1, 2009, from http://www.pbs.org/newshour

American Airlines Post 9/11 Commercial. (2001). Retrieved June 16, 2009, from http://www.youtube.com

Brown, W. (2001). *San Francisco open for business: A message from the mayor*. Retrieved June 16, 2009, from the San Francisco Chamber of Commerce Web site: http://www.sfvirtualshop.com/mayor_brown.htm

Campbell, C. (2003). Commodifying September 11: Advertising, myth and hegemony. In S. Chermak, F. Bailey, and M. Brown (Eds.), *Media Representations of September 11* (pp. 47–66). Westport, CT: Praeger.

Frascina, F. (2003). *The New York Times*, Norman Rockwell, and the new patriotism. *Journal of Visual Culture, 2*(1), 99–130.

Gaffney, J. (2002, August 28). Nextel to sponsor CBS 9/11 special. *Online Media Daily*. Retrieved from http://www.mediapost.com/publications

General Motors. (2001). *Keep America rolling* [Television commercial]. Retrieved from http://
     www.coloribus.com/adsarchive/tv-commercials/general-motors-keep-america-rolling
     -118972/

Horovitz, B. (2008, February 10). 20 highlights in 20 years of Ad Meter. *USA Today*.
     Retrieved from http://www.usatoday.com

Howard, T. (2002, December 30). Advertisers and viewers agree: It's OK to be funny again.
     USA Today, 3B.

Magenheim, H. (2001, October 18). Ad messages focus on patriotism, reassurance. *Travel
     Weekly*, p. 4.

Meredith, R. (2001, October 29). What's good for General Motors . . . *Forbes*. Retrieved from
     http://www.forbes.com

Millard, P. (2001, November 30). Patriotism becomes a trendy advertising theme. *The Business
     Journal-Milwaukee*, p. 8. Retrieved from http://milwaukee.bizjournals.com/milwaukee/

Sampey, K. (2003, September 8). G2 Worldwide creates 9/11 tribute ad. Adweek. Retrieved
     from http://www.adweek.com

United Airlines. (2001). *We are United* [United Airlines post-9/11 television commercial].
     Retrieved June 16, 2008, from http://www.youtube.com

SPOTLIGHT ESSAY/EVERYDAY LIFE: COMFORT FOOD

Of the many responses to September 11, one of the most meaningful, yet simple, was
the use of food to nourish, comfort, and console. At Ground Zero, food became
not only essential sustenance to weary rescue personnel but a means for everyday
volunteers—who cooked and served—to contribute to the recovery process. Food
became important in other parts of the country as well, where the nation's anxiety
and distress over the events led many individuals to seek solace and relief in their
favorite comfort foods.

After the September 11 attacks, the need for the physiological and psychological
benefits of comfort food was almost immediate. Part of this need stemmed from the fact
that "food not only nourishes but signifies" (Fischler, 1988, p. 276). For the volunteers
at Ground Zero, for example, the food they served symbolized their caring and concern
for the victims, their families, and the rescue workers. By preparing and serving food in
nearby hotels, restaurants, partially destroyed buildings, or tents, volunteers participated in the humble act of offering a hot meal—and perhaps comfort and hope—to
the police officers, firefighters, rescue workers, medical personnel, construction
workers, and others contributing to the relief efforts. As Iannolo (2004), one of the
many volunteers who helped prepare and serve these meals, explained, "A hot meal
can lend solace when we truly need it, and providing such a meal can be the most
effective way to show one's caring for another human being" (para. 15).

Other volunteers offered similar testimony. In "A Visit to Ground Zero Just after
9/11," one volunteer recounts that although they had set up a makeshift cafeteria with
folding tables and chairs in a partially destroyed restaurant, the food that they offered
included "salmon, lamb, ratatouille . . . green beans, sweet potatoes, fried chicken" (p. 3).

These foods were carefully prepared and served to provide the most nourishing and heartening meal possible under the circumstances.

Food providers came from across the country to offer food and comfort to rescue workers and others. The Gumbo Krewe from Louisiana, for example, served "thousands of free bowls of steaming hot gumbo and spicy jambalaya" (Ratnesar & Stein, 2001, p. 2), and a California pizzeria owner traveled to Manhattan to help prepare meals in "a makeshift tent little place down by the piers," cooking up pots of soup, chili, chicken, and pasta (Burns, 2001, para. 6).

As Kendra and Wachtendorf (2002) describe, other well-meaning individuals brought in foods ranging "from home-baked goods to hot meals, typically pasta," (p. 13), but ironically some of the food intended to be comfort food instead became a security risk. The "terms 'rebel food' and 'renegade supplies' were used to refer to food and other items that were brought into the impact area on an ad hoc, uncontrolled basis, sometimes by people who were known to the recipient, but often not," bringing "issues of access, health and safety, and security" (p. 13). Whether or not the food could contain harmful ingredients was a key issue; another issue was whether the food had been properly stored, because if not, it could become contaminated, posing a health risk to those who consumed it (p. 14). Although it was meant as comfort food, the realization that food now posed a security threat affected the level of reassurance meant to be offered along with the food itself (Kendra and Wachtendorf, 2002, p. 14).

As relief efforts continued, restaurants in the area began filling more requests for comfort foods. As Thorn (2001) explains, requests for burgers, lasagna, and other home-style dishes increased once diners returned to the restaurants, even causing some upscale restaurants to add such items to their menus to meet customer requests. The Tribeca Grand Hotel even replaced its more upscale menu with simpler foods like pasta, in addition to adding a children's menu after it became temporary housing for families (Thorn, 2001, para. 18).

The need for comfort foods was significant not only in New York City, but across the country as Americans turned to their favorite foods to overcome the fear, anxiety, and helplessness caused by the terrorist attacks. Restaurants from New York to California reported that diners were ordering more comfort foods such as burgers, chili, and chicken pot pie; some restaurants even added comfort food selections such as "grown-up" versions of items such as chocolate pudding and grilled cheese sandwiches to meet their customers' requests (Thorn, 2001, para. 6, 19). As John Hurley, the owner of Home, a San Francisco restaurant, stated, "After September 11, people want to feel more comfortable. . . . They don't want fancy foods. They just want foods that they know and trust. And you can really trust meatloaf, mashed potatoes, and macaroni and cheese" (Farley, 2002, para. 6).

The events on September 11, 2001, had a profound impact on American culture, and comfort foods played a significant role in the nation's psychological recovery. Although there was some concern about food being contaminated, overall comfort foods provided a tangible form of consolation and assurance that was citizens so desperately needed after the 9/11 tragedy, both in New York City and across the country.

—*A. A. Hutira*

References

"A visit to Ground Zero just after 9/11." (2007, September 19). Retrieved from www
    .scribd.com

Burns, K. (2001, November 3). Pizzeria owner cooks for workers at Ground Zero. *North
    Country Times*. Retrieved from http://www.nctimes.com

Farley, D. (2002, January). Comfort food nation: We put down our turkey drumsticks
    and meatloaf long enough. *The Wave Magazine*. Retrieved from http://www
    .thewavemag.com

Fischler, C. (1988). Food, self, and identity. *Social Science Information, 27*, 275–292.

Iannolo, J. (2004, September 9). Comfort food. *TheAtlasphere.com*. Retrieved from http://
    www.theatlasphere.com

Kendra, J. M., & Wachtendorf, T. (2002, August 17). Rebel food . . . renegade supplies: Con-
    vergence after the world trade center attack. (Preliminary Paper 316). Newark, DE:
    Disaster Research Center, University of Delaware. Retrieved from http://www
    .udel.edu

Ratnesar, R., & Stein, J. (2001, December 23). Out of the ruins. *Time.com*, 1–4. Retrieved
    from http://www.time.com

Thorn, B. (2001, October 15). Seeking comfort, diners indulge in feel-good fare. *Nation's
    Restaurant News*. Retrieved from www.nrn.com

SPOTLIGHT ESSAY/EVERYDAY LIFE: HATE CRIMES AND PROFILING

As Americans learned that the World Trade Center and the Pentagon had been hit by hijacked airliners it was impossible not to wonder, "Who could have done this? Who were the hijackers?" Images that came to mind were fueled by earlier attacks—the Egyptian "cleric" who was convicted of masterminding an attack on the World Trade Center in 1993, or Timothy McVeigh, who brought down the Alfred P. Murrah Federal Building in Oklahoma City in 1995. Three days after 9/11, the FBI announced the names of the 19 hijackers: All of them were Arab, Muslim men who were later confirmed to be from the United Arab Emirates, Saudi Arabia, Lebanon, and Egypt.

Following this announcement, the media began flooding American televisions with images of Osama bin Laden and other dark-skinned men wearing checkered scarves (*kaffiyeh*), turbans, and beards, giving credence to the derogatory term, "towel head." In 2004, a report by the Media and Society Research Group at Cornell University noted that Americans who paid more attention to television news programs were more likely to fear terrorism and have negative views of Muslims. Forty-four percent of those surveyed agreed with statements such as, "U.S. government agencies should profile citizens as potential threats based on being Muslim or having Middle Eastern heritage," and "All Muslim Americans should be required to register their where-abouts with the federal government" (Nisbet & Shanahan, 2004, p. 6).

Muslim women wearing *hijab*—modest dress that commonly includes a head covering—also became highly visible targets of harassment. Researchers at the City

University of New York noted that "veiled women were cursed, yelled at with racial slurs and death threats, spit at, hit with a stick, kicked, asked to remove the *hijab* in public, and prevented access to their destination" (Bakalian & Bozorgmerh, 2005, p. 218). In the early months after the attacks, many women were encouraged by well-intentioned family members to remove their head coverings or adopt something less conspicuous such as a hat and turtleneck (Lewin & Niebuhr, 2001, p. 5). Others were inspired to stand up to the backlash by converting to Islam or even wearing hijab for the first time. Discussing this topic on a blog, one woman observed that she had converted in July 2001, but did not immediately change her style of dress. After September 11 she decided to wear hijab because "I felt like I had to be strong and to let others know that Islam is a beautiful religion" (Maryam01, 2006).

Six days after 9/11, President George W. Bush held a press conference at a mosque in Washington D.C., urging Americans to treat Muslims with respect ("Bush Denounces," 2001). At the same time, he cautioned Americans to be on the lookout for "suspicious" people and activities without clarifying what to look for. As a result, thousands of men and women with Arab names or a "Middle Eastern" appearance were subjected to hate crimes and harassment, particularly around mosques and airports. This kind of profiling became official policy in 2002 under the Terrorist Information and Prevention System (TIPS), which engaged thousands of truck drivers, bus drivers, and mail carriers to serve as "citizen observers" (Bakalian & Bozorgmerh, 2005, p. 224). In 2006, an activist was denied boarding at John F Kennedy International Airport (JFK airport) in New York simply for wearing a T-shirt that said, "We will not be silent" in English and Arabic. An airline official told him, "Going to an airport with a T-shirt in Arabic script is like going to a bank and wearing a T-shirt that says, 'I'm a robber'" ("Airline Passenger," 2006).

Although Muslims also experienced discrimination after the attempted bombing of the World Trade Center in 1993 and the bombing of the Alfred P. Murrah Federal Building in Oklahoma City in 1995 (an act initially blamed on Muslims), the Council on American-Islamic Relations (CAIR) observed that "the post-September 11 anti-Muslim backlash has been the most violent" (2002, para. 2). In April 2006, for example, a Muslim student at Baylor University in Texas was attacked by a white man in his 30s, who "pushed, slapped, and kicked her while using racial and anti-Muslim slurs and pulled off her headscarf" (CAIR, 2007, p. 9). The woman had to be treated at a hospital for a dislocated shoulder. Later that year in Fremont, California, Alia Ansari, an immigrant from Afghanistan, who always wore an hijab when she left her house, was walking with her three-year-old daughter to school when a man jumped out of a car, shot her at point-blank range and sped away. Since nothing was taken (and she was not carrying a purse), relatives and local leaders said "the only motive they could see, outside of insanity, would be hatred" (Kuruvila & Lee, 2006, p. B1). CAIR, which has gathered thousands of discrimination complaints since September 11, 2001, has observed that common "triggers" for these incidents include being from the Middle East or South Asia, having a Muslim name, requesting time off from work for prayers, and wearing a beard, turban, *kufi* (skullcap), or hijab (CAIR, 2007, p. 20).

Some people who simply resembled Muslims were also affected. Balbir Singh Sodhi, for example—a devoted member of the Sikh religion who wore a beard and a turban as part of his faith—was the first reported victim of a hate crime in the aftermath of 9/11. On September 15, 2001, he was planting flowers outside his gas station when he was shot and killed by Frank Roque, a man who called himself "a patriot" (Goodstein & Lewin, 2001, p. 1) and declared that "all Arabs had to be shot" (Ritter, 2002, p. 4a). A tribute to Sodhi on www.sikhnet.com notes that "he was killed simply because of the way he looked" (Khalsa, 2001).

After September 11, 2001, any reminders of the 9/11 hijackers, including beards, scarves, and head coverings took on dramatic new meanings in American society. Without more education about Muslim cultures and dress, it could take many years for these attitudes to change.

—*Heather Marie Akou*

References

Airline passenger told to conceal Arabic T-shirt. (2006, August 30). *MSNBC.com*. Retrieved from http://www.msnbc.msn.com

American-Islamic Relations (CAIR). (2002). *The status of Muslim civil rights in the United States 2002: Stereotypes and civil liberties*. Retrieved from http://www.cair.com

American-Islamic Relations (CAIR). (2007). *The status of Muslim civil rights in the United States 2007: Presumption of guilt*. Retrieved from http://www.cair.com

Bakalian, A., & Bozorgmerh, M. (2005). Discriminatory reactions to September 11, 2001 terrorism. In P. G. Min. (Ed.), *Encyclopedia of racism in the United States* (pp. 213–231). Westport, CT: Greenwood Press.

Bush denounces Muslim harassment. (2001, September 17). *CNN.com*. Retrieved from http://archives.cnn.com

Goodstein, L., & Lewin, T. (2001, September 18). A nation challenged: Violence and harassment; Victims of mistaken identity, Sikhs pay a price for turbans. *The New York Times*. Retrieved from www.nytimes.com

Khalsa, E. O. K. K. (2001). *Balbir Singh Sodhi honored*. Retrieved from http://fateh.sikhnet.com/s/BalbirSodhi

Kuruvila, M. C., & Lee, H. K. (2006, October 21). Religious hate seen as motive in killing. *San Francisco Chronicle*, p. B1.

Lewin, T., & Niebuhr, G. (2001, September 18). A nation challenged: Violence; attacks and harassment continue on Middle Eastern people and mosques. *The New York Times*. Retrieved from www.nytimes.com

Maryam01. (2006, April 26). *Conversion stories*. Revert Muslims Association. Retrieved from http://revertmuslims.com

Nisbet, E. C., & Shanahan, J. (2004). *MSRG special report: Restrictions on civil liberties, view of Islam, & Muslim Americans*. Retrieved from Cornell University, Media and Society Research Group Web site: http://www.yuricareport.com/Civil%20Rights/CornellMuslimReportCivilRights.pdf

Ritter, J. (2002, September 12). Hate crimes born out of tragedy added victims. *USA Today*, p. 4a.

SPOTLIGHT ESSAY/EVERYDAY LIFE: GREETING CARDS

National tragedies often produce a need to connect with others, a need to feel a sense of belonging and unity. In the weeks following 9/11, sales of greeting cards increased as people used the cards to reach out to other people, renew the bonds of family and friendship, and offer comfort to survivors and families who had lost loved ones in the attacks. The sending of greeting cards provided a tangible emotional release for both the senders and the receivers, offering words of encouragement and hope during a time when many individuals had difficulty finding words of their own to express what they were feeling. Those who received the cards found a source of comfort in the words and in their acknowledgment. The cards—many of which were created and sold specifically for the purpose of meeting the needs of post-9/11 life—were also tangible keepsakes. Overall, greeting cards played an important role in helping many Americans deal with the complex and overwhelming emotions that many individuals were experiencing in the wake of the 9/11 attacks.

Historically, greeting cards have been used as a way to get through times of national crisis—such as World War II, the Great Depression, and the Gulf War—so it was only natural that more greeting cards would be sent after 9/11. This buying and sending of cards during times of grieving and crisis, Jackson (2005) states, serves as a form of "psychological first aid for a distressed nation," since "[g]reeting cards constitute a socially acceptable and tangible way to express emotion and concern" (p. 13).

Sales of greeting cards increased in the weeks following 9/11, suggesting that for many Americans, greeting cards provided a way to cope with the overwhelming emotions they were feeling, as sending greeting cards expresses love, encouragement, concern, and other positive emotions. As Hallmark spokeswoman Rachel Bolton commented shortly after the attacks, "As a culture, we got jerked back into reality; it's a good time to tell people how much you care" (Dunn, 2001, para. 5).

The types of cards that were sent after 9/11 reflected the shift in the nation's concerns and values regarding the holidays after 9/11. As Doup (2001) explained, consumers wanted patriotic-themed cards to express the emotions that they were feeling, and companies such as American Greetings provided cards in various designs, "including one adapted from an American Red Cross poster . . . [featuring] a crowd of people amid waving flags"; Hallmark's cards included one with "a red, white, and blue wreath and a snowman holding a flag" (paras. 10–11).

Both large and small greeting card companies responded by blending traditional holiday images together with the U.S. flag, as well as replacing the traditional red and green colors of the Christmas season with the red, white, and blue colors of American patriotism. In addition, other images from 9/11 were incorporated into cards. Smith (2001) describes a particularly poignant card that "shows a silhouetted firefighter and police officer gazing at an American flag. Its message: 'It is in life's hardest moments our heroes shine the brightest' " (para. 15). Another image that was in demand was the World Trade Center itself; Ira's Peripheral Visions, which produces World Trade Center cards, reported a dramatic increase in the demand for their merchandise, including requests in custom orders that included the New York skyline or the World Trade Center along with holiday sentiments in red, white, and blue (Smith, 2001, paras. 21–22).

The writers, artists, and others involved with creating and producing greeting cards worked quickly to develop new lines of cards and products with patriotic themes, viewing their involvement as a way of helping themselves and the nation recover. As Andrea Liss, the owner of Hannah Homemade Cards, explained, "I think, like all Americans, I felt helpless but wanted to do something . . . And what I do is make cards" (Doup, 2001, para. 7). The greeting card industry met the public's requests for cards and gifts that expressed hope, encouragement, and patriotism by bringing out new lines of products that included cards, stationery, pins, stickers, and ornaments. The industry expressed its concern further by contributing to the relief funds of organizations like the American Red Cross and the Salvation Army, either by donating a portion of the proceeds of the new patriotic lines or through direct donations, often matching the donations of their employees.

The emotional impact felt in the wake of 9/11 took a powerful psychological toll on the nation, leaving many with a need to express their feelings and begin the healing process in a positive way. Greeting cards represented a personal, tangible way to connect emotionally with family and friends while focusing on the positive feelings of hope, concern, unity, and patriotism during a time of national crisis, and all through the simple yet powerful act of sending a greeting card.

—*A. A. Hutira*

References

Doup, L. (2001, October 17). Greeting card companies rush patriotic holiday arts to store shelves. *South Florida Sun-Sentinel*. Retrieved from http://www.sun-sentinel.com/

Dunn, J. (2001, October 7). Sales climb for greeting cards. *The New York Times*. Retrieved from http://www.nytimes.com

Greeting card writers help Americans during national crisis. (2001, October 17). *PR Newswire*. Retrieved from http://www.highbeam.com

Jackson, K. M. (2005, March). Psychological first aid: The Hallmark company, greeting cards, and the response to September 11. *Journal of American Culture, 28(1)*, 11–28.

Smith, J. (2001, November 2). Greeting card businesses offer patriotic cards. *The Kansas City Star*. Retrieved from http://www.kansascity.com/

SPOTLIGHT ESSAY/EVERYDAY LIFE: FIREFIGHTERS

In the wake of 9/11, the firefighters who risked their lives to save others in the World Trade Center became America's heroes. The FDNY lost 341 firefighters and 2 paramedics that day, making them the emergency service to sustain the greatest number of causalities as a direct result of the attacks. Stories and images of firefighters' bravery—for example, climbing up the stairs of the North Tower while everyone else fled downward—only added to the widespread admiration people felt for those who risked their life that day. Their actions and images upheld American ideals of selflessness and courage unto death, and they became symbols of September 11.

Perhaps the most powerful images linking the firefighters to the attacks were two photos of firefighters in poses reminiscent of Joseph Rosenthal's famous "Raising the Flag on Iwo Jima." The photos, one taken by Thomas E. Franklin and the other by Ricky Flores, depict three firefighters raising the U.S. flag over the remains of the fallen Twin Towers. According to Robert Rue's *D-day: The Total Story* (2004) in this picture, "what Flores's editors saw was the chance to make meaning out of incoherence, the chance, perhaps to create the first myth of 9/11: Americans love America, and its citizens will be as heroic and resilient as soldiers in assuring its survival" (p. 1).

The firefighter image began to appear in other areas of popular culture as well. At the Mall of America in Minneapolis, an entire kiosk, named the 911 Marketplace, opened selling souvenirs of firefighters. Toys were also influenced. As one writer described, "Terrorism has changed the way U.S. children play, since the [September 11] attacks. The violence that once seemed like make-believe has suddenly become so real to American children that they and their parents now [favor] toy characters that save lives instead of destroy them" (Markham-Smith, 2001, para. 1). A month after September 11, firefighter costumes were the number one request among children for Halloween. Reflecting this new interest in the firefighter, demand for the costumes was so high that manufacturers could not keep up and actually exhausted requests long before Halloween (Gill, 2001).

Children were not the only ones who became enamored with the firefighter image. Adult T-shirts, figurines, beer steins, and even a television drama starring Denis Leary, aptly titled *Rescue Me*, became popular in the years following September 11. The show focuses on a group of New York firefighters working in New York City after September 11. Movies about the 9/11 firefighters, including *World Trade Center* (2006), photo books such as *Brotherhood* (2001), and Web sites such as 9-11 Heroes (http://www.9-11heroes.us) further reinforced the iconic status of firefighters after 9/11. One of the most familiar September 11 memorials—the FDNY Memorial Wall—was "dedicated to the 343 members of the NYC Fire Department, as well as volunteer firefighter Glenn J. Winuk, a partner at Holland & Knight who died on that tragic day . . . located at FDNY Engine 10 Ladder 10, directly across from the World Trade Center site" ("FDNY Memorial Wall," 2009, para. 1).

After the terrorist attacks in 2001, firefighters gained new status as icons in American culture. They came to represent an American ideal of valor and nobility, one easily marketed as a new kind of superhero, but one without super powers. As the special edition of *Spider-Man* (#36) would suggest, no superhero would come to the rescue during the dark days of September 11, but flesh and blood men and women were simply, quietly, doing precisely what they had been trained to do. Americans began to refine their definitions of heroism, and in so doing, began to look for heroes who were more literally all around them.

—*Yvonne D. Sims*

References

FDNY Memorial Wall. (2009). *FDNY Ten House*. Retrieved from http://www
.fdnytenhouse.com/

Gill, J. (2001, September 26). This year's Halloween's hit: To be a hero. *BusinessWeek*.
Retrieved from http://www.businessweek.com

Markham-Smith, I. (2001, October 24). US toy trends break with the past after 11th September
attacks. *International Market News*. Retrieved from http://www.hktdc.com

Rue, R. (2004, April 27). *D-day: The total story*. Retrieved from http://www.popmatters.com

SPOTLIGHT ESSAY/EVERYDAY LIFE: HUMOR

As inappropriate as it may have seemed, topical humor addressed the terrorist attacks of September 11 soon after the tragedy. The link between humor and tragedy is not new, in fact current events are the central focus of topical humor, and it is something of a national tradition to make jokes about tragic events. For example, topical humor helped reestablish unity after the Civil War (Rourke, 1931, p. 220); it helped the nation deal with the burdens of World War II (Osgood, 2002); and, more recently, the assassination of President Kennedy and the crash of the *Challenger* space shuttle both inspired a cycle of "sick jokes" as a means to process the tragedies (Dundes, 1987; Morrow, 1987).

In the first four months after September 11, humor focused primarily on those groups and individuals who were perceived to be the enemies of America. Historically, national enemies are safe topics of humor (Klein, 2001), and after noting the importance of humor to the United States in their initial show, topical humorists began to aim their comic correctives at Osama bin Laden and other enemies of the United States.

The Center for Media and Public Affairs' quantitative analyses (2002) of the jokes made on *The Late Show with David Letterman*, *The Tonight Show*, and *Late Night with Conan O'Brien* in 2000 and after September 11, 2001, point to some interesting trends. The top 10 joke targets in 2000 were focused on political figures such as George W. Bush, Bill Clinton, Al Gore, Hillary Clinton, Dick Cheney, Monica Lewinsky, and Rudolph Giuliani (The Center for Media and Public Affairs, 2000). In contrast, from September 11 to December 31, 2001, the top objects of humor included Osama bin Laden, Bill Clinton, the Taliban Militia, and Geraldo Rivera (The Center for Media and Public Affairs, 2002). The time frame is shorter in the latter survey, which may suggest that some topics were privileged only because they were part of the news cycle (e.g., Lindh, Rivera). But the decrease in frequency of George W. Bush and Dick Cheney jokes as compared to Bill Clinton and Al Gore is considerable, even accounting for the fact that Bush and Cheney were in positions of power in 2001. After all, Clinton and Gore jokes outnumbered Bush and Cheney jokes when they were still in power in 2000, indicating that the targets of humor changed after 9/11.

Jay Leno addressed this change in his typically humorous manner: "We can't do Bush jokes anymore," he quipped, "he's smart now" (Kurtzman, 2002). Part of the reluctance to mock President Bush and Vice President Cheney stemmed from the belief that leaders should not be criticized during a time of war. Topics such as a sex scandal or a speaker's lack of animation reminded audiences of simpler times, times when terrorist activities were not the main topic of concern within the country. David Letterman consciously noted this on October 2, 2001, when he stated: "You know what the country needs right now? A good old-fashioned Bill Clinton sex-scandal" ("The Hotline: Laugh Track," 2001). Both Letterman and Leno found a "safe" target in President Bill Clinton, likely because such jokes reminded viewers of an object of humor that was popular before the attacks, thereby creating a bridge between a pre- and post-9/11.

Leno also made frequent comparisons between U.S. and Middle Eastern cultures. On September 23, he reported that Osama bin Laden had increased his wealth through "construction, smart investments and gas and oil investments" in order to wage war on capitalism ("The Hotline: Laugh Track," 2001). On October 18, 2001, Leno stated that children were hoarding the meals dropped from U.S. planes and selling them for profit in the city and then queried, "Who says the American way of life couldn't catch on here?" ("The Hotline: Laugh Track," 2001). Leno also compared U.S. sports teams and the Taliban: On October 9, 2001, he noted that neither the Redskins nor the Taliban would be around for the playoffs ("The Hotline: Laugh Track," 2001).

Such cultural comparisons create analogies that help audiences understand foreign threats by framing them in familiar terms. The use of sports is a straightforward way to make such connections. The references to capitalism refer to a commonly cited reason for the attacks: Al Qaeda and Osama bin Laden hate the way of life in the United States, an existence that privileges accumulating wealth over spiritual enlightenment. Leno noted that bin Laden and the children of Afghanistan engage in capitalistic endeavors when it suits their needs, thus dismissing such critiques as hypocritical. These jokes can also be understood as advancing a sense of American superiority: "They" say they hate our way of life, yet mimic our economy when they have the chance, proving the preeminence of the U.S. lifestyle. Depending on the level of reflection afforded to these jokes, such humor can be enjoyed for making bin Laden look ridiculous or for presenting the United States as superior because of its market economy. At the same time, categorizing an entire nation with the term "they" reduces them to a single category easily labeled as "other" than American.

Not all comedians' remarks were viewed as appropriate, however, as Bill Maher, host of ABC's *Politically Incorrect* learned all too well. Just days after the attacks, Maher challenged the ways in which the word "coward" was being used in reference to 9/11, suggesting that it was more cowardly to bomb another country from the safe distance of thousands of miles away than to fly a plane into a skyscraper. The statement struck audiences and politicians wrong, in part because there was little if any room in post-9/11 culture either to raise doubt about American actions or suggest that there was anything heroic in the terrorists' behavior. Maher quickly apologized for his remarks but some advertisers withdrew their support and local networks temporarily dropped the program. The show was cancelled in June 2002, and although ABC claimed there was no connection to Maher's post-9/11 gaff, many believed this was a direct result (Associated Press, 2002).

Just a brief look at topical humor after the attacks of 9/11 illustrates the cultural importance of this discourse in helping the nation to process the occurrence of such a tragedy. Topical humor in the United States reflects and questions national values as a means to clarify our ideals and establish a common culture. This occurs through the simultaneous referencing and mocking of shared social values. Topical humorists are especially vital in this regard as they bring current events into a broader context with past events and contemporary values. Specifically, topical humor in the aftermath of 9/11 helped audiences to transcend the immediate tragedy. In doing so, they allowed for an emotional release of fear and anxiety and facilitated an adjustment to a changed world. Topical humorists on late night television provided both relief and the tools to adapt to an ever-changing world after 9/11.

—*Elizabeth Benacka*

References

Associated Press. (2002, June 29). Maher tapes final episode of "Politically Incorrect." *USA Today*. Retrieved from http://usatoday.com

Center for Media and Public Affairs (2000, March 1). McCain goes on Leno but Bush is top joke target. Election Watch [report]. Retrieved May 18, 2010 from http://www.cmpa.com/PressRel/Archive/2000/2000.03.01.%20MCain%20Goes%20On%20Leno%20But%20Bush%20Is%20Top%20Joke%20Target.pdf

Center for Media and Public Affairs (2002, May/June). Political humor on late night TV 1989–2002. Media Monitor, XVI (3), 1–6. Retrieved August 22, 2006 from http://www.cmpa.com/files/media_monitor/02mayjun.pdf

Dundes, A. (1987). At ease, disease—AIDS jokes as sick humor. *American Behavioral Scientist, 30*(3), 72–81.

The hotline: Laugh track. (2001, September 12–October 12). *National Journal*. Retrieved August 22, 2006, from http://www.nationaljournal.com/pubs/hotline

Klein, A. (2001). The day the laughter returned part II. *Humor and September 11*. Retrieved August 22, 2006, from http://www.allenklein.com/articles/humor9-11part2.htm

Kurtzman, D. (2002, September 8). 4 iconoclastic views of 9/11 and its aftermath. *San Francisco Chronicle*, C1.

Morrow, P. (1987). Those sick challenger jokes. *Journal of Popular Culture, 20*(4), 175–184.

Osgood, C. (2002). *Kilroy was here: The best American humor from World War II*. New York: Hyperion.

Rourke, C. (1931). *American humor: A study of the national character*. New York: Harcourt Brace Jovanovich.

SPOTLIGHT ESSAY/EVERYDAY LIFE: PATRIOTIC PRODUCTS

On the evening of one of the most heart-wrenching, confusing, and frightening days many Americans have ever experienced, citizens turned to their nation's leader for words of hope, encouragement, and perhaps even explanation. Many people were feeling helpless and found themselves looking for guidance or suggestions of ways to cope; looking for ways to help their fellow citizens in need; looking for how to help their country heal. On September 11, 2001, at 8:30 p.m. eastern standard time, President George W. Bush finally addressed the nation and proclaimed, "Our financial institutions remain strong and the American economy will be open for business as well." In other words, in their moment of need, Americans were told by the president of the United States to go shopping.

Knowing that Americans were being pointed in their direction, many businesses immediately began marketing their products, as well as themselves, as patriotic. In part to express support for the country in a time of need, and in part to reap the largest amount of profits possible, corporations used the concept of branding to make their product or company synonymous with patriotism. In general, the concept of branding works on the premise that there are specific values and beliefs associated with the image of the product, as well as the company that produced it. When consumers purchase a brand-name product they are, by the act of buying, endowed with its qualities. A particularly effective brand-name product is one that instantly connects its implied meaning to the producer and purchaser of the good.

In the case of September 11, an array of companies began including patriotic images in the advertisements of their usual products. Thus, when consumers purchased a commodity laden with patriotic imagery they were investing in "brand America" and as a result could feel as though they performed their patriotic duty in the aftermath of September 11. For example, General Electric's post-9/11 full-page ad featured a sketch of the Statue of Liberty in the act of leaving her pedestal and rolling up her sleeves. At the top of the page was the headline "We will roll up our sleeves. We will move forward together. We will overcome. We will never forget." The ad works by encouraging consumers to believe that GE is on their side, supporting the country in a time of need. Other companies followed suit.

For example, the advertisement for Perfect Beauty's patriotic twinkle tweezers, which were red, white, or blue stainless steel decorated with three rows of red, white, and blue Swarovski crystals, read "Tweeze with Pride! God Bless the USA!" Similarly, formal dress designer, Jessica McClintock, created patriotic prom dresses for her spring 2002 line. These dresses were known as "the American Collection" and featured red, white, blue gowns covered in red, white, and blue rhinestones. In a 2002 interview with the *Wall Street Journal* about 9/11, McClintock stated, "I was very shaken by this event like everyone" (de Lisser, 2002, p. 1) which resulted in her conscious choice to create dresses that were representative of American pride. Likewise, shoe designer Steve Madden created a white athletic shoe emblazoned with the U.S. flag and called "The Bravest," a phrase that, in the aftermath of the attacks, explicitly evoked the bravery of firefighters, police officers (Barstow and Henriques, 2002), and other emergency personnel who served the country on September 11. Perfect Beauty, Jessica McClintock, and Steve Madden are just a few additional examples of products created to capitalize on post-9/11 patriotic fervor.

Post-9/11 culture provided an opportunity for companies to rebrand themselves and their products as American. In doing so, they supported the president's directive to consume, gave Americans a concrete way to express their support for their country, and made a tidy profit in the process.

—*Lori Bindig and M. Bosau*

References

Barstow, D. & Henriques, D. (2002 February 2). 9/11 tie-ins blur lines of charity and profit. The New York Times. Retrieved from http://www.nytimes.com
Bush, G. W. (2001, September 11). *Statement by the President in his address to the nation.* The White House, Washington, D.C. Retrieved from http://www.whitehouse.gov
de Lisser, E. (2002, February 5). Shoes, diapers salute the flag. *The Wall Street Journal,* B1.

SPOTLIGHT ESSAY/EVERYDAY LIFE: SOCIAL NETWORKING

The classification of government documents and sealed court records increased after September 11, 2001; however, during the same period, the use of social networking sites experienced explosive growth. This increase in social networking contradicts the idea that safety comes from secrecy and instead shows that Americans tend to find routes of public expression in the absence of public discourse.

Government document classification increased 40 percent between September 11, 2001, and 2003, and the government spent more than $6.5 billion managing classified documents (Weitzal, 2004). To justify government restriction of documents, public information was said to provide terrorists a "road map" for future attacks; however, the Reporters' Committee for Freedom of the Press pointed out the absence of causal links between government openness and 9/11 (Dalglish & Leslie, 2005; Roberts, 2006). Furthermore, the U.S. press, previously charged with open, investigative reporting encountered roadblocks that minimized their role as impartial managers of public discourse (Weitzal, 2004). Tied to the terrorist attacks of 9/11, the government's withdrawal of information from the public sphere and journalism's lack of reporting diminished the ability of everyday Americans to participate in public civil rights, terrorism, and immigration discourse.

In contrast, the burgeoning social networking movement saw people clamor to express themselves in a public forum with little secrecy. For example, Friendster launched in 2002, and one million users registered on LiveJournal in 2003 (Searcher, 2007). Facebook connected university students initially and now boasts more than 200 million users (Facebook, 2009). The historic avenues of public engagement, such as the press, unavailable to citizens because of government secrecy, were re-created online.

As government and journalistic institutions backed away from the open dialogue of healthy democracy, Internet users created areas of their lives where a feeling of openness existed. Studies of everyday living and popular culture have shown that government efforts to maintain control are counteracted by the tactics of a populace seeking small areas of control (De Certeau, 1984). In this case, open participation in social networking can be seen as an outgrowth and response to government secrecy and its restriction on public discourse. Further evidence shows that Americans desire government openness: Freedom of Information Act requests in 2003 increased 36 percent from the previous year (Weitzal, 2004, p. 84). Although social networking users participate in a variety of online dialogues, these networks at the very least reveal a desire for transparent government, but ultimately show an approach to information that privileges openness, not secrecy.

—*Stephanie C. Plummer*

References

Dalglish, L., & Leslie, G. (Eds.). (2005, September). The rollback in state openness. *The Reporters Committee for Freedom of the Press. Homefront confidential: How the war on terrorism affects access to information and the public's right to know, 6*. Retrieved from http://www.rcfp.org

De Certeau, M. (1984). *The practice of everyday life*. Berkeley: University of California Press.

Facebook. (2009). Statistics. *Facebook*. Retrieved June 26, 2009, from http://www.facebook.com/press/info.php?statistics

Roberts, A. S. (2006). *Blacked out: Government secrecy in the information age*. New York: Cambridge University Press.

Searcher. (2007, July/August). Social networking timeline. *Searcher, 15*(7), 38.

Weitzal, P. (2004, Fall). The steady march of government secrecy. *Nieman Reports, 58*(3), 84–88.

SPOTLIGHT ESSAY/EVERYDAY LIFE: SPORTS

Not long after the terrorist attacks of September 11, 2001, the parking lot at Shea Stadium, home field of the New York Mets, was converted into a staging area for emergency workers and the collection of relief supplies. Ten days later, the parking lot was returned to its regular purpose as fans arrived for the first professional baseball game to be played in New York after the attacks. But the consolation of the game, including the patriotic emotion of pregame ceremony and the Mets choosing to wear baseball caps in honor of the fallen members of the New York City emergency services agencies, was tempered by a score that favored the visiting team going into the bottom of the eighth inning.

With his team losing, Mets superstar catcher Mike Piazza, who had earlier visited with relief workers and victims at the Shea Stadium staging area, came to bat. He swung on a pitch that, when hit, landed beyond the left-centerfield wall. The home run proved to be the game-winning hit, and was immediately recognized in the context of city-wide comeback and recovery (Kepner, 2001). Baseball, "America's Pastime," had reaffirmed the nation's values and way of life in a turbulent new reality.

When the terrorist attacks occurred on September 11, the Mets and other Major League Baseball (MLB) teams were nearing the end of their regular season. The National Football League (NFL) had also been in-season, having just completed its opening weekend slate of games. In both sports, some owners, coaches, players, and fans reasoned for a postponement of upcoming games while others maintained that the games would assert a sense of "normalcy." After deliberation, the MLB announced it would postpone all games through the following Sunday after the NFL had chosen to postpone its following week of scheduled games (Brown, 2004; Chass, 2001).

There has been a legacy of debate over whether professional sports competition, which is oftentimes perceived as a trivial dimension of American society, should be postponed out of respect for significant and acute national crises. Such was the case with some professional football league games scheduled on the Sunday following the assassination of President John F. Kennedy (McDonough, 2001; Povich, 2005). Yet whenever sports schedules have been suspended, the games, when resumed, have emphasized the function of sports in the life of American community and society.

More than 150 years ago, Tocqueville (1840/2004) observed and wrote, "Americans of all ages, all conditions, and all minds are constantly joining together in groups. . . . If, finally, they wish to publicize a truth or foster a sentiment with the help of a great example, they associate" (p. 595). Indeed, membership and involvement in groups is still today a fundamental characteristic of the American way of life. It is, further, a human tendency to identify and flaunt one's association with a successful group enterprise as a means toward enhancing self-worth, confidence, and performance (Drucker, 1998; Cialdini, et al. 1976; Maslow, 1962), including in times of despair, when one needs to overcome feelings of disillusion, loneliness, and alienation, and seeks a return to a "normal" way of life.

The above requirements were filled by the resumption of the MLB and NFL seasons at stadiums throughout the country. However with heightened security in, around, and above the facilities ("United States," 2001), each provided a sanctuary for free and voluntary group identity and action amidst chaos and confusion. They provided constructive community. And they offered a proving ground for patriotism.

For Americans, patriotism instills a love of country because "it is the palladium of human liberty—the favored scene of human improvement" (Wright, 1829, p. 181). Sports personify that sentiment. During the week following September 11, when MLB returned to its season in-progress, the stadiums and fields of "America's Pastime" were awash in emblematic red, white, and blue colors, and U.S. flags were affixed to players' uniforms and waved by fans. Moments of silence were counterbalanced by the chords of "The Star-Spangled Banner," which has been performed at the start of baseball games since the time of the World War I (Ward & Burns, 1994), while "God Bless America" replaced the standard "Take Me Out to the Ballgame" during the seventh-inning stretch (Krause, 2003). When the first post-September 11 NFL games were played on Sunday, September 23, similar ceremony was accorded: On every player's helmet was affixed a U.S. flag decal, enormous U.S. flags were unfurled on the field, and fans waved small ones in the stands, and "The Star-Spangled Banner," "God Bless America," and "America the Beautiful" were sung at different points during the games (Mihoces, 2001).

Some weeks later, the MLB World Series, held in late October, featured the New York Yankees and the Arizona Diamondbacks. At the first World Series game to be played at Yankee Stadium, after a moment of silence and the national anthem, and with a tattered U.S. flag recovered from Ground Zero flying over the stadium, President George W. Bush strode to the pitcher's mound to throw out the ceremonial first pitch (Greenburg, Bernstein, & Shapiro, 2004; Milbank, 2001). Amidst enormous ovation, the president, wearing a FDNY warm-up jacket over a bulletproof vest, saluted the crowd in attendance with a thumbs-up gesture and then threw a strike to the catcher crouched-in-waiting behind home plate.

Going forward, as Americans sought context for reviving the national mood after the September 11 attacks, sports events—from the New York City Marathon to the Super Bowl to the Olympic Games—continued to be a formative influence on the national identity. Although the manner of patriotic response has toned down as a "normal" way of American public life has since been increasingly restored, professional sports—to say nothing of the deep-rooted tradition of amateur sports—has consistently expressed a dominant feature of the American experiment: the voluntary and organized interaction between competition and cooperation. In a period of great upheaval, sports were an organ through which a free and functioning society could reaffirm its basic values.

—*Lee H. Igel*

References

Brown, R. S. (2004). Sport and healing America. *Society, 42*(1), 37–41.

Chass, M. (2001, September 12). Selig, in a sense of mourning, cancels baseball games. *The New York Times*, p. C15.

Cialdini, R. B., Borden, R. J., Thorne, A., Walker, M. R., Freeman, S., & Reynolds Sloan, L. (1976). Basking in reflected glory: Three (football) field studies. *Journal of Personality and Social Psychology, 34*(3), 366–375.

Drucker, P. F. (1998). Civilizing the city. *Leader to Leader, 7*, 8–10.

Greenburg, R. (Producer), Bernstein, R. (Producer), & Shapiro, O. (Director). (2004). *Nine innings from Ground Zero* [Film]. Home Box Office.

Kepner, T. (2001, September 21). Mets' magic heralds homecoming. *The New York Times*, p. D1.

Krause, R. S. (2003). A shelter in the storm: Baseball responds to September 11. *NINE: A Journal of Baseball History and Culture, 12*(1), 88–101.

Maslow, A. H. (1962). *Toward a psychology of being*. Princeton, NJ: Van Nostrand.

McDonough, W. (2001, September 16). They played through pain in '63. *The Boston Globe*, p. C1.

Mihoces, G. (2001, September 24). Emotional day for NFL. *USAToday*, p. C1.

Milbank, D. (2001, October 31). At Yankee Stadium, President makes a pitch for normalcy. *The Washington Post*, A20.

Povich, S. (2005). *All those mornings . . . at the Post: The 20th century in sports from famed Washington Post columnist Shirley Povich*. New York: PublicAffairs.

Tocqueville, A. (2004). *Democracy in America* (Arthur Goldhammer, Trans.). New York: Library of America. (Original work published 1840)

United States: Getting to grips with evil. (2001, September 22). *The Economist*, p. 28.

Ward, G. C. & Burns, K. (1994). *Baseball: An illustrated history*. New York: Knopf.
Wright, F. (1829). *Course of popular lectures as delivered by Frances Wright*. New York: Office of
    the Free Enquirer.

SPOTLIGHT ESSAY/EVERYDAY LIFE: SOUVENIRS

In the years following September 11, numerous material responses in the forms of spontaneous shrines, memorials, and even an entire market of consumer goods emerged. Within this market, a number of products—from commemorative coins, bumpers stickers, snow-globes, plaques, pins, cufflinks, and T-shirts—have sold untold numbers, and are a physical and ritualistic way through which Americans can display their patriotism. Sometimes called "sacred consumerism," this process builds a participatory community—like a community of believers—that has experienced, through the simple act of purchasing an item related to the place or trauma, the events of September 11. According to Damphousse, Hefley, and Smith (2003), "The goal is to become transformed by the visit into someone who has 'experienced' the event" (p. 4). And, indeed, the possession of these goods—purchasing the objects as a memory rite—allows practitioners to see themselves as having participated in the community of those who have experienced, in some fashion, the attacks.

One object that offered people the chance to participate in sacred consumerism is the September 11 commemorative coin designed and distributed by the National Collector's Mint. Minted from silver that was housed in a vault beneath the World Trade Center towers, the coin features a gold bust of the World Trade Center towers that pops up to stand perpendicular to the coin when a tab is pressed on the coin itself. In its physical representation of the fallen towers, the coin connects the purchaser to the event much like religious relics or souvenirs because it is actually made from material from the disaster site. The bust of the towers standing on the coin, and standing in for the real towers which no longer exist, is symbolic of a set of American ideals—that are supposed to bind together a community who shares those ideas. By purchasing the coin, individuals imaginatively participate in that community and uphold those ideas (Anderson, 1991). More specifically, by purchasing this 9/11 commemorative coin, or any one of the many like it, is a means of identifying with or experiencing the events of September 11.

All of these purchasable relics—the commemorative coin, the snow-globe, the "I Heart NY" T-shirt, or even a "Support Our Troops" magnetic ribbon—are meant to be identified with, and to imbue their beholders with, a national identity as Americans. More than this, because the objects are instilled with a sense of sacredness, they give the memory of September 11 more meaning. This in turn lends sanctity to the institutions that were threatened by the attacks reinforcing the sense of patriotism and nationalism that increased so steadily in the aftermath of the attacks.

Sacred consumerism, the buying and selling of these consumer goods, is a ritual of consumption in which those individuals who participate create a specific, if imagined, community. In many ways, the purpose of a ritual like this sacred consumerism is to identify one's self with an event, like any other religious or traumatic experience. What is unique in the case of this set of responses to September 11 is that it is done through consumerism, however it shares the same goal of all commemoration—to form a usable past in hopes of creating a meaningful present and future.

—*Anthony J. Kolenic*

References

Anderson, B. (1991). *Imagined communities: Reflections on the origin and spread of nationalism* (New ed.). London and New York: Verso.

Damphousse, K. R., Hefley, K. S., & Smith B. L. (2003, August). *Creating memories: Exploring how narratives help define the memorialization of tragedy.* Paper presented at the annual meeting of the American Sociological Association, Atlanta, GA. Retrieved from http://www.allacademic.com/meta/p107083_index.html

SPOTLIGHT ESSAY/EVERYDAY LIFE: *TRACKING TRANSIENCE* BY HASAN ELAHI

During the months following September 11, Bangladeshi-American Hasan Elahi, a professor and artist, was working overseas and traveling as he usually did. On his return to the United States in 2002, agents at the Detroit International Airport stopped Elahi to question him about his activities. The immigration official who inspected Elahi's passport seemed frightened, and later it was found that the owner of Elahi's storage facility reported him to authorities for possessing explosives and abruptly leaving the country.

While the tip that led to his detainment was never proven, it did not stop the FBI from repeatedly interviewing Elahi, giving him a lie detector test, and requiring him to inform them of his future travels. Elahi was never officially cleared from suspicion and instead was told to check in with the FBI whenever he traveled. The reasoning behind this request was to prevent detainment at airport checkpoints and borders. So, for the next few years he did just that, contacting an FBI agent each time he traveled for an exhibition or speaking engagement (Raza, 2005; Regine, 2006; Zuckerman, 2006).

Hassan's experience rose directly from the post-9/11 USA Patriot Act. Passed quickly after the attacks, the Patriot Act gave the government greater authority to investigate, detain, and track American citizens. While the legislation is meant to help prevent future terrorist attacks, it has also been widely criticized for the authority it grants the U.S. government to gain information about the lives of private citizens through increased surveillance. While some Americans have responded to the Patriot Act with apprehension or even hostility toward government, others have chosen to subvert the intentions of the Patriot Act legislation by producing making every detail of their lives available to anyone. Professor and artist Hasan Elahi's response was to create a multimedia artwork known as *Tracking Transience* (Elahi, 2008).

Tracking Transience, Elahi's ongoing creation, illustrates the details of his life in minutiae. Every meal he eats, every airport he goes through, and every public bathroom he uses is diligently documented. These digital photographs are uploaded to his Web site, along with detailed credit card records and a photograph taken at his current location. While Elahi's Web site is largely the means he uses to communicate personal details, his photographs also appear in gallery exhibitions all over the world, allowing people without Internet access to understand the full scope of his self-surveillance.

In addition to the photographic evidence of his habits, Elahi's Web site also documents his geographic location by way of a global positioning system (GPS) monitor kept on his person. The coordinates are posted to Trackingtransience.net (http://trackingtransience.net/) and are shown on a satellite map with an arrow pointing directly to his location. Superimposed over the map are 18 squares highlighted in red. By clicking on the square farthest to the right, one changes the map to a global view. Clicking on each box from the right to the left focuses the map closer and closer until trees and automobiles become discernible. At that point, it becomes apparent that the photograph at the top of the screen was taken from the position indicated on the map.

While the map and large photograph give a glimpse into Elahi's present tense, the Web site also shows Elahi's past. At the bottom of the screen are 10 photographs that change throughout the day. The images are linked to small windows that when clicked appear showing even more photographs, lists of airport codes and flight numbers, or detailed lists of credit card purchases. The airport codes link to photographs of the airport itself and the flight numbers link to images of Elahi's in-flight meals. The photographs on the main page, however, do not link to the same windows each time. Curiously compatible, Elahi's information is mirrored by sections of the Patriot Act, which inadvertently deal with the past and the present. Current actions illustrated through Elahi's GPS location and past activities demonstrated by credit card records reflect two aspects of the Patriot Act, search and seizure as an action toward the past and wiretapping as an action within the present.

Like surveillance, looking through someone's personal information such as that presented on Elahi's Web site can result in random and unexpected conclusions. Because this information is available to individuals viewing *Tracking Transience* from all over the world, different meanings and conclusions are inevitable. Unlike the single interpretation of a policing agency, multiple viewpoints both diminish the power of federal agencies to create one specific truth and also protect Elahi from potential prosecution (Zuckerman, 2006). Furthermore, presenting this information on his Web site alters the power structure between Elahi and the federal government. In other words, Elahi removes the power inherent in surveilling from the hands of the government and injects his own agency into his surveillance.

As a result of the fact that Elahi began this project in 2002, the amount of information available on *Tracking Transience* is extensive. Undoubtedly, the Federal Bureau of Investigation or any federal agency has the resources to comb through such information. However, for every photograph of an airport terminal there seems to be another photograph of a public toilet Elahi used or a credit card entry from a 7-11 store. This forces any investigation to treat all information, even the most mundane, with equal amounts of time and consideration.

In an interview on the satirical television program *The Colbert Report*, Elahi (May 7, 2008) said that his Web site uses market forces to make personal information worthless. According to Elahi, information has value because it is generally secret and hard to obtain. By flooding the world with personal information, it becomes worthless to investigators. While Elahi's artwork certainly demonstrates this, the ability to undermine the Patriot Act by working with technology is not available to all citizens. However, along with Elahi, any ordinary American or world citizen who visits www.trackingtransience.net, negotiates the purpose, meaning, and effect of surveillance and thus the Patriot Act.

—*Stephanie C. Plummer*

References

Elahi, H. (2008, May 7). *The Colbert Report* [Interview]. Comedy Central.

Elahi, H. (2008). *Tracking transience* [Internet, GPS, photographs]. http://www.tracking-transience.net

Raza, S. (2005, October 28). *Art in security and security in art*. Retrieved from http://www.elastic.org.uk/KISSS/saraRaza.html

Regine. (2006, September 11). *Orwellian projects*. Retrieved from http://www.we-make-money-not-art.com

Zuckerman, E. (2006, October 19). *Tracking Hasan Elah*. Retrieved from WorldChanging: http://www.worldchanging.com

SPOTLIGHT ESSAY/EVERYDAY LIFE: TRAVEL CATALOGS

After the 9/11 attacks, Americans' attitudes toward, and concerns about, travel changed. Many Americans who might have otherwise traveled abroad altered their travel plans in the light of ongoing restrictions, troubling nightly news footage, and continued reports of international lawlessness and threats to Americans in particular. This shift in American thinking also meant that the travel industry had to renegotiate its significance for the American consumer and find new ways to access the American travel dollar. One company in particular has responded to this challenge by reinventing the American traveler as a well-prepared target.

Faced with the industry downturn, the Magellan's travel goods company made use of the 9/11 attacks by playing on American travel fears and suspicions of foreign space and peoples. Each catalog began with a letter from the CEO that helped transform customer fears into travel "wisdom." For example, the Spring 2002 catalog introduction listed a variety of Magellan's goods designed "to ward off unhealthy airborne and waterborne biological hazards" and highlights "many safety and security products (noted with our Safer Travel logo [a U.S. flag]) that add peace of mind to your travels" ("Magellan's," p. 2).

This statement captures the company's post-9/11 approach to the American traveler. By positioning its customers as potential targets of "foreign" threats, and suggesting that travel outside the United States is a hazardous business, Magellan's offers products that "protect" the consumer from the outside world.

The cover images of overseas destinations, the introductory references to "remote areas of the world" ("Magellan's," 2002, p. 2), and the repeated use of the word "foreign," reinforce *international* destinations as the focus of the company's products, most of which are designed to negate the need to meet the locals, drink their water, breathe their air, or use their cups, plates, cutlery, or bathrooms. Some of the Magellan's product descriptions are more extreme than others, but the cumulative message is clear: If you *must* travel away from the United States, for heaven's sake, heed the lessons of 9/11 and be prepared for the inevitable dirt, corruption, disease, and unpleasantness of your foreign destination. The following examples illustrate this message.

The 9/11 attacks were immediately followed by a number of communicable disease threats, most notably, the appearance of anthrax in the U.S. postal system, and 9/11-linked stories about foreign disease conspiracies (biological weapons, severe acute respiratory syndrome [SARS], and bird flu among others). Not surprisingly, Magellan's was quick to exploit American fears of foreign germs by offering an extensive range of health and hygiene products. Collectively, these items build an image of the world outside the United States as so overrun with disease and disease vectors that leaving home without at least one "Developing Country First Aid Kit" would constitute self-endangerment. A prime example of Magellan's construction of American hygienic and moral superiority is the "Travel Comfort Set"—"many of us avoid airplane pillows and blankets for fear of exposure to germs left behind by other passengers" ("Magellan's," 2004, p. 28). Other products include "Our Refreezable Ice Cubes [for use where] the water is 'questionable' " (Spring 2002, p. 28); "Snac Pac . . . nesting utensils, a welcome alternative to . . . the 'iffy' silverware we've seen at times" (2002, p. 28); the "Uri-Mate," which allows "women [to] stand with minimal undressing, at those filthy, hole-in-the-floor toilets around the world" (2002, p. 12); "SANITAIRE [aerosol spray], a convenient way to kill viruses, bacteria and other harmful organisms on telephones, door-handles, lavatory tops, toilet seats and other hard surfaces" (2002, p. 35); "Emer'gen-C [dissolvable crystals] . . . for dealing with the stresses of travel [such as] jet lag, strange customs, languages, foods, and much-too-close proximity to hundreds of people" (2002, p. 42); and the "Insect Barrier" shirt, hood and pants, reminiscent of the HazMat suits that characterized post-9/11 news footage (2002, p. 38).

Disease is not the only threat to Americans, however. Magellan's hints at a world so changed by the 9/11 attacks, and subsequent diminution of U.S. authority, that travelers may well need to prepare for the apocalypse. Starting with the possibility that the hotel furniture could steal one's loose rupees: "For safety's sake, organize your . . . coins, keys, wallet, jewelry and eyeglasses . . . in our Travel Tray" ("Magellan's," 2002, p. 41), Magellan's goes on to warn travelers that bags can be stolen in " 'cut-and –run' thefts," which are thwarted by steel cable-reinforced straps; hotel doors can be forced open and are prevented by the "Door Stop Alarm," which emits a "shrill, pulsating, siren" when tripped (2004, p. 20). Buildings can burn down so be sure to pack the "Evac-U8 Smoke Hood" (2004, p. 20). One can be attacked anywhere and anytime (however, the Magellan's traveler will be protected by "Our Personal Security Alarm." Just pull the "grenade-style" pin to "startle . . . assailants" [2002, p. 17]). One could be interned in a concentration camp (better pack a windup "Info Mate Short-Wave Radio" [2002, p. 17]); or polar ice-caps could form (don't take just one "Emergency Blanket"! [2002, p. 35]).

Obviously, Magellan's does not want Americans to cancel their travel plans. Their business relies on its customers' need to travel. But by repeatedly invoking American travelers' "peace of mind," Magellan's helped to characterize the post-9/11 world *outside* the United States as culturally separate, morally inferior, and microbially overrun. As a major vendor of travel goods, it is unfortunate that the Magellan's catalog neither encourages a positive view of international travel nor affirms its American customers as equal and contributing members of the international community. At a time when Americans most need to reconnect with the world, Magellan's is instead encouraging a culture of distance and suspicion. Furthermore, Magellan's overlooks the reality that the event that they invoke as the reason for traveling "more carefully" actually occurred in the United States; in fact, it could be argued that Magellan's customers might be safer overseas than at home.

—*Gabrielle Watling*

References

Magellan's: America's Leading Source of Travel Supplies. Catalog. (2002, Spring).
Magellan's: America's Leading Source of Travel Supplies. Catalog. (2004, Fall).

SPOTLIGHT ESSAY/EVERYDAY LIFE: URBAN LEGENDS

In the hours immediately following 9/11, urban legends began being transmitted across the nation along with news reports, rumors, and speculation. These stories—which spontaneously arise and are typically false—dealt with various aspects of 9/11, including the idea that that there were angelic and demonic images in the smoke as the towers collapsed, that Nostradamus predicted 9/11, and that if a $20 bill was folded properly, a picture of the towers burning would be produced. The way in which these urban legends were quickly circulated and frequently discussed demonstrates how our culture responded to and attempted to find meaning in 9/11, showing that urban legends are still a significant part of our history, folklore, and our everyday lives.

Urban legends are narratives or stories that describe specific events, from natural and supernatural events to bizarre or coincidental occurrences, often to provide a moral or meaning. Urban legends are presented as true and are meant to be believed, even though they can contain strange or extraordinary details about unexplainable or unnatural occurrences. Although urban legends are often false, they "do tell one kind of truth. They are a unique, unselfconscious reflection of major concerns of individuals in the societies in which the legends circulate" (Brunvand, 1981, p. xii). These concerns include the hopes, fears, and anxieties shared by a culture, and because the events of 9/11 were so shocking, it was inevitable that dozens of urban legends about these events would be created and shared.

One of the first urban legends that received attention stated that in photographs and video footage taken as the towers collapsed, images of an angel and a demon could be clearly seen. While parts of these photographs do seem to take these shapes, the meaning behind the images is subjective and can be interpreted as merely shocking or as having spiritual significance. The angel can be seen as a symbol of hope in the midst of the evil the demon face represents, and by sharing and discussing these images, the extreme emotions felt by many could be processed and dealt with in a more productive manner. These images also tie into Brunvand's (1981) assertion that legends "embody social stresses and attempt to define ambiguous feelings of threat in vivid, dramatic form" (p. xiv). Few images could be more dramatic in the representation of 9/11 than angels and demons, and an urban legend dealing with the battle between good and evil could be a productive way to put the events of 9/11 into a context that could promote discussion and a sense of meaning to alleviate some of the social stresses caused by 9/11.

Another urban legend that received almost immediate attention involved an e-mail that involved a quatrain supposedly written by Nostradamus that predicted 9/11. The quatrain tells of "a great thunder" that would tear "[t]wo brothers" apart, which seems to refer to the destruction of the Twin Towers; it also predicted that "the third big war will begin when the city is burning," which can be interpreted as the beginning of World War III. However, as Emery (2007) shows, this was easily proven to be a hoax as the quatrain cannot be found in any of Nostradamus's writings. Yet the speed at which it was circulated via e-mail and the fact that many did not question its veracity reflects the opinion held by many that 9/11 should have been prevented, that there should have been some warning signs. It also relays societal fears regarding the military retaliation by the United States and the possibility of World War III, which relates to fears about nuclear war. Probably the most bizarre aspect of this prediction is that it was actually part of an essay written in 1996 by a college student who was demonstrating how a prediction could be written in such a way that its meaning could fit almost any situation one wanted (Emery 2007).

Another urban legend open to interpretation involves folding the new U.S. $20 bill (issued in 1998) in such a way that images are produced that can be interpreted as showing the Pentagon and the Twin Towers burning. This urban legend gained momentum when it was discovered that by folding every bill (from the $1 to the $100) in the same way, a series of images showing the Towers before, during, and after the attacks are seemingly produced. While the images can be interpreted in this manner, the significance of this urban legend lies more in the fact that it represents our culture's continuing effort to find meaning in 9/11, as many believe that these images are a commemoration of 9/11 and a way to honor those who died, since individuals should remember 9/11 every time they look at paper money.

Urban legends are still a significant part of our culture and heritage, a way for society to deal with certain anxieties or fears by placing them in the less threatening context of a legend, enabling individuals to interpret the meaning as they see fit and thus exert some control over the anxieties and fears that created the urban legend in the first place.

—A. A. Hutira

References

Brunvand, J. H. (1981). *The vanishing hitchhiker: American urban legends and their meanings.* New York: W. W. Norton.

Emery, D. (2007). *Did Nostradamus predict the 9/11 attacks?* Retrieved July 11, 2008, from http://urbanlegends.about.com/cs/historical/a/nostradamus.htm

Chapter 2

NEWS AND INFORMATION

INTRODUCTION: NEWS, INFORMATION, AND SEPTEMBER 11, 2001

During crises situations, the public relies heavily on news media to provide information and sometimes instruction. Since the integration of television into the American household, there have been a handful of historical crises (e.g., President Kennedy's assassination; the *Challenger* explosion; the Oklahoma City bombing) whereby the television in particular was central to the public's understanding of unfolding events. Given the unprecedented widespread nature of the attacks that took place on September 11, 2001, the media was challenged to cover a never-experienced situation that at the time was not fully understood and was happening as it was being covered. Several years later, a picture of the ways the news media covered the situation as it unfolded in real time on September 11 has emerged.

Identifying the media's role in a time of crisis is not a new concept. Graber (1980) claims that during crises there are three notable stages in news media coverage. First, the media provides information to the general public and public officials. Second, the media tries to make sense out of the situation. Third, the media begins to frame and discuss the crisis in long-term and big-picture perspectives. Similarly, the National Research Council Committee on Disasters and the Mass Media (1980, p. 10) identifies six functions of the media during crisis situations: warning of predicted or impending disasters; conveying information to officials, relief agencies, and the public; charting the progress of relief and recovery; dramatizing lessons learned for the purpose of future preparedness; taking part in long-term public education programs; and defining slow-onset problems as crises or disasters (as seen in Li, 2007, p. 671). Additionally, in crises situations the media may also provide consolation and guidance (Li, 2007). On and after September 11, 2001, the media demonstrated its capabilities of distributing, collecting, and archiving information in ways the American people had not seen before.

Broadcast News

On September 11, 2001, television news networks and cable channels were in the midst of regularly scheduled programming when the first plane, American Airlines Flight 11, hit the North Tower of the World Trade Center at 8:46 a.m. While the main news networks interrupted programming to cover the crash, reporters both gathered and reported information simultaneously, often in ways that were visible to the viewing public. For example, on ABC's interrupted *Good Morning America* (GMA), Diane Sawyer and Charlie Gibson began reporting on the fire in the North Tower shortly after the crash. As GMA broadcasted the image of the burning section of the tower, the reporting of the cohosts relied on witness testimony and information that was being gathered in the field. Unsure what exactly had just transpired, GMA did its best to inform the viewing public what was happening as quickly as they sorted through the unfolding events.

In the midst of covering the story live, with images of the North Tower behind them, the broadcast captured the second plane, United Airlines Flight 175, as it flew into the South Tower at 9:02 a.m. To clarify what had just occurred, ABC immediately rewound the footage and played it again live so the reporters and the viewers could confirm for themselves that another plane had flown into the South Tower. Eyewitness testimony—testimony that at the time described the planes as "small" ("The September 11 Collection [ABC News]," 2008)—supplemented the footage. Similarly, on CBS, Bryant Gumbel was interviewing a witness to the first plane crash when the second plane flew into the South Tower. Like ABC, CBS rewound their tapes to confirm what had happened ("The September 11 Collection [CBS News]," 2008). Although some speculated that the first plane crash was intentional, the presence and live confirmation of the second plane crash indicated to the news organizations and the viewing public that New York City was most likely under attack.

Once it seemed clear that the plane crashes in New York were not accidental, television news organizations officially began their around-the-clock coverage and began working together to convey information to the public. The attacks immediately changed how the major news organizations did business. According to *USA Today*, shortly after the crashes ABC, CBS, and NBC began sharing individually obtained video and satellite images (Bianco, 2001). Such collaboration was unprecedented. Other media resources were also pooled as the day progressed, and concerns over ratings and sponsorship were set aside as the networks prioritized working with one another across media lines in order to understand, make sense of, and convey the most accurate information available (Zelizer & Allan, 2002). As the events unfolded quickly, television journalists tried to keep up. News reporting expanded to Washington, D.C. when reports of American Airlines Flight 77's crash into the Pentagon began to surface. Robert Bianco (2001), a *USA Today* reporter noted: "As ABC was reporting the news of the Pentagon attack from a New York rooftop at 10:02 a.m. ET, viewers could see the collapse of the Trade Center's South Tower in the background. That was followed, almost unimaginably by the collapse of the North Tower—once again, caught live on television" (para. 9). Although television feeds were picked up by many radio networks and television cable stations—and although National Public Radio (NPR) began broadcasting live 24 hours a day—the majority of citizens used television as their main source of news in the immediate aftermath of the attacks (Zelizer & Allan, 2002). However, in the weeks following September 11, listenership to radio was higher than usual both in terms of news programming and radio talk shows (Carey, 2003).

By most accounts, the live broadcast coverage of 9/11 was considered to be exceptional, and the teamwork exhibited by journalists was viewed as a public service that underscored the importance of news in a time of crisis. Programming schedules were canceled and, instead, live coverage of the attacks and their aftermath continued commercial free on the major networks for four days (Zelizer & Allan, 2002). Some mistakes were made in this crisis-driven reporting environment, however. For example, ABC News, followed by CNN, incorrectly reported an explosion at the U.S. Capitol Building and, at one point CNN, reported live from Kabul, Afghanistan, falsely implying that the United States was retaliating with cruise missiles (Bianco, 2001). In addition, as reporters tried to make sense of the information they were compiling as the day progressed, incorrect rumors were disseminated on television broadcasts, and journalists veered from the guidelines that often inform their practice. At times, journalists violated standard news practice by reporting unsubstantiated rumors, using anonymous sources, and personally reflecting on the day's events (Reynolds & Barnett, 2003). At least 12 different rumors were later proved false, including reports that a missile hit the North Tower, an aircraft crashed at Camp David, a car bomb was found at the State Department, and that a hijacked airplane was being escorted by military jets to an airport. Although these deviations from standard reporting practices were problematic, the percentage of these lapses in judgment were low especially given the context of the day (Reynolds & Barnett, 2003).

Newspapers

Despite the fact that print media takes longer to produce than live-crisis television and radio coverage, newspapers responded quickly to the events of September 11 as well, with many publications producing special late editions of their paper distributed that afternoon. The national newspapers published on September 11 and September 12, 2001, used large, bold type and short powerful headlines to convey the scale and intensity of what was happening. Examples of frontpage headlines included: "DEVASTATION" (*Baltimore Sun*), "New Day of Infamy" (*Boston Globe*), "U.S. Under Attack" (*Chicago Tribune*), "TERROR" (*Los Angeles Daily News*, among many others), "Terror Attack" (*Los Angeles Times*), "BASTARDS" (*San Francisco Examiner*), "HORROR" (*Washington Times*), and "Act of War" (*USA Today*). Other visual changes were made as well: *USA Today* dropped its cover layout, the *Atlanta Constitution* had just one story on its front page, and the *New York Times* ran many prominently displayed pictures (Zelizer & Allan, 2002).

Within a week after the attacks, newspapers became journalistic leaders in reporting on post-9/11 stories, usurping the television networks (Carey, 2002). Although television reporting was taking place around the clock during the few days following the attacks, networks soon returned to their schedules, leaving newspapers to provide deeper and more comprehensive coverage. The *New York Times* responded to the crisis by expanding their coverage to meet the needs of New Yorkers and the nation. Specifically, the paper established an advertising-free section of the paper titled "A Nation Challenged," which ran for 15 weeks and contained coverage of the multiple components of the terrorist attacks, the aftermath, and the resulting war in Afghanistan. Stories were diverse in their subject matter and perspectives, while special attention was given to those grieving in the city. As part of "A Nation Challenged" the *Times* also expanded their obituary section to provide space for every family who had one member confirmed dead as a result of the attacks. Families could publish a photo and personal, descriptive commentary of their loved one. Called "Portraits of Grief," this section elicited reader responses like none other in the history of the *New York Times* (Raines, 2002). It was later published as a memorial book entitled, *Portraits 9/11/01: The Collected "Portraits of Grief" from the New York Times* (2002).

COMIC STRIPS

Comic strips, or "funnies," had a unique challenge in responding to the September 11 attacks. Standard practice in the industry is for creators to write and draw comic strips weeks in advance. Therefore, it was difficult for comic strip creators to respond to the tragedies immediately. The National Cartoonists Society president, Steve McGarry, suggested Thanksgiving as the day that artists would respond the attacks and direct readers to Networkforgood.com, which raised $50,000 for victims (Walker, 2002, p. 326). On this day, most comic strips effectively became political cartoons. The result was a funnies page that was partially thanking heroes for the sacrifice, partially encouraging readers to donate to charities, and partially meeting the traditional role of already completed Thanksgiving strips. The page showed the wide variety of ways that the United States responded to the attacks and a full gamut of emotion. Some examples include Willy 'n Ethel painting their roof into a flag (Martin, 2001), Heathcliff getting stuck in a tree "so he can see a real hero" (Gallagher, 2001), Blondie characters all saluting the U.S. flag (Walker, 2002), and Jeffy from The Family Circus crying about a crumbled tower of blocks with his sister Dolly saying they could rebuild it "the 'merican way" (Walker, 2002, p. 326).

—*Ora C. McWilliams*

References

Gallagher, P. (2001, November 22). Comics and cartoons. *Creators Syndicate*. Retrieved from http://www.chron.com

Martin , J. (2001, November 22). Comics and cartoons. *Universal Press Syndicate*. Retrieved from http://www.chron.com

Walker, B. (2002). *The comics: Since 1945*. New York: Abrams.

Coverage of September 11 and its aftermath dominated national newspapers in the months to follow. Although the New York, Washington, D.C., and Pennsylvania papers tended to focus more on victims and their families than papers in areas not witnesses to, or directly impacted by, the attacks, references to September 11 became ubiquitous in all newspapers as the resulting actions such as the establishment of the Department of Homeland Security, the passing of the Patriot Act, and the creation of the National Commission on Terrorist Attacks upon the United States (9/11 Commission) took place.

The Internet

The use of the Internet was not as pervasive in 2001 as it would become in the following years. However, the popularity and reliance on the Internet as an information tool was immediately apparent on September 11 and the time following. In the early hours of the attacks, the mainstream news Web sites (CNN.com, ABCNews.com, MSNBC.com, CBS.com, and FoxNews.com) were largely inaccessible because of tremendous user traffic and demand. No previous event had impacted the performance, or lack thereof, of the Internet; not even the release of the *Starr Report* in 1998 or the 2000 U.S. presidential election halted Internet access to the extent seen in September 2001 (Allan, 2001).

A major challenge for online news sites was the fact that Internet servers could not handle the number of users attempting to access their sites. Online news sites responded quickly to the access problem by eliminating photographs and graphics to ease the demands on their servers (Carey, 2003). In addition, in an effort to support their servers and keep their sites up and running, news sites borrowed server space from Web sites anticipated to have little traffic. For example, ABC.com drew from the ESPN.com server capacity because they expected few people would be looking for sports information that day (Carey, 2003). While these were helpful steps they did not always solve the challenge of accessing news online during the attacks.

As a result of the fact that the news sites were virtually inaccessible, those searching the Internet looked elsewhere for information. At the same time, nonnews sites began posting information about the attacks, often authored by citizens who acknowledged that they were doing so because the mainstream news sites were not available. As the events unfolded, through web logs, comment pages, and photo galleries, the Internet provided a virtual space for users to interact, discuss, and process the developments as they happened (Allan, 2001).

Eventually, news outlets established separate Web sites that focused on September 11. Several key elements were present on many of the sites, including a timeline of events that was updated frequently, links to pages that provided information on the War on Terror, links to information about terrorism, information on Osama bin Laden, chat rooms designed for the public to interact with news staff and experts, emergency information, photo essays and slide shows, video and audio footage, and animated graphics (Brown, Fuzesi, Kitch, & Spivey, 2003, p. 108). The sites were not commercial

SEPTEMBER11NEWS.COM

The Internet site September11News.com has archived national and international news coverage of September 11 and the days, weeks, and years that followed ("Complete International Archives," n.d.). The Web site's creator and editor, Canadian resident A. D. Williams, began building the Web site on September 11 and has continued to do so, adding relevant links and resources as they become available. The extensive collection of news archives include timelines, national and international newspapers and magazine images, photography, September 11 mysteries, and information on the search for Osama bin Laden. The site was honored by the History Channel in 2002 as an Affiliate of the Month. It also has been recognized by the Library of Congress and is part of the Library's *September 11 Historic Internet Collection* (September11 news.com).

—Amy M. Damico

Reference

Complete international archives of September 11, 2001. (n.d.). *September11News.com*. Retrieved from http://www.september11news.com

---

free—banner advertisements and pop-up ads for magazines, cell phones, security systems, and investment firms were also present. Within a year of the attacks, many of these Web sites and others were moved into archival formats available as digital records of September 11.

The extensive digital archives of materials related to September 11 represents how new technology allows for both institutional and private collections of materials to be made available to a wide audience. In the years following the attacks media outlets, museums, private parties, and educational institutions created extensive collections of September 11-oriented materials—videos, newspaper articles, images, interactive features, and memorials. The reputable archival sites are extensive in their contents and often contain hyperlinks to other Web sites containing additional material.

In addition to digital archives, online technologies were used as vehicles to talk about the terrorist attacks. In the days and weeks following September 11, users posted comments about news stories in online forums, private parties created memorial Web sites, and people e-mailed one another links to news stories. Within a day of the attacks, a number of digital disaster jokes focusing on 9/11 surfaced online (Kuipers, 2005), and as time passed, citizen-generated viral videos ranging from humorous reenactments of government responses to 9/11 to theories about 9/11 conspiracies were produced and disseminated.

As new technologies evolved over the years, September 11-oriented content became integrated into new platforms of communicating and sharing information. Social networking sites have numerous pages devoted to aspects of September 11. For example, Facebook and MySpace each have many pages dedicated to various aspects of

---

DIGITAL DISASTER JOKES

Disaster jokes after 9/11, Kuipers (2005) notes, fell into several categories. Hostile and aggressive jokes included ones that honed in on Osama bin Laden as evil and threatened him and the Taliban through imagery, as with an illustration of bin Laden's head being eaten by an American eagle. Other jokes juxtaposed references to popular culture with an aspect of September 11; for example, a digital image of *Sesame Street*'s Bert flying a plane into the World Trade Center or a parody of *Star Wars* titled "Tali Wars America Strikes Back," whereby members of the government assume likenesses of those fighting a bin Laden Darth Vader. Many digital images displayed patriotic symbols in their approach, such as an image of the Statue of Liberty holding up the head of Osama bin Laden. Several of these digital disaster jokes were static images, some were textual and others took the form of a short digital video.

—*Amy M. Damico*

Reference

Kuipers, G. (2005). "Where was King Kong when we needed him?" Public discourse, digital disaster jokes and the functions of laughter after 9/11. *Journal of American Culture, 28*(1), 70–84.

September 11, such as remembering those who were lost, celebrating survivors, honoring heroes, criticizing news coverage, and discussing conspiracy theories. In addition, a number of the September 11-oriented institutions, such as the September 11 memorial and the Ground Zero Museum Workshop, can be followed on Twitter, whereby the organizations "tweet" to followers. Finally, the Internet became a platform for citizens to express their views on the Bush administration's post-9/11 military policies, the implementation of the Patriot Act, and the published *9/11 Commission Report*.

Magazines

In the attacks' aftermath, the highest circulating weekly news magazines—*Time, Newsweek*, and *U.S. News & World Report*—published advertising-free special issues that covered the crisis. These special issues broke previous circulation records. For example, *Time* printed 3 million more copies of its special issue than its usual 155,000 run for newsstands, and bookstores such as Barnes & Noble and Borders Books and Music, reported selling out of all special issues within hours of their release (Loohauis, 2001). In the weeks and months following the attacks, these magazines focused on the aftermath of September 11 events, Osama bin Laden, the war in Afghanistan, the anthrax scare, and the War on Terror, including plans to consider invading Iraq. Other magazines also altered their previous publishing plans to include content related to the terrorist strike. For example, the September 24, 2001,

Sports Illustrated featured a cover image of the U.S. flag draped in a seated position over a chair. The image suggested that American sports, too, had been impacted by September 11, and the issue included articles that examined the attacks' effect on sports and athletes. The *New Yorker*'s (September 24, 2001) first issue following 9/11 was revised to focus mainly on the attacks at the World Trade Center and contained stories that addressed how DNA technology could be used to locate victims' remains and thoughts about the restoration of the New York City skyline. The *New Yorker* cover was a solid black with the date September 11, 2001, appearing in red, printed vertically up the page. *Business Week* (September 24, 2001) released a special report that discussed the economic results of the attacks, and *Forbes, Vogue*, and *Good Housekeeping* all made last-minute changes to acknowledge the disaster in some way. Doing so was something of a challenge because magazines are sent out for printing weeks in advance of their publication dates. For example, *Good House-keeping*'s November 2001 issue was already at the printer when the attacks happened; nonetheless, Editor-in-Chief Ellen Levine decided to attach a memorial card to the front of the issue before it was mailed to subscribers (Fabrikant, 2001).

As the weeks unfolded, news and reaction to September 11 was featured prominently in other magazines as well. For example, *Rolling Stone* magazine published a special issue dated October 25, 2001, that featured articles such as "The Realities of Ground Zero," "Heroes of New York," and "Inside the Holy War." Instead of their traditional cover, the *Rolling Stone* cover text was generated in red and blue (instead of the magazine's usual red), and the cover featured an image of the flag with the text "9.11.01." *People* magazine's cover story on September 24, 2001, was "The Day That Shook America"; in the place of the usual celebrity photo, the magazine cover was a picture of the Twin Towers burning.

Relatively quickly, magazines moved on from mourning the day of the attacks to offering readers encouragement and optimism. On October 8, 2001, for example, *People*'s cover was "The Stars Pitch In," and imagery of celebrities working toward 9/11-related causes were featured on a red cover. *Fortune* magazine's October 8 issue included an image of a New Yorker covered in soot with the copy "Up from the ashes. Rebuilding Wall Street. How the world will change. What now for investors?" *Entertainment Weekly*'s September 18, 2001, cover depicted the U.S. flag and the headline "What Lies Ahead: The Challenge to Our Culture." Over the weeks to follow, *Entertainment Weekly* highlighted ways popular culture was connected to the current climate. Cover stories included: "After the Attacks: Can Comedy Still Be Funny," "The West Wing: Inside the Oval Office," and "The Movies Go to War: *Behind Enemy Lines* Leads the Charge as Hollywood Marches toward a New Patriotism."

Talk Shows and News Programs

In the days following the terrorist attacks, radio talk show calls from listeners increased by 50 percent or more, suggesting that the medium provided another way to discuss their reactions to the events (Hume, 2003). Morning news and information shows incorporated many segments related to September 11 and the aftermath, segments about the recovery efforts, survivors, victim's families, and the government's actions were daily features on NBC's *Today*, ABC's *Good Morning America*, and CBS's *The Early Show*. Eventually, these segments were phased out or became less frequent, marking the annual anniversary or occasional special topic reports. However, several morning shows crafted accompanying September 11 Web sites where archived news was organized with an emphasis on human-interest type stories. For example, NBC's *Today* September 11-page features a video timeline titled "The Darkest Day," several stories on heroes, witness accounts, and a "Know 9/11?" quiz.

In time, television talk shows also integrated September 11-oriented topics into their programming. *The View* dedicated several segments to 9/11 rescue workers, the evolving situation at Ground Zero, and 9/11 conspiracy theories. Popular television talk show host Oprah Winfrey hosted approximately 40 programs about 9/11 and its aftermath, including Mother's and Father's Day tributes, interviews with survivors, discussions with reporters, and features led by Dr. Phil (McGraw) about helping people handle grief, loss, and fear (Kaplan, 2007). In 2007, Winfrey recorded a show in New York City to spotlight those who lived through a personal tragedy on September 11 and found a way to use the experience to help others.

Nightly news programming integrated September 11-oriented segments into their shows as well. For example, NBC's *Dateline* featured an interview with widow Lisa Beamer, whose husband Todd died on United 93. *Primetime Live* produced episodes on pregnant widows and their babies born after the terrorist attacks. In the weeks, months, and years to follow, radio talk shows and radio and television news programming also addressed government reactions to September 11. Most outlets broadcasted and discussed President Bush's speeches to Congress and at the Pentagon and sought reaction from a variety of pundits and citizens. Significant discussion centered around Congressional support of the newly created Department of Homeland Security and the Patriot Act. As the months and years passed, topics such as the passing of the Patriot Act, the clean up in New York City, the rebuilding of the Pentagon, the release of *The 9/11 Commission Report*, as well as many other subjects related to the terrorist attacks became commonplace on informational programming.

Information for Young People

After the attacks, organizations and institutions began compiling resources for parents and young people. A number of national organizations, such as the American Academy of Pediatrics and the American Academy of Child and Adolescent Psychiatry, published guidelines on their Web sites with suggestions on how to discuss with young people the terrorist attacks, loss, and going to war. Other organizations, such as AboutOurKids.org and PBS, provided a number of resources for parents and young people about the events of September 11, how to identify stress in children, and how to begin discussions about difficult topics. Several Web sites also provided talking

A SCARY THING HAPPENED

In 2003, the Federal Emergency Management Agency (FEMA), produced and made available on its Web site a coloring book titled, *A Scary Thing Happened*. Subtitled *A Children's Coloring Book to Help Cope with Disasters*, the book depicts an image of a plane flying toward one of the towers while the other burns. In addition to other drawings, the coloring book contains three images of the World Trade Center towers burning for children to color (Orr, 2009). The book was created by the Freeborn County Crisis Response Team after tornados struck Glenville, Minnesota, with the intent of helping children deal with trauma and has been used in different areas of the country (Walsh, 2009). The coloring book was removed from the FEMA Web site in April 2009 after complaints about its content.

—Amy M. Damico

References

Orr, J. (2009, April 30). FEMA removes 9/11 coloring book for children from Web site. *The Christian Science Monitor*. Retrieved from http://www.csmonitor.com

Walsh, P. (2009, April 30). FEMA pulls Minnesota crisis coloring book. *Star Tribune*. Retrieved from http://www.startribune.com

points for parents of teens and children, as well as tips and video clips to assist caregivers in comforting young children and helping them feel safe.

Other organizations provided summaries of information that could be helpful to parents of young children. For example, PBS Kids produced material to assist parents in helping their children deal with scary news; the National Education Association provided a summary of how children understand death at different ages; and the American Red Cross provided guidelines regarding how to address dealing with trauma with children of different ages. The challenges of parenting during this time were also discussed in national news magazines such as *Time* and *U.S. News & World Report* in addition to education and parent-oriented publications and Web sites.

Resources were also developed specifically for older children. Public libraries compiled lists and sections of September 11 materials for young adults. Often posted on their Web sites, libraries organized their information around topics such as September 11 timelines, heroes, Islam, the Taliban, and perspectives on the Middle East. News organizations whose target audience was young people produced September 11 content that summarized current information, reported about developing stories, and often provided lesson plans for middle school and high school teachers. For example, Channel One, the syndicated news broadcast for a predominantly high school audience, began reporting on the terrorist attacks on September 12, beginning with a summary of the previous day's events. The cable network CNN published September 11-oriented articles and accompanying lesson plans on their student news Web site CNNfyi.com (now called

---

SESAME STREET'S RESPONSE TO 9/11

When the events of 9/11 unfolded, all but four of *Sesame Street*'s (1969 to present) fifty shows of the season were already written. Sesame Workshop developed the final four episodes aimed at addressing important life lessons that could be taken from the events, as well as to model strategies for dealing with difficult situations. The episodes were titled, "Firefighters," "Discrimination," "Loss," and "Bullying."

In "Firefighters," Elmo sees and is frightened by a grease fire at the Hooper's store lunch counter. He is reassured by the firefighters who help put out the fire and later visits a fire station to learn about firefighters and firefighting. In "Discrimination," Big Bird's pen pal, Gulliver, visits Sesame Street and refuses to associate with anyone who is not a bird. Gulliver is surprised that Big Bird has friends who are not birds, and Big Bird tells Gulliver that if he refuses to play with all of Big Bird's friends, regardless of who they are, then Big Bird will not play with Gulliver. The end of the program depicts Gulliver's new understanding that differences between people can be wonderful. "Loss" shows the pain Big Bird feels when his pet turtle walks away to return to his natural environment. Other characters on the program comfort Big Bird by giving him hugs and asking him to talk about his former pet. Finally, "Bullying" depicts a sharing conflict between Telly and his cousin, Izzy. The program models ways to address sharing conflicts that do not involve hitting or grabbing.

These four episodes were aired again in the Fall of 2002 and corresponding materials in the *Sesame Family Newsletter* and on the *Sesame Street* Web site provided strategies and advice for talking about 9/11 with children of various ages (Daniel, 2002).

—Amy M. Damico

Reference

Daniel, J. (2002, September). Talking with kids about 9/11: One year later. Sesame Family Newsletter. *Sesame Workshop*. Retrieved June 23, 2008, from http://www.sesameworkshop.org

---

CNN Student News). PBS's NewsHour with Jim Lehrer produced web content for young people including a package titled "Life After 9.11" that included articles about the terrorist attacks, the response made by the United States, and how the "mood of the nation" influenced choices made by the entertainment industries.

Conspiracy Theories

The sheer enormity and complicated nature of the events surrounding 9/11 prompted conspiracy theories to be crafted and disseminated almost immediately following the terrorist attacks. The presence of conspiracy theories is not unusual given that in American culture, conspiracy theorists have routinely addressed many important events in U.S. history. However, the fact that such theories emerged so quickly was surprising to some given that usually conspiracy theories take about 10 years to surface (Atkins, 2008).

Atkins (2008) describes two of the prominent conspiracy theories that emerged shortly after the terrorist attacks. The first, authored by French activist Thierry Meyssan, suggests that the 9/11 attacks were part of a plot by the American government to discredit its enemies and increase the defense budget. The second, authored by Canadian professor emeritus A. K. Dewdney, also claims that the attacks were planned by the American government and that remote-controlled planes flew into the Twin Towers and the Pentagon. In addition, Dewdney claims that the passengers from all four planes involved were forced to board United 93 and were later shot down in Pennsylvania. The main conspiracy theorist groups in the United States are called Scholars for 9/11 Truth and Scholars for 9/11 Truth and Justice. Initially these groups were united as one, but disagreements over how to determine what really happened on 9/11 prompted the split.

Conspiracy theories surrounding September 11 spread quickly via the Internet and were addressed and challenged in mainstream media. The proliferation and pervasiveness of conspiracy theories prompted *Popular Mechanics* to investigate and eventually publish a report titled "9/11: Debunking the Myths" in March 2005. This article was used as a source on a number of television news and talk programs as well as on National Public Radio. According to the *Popular Mechanics* Web site, this report has been the most frequently read article and has been printed out more than 850,000 times. The response to the story, including questions from readers and criticism, prompted *Popular Mechanics* to expand on their original article and publish a book in 2006 titled, *Debunking 9/11 Myths: Why Conspiracy Theories Can't Stand Up to the Facts.*

Conclusion

Like the rest of the country, the news media was caught off guard on September 11, 2001. After it became clear that the first plane crashes in New York City were not accidental, the news media worked together to convey information about the unfolding events to the public, pooling resources in unprecedented ways to do so. In the attacks' aftermath, the events of September 11 maintained a presence on television, radio, newspapers, and the Internet evolving over time from around-the-clock broadcast coverage to daily stories to routine coverage. Digital archives of September 11-oriented material were created, and along with numerous Web sites, maintain an online presence today as available resources. News related to September 11 has been deemed so significant to the nation's history that an entire exhibit focused on the subject is in Washington, D.C.'s Newseum.

—*Amy M. Damico*

Partial List of Internet Archives of September 11 News

America Transformed: NPR Coverage, September 11—October 8, 2001
    http://www.npr.org/news/specials/americatransformed/
The September 11 Television Archive
    http://www.archive.org/details/sept_11_tv_archive

September11news.com
   http://www.september11news.com/
The Center for History and New Media/American Social History Project 9/11 Digital
   Archive
   http://911digitalarchive.org/guide.php?content=news
The Gotham Gazette's Rebuilding New York
   http://www.gothamgazette.com/rebuilding_nyc/features/previous_features.shtml
New York Magazine archive
   http://nymag.com/news/articles/wtc/
CameraPlanet 9/11 Archive
   http://www.911archive.net/Google
Times Topics: September 11, 2001 (*The New York Times*)
   http://topics.nytimes.com/top/reference/timestopics/subjects/s/sept_11_2001/index
   .html
One Year Later: *The Washington Post* Archive
   http://www.washingtonpost.com/wp-srv/nation/specials/attacked/remembrance/
   front.html
Library of Congress September 11th Web Archive
   http://web.archive.org/collections/sep11.html
USA Today: Remembering September 11 Archive
   http://www.usatoday.com/news/sept11/year-later-index.htm

References

Allan, S. (2001). Reweaving the Internet: Online news of September 11. In B. Zelizer &
      S. Allan (Eds.), *Journalism after September 11* (pp. 119–140). London: Routledge.
Atkins, S. (Ed.). (2008). *The 9/11 encyclopedia*. Westport, CT: Greenwood.
Bianco, R. (2001, September 11). Attack and chaos unfold on national TV. *USA Today.*
      Retrieved from http://www.usatoday.com
Brown, M., Fuzesi, L., Kitch, K., & Spivey, C. (2003). Internet news representations of
      September 11: Archival impulse in the age of information. In S. Chermak, F. Bailey, &
      M. Brown (Eds.), *Media representations of September 11* (pp. 103–116). Westport, CT:
      Greenwood.
Carey, J. (2002). American journalism on, before, and after September 11. In B. Zelizer &
      S. Allan (Eds.), *Journalism after September 11* (pp. 71–90). London: Routledge.
Carey, J. (2003). Media during the September 11 crisis. In A. Michael Noel (Ed.), *Crisis com-
      munications: Lessons from September 11* (pp. 1–16). Oxford: Rowman & Littlefield.
Fabrikant, G. (2001, September 17). After the attacks: The magazines; editors rush to revise
      long made plans. *The New York Times.* Retrieved from http://www.nytimes.com
Graber, D. A. (1980). *Mass media and American politics*. Washington, DC: Congressional
      Quarterly.
Hume, E. (2003). Talk show culture. In D. Johnston (Ed.), *The encyclopedia of international
      media and communications*. San Deigo, CA: Academic. Retrieved from http://www
      .ellenhume.com
Kaplan, D. (2007, August 30). Apple bound Oprah to do 9/11 show. *The New York Post.*
      Retrieved from http://www.nypost.com

Kuipers, G. (2005). "Where was King Kong when we needed him?" Public discourse, digital disaster jokes and the function of laughter after 9/11. *Journal of American Culture, 28*(1), 70–84.

Li, X. (2007). Stages of a crisis and media frames and functions: U.S. television coverage of the 9/11 incident during the first 24 hours. *Journal of Broadcasting and Electronic Media, 51(4)*, 670–687.

Loohauis, J. (2001, September 18). U.S. magazines print special editions to cover terrorist attacks. *Milwaukee Journal Sentinel*. Retrieved October 23, 2008, from http://www.accessmylibrary.com

Raines, H. (2002). Forward. In *Portraits 9/11/01: The collected "Portraits of Grief" from the New York Times (2003)*. New York: Henry Holt.

Reynolds, A., & Barnett, B. (2003). This just in . . . How national TV news handled the breaking "live" coverage of September 11. *Journalism and Mass Communication Quarterly, 80*(3), 689–703.

The September 11 Collection. (2008). *September 11 television archive*. Retrieved from http://www.archive.org/details/sept_11_tv_archive on September 18, 2008

Zelizer, B., & Allan, S. (2002). Introduction: When trauma shapes the news. In B. Zelizer & S. Allan (Eds.), *Journalism after September 11* (pp. 1–24). London: Routledge.

SPOTLIGHT ESSAY/NEWS AND INFORMATION: 9/11 GALLERY AT THE NEWSEUM

One of the most interesting exhibits at the Newseum, "the world's only interactive museum of news," is its 9/11 Gallery, which tells the story of how news media all over the world responded to the attacks, and honors the public service and personal sacrifice of those journalists who courageously faced danger in order to provide the public with eyewitness accounts. Located adjacent to the National Mall in Washington, D.C., the Newseum, a project of the Freedom Forum, a nonprofit foundation with ties to the news industry, is meant both to educate and to entertain, to be both a repository for rare press artifacts and a high-tech tourist attraction. The Newseum's sponsors and staff feel that the public has steadily come to hold a distorted conception of the news profession, in part because of often unflattering popular cultural representations, and see the Newseum as a means to project an alternative representation of news and the professionals who provide it.

The Newseum's 9/11 Gallery space features a memorial to the courageous photojournalist William Biggart, whose story is told by a brief film narrated by his widow, telling of his deep commitment to covering the news. The memorial also features his dusty, damaged camera preserved behind Plexiglas, as well as a dozen or so of the spectacular photos Biggart took just before he was killed when the second World Trade Center tower collapsed. Anchoring the various displays and dominating the space, in the center of the gallery one encounters the mangled remains of a massive broadcast antenna that formerly stood atop the North Tower. The dramatically malformed antenna, even in its misshapen, reduced state, still stands an imposing 40 feet high, and its ravaged condition, with shards and fragments protruding at extreme angles, speaks to the almost unimaginable violence of that day. Lining the enveloping 9/11 Gallery walls, newspaper front pages from around the world express horror at the carnage, and sympathy at the loss.

The gallery's spatial arrangement and the antenna's massive size and spectacular disfigurement work to designate the antenna as the symbolic center of the tragedy. But what, precisely, does it memorialize? Is the antenna supposed to represent the people who lost their lives that day? Another 9/11 memorial, the Tribute in Light (a display at Ground Zero that re-created the towers temporarily in blue light) was widely celebrated as a powerful statement of loss, as it was itself ephemeral and mournfully invoked both presence and absence. But it generated a fair amount of criticism from those who said it memorialized the towers themselves rather than the dead (Sturken, 2002, pp. 376–377). The same criticism could be directed at the Newseum's display of the World Trade Center antenna. However, the presence within the gallery of the exhibit memorializing the fallen photojournalist William Biggart effectively counters this potential criticism, and leaves the antenna free to symbolize, at a more abstract level, the news media and news consumers it served. The displaced and disfigured antenna evokes the vulnerability of the nation, but most particularly it gestures to the vulnerability of our open news system and the democracy it is meant to serve.

For a time, the antenna stood at the nation's very pinnacle—it was literally the nation's highest achievement. Now, the antenna stands eerily at ground level, in uncomfortable proximity to visitors. At one time, the antenna was just that—simply a powerful antenna working on behalf of a consortium of broadcasters. Now, as a technology of memory, it can create different and perhaps even more powerful effects, as it works to reshape collective memory. The visitor's encounter with the Newseum's 9/11 memorial conjures powerful memories of 9/11 and tries to extend the 9/11 moment, a moment when we turn to the news media not just for information but also for reassurance and guidance. By conjuring the 9/11 moment, the antenna would have us forget the factors that have led to growing public unease with the work of the news media (including, for example, corporate consolidation and conglomeration, and the steady blurring of boundaries between news and entertainment).

In its diminished state, the 9/11 antenna represents a powerful plea for restoration. Although the antenna itself will, of course, never be repaired, more fundamentally it represents a plea for restoration of public trust in the news media, without which the news media will be unable to perform its assumed work of safeguarding democracy. If visitors to the Vietnam Memorial actively redefine memory of that conflict, and act to heal its wounds, by means of placing poetry, dog tags, letters, or other memorial items at the base of the memorial, Newseum visitors can, in similar fashion, help to heal some of the trauma of 9/11 by undertaking the kinds of actions, and in particular making the types of choices as news consumers, that will express a restored trust in the news media, a trust newly predicated on memories of 9/11. Memories of 9/11 will then have become an active force within our current (and future) relationships to the news media.

—Mark Nimkoff

Reference

Sturken, M. (2002). Memorializing absence. In C. Calhoun, P. Price, & A. Timmer (Eds.), *Understanding September 11* (pp. 374–384). New York: New Press.

SPOTLIGHT ESSAY/NEWS AND INFORMATION: CHANNEL ONE NEWS COVERAGE

Channel One broadcasts a student news program to middle and high schools across the country. Because of its mandatory inclusions of commercials and what some characterize as simplistic news content, Channel One has been controversial from its creation. It has been the subject of both scholarly criticism (Austin, Chen, Pinkleton, & Johnson, 2006; De Vaney, 1994; Greenburg & Brand, 1993) and public hearings in Congress ("Channel One, Educational Television," 1991). Paying particular attention to Channel One's coverage of 9/11 provides a window into the media to which many students were exposed in the wake of the attacks. Overall, Channel One's initial coverage of 9/11 was not substantially different than what students would have been seeing in other media outlets with one exception: Channel One elected not to show much of the raw footage of the attacks.

Channel One first addressed the terrorist attacks on September 12 in a newscast titled "The Day After" (Channel One, 2001). Mirroring the choices national television networks made, reporters for Channel One announced they would provide uninterrupted coverage, which differs from their common structure of news and commercials. During the introduction to the programming, a U.S. flag waved across the screen as images of the attacks cycled past the viewer. This patriotic display paralleled the choices of the mainstream news outlets to use patriotic imagery as well. Such imagery was the impetus for criticism in later years regarding what role the news media should play in times of crisis and if displaying patriotic symbols suggest acceptance of government assertions and actions.

As the report proceeded, the anchors reviewed what few facts were known at the time and then moved to discussing where the planes took off from until they were diverted. The reporting displayed the hesitance the producers must have had in showing images of the airplanes striking the buildings, as the World Trade Center towers were pictured accurately, but the planes were depicted only by arrows. A brief clip of a video feed showed a portion of the second impact, but this was a fleeting and partially obscured view. Given that Channel One's audience consists of middle school and high school students, the network seemingly decided that making conservative choices regarding what images were appropriate to show was the proper course.

The next part of the news segment depicts President Bush in Florida at a school where he is working on his main policy issue to that point in his administration—education (Bush, 2001). There is no mention of the amount of time between his hearing that "America is under attack," the reading of *The Pet Goat*, and his final departure from the classroom. Like mainstream media coverage, Channel One's reporting suggested that President Bush left the elementary school classroom directly after he heard about the attacks from his aides to deal with the situation. Most media sources did not widely report on how long President Bush spent in the classroom after hearing about the second plane's crash into the World Trade Center; this issue was later documented in *The 9/11 Commission Report* (2004) and Michael Moore's *Fahrenheit 9/11* (2004).

In moving to the attacks on the Pentagon, Channel One news again used an arrow to represent the plane that struck the building. In this section of the broadcast, the viewer hears shouts to get back from the Pentagon site as the attacks were still rapidly unfolding. The reporter then describes the fall of the World Trade Center's South Tower, but footage of the tower's fall was not used. The students instead saw the horrific dust and debris storm that was generated by the collapse. The report wrapped up with an interview of several witnesses to the attacks followed by a brief discussion with a social worker on the coping and grieving processes many students might have been experiencing as a result of having been exposed to such frightening images.

In the years since the attacks, Channel One continued to cover aspects of September 11 and produced several segments related to the attacks and the war on terrorism, including a five-year-anniversary special where a young reporter interviewed Secretary of State Condoleezza Rice. The Channel One Web site houses archival material on September 11 including newscasts, information on the Middle East, Islam, and terrorism.

—*Aaron Cooley*

References

Austin, E. W., Chen, Y., Pinkleton, B., & Johnson, J. (2006). Benefits and costs of Channel One in a middle school setting and the role of media-literacy training. *Pediatrics, 117*(3), 423–433.

Bush, L. (2001). Mrs. Bush's remarks to the Hoover institution. Retrieved September 15, 2008, from http://www.whitehouse.gov/briefing-room/statements-and-releases

Channel One. (2001). *The day after*. Retrieved September 13, 2008, from http://www.channelone.com/

Channel One. (2006). *9/11 five years later*. Retrieved September 13, 2008, from http://www.channelone.com/

Channel One, Educational Television and Technology. Hearing on examining current educational television programming and to examine new technologies which could impact the future of educational television, focusing on Channel One, a news and information program designed for a teen-age audience, before the Subcommittee on Education, Arts, and Humanities of the Committee on Labor and Human Resources, *United States Senate*, 102d Cong., 1. (1991). Washington, DC: U.S. Government Printing Office.

De Vaney, A. (Ed.). (1994). *Watching Channel One: The convergence of students, technology, and private business*. Albany: SUNY Press.

Greenburg, B., & Brand, J. (1993). Research note: Television news and advertising in schools: The "Channel One" controversy. *Journal of Communication, 43*(1), 143–151.

SPOTLIGHT ESSAY/NEWS AND INFORMATION: THE 9/11 TRUTH MOVEMENT

Conspiracy theories, or alternative versions to the official account of the September 11, 2001, events, appeared immediately after the attacks, and some proliferation of these theories continues today. In fact, some have gained new momentum long after 9/11. There are different conspiracy theories regarding 9/11, some of which insist on different accounts of the events of September 11 itself, while others refer only to different motives and or to different alleged culprits. The spread of conspiracy theories after 9/11 happened quickly, and in some cases, the believers in those theories were also mobilized to collective action, the most conspicuous example of which is the 9/11 Truth movement.

There are several explanations about what motivates conspiracy theories and the type of people who believe in them. Some view conspiracy theories simply as hate-driven irrationality while others assert that they express distrust in the existing political and social system (Knight, 2003). Believers in conspiracy theories also tend to attribute excessive powers to institutions, groups, or individuals—which they may or may not posses in reality. In many cases conspiracy theories are explanations of the powerless regarding those they consider powerful. Conspiracy theories can be developed by various groups in society—some powerful, others not, which have their own interests in publicizing the theory. This is sometimes done to raise hostility toward a certain group or a specific individual and to create mass hysteria. Many conspiracy theories, for example, rely on a mythical "enemy" that initiated the event (e.g., Jews, Illuminati, witches). The believers are mobilized into action against this perceived "enemy," which might prevent the public from engaging in other types of collective action that might improve their situation.

The 9/11 Truth movement is a loose network of individuals and groups who believe in conspiracy theories related to the September 11 attacks. The movement's activity is not systematically coordinated, nor are there any individuals who can be pinned as the "leaders" of the movement (although some activists are more vocal and are featured more often in the mainstream media). Some of the members of 9/11 Truth framed themselves as professional experts in construction, aeronautics, or security as a means of advancing the credibility of their claims; other prominent supporters lost loved ones in the attacks. The movement led believers into collective action against the Bush administration by way of organizing protests and communicating their conspiracy theories via a number of media outlets including their extensive Web site.

Several conspiracy theories regarding the events of September 11 were advanced by this group and numerous articles that question aspects of September 11 are found on the Web site, 9/11truth.org. For example, some claim that the Bush Administration either "let" the attacks happen on September 11, 2001, or was directly involved in planning and operating the attacks. They question the failure of the air defense system to prevent the attacks, as well as President Bush's behavior throughout the events.

Some members question the nature of the collapse of the World Trade Center towers, suggesting that the towers did not collapse because of the collision with the planes, but as a result of controlled demolition. Others believe the damage to the Pentagon does not correspond with that of a plane collision into the building. In addition, some members of 9/11 Truth alleged that the Bush Administration's instatement of the Patriot Act and its attacks on Afghanistan and Iraq were a means to creating a new world order (Anonymous, 2009; 9/11 Truth movement, 2009).

The Internet plays an important role both in the mobilization and organization of the 9/11 Truth movement and in proliferation of other conspiracy theories. Internet sites, including 911truth.org, publish alternative accounts and encourage visitors to become active in revealing what they believe to be the truth. The Internet also plays an important role in proliferating films, which allegedly feature the faults of the official account and the "truth" behind the events. One of the most popular films of this genre, *Loose Change* (2005), interviews members of the 9/11 Truth movement, who label themselves as experts, and integrates this with clips from news reports of the events.

The 9/11 Truth movement's ideas provide alternative explanations to the official and generally accepted interpretations of what happened on September 11, 2001. The 9/11 attacks have invoked, as in many previous traumatic moments in history, certain assumptions about how the society and the government system work. The 9/11 Truth movement's alternative explanations presuppose a deliberated attempt to hide the "truth," as the supporters of the conspiracy theories view it. Although the organization questions many different aspects of September 11, many theorists still maintain links to the wider framework of the "conspiracist worldview" (Knight, 2001), which interprets the trauma within preset beliefs such as antigovernmental views, suspicion toward "big business" and globalization, and resentment toward specific nations or minorities.

—*Tamar Gablinger*

References

[Anonymous]. (2009). *The top September 11 conspiracy theories*. America.gov. Retrieved from http://www.america.gov

Knight, P. (2001) *Conspiracy culture: From Kennedy to the X-Files*. London: Routledge.

Knight, P. (Ed.). (2003). *Conspiracy nation: The politics of paranoia in postwar America*. New York: New York University Press.

9/11 Truth Movement. (2009). Retrieved August 13, 2009, from http://www.911truth.org/

SPOTLIGHT ESSAY/NEWS AND INFORMATION: EDITORIAL CARTOONS

In the days and weeks after September 11, the nation experienced a roller coaster of emotions. Somewhat mirroring this response, political cartoons followed an emotional path from shock to sadness to anger. This trajectory can be seen by examining the illustrated editorial cartoons of the *Chicago Tribune;* the paper acts as a good barometer of the nation's climate because it routinely reprints syndicated cartoons from other newspapers.

The "first responder" comics—those printed immediately after the attacks— were the editorial cartoons of September 12 and 13. The emotion expressed within these two days was one of absolute shock. Foreigners attacked America within its own borders for the first time in more than 50 years, and the feelings that accompany such an experience ran through the nation's streets and in its cartoons. The first image that appeared in the *Chicago Tribune*—a cartoon depicting a child and an older man, presumably a father and son, with their arms around each other, staring wide-eyed into a store window through which they watch the attacks displayed on several televisions—captured this feeling of shock when it ran on September 12 (Anderson, 2001). The shock is evident on the characters' faces who, both young and old, represent the feelings of helplessness. Unable to shut off the images and the devastation before them, they are drawn as physically and metaphorically stuck behind the glass as they watch the tragedy. The cartoon also records the fact that the majority of the nation experienced the events of September 11 through the television, rather than in person.

The next day, Thursday, September 13, a cartoon in the *Tribune* showed another image of shock as a wide-eyed Statue of Liberty watches Manhattan with the smoking Twin Towers reflected in her eyes (Luckovich, 2001). Much like the father and child in the previous day's cartoon, Lady Liberty is symbolic of the nation helplessly watching as the attacks occurred. A small tear in her eye suggests the grief that will follow the shock. In fact, over the following days cartoons began to convey sadness and even acceptance. For example, the *Tribune* reprinted a different crying Statue of Liberty image on September 15 (Ariail, 2001a). This Statue of Liberty is devastated. Her head is buried in her hand, and she is unable to look at the aftermath of the attacks; the devastation is behind her but also within her. Other editorial cartoons also conveyed feelings of sadness and regret. In response to politicians' calls to honor the fallen, the *Tribune* ran another cartoon on September 15 depicting two statues standing side by side. The statue on the left is of Nathan Hale, a soldier in the Revolutionary war, who is famously quoted as saying, "I regret that I have but one life to lose for my country." The second statue includes the same quote, however the word "I" is changed to "we," and Hale's likeness is replaced with images of the passengers of United Flight 93, who were recognized as heroes after preventing the plane's hijackers from attacking another site in Washington, D.C (Stayskal 2001).

Editorial cartoons also honored heroes and rescue workers. For example, the *Tribune* published a cartoon on Friday, September 14, with the caption "New York's Twin Towers." The cartoon depicts two men, as physical representations of the now destroyed World Trade Center towers, standing in rubble alongside the words "courage" and "strength" (Handelsman, 2001). On Sunday, September 16, another cartoon showed police and firefighters raising the U.S. flag in a way that mirrored the famous Iwo Jima pose from World War II (Ariail, 2001b). The editorial cartoon published on Monday, September 16, depicts firefighters running into a smoldering skull with the word "terrorism" across its head and a caption that says "war heroes" (Anderson, 2001).

By the end of the week, new sentiments appeared in editorial cartoon imagery. Moving past shock and grief, the cartoons reflected the nation's anger and desire for revenge; revenge meant war. In Saturday's edition of the *Tribune*, two images, one by Chip Bok and one by Nick Anderson, compared the 9/11 attacks to the attack on Pearl Harbor. The Bok image shows two smoldering fires with each of the historic dates captioned above them and the subtitle "Infamy II" (Bok, 2001). The Anderson image also shows a smoldering fire in the New York skyline and a quote from a Japanese admiral about "waking a sleeping giant" (Anderson, 2001). By Monday, September 17, President Bush declared that he wanted justice. As a result, the imagery in political cartoons began to change again. Whereas the earlier images often used the Statue of Liberty, these later images frequently featured images of Uncle Sam. For example, on Tuesday, September 18, the *Tribune* published a cartoon that showed Uncle Sam rolling up his sleeve (Ramirez, 2001). The shift from female to male imagery, and from the welcoming symbolism of Lady Liberty to the more aggressive stance of Uncle Sam reflected the country's changing emotions after the 9/11 attacks.

As a final remembrance of those who died on September 11, and just before to going to war September 19, a cartoon comprised simply of 5,000 dots asked readers to remember what that number—the number of estimated dead—feels like (Ohman, 2001). On Thursday, September 20, the *Tribune* ran the final 9/11-related image of two people in bed comforting one another with newspapers on the floor that say "attacked" and "war." This couple symbolizes the fatigue that the nation was feeling (Borgman, 2001). After September 20, the political cartoons slipped back into a "business as usual" mode with more pithy commentary and with fewer allusions to the imagery of September 11. Editorial cartoons began to focus more on War on Terror imagery such as drawings of bin Laden.

Cartoons after September 11 reflected the wide range of emotions experienced throughout the nation during the aftermath of the terrorist attacks. As with other media forms, cartoons recognized the gravity of the event, expressed appreciation for rescue workers, and conveyed sadness for lives lost. Recognizable images, such as the Statue of Liberty, the U.S. flag, and Uncle Sam were commonly used within the cartoons to depict the nation's shock, grief, sentiments for revenge, and, ultimately, its march toward war.

—Ora C. McWilliams

References

Anderson, N. (2001, September 12). [9/12 editorial cartoon]. *Chicago Tribune*, sec. 1, p. 22.

Ariail, R. (2001a, September 15). [9/15 editorial cartoon]. *Chicago Tribune*, sec. 1, p. 23.

Ariail, R. (2001b, September 16). [9/16 editorial cartoon]. *Chicago Tribune*, sec. 1, p. 22.

Bok, C. (2001, September 15). [9/15 editorial cartoon]. *Chicago Tribune*, sec. 1, p. 23.

Borgman, J. (2001, September 20). [9/20 editorial cartoon]. *Chicago Tribune*, sec. 1, p. 28.

Handelsman, W. (2001, September 14). [9/14 editorial cartoon]. *Chicago Tribune*, sec. 1, p. 30.
Luckovich, M. (2001, September 13). [9/13 editorial cartoon]. *Chicago Tribune*, sec. 1, p. 26.
Ohman, J. (2001, September 19). [9/19 editorial cartoon]. *Chicago Tribune*, sec. 1, p. 30.
Ramirez, M. (2001, September 18). [9/18 editorial cartoon]. *Chicago Tribune*, sec. 1, p. 8.
Stayskal, W. (2001, September 15). [9/15 editorial cartoon]. *Chicago Tribune*, sec. 1, p. 22.

SPOTLIGHT ESSAY/NEWS AND INFORMATION: THE INTERNET AND 9/11

The development of digital video has altered the way people can obtain and share information. No longer dependant on professionals for the news of the day, anyone with the easily accessible technology can record images, upload them on YouTube, publish a written piece on the Internet and e-mail content to friends and strangers. Such historical recording capabilities have influenced the representation of the 9/11 World Trade Center attacks. Thousands of videos were posted on YouTube by witnesses to the horror in Manhattan. Often filmed through dust-sheeted windows and lenses, the amateur recordings attest to the inextricable link between modern technologies of catastrophe (such as the attacks on skyscrapers in one of the world's largest and most modern cities), hi-tech media, and instant historiography (the creation of history).

The way the events of 9/11 have been documented on the Internet demonstrates the soaring success of Web 2.0 media in recent years, from the proliferation of small screen feeds and handheld cameras to the growing interest shown by storing and archiving facilities (such as the Library of Congress, which houses one of the largest 9/11 digital archives) that offer an easily accessible database of textual and visual material related to the historical event, its reception and memorialization. The transition from photography to television and finally to user-generated content online culminated with the revolution in digital photography and handheld devices (Friend, 2006).

User-generated content created with these new technologies comprises many September 11-oriented Web sites. The most ubiquitous coverage of the 9/11 facts (and fictions) can still be found on so-called conspiracy Web sites, which feed on the prevalent climate of paranoia in contemporary America that has characterized American culture ever since World War II. In contrast to the conspiracy-oriented sites, amateur videos of the events emphasize the process of witnessing involved in the close encounter with mass destruction and the emotional impact on the spectator. In doing so, they reinforce the idea that web services for sharing video files, as well as countless blogs and social networking Web sites, are charting a parallel account of history that focuses less on the actual development of the tragedy than on its impact—in painstaking chronological sequence—on those personally involved. The prevalence of confessional clips among YouTube's most popular 9/11-themed videos also attests to increasing discussions about death (Egan, 1999) in the aftermath of 9/11, reflected in the numerous "accidental memoirs" centered on the private experience of a historical public trauma (Wyatt, 2004).

Some argue that the media coverage of 9/11 produced a specific American collective identity through a melodramatic plotline, which allowed the United States to emerge as a morally powerful victim forced to transform victimization into heroic retributive action (Anker, 2005). The bulk of 9/11 materials on video platforms perpetuate these melodramatic scenarios and rely on demonizing an enemy whose threats must be fought or ridiculed (see, for example, the countless video jokes at the expense of Arab characters or mascots on YouTube). However, other uses of web content keep with the initial digital coverage of 9/11 as highly personal, affect-laden disaster. On the streets of lower Manhattan on 9/11, passers-by stopped to look at the posters of missing persons, read the captions attached to the images, and scribbled notes of support and empathy in between the pictures on the walls—very much like an Internet viewer would pause to comment on a video that caught his or her attention.

Perhaps the most controversial and ethically questionable images disseminated through current Internet platforms are videos of the World Trade Center "jumpers"— many of which reproduce in high resolution the profoundly personal drama of about 200 people who were either ejected from the towers by the force of the explosions and gradual collapse of the buildings or opted to jump to certain death rather than be burned alive. "The jumpers," Tom Junod (2003) notes in a definitive article on Richard Drew's iconic picture of the "falling man," "were relegated to the Internet underbelly, where they became the provenance of the shock sites . . . where it is impossible to look at them without attendant feelings of shame and guilt. It was as though the jumpers' experience, instead of being central to the horror, was tangential to it, a sideshow best forgotten" (pp. 178–179). However, visual forgetfulness of such images is exactly what platforms of amateur historiography are now calling into question. Videos of World Trade Center victims plummeting to their deaths have mushroomed into a network of exploitative clips whose very multiplicity and ready accessibility seem to gloss over the horrific loss of life. Some even falsely proclaim to depict what could never have been caught on camera, because of the dangers of approaching the towers with handheld devices and to the subsequent collapse, namely the bodies of the jumpers strewn on the ground. Undoubtedly, the attraction of these videos is increased by their sensational content and prurient appeal, which belong to the staples of Internet enjoyment and its privacy.

In conclusion, the events of September 11 demonstrated how new technologies could be used in various ways to discuss and document disasters. Whereas some uses of the Internet contribute to the creation of easily accessible vast archives of information, other uses demonstrate more personal, private ways of sharing feelings in a public setting. The use of sharing of September 11 related content does raise some ethical issues. The use, misuse, and overuse of these technologies should be examined to ensure the public's ability to distinguish between affective memorialization and destructive perpetuation of terror-related media.

—*Georgiana Banita*

References

Anker, E. (2005). Villains, victims, and heroes: Melodrama, media, and September 11. *Journal of Communication, 55*(1), 22–37.

Egan, S. (1999). *Mirror talk: Genres of crisis in contemporary autobiography.* Chapel Hill: University of North Carolina Press.

Friend, D. (2006). *Watching the world change: The stories behind the images of 9/11.* New York: Picador.

Junod, T. (2003, September). The falling man. *Esquire,* 178–179.

Wyatt, D. (2004). *And the war came: An accidental memoir.* Madison: University of Wisconsin Press.

SPOTLIGHT ESSAY/NEWS AND INFORMATION: ISLAMIC DRESS AND THE WAR ON TERROR

An opinion poll released a week after the tragedies of September 11, 2001, found that although most Americans wanted some sort of action against the terrorists and favored the assassination of Osama bin Laden, many did not like the idea of military operations in a country they had never heard of; people were uncomfortable with the bombing of a distant nation. To appease these skeptics, the George W. Bush administration decided to use what today has become a common and recognizable image—the image of a burqa-clad Afghani woman. Video news packages released by the White House featuring the shrouded women were immediately picked up by mainstream as well as by alternative news outlets such as feminist Web sites and magazines. The images of these women were so racially charged that within a few days another poll showed that a majority of Americans were now in favor of the war.

To understand the power of images of the burqa-clad Afghani woman, it is useful to understand a little history regarding how women from Eastern nations have been portrayed in imagery created by the West. Edward Said's book *Orientalism* (1978) and his more mature work *Culture and Orientalism* (1993) provide an analytical framework, called Orientalist scholarship, from which the image of the burqa in the American media can be examined. Said argues that eighteenth- and nineteenth-century European scholarship and travel writing constructed a very careful and specific image of the East, or the Orient. In contrast to the West, the East was depicted as unchanging, mysterious, indolent, and steeped in traditions that kept them backward (Abu Odeh, 1993; Kabbani, 1994; Lewis; 1996, Lowe, 1991). The post-September 11 media images of the burqa-clad Afghani woman can be viewed as an example of Said's argument; that these images suggest that Eastern women are stuck in a "backward" culture and need help from the West, or the United States.

After September 11, mainstream and feminist media suggested that the Afghani woman were helpless and weak by the use of a number of photographs. At the height of the bombing in Afghanistan, *Ms. Magazine* (see Vol. XII, No. 1, December 2001–January 2002; Vol. XIII, No. 2, Summer 2003, etc.) and *Off Our Backs* published several photographs of Afghani women in their burqas. Often the women were shown alone in a barren landscape, and at times no text accompanied the image. Readers were never told who the women in the images were, where they came from, how representative they were of women in their country, and whether they were wearing the burqa by choice or by force. In photograph after photograph, the Afghani women were seen as hapless, helpless victims—victimized by their own faith, culture, and men (see Ong, 1994; Mohanty, 2000 for context).

The November 2001 issue of the feminist publication *Off Our Backs*, featured six women in their burqas on the cover. The women were lined up so that only the full front of two of the women was visible. The black and white photograph was accompanied by the headline: "Will Bombing Help These Women?" The photograph was cropped so closely that we cannot see where the women are situated or headed. Other than what some see as the "offending" burqa, there was nothing in the image to suggest that these women needed any help. These photographs, shown without any information about the women themselves, their history, their perspectives, their opinions about what they are wearing, lead to the veil then becoming a one-dimensional indicator of gender oppression, marking the Muslim woman as different and in need of Western help.

The use of these images may have functioned to increase support for the war after September 11, when the United States began its military operations in Afghanistan. The images of women in burqas may have suggested to readers that all Afghani women were victims, oppressed, and hoping to be liberated. Additionally, the photographs, particularly the ones without accompanying narratives, do not require readers to think about the women's own stories, history, and opinions—perhaps one of the first steps in attempting to understand another's culture.

—Sanjukta Ghosh

References

Abu Odeh, L. (1993). Post-colonialism, feminism, and the veil: Thinking the difference. *Feminist Review, 43*(1), 26–44.

Kabbani, R. (1994). *Imperial fictions: Europe's myths of the Orient.* New York: Pandora.

Lewis, R. (1996). *Gendering orientalism: Face, femininity and representation.* London: Routledge.

Lowe, L. (1991). *French and British colonialisms.* Ithaca: Cornell University Press.

Mohanty, C. (2000). Under Western eyes: Feminist scholarship and colonial discourses. In A. Tripp (Ed.), *Gender: Readers in cultural criticism* (pp. 51–70). New York: Palgrave.

Ong, A. (1994). Colonialism and modernity: Feminist representations of women in non-Western societies. In A. C. Herrmann & A. J. Stewart (Eds.), *Theorizing feminism: Parallel trends in the humanities and social sciences* (pp. 281–372). Boulder: Westview.

Said, E. W. (1978). *Orientalism.* New York: Pantheon Books.

Said, E. W. (1993). *Culture and imperialism.* London: Chatto & Windus.

SPOTLIGHT ESSAY/NEWS AND INFORMATION: NEWSPAPER HEADLINES

Newspapers reacted quickly to the events on September 11, many producing late editions of their publications. Given the unprecedented nature of the attacks, newspapers used their headlines to commemorate the day's devastation. The initial headlines called attention to 9/11 in a variety of ways and, in so doing, prioritized certain aspects of the events while excluding others. A sample of headlines published in the immediate aftermath of the attacks demonstrates some of the ways newspapers characterized the events.

A number of initial newspaper headlines conveyed the idea that what had happened was incomprehensible. By using phrases and words such as "BEYOND BELIEF" (*Minnesota Pioneer Press*) and "UNTHINKABLE" (*Salt Lake Tribune*), these headlines emphasized the feeling that readers had witnessed an unforeseen and exceptional tragedy. Resonating seamlessly with President Bush's (2001) earlier claim that, "The pictures of airplanes flying into buildings . . . have filled us with disbelief," a powerful narrative of "AMERICA IN SHOCK" (*Nashville City Paper*) very quickly emerged.

At one level, it is easy to understand the appeal of this framing. Beyond the realm of disaster movies, the devastating, spectacular impact of those crashes was, perhaps, without parallel. By so vividly underscoring the attacks' exceptional nature, however, this particular story also worked to camouflage alternative understandings of those events. The first newspaper headlines emphasized *and* excluded certain themes. As Jackson (2005) argued, there was simply no space in this version of story for contextualizing 9/11 within a long history of violence between Al Qaeda and the U.S. government, a history that incorporated attacks on the USS *Cole*, and American embassies in East Africa, as well as a history that included U.S. bombings in Afghanistan and Sudan. A complex and multifaceted historical event was reduced, quite simply, to a sudden moment of rupture captured succinctly in the *New York Daily Record*'s dramatic "9/11/01" headline.

In addition, headlines did not contextualize 9/11 through any distinctively political lens. While emphasizing the incomprehensible nature of the attacks, the headlines also refer to them and their perpetrators simply, not addressing or even acknowledging motives for such destruction. In combination with the more direct condemnations of these "EVIL ACTS" (*Montana Billings Gazette*) and the "BASTARDS" (*San Francisco Examiner*) behind them, this version of the story reduced those events to, simply, an unintelligible "OUTRAGE" (*Atlanta Constitution*).

However we may wish to condemn 9/11, this characterization of the attacks as little more than a "DESPICABLE" (*Macon Telegraph*) "HORROR" (*Los Angeles Daily News*) offered an unsatisfactory framework for doing so. In the first instance, this framework represented a denial of the repeatedly stated political demands motivating Al Qaeda's campaigns of violence. It also blocked any meaningful discussion of the appropriate strategies for confronting those "Bastards." "Evil" cannot be reasoned with or engaged in dialogue. By framing the attacks through this particular lens, the early headlines may have contributed to legitimizing the subsequent, devastating, military operations in Afghanistan and Iraq. With "ACTS OF WAR" (*USA Today*) thus committed, it was perhaps unsurprising that further "acts of war" soon followed.

These headlines demonstrate how newspapers initially characterized the September 11 attacks. Other headlines reflected on the future impact and consequences of the attacks—a reflection, grounded in their very immediate aftermath. What did headlines such as "NOTHING WILL EVER BE THE SAME" (*Philadelphia City Paper*) and "AMERICA SAVAGED, FOREVER CHANGED" (*Detroit News*) tell readers about 9/11? What, again, did they exclude or conceal?

The first point to note here is that these discussions of transformation fitted remarkably neatly with the above accounts of trauma and rupture. By informing us solemnly, assuredly, that everything had changed on that day, these headlines again reminded us that something incredible—something unbelievable—had taken place. Yet, what precisely did change on 9/11? For the attacks' immediate victims and their families, this violence no doubt irrevocably altered the trajectory, perhaps meaning, of the rest of their lives. For many other individuals in the United States and beyond, however, this sense of radical change may have seemed rather too hasty. As Halliday (2002) argued, "Many of the greatest threats to the world, and many of the problems which are least susceptible to traditional forms of state control (the environment, migration, the drugs trade, AIDS), long-predated September 11" (p. 235). That these less dramatic, yet similarly devastating, security challenges continued unabated after those attacks should again encourage our thinking carefully around the media headlines that grapple for our attention. If those headlines do, indeed, prioritize and camouflage aspects of reality as argued above, a patient reading of this sort is likely to open considerable space for a fuller, more detailed, understanding of important events.

—*Lee Jarvis*

References

Bush, G. (2001). *Statement by the president in his address to the nation: 11 September 2001.* Retrieved September 14, 2005, from http://www.whitehouse.gov/briefing-room/statements-and-releases

Halliday, F. (2002). A new global configuration. In K. Booth & T. Dunne (Eds.), *Worlds in collision: Terror and the future of global order* (pp. 235–241). Basingstoke: Palgrave.

Jackson, R. (2005). *Writing the war on terrorism: Language, politics and counter-terrorism.* Manchester: Manchester University Press.

Poynter Institute. (2001). *September 11, 2001: A collection of newspaper front pages selected by the Poynter Institute.* Kansas City: Andrews McMeel.

SPOTLIGHT ESSAY/NEWS AND INFORMATION: NEWS PHOTOGRAPHY

Photography is a process of knowledge production—to view photographs is to know something (White, 1996). But what is it that we know? Newspapers, magazines, and television provided us with images of 9/11 making us constantly aware of the event even weeks later. But were these images, repeated again and again, helpful in understanding—of knowing better—the events of September 11, 2001? Hayden White (1996) suggests that understanding of history is constituted by its images being shown and reproduced over and over again. The use and reuse of similar sets of images that emerged from the photographic coverage of September 11 contribute to a specific collective memory of the event that focuses on the World Trade Center towers, frightened New Yorkers, and firefighters as celebrated rescue workers.

In the United States, the newspapers dispatched on the evening of 9/11, and in the immediate days following, headlined with photographs of the tragedies that occurred earlier that morning. On the following day most of the major news publications—including but not exclusive to the *New York Times, Los Angeles Times*, the *Baltimore Sun*, the *Charlotte Observer*, and *Kansas City Star*—depicted one or both of the World Trade Center towers in flames as they billowed smoke. Other publications depicted the trauma of the event by showing the emotions of individuals or groups. For example, the *Salt Lake Tribune* and the *Columbia Daily Tribune* chose to use images of people fleeing away from the burning towers and toward the reader. Here, the image of the World Trade Center was secondary to photographs of fleeing people who literally were attempting to run out of the photographic frame (www.september11 news.com). Still other newspapers—*Seattle Post Intelligencer* (September 13, 2001) and *Chronicle Tribune* (September 16, 2001)—sought to console the nation by depicting the heroic work of the New York City firefighters at Ground Zero through a nostalgic and patriotic reinterpretation of the now famous photograph of U.S. soldiers lifting the U.S. flag at Iwo Jima (www.september11news.com). Finally, some newspapers tried to grapple with the enormity of the event through an appeal to humanity. For example, a chilling image of portrait-style photographs aligned in rows and columns found their way onto the front pages of some newspapers such as the *Cleveland Plain Dealer* (September 16, 2001; www.september11news.com). This choice was an early recognition of the enormous effect September 11, 2001, would have to a nation just beginning to mourn.

The events of 9/11 could have been covered from a number of different camera angles and from a variety of sources. Instead, most news coverage opted to use a finite number of images to re-create and tell the events of 9/11, which insured that everyone would be receiving, at least visually if not rhetorically, the same story. Those learning about 9/11, or any part of history, rely in part on photographs to "say something" about the event they are trying to understand (Sontag, 1977; White, 1996; Zelizer, 1998). Photographs become part of the evidence that an event took place and convey a particular narrative, sometimes excluding other parts of the story by virtue of a lack of images or digital manipulation of present photographs. The mainstream images of 9/11 conveyed that the World Trade Center towers burned and then collapsed, that people were fearful for their lives, and that firefighters played a prominent role in rescue and recovery operations. Photographs of 9/11 secure ideas that an event did take place, that individual lives were lost, and that a whole nation was affected by the destruction and damage to buildings that were symbols of financial wealth and military dominance.

The event of 9/11 will be largely remembered by the nation through the finite number of images that were chosen as representative of the event itself. News photographs constructed 9/11 as towering infernos, people in chaos, and firefighters covered in ashes. Has a disservice been done in constructing 9/11 through a limited number of images in terms of 9/11 remembrance? Would more variations of images from September 11 offer a better understanding of the events or a more complicated collective memory? Was it, in order to create nationalistic feelings of pride and patriotism, necessary for a nation in shock and mourning to see the same images that their neighbors saw? There are many questions that could be asked about the role of images in creating historical memory and knowledge; now it remains to ask them.

—*Robin Anderson*

References

September 11 news.com. (2001–2008). *September 11 archival news*. Retrieved from http://www.september11news.com

Sontag, S. (1977). *On photography*. New York: Farrar, Straus, and Giroux.

White, H. (1996). The modernist event. In V. Sobchack (Ed.), *The persistence of history: Cinema, television, and the modern event* (pp. 17–38). New York: Routledge.

Zelizer, B. (1998). *Remembering to forget: Holocaust memory through the camera's eye*. Chicago: University of Chicago Press.

SPOTLIGHT ESSAY/NEWS AND INFORMATION: PERSPECTIVES ON NEWS COVERAGE AFTER 9/11

A number of themes are present in analysis of news after September 11, 2001. Over the years and with the benefit of hindsight, numerous scholars have analyzed how the news media covered the attacks on the United States and the aftermath in the days, weeks, months, and years that followed. Media scholars wonder if the terrorist attacks on September 11 influenced the way news was reported to the American people. Many books, reports, and academic journal articles address numerous facets of news coverage on and after September 11, discussing topics such as news bias, quality of reporting, appropriateness of sources, and the presence of American ideals in news content. A number of topics continue to be addressed in ongoing analyses of news after the terrorist attacks.

One theme that can be examined is whether or not post-9/11 news coverage served the political goals and agenda of the Bush administration. For example, an analysis of 9/11 television coverage indicated that images and narratives were present in ways that reinforced American patriotism and unification as country (Martin & Phelan, 2003). This unification was the first step to garnering American support for a war or military strike and that media coverage was constructed in such a way to gain such support (Martin & Phelan, 2003). Similarly, an analysis of CNN's coverage of September 11 documents several examples of unity that appeared within the first 12 hours of reporting (Reynolds & Barnett, 2003). The main theme of unity on CNN suggested that the two political parties were united and were going to support the president. Reynolds and Barnett (2003) argue,

> It is noteworthy that unity was defined in such a narrow way. CNN gave viewers the perception that because government leaders from the two dominant American political parties were unified, the entire country was unified. While this most likely accurately reflected a majority view, it discounted many other available viewpoints that in theory might have altered, or at least encouraged some substantive debate. CNN's sources repeatedly connected the keyword "America" with freedom and other American ideals, which included the implied notion that it would be un-American to voice political dissent given the magnitude of the day's events. (p. 95)

Reynolds and Barnett make it clear that CNN was not "conspiring" with the administration to craft a particular picture of unity in its coverage but rather that the current corporate and ideological structure of news gathering and reporting supports the favoring of the status quo.

Another theme discussed in analyses of post-9/11 news coverage is whether or not the U.S. news media sufficiently discussed the government's decision to go to war. For example, well-known media scholar Robert McChesney (2001) argues that the lack of debate about whether or not to engage in war was noticeably absent from U.S. news coverage after the attacks. McChesney points out that after September 11, the president was not challenged or criticized by the press, that military and intelligence community members provided "expert analysis" in media reports, and discussion of who benefits economically from a war on terrorism was absent from mainstream media. McChesney also points to the fact that CNN clearly played a part in garnering American support for the war; the network produced two separate newscasts. The domestic CNN news presented content that suggested that the war on terrorism was necessary: "[CNN president Walter Isaacson] instructed the domestic CNN to be certain that any story that might undermine support for the [United States] was needed to be balanced with a reminder that the war on terrorism was a good war" (p. 94). In contrast, Isaacson allowed the global CNN news to present a more critical approach to the war given that international audiences would "not watch CNN if it were seen as a front for the Bush administration" (p. 94).

The concept of whether the U.S. media was taking on the form of a "patriotic press," a term that refers to news content as representative of the views of the government in order to ease concerns in times of war or uncertainty, was also discussed after September 11. A Project for Excellence in Journalism (2002) report published about the post-9/11 media coverage noted that although in the weeks following the attacks many of the stories in the newspapers and television programs they analyzed were factual in nature, by November 2001, media coverage had shifted to more analysis, speculation, and opinion-based content. Within the speculative and opinion-driven content, aspects of patriotic journalism were identified. Complementing this shift in content was the decision of many television stations to display patriotic symbols or use patriotic slogans in their reporting. Shortly after the attacks, many cable news programs were using flags in their broadcasts. Many local television stations followed the lead of their networks in choosing to display symbols of a patriotic nature, such as flag lapel pins and flag or red, white, and blue backdrops, or use patriotic slogans such as "America Stands Together," "America Fights Back," and "The Spirit of America" (Lambe & Begleiter, 2002). This marked a change in broadcast policy; during the Gulf War in 1991 television journalists did not wear flags on their person, and patriotic colors and the U.S. flag were not used in newscasts. Not since World War II had American viewers seen overt displays of patriotism on their television news screens (Lambe & Begleiter, 2002).

In conclusion, a few studies have analyzed whether television news has changed since September 11, 2001. The content of local television news changed a bit, largely because of the integration of more international news (Dean & Brady, 2002; Phipps, 2002). However, this change did not impact the basic content of local news since the attacks because crime on local news channels still took priority in the broadcasts (Dean & Brady, 2002). On the network news front, a Project for Excellence in Journalism (2006) study that examined network news in the five years following the attacks found significant difference in news coverage. In comparing the four years prior to 2001 and the four years since 2001, the Project for Excellence in Journalism noted that minutes devoted to coverage of terrorism was up 135 percent, foreign policy was up 102 percent, and armed conflict was up 69 percent. Coverage of domestic issues decreased. Crime coverage dipped by 47 percent; science and technology decreased by 50 percent. Coverage of alcohol and other drug issues decreased by 47 percent. However, the Project for Excellence in Journalism pointed out that the tone of newscasts did not change much; minutes devoted to hard news stories increased just 2 percent and soft news decreased 4 percent.

—*Amy M. Damico*

References

Dean, W., & Brady, L. A. (2002). After 9/11 has anything changed? *Columbia Journalism Review, 41*(4), 94–96.

Lambe, J., & Begleiter, R. (April 2002). *Wrapping the news in the flag: Use of patriotic symbols by U.S. local TV stations after the terrorism attacks of September 11, 2001.* Paper presented at the Broadcast Education Association Convention, Las Vegas, NV.

Martin, P., & Phelan, S. (2003). History and September 11: A comparison of online and network TV discourses. In A. Michael Noel (Ed.), *Crisis communications: Lessons from September 11* (pp. 167–184). Oxford: Rowman & Littlefield.

McChesney, R. (2001). The structural limitations of U.S. journalism. In B. Zelizer & S. Allan (Eds.), *Journalism after September 11* (pp. 91–100). London: Routledge.

Phipps, J. (2002). Stations share lessons learned from 9/11. *Electronic Media, 21*(36), 15–16.

Project for Excellence in Journalism. (2002). *Return to normalcy? How the media have covered the war on terrorism. New York.* Retrieved from http://www.journalism.org

Project for Excellence in Journalism. (2006). *How 9–11 changed the evening news: PEJ analysis.* Retrieved from http://www.journalism.org

Reynolds, A., & Barnett, B. (2003). "America under attack": CNN's verbal and visual framing
    of September 11. In S. Chermak, F. Bailey, & M. Brown (Eds.), *Media representations
    of September 11* (pp. 85–101). Westport, CT: Greenwood.

SPOTLIGHT ESSAY/NEWS AND INFORMATION: PORTRAITS OF GRIEF

As part of the special newspaper section "A Nation Challenged," the *New York Times*
created a subsection called "A Nation Remembers," where they published "Portraits
of Grief," short, actively written memorials of those killed in the attacks. *The Times*
committed to publishing a Portrait for any family wanting their loved one who died
on September 11 memorialized in this way, including those who died on United
Flight 93 or at the Pentagon. "Portraits of Grief" quickly became one of the most
highly regarded artifacts that emerged after the terrorist attacks.

Metro news reporter Janny Scott (2002) explained that the "Portraits of Grief" came
about when the *Times* realized that a confirmable list of those who died at the World
Trade Center site would be unavailable for quite some time. Even though there were
only a few identifiable bodies found at the former site of the World Trade Center towers,
there were thousands missing, and handmade missing-person flyers were being posted
near the site. Hundreds were presumed dead, although family members and friends
posted flyers near the World Trade Center in the hopes that their loved ones would be
found alive. Given these unique circumstances, the paper made the decision to write
about the missing one by one. Reporters began calling phone numbers posted on the
missing-persons flyers and used collected facts and anecdotes to create "snapshots" of
loved ones. According to Scott, the portraits were never intended to be obituaries,
although in many ways they evolved to fulfill a purpose. The Portraits were described
by readers as incredibly moving, and Scott (2002) claimed that "reading the profiles
became a daily ritual" for many people, and a "source of connection and consolation,
a poignant reminder of the individual humanity swallowed up by the dehumanizing
vastness of the toll, a focus for the expression of unfocused sorrow" (p. ix).

"Portraits of Grief" was featured in national news programming—including segments on ABC's *Nightline* and *Good Morning America*, NBC's *Nightly News*, and CNN's
Live Today ("Portraits," n.d.)—and won a 2001 Pulitzer Prize. Its importance was recognized by the Library of Congress, who hosted a panel discussion with *New York Times*
staff around the first-year anniversary of the attacks. The *New York Times* Executive Editor Howell Raines (2002) explained his understanding of the Portraits' popularity by
stating "I'm convinced that the core of the portraits' appeal lies in our metropolitan
desk's decision to cast these stories as snapshots of lives interrupted as they were actively
being lived, rather than the traditional obituary form" (p. vii). Although the final daily
edition of "Portraits of Grief" ended on December 31, 2001, additional portraits were
published periodically in the *New York Times*, and all the Portraits remain archived on
the *Times* Web site. By the end of 2001, 1,800 portraits were published, and the project

---

EXCERPTS FROM THE *NEW YORK TIMES,* "A NATION REMEMBERS: PORTRAITS OF GRIEF"

Deanna L. Galante: A Knack for Hair

Deanna L. Galante had such a knack for styling hair that she attended beauty school after high school in Sheepshead Bay, and when she ran out of heads to practice on among family members, she used her own. It was her second career, and she kept up with the trends. Braids, beads, perms, and shavings, she did them all.

On Wall Street, Ms. Galante, 32, worked for Cantor Fitzgerald's eSpeed division as a personal assistant. At home on Staten Island, where she lived with her husband, Anthony, she did puzzles to unwind and was busy redecorating in anticipation of their first child; she was six weeks away from going on maternity leave. "She was already like a second mom to my 12-year-old," said her sister, Tina. "They were always doing their hair and nails." (Excerpt published September 25, 2001; retrieved from http://www.nytimes.com/pages/national/portraits/)

Michael Esposito: Regular Guy, and a Leader

"My Mel," her voice quivered. "Oh my Mel. He was a regular guy. But he was so much more than that."

Those are the words of a woman asked to describe the man she made a life and two children with.

His name was Michael Esposito. He was 41 and a lieutenant at the elite fire and rescue company Squad 1, stationed in Park Slope, Brooklyn. Her name is Denise. The children are Andrew, 15, and Michael, 12.

"When you say regular guy that's an inside joke," she said. "What it means is that he just helped people and asked for nothing in return." (Excerpt published December 17, 2001; retrieved from http://www.nytimes.com/pages/national/portraits/)

---

continued into 2002. Additionally, the *New York Times* published a book of all of the portraits in 2002, which was revised in 2003.

—*Amy M. Damico*

References

Portraits of grief: Glimpses of some of the victims of the September 11 attacks. (n.d.). *The New York Times*. Retrieved June 30, 2009, from http://www.nytimes.com/pages/national/portraits/

Raines, H. (2002). Foreword. In *Portraits 9/11/01: The collected "Portraits of Grief" from the New York Times (2003)*. New York: Henry Holt.

Scott, J. (2002). Introduction. In *Portraits 9/11/01: The collected "Portraits of Grief" from the New York Times (2003)*. New York: Henry Holt.

SPOTLIGHT ESSAY/NEWS AND INFORMATION: PRESIDENT BUSH'S SEPTEMBER 11 SPEECHES

As the news organizations and citizens around the world tried to make sense of the events that took place on September 11, 2001, U.S. president at the time, George W. Bush, delivered three key speeches in the immediate aftermath of the terrorist attacks that highlighted themes his administration believed captured the historic moment. Given the gravity of the events, these addresses to the nation—watched by thousands and covered on a multitude of broadcast outlets—allowed Bush the opportunity to define his presidency in particular ways. The three 9/11 speeches reveal President Bush becoming aware that his presidency was going to be part rescue and part revenge story.

President Bush's first speech, "Remarks by the President After Two Planes Crash into World Trade Center," shows a quick response to the events of 9/11 which, at 9:30 a.m., was already taking place. Bush's initial sentence—"This is a difficult moment for America"—seems in hindsight a great understatement, but Bush is cautious in initially characterizing the unfolding story of 9/11. In a rehearsed speech, we would expect Bush to explain the "difficult moment." Atypically, Bush thanks the school he was visiting at the time of the attacks in mid speech (rather than at the beginning or end), apologizes that he must return to Washington, and then, abruptly, returns to mentioning the "difficult moment." This nonlinear arrangement suggests that Bush is still not cognizant of the unfolding details of the story and that he is dealing with two simultaneous impulses: one to respond to the audience before him and the other to synthesize the data as it comes in. At this point, the details of the attack are unknown; as evidenced by Bush's statement that "two airplanes have crashed into the WTC," a statement that does not indicate that the crashes were intentional. Even so, Bush is aware that a rescue-oriented response is needed by government and local officials.

About three hours later, as shown in his "Remarks by the President upon Arrival at Barksdale Air Force Base," Bush's characterization of the 9/11 story is clearer but still not lucid. There is confusion in President Bush's inability to explain who the enemies are and why the United States was attacked. For example, Bush refers to the attacks in the singular. At 1 p.m. on September 11, it was obvious that many terrorists were involved, yet Bush begins by saying "Freedom itself was attacked by a faceless coward." At this point in the afternoon, 9/11 has bestowed on Bush a revenge story in which an enemy has clearly surfaced, and the need for revenge is at hand, but it is still too premature to take vengeance. In this speech, Bush wrestles between abstract and literal language. The tangible Twin Towers, the physical objects that were struck, become symbols of "Freedom." This freedom, rather than people in financial buildings, was attacked. In short, the speech points to revenge as necessary and justified, but whom to seek revenge upon is still the question.

By 9 p.m. when Bush delivered his "Address to the Nation," all was evident. The terrorist attacks were no longer apparent; they were "deliberate and deadly." This third speech of the day saw Bush as defining the early part of his presidential term as a mission of retaliation. At this point in the evening, the perpetrators are nearly known; and although it would take more time to name bin Laden and Mohamed Atta, the government confirmed that the attacks were from terrorists. In his remarks, Bush defines the attacks as "mass murder," a phrase usually reserved for domestic killings or atrocities of war, but which, to the majority of Americans during the "Pearl Harbor" of our times, was appropriate. Bush views the United States as willing to support these rescue- and revenge-oriented responses; to join in the rescue by refreshing strangers with our own donated blood as Bush points out in his evening address; and to join in the revenge by a majority of support for the initial wave of attacks in Afghanistan. Bush's two terms are no doubt beleaguered with controversy, mostly because the retaliation for September 11, 2001, extended beyond a war in Afghanistan into a lengthy and costly war in Iraq. Yet the events of September 11 provided Bush with a chance to define his presidency. It forced him to make that presidential story one of rescue and revenge.

—*Daniel R. Fredrick*

References

Bush, George W. (2001). *First inaugural address*. Retrieved from http://www.whitehouse.gov/briefing-room/statements-and-releases

Bush, George W. (2001). Remarks by the president after two planes crash into world trade center. Retrieved from http://www.whitehouse.gov/briefing-room/statements-and-releases

Bush, George W. (2001). Remarks by the president upon arrival at Barksdale Air Force Base. Retrieved from http://www.whitehouse.gov/briefing-room/statements-and-releases

Bush, George W. (2001). *Statement by the president in his address to the nation*. Retrieved from http://www.whitehouse.gov/briefing-room/statements-and-releases

SPOTLIGHT ESSAY/NEWS AND INFORMATION: WOMEN'S MAGAZINES AFTER 9/11

In the aftermath of September 11, 2001, women's magazines were put in a difficult position: Their normal fare did not include extensive coverage of political events. At the same time, magazines such as *Ladies Home Journal, O: The Oprah Magazine*, and *Marie Claire*, recognized they could not ignore the terrorist attacks and creatively incorporated aspects of the events of September 11 into their own larger themes and concerns. Articles from women's magazines in the year following 9/11 included such varied stories as how to help your children deal with nightmares after watching the World Trade Center towers collapse on television (Brophy, 2002); how widows and survivors of 9/11 cope with their grief (Bakalian, 2002; Casey, 2002); personal recollections by editors and writers, many of whom were located in New York City (Tuhy, 2001; Levine, 2001); and what kind of emergency kits you should pack in the event of another national attack (Chin, 2002). Other articles featured stories of high school students in the area of the World Trade Center who painted murals to help them deal with their grief, school children who made their own flags (Levine, 2002), and even articles that gave their readers a quiz to find out whether they were clinically depressed or simply grieving as part of a sense of national loss ("How Do You Feel," 2001).

While there were many different kinds of stories that arose in the wake of September 11, three larger themes emerged in women's magazines as a way to help their readers assimilate the enormity of the events. The first broad theme explored how this large-scale political event could be translated into life-affirming stories that followed the arc of initial grief followed by some kind of personal transformation. The second broad theme included a reexamination of family, in both an individual and collective sense. Finally, there was the more progressive theme of how, despite the political climate of patriotic jingoism and the accompanying prejudice that might occur, it was necessary to be more tolerant of those are different.

The first theme—using tragedy to assist in personal transformation—was found in stories that sought to support and encourage women to make positive changes in their lives. For example, in *O: The Oprah Magazine*, an interview with Philip McGraw, or "Dr. Phil," on "What Do You Pledge to Focus on Now," looked at ways that individuals can draw on their personal and collective experiences for personal growth (McGraw, 2001). These experiences or "moments" could be personal, but also collective. In this context, McGraw raised September 11 as one of those collective experiences—the "now" referred to in the article's title—that might also define who we are. Another example of this was a *Real Simple* profile on five women moving forward after the terrorist attacks (Schultheiss, 2001).

A second theme related to the notion of family and how readers might redefine our sense of who a family is in the wake of a national tragedy. In another article from *O: The Oprah Magazine* entitled, "Family: Now More Than Ever," the editor describes all the people who lost their lives in the "ashes" of the World Trade Center as part of our family ("Family," 2001). The editorial then urges its readers to take the message of the importance of family, and of honoring those bonds, and to learn from the experiences of these individuals for whom it was too late.

A third theme focused on prejudice and even violence against "dark-skinned" women and their families and a plea for ending their discriminatory treatment. In one article from *Marie Claire* entitled, "My Husband Was Killed Because He Looked Arab," a woman who was Sikh described what happened to her husband, who was killed by a white racist (Polaneczky, 2002). Another piece in *Good Housekeeping* explored racial differences (Divakaruni, 2002). In these articles, there is a plea to American women not to fall prey to prejudice as a result of September 11. They are appealing to American women as wives and mothers, and showing examples of other Americans who stood up against this kind of discrimination.

In the end, despite the enormity of the event, many women's magazines did their best to speak to their readers, to address their fears and anxieties, and to offer them strategies for transforming their personal grief into something that might make their lives more reflective and meaningful. Ultimately, however, like other areas of popular culture after 9/11, these stories were more successful in raising the problems, rather than attempting to voice any meaningful collective action to respond in a positive way to the events of 9/11.

—Margaret J. Tally

References

Bakalian, E. (2002, September). A year without Jeff. *Ladies Home Journal, 119*(9), 48.

Brophy, B. (2002, January). Mommy, it was really scary. *Good Housekeeping, 234*(1), 74.

Casey, K. (2002, October). Todd was our hero. *Ladies Home Journal, 119*(9), 88.

Chin, P. (2002, May). Are you prepared for an emergency? *Ladies Home Journal, 119*(5), 108.

Divakaruni, C. (2002, January). Being dark-skinned in a dark time. *Good Housekeeping, 234*(1), 89.

Family: now more than ever. (2001, December). *O. The Oprah Magazine, 2*(12), 33.

How do you feel about America now? (2001, December). *Marie Claire* (U.S.), *8*(12), 94.

Levine, E. (2001, December). The day we'll never forget. *Good Housekeeping, 233*(6), 18.

Levine, H. (2002, February). Hope and healing. *Ladies Home Journal, 119*(2), 72.

McGraw, P. (2001, December). Dr. Phil: What do you pledge to focus on now? *O. The Oprah Magazine, 2*(12), 54.

Polaneczky, R. (2002, January). My husband was killed because he looked Arab. *Marie Claire* (U.S.), *9*(1), 63.

Schultheiss, S. (2001, December). Changing times, changing priorities: It's a new year and a new world these five women have resolved to find happiness there. *Real Simple, 2*(10), 108.

Tuhy, C. (2001, November). Editor's Note. *Real Simple, 2*(9), 22.

Chapter 3

BOOKS

INTRODUCTION: BOOKS AND SEPTEMBER 11, 2001

Many witnesses of the September 11 attacks on the World Trade Center describe the paper that flew through the air like snow after the first plane tore a hole into the side of the North Tower: memos, faxes, and accounting documents; payroll sheets, vacation day requests, and "To Do" lists. The poignancy of the image of the written word surviving what the steel and glass structures could not is just one of countless images that mark the date. At the same time, the idea that paper—and therefore writing—survived to tell the tale of the day also suggests the role writing plays in a culture. Writing shapes perception, and even reality, by giving voice to one's experience, articulating what seems inexpressible, ordering what feels chaotic, and shaping a collective narrative out of many stories. It is through writing that a nation can begin to understand an event and incorporate it into the larger tale of the nation's past, present, and future. As Don DeLillo wrote in December 2001, tying the fallen Twin Towers to the purpose of writing, "There is something empty in the sky. The writer tries to give memory, tenderness, and meaning to all that howling space" (p. 36).

Given the part writing plays in responding to crisis, it is not surprising that written words became an integral part of September 11 within hours of the attacks. From posters of the missing, to poems of grief, words were pasted on every available space becoming the first memorials in a city reeling from loss. This "spontaneous burgeoning of poetry," Ulrich Baer (2002) writes, "responded to a need—a need for words that then took the form of written scrolls hung on fences and walls along with donated pens and markers, allowing anyone to offer the language of poetry where little could be said" (p. 2). Within hours, editorials and letters in local newspapers similarly attempted to process and respond to the attacks. In each instance, everyday people turned to the written word as an outlet for their fear, grief, rage, and sadness.

Words were not only written, but read by readers searching for knowledge and insight, ways to make sense of the attacks. In the days immediately following 9/11, previously published books on terrorism and the World Trade Center surged to the top of best-seller lists reflecting readers' desire to learn more about the reasons for, and sites of, the attacks. Within months, books memorializing the day—especially the victims and heroes of it—recorded the national sense of mourning, loss, and patriotism. Plays, memoirs, comic books, and graphic novels were also written and published after 9/11, many of them grappling with how to represent the events and their impact. As time went by, analysis of September 11—including documented findings by *The 9/11 Commission Report* (National Commission, 2004) and political treatises on Al Qaeda—suggested a shift in readers' attention from the emotional to the intellectual. Eventually, novels were written that approached the event in diverse ways, often incorporating 9/11 into the narrative as a metaphor, analogy, or motivating plot point.

From the words that scattered across the sky on September 11, to the words that expressed grief, shared knowledge, or challenged beliefs in the months and years afterwards, written works responded to the attacks in an effort to incorporate the tragedy into national consciousness. By examining what people read, the types of books that were published, and the new forms of writing that grew out of 9/11, the process by which the country moved from shock to comprehension can begin to be charted.

Seeking Solace and Information

In the immediate aftermath of the attacks, publishing companies and booksellers across the country found themselves in uncharted territory. Books that just the day before had seemed innocuous—thrillers about terrorism or disasters, for example—suddenly seemed less than appropriate to display or promote. Book covers with images of cities under attack, plane crashes, or other destructive themes seemed too close to the very real images running over and over on television screens and in newspapers. Publishers, aware of the impact such pictures could have on potential readers, made changes to book jackets. *Headwind* (2001), for example, a thriller by John Nance, was released in hardcover six months before the attacks. The cover illustration showed an airplane careening downward with a blaze of fire pouring from its tail. The paperback version, released five months after the attacks, depicted the same plane flying in a takeoff position without the fiery tail (Milliot, Zeitchik, & Baker, 2001).

Publishers and booksellers also reacted quickly in terms of the books they stocked and displayed. Titles from backlists were pulled to storefronts. Out-of-print books about the World Trade Center, terrorism, and the Middle East were quickly reissued. University presses issued online lists of books they believed would be of interest to readers—on topics from terrorism and Islam to airline security and Osama bin Laden (Milliot, Zeitchik, & Baker, 2001). Publishers also printed "instant books"—books published quickly after a significant event occurs. Scholastic, for example, printed several instant patriotic children's books including *America the Beautiful* (2001) and *We Dreamed of a World* (2002). Other publishers quickly ushered out *The Day That*

Was Different: September 11, 2001—When Terrorists Attacked America (2002) and *The Breadwinner* (2001), a story aimed at promoting tolerance through its focus on a young Muslim girl living in Kabul, Afghanistan, with her family (Roback & Britton, 2001).

Reflecting the public's interest in learning more about how and why the attacks had happened, in the weeks after 9/11 book sales increased around topics related to the Middle East, the Taliban, Islam, and terrorism. Other popular reading topics were related to grief and loss as readers sought ways to cope with such a dramatic, unexpected day in U.S. history. Prophetic books about Nostradamus, who was said to have predicted the disaster, also found a wide reading audience (Abbott, 2001). Escapist fiction rose in sales, and bookstore owners across the country shared the sentiment that books were appropriate to a nation of people who were "looking more inward and toward home" (Mutter, Howell, & Nawotka, 2001, p. 16).

Religious books were also very popular in the immediate aftermath of 9/11. Sales at Family Christian Stores increased 30 percent and pocket Bible sales increased by 150 percent (Fitch, 2001, p. 28). By September 17, titles like the *Prophecy Study Bible* (1997) had increased in sales by 80 percent; by September 21, Bible publisher Zondervan doubled its shipment of Bibles to 1 million copies. Books on non-Christian religions found new audiences, especially copies of the Koran (Ford, 2001, p. 37). Religious-based stories were also sought after. In November, *Desecration: Antichrist Takes the Throne* (2001), the ninth installment in the popular Left-Behind series with its end-of-times theme, "had the best opening week tally for any book since the September 11 attacks" (Maryles, 2001, p. 16).

In contrast to these areas of increased interest, travel books fell in popularity as Americans adjusted to a world that felt less safe and more unpredictable than ever before. Many people chose to remain close to home because of uncertainty about another attack, making travel guides and other materials seem irrelevant to fearful readers. As part of what became known as the "cocoon" effect—the tendency to stay safely at home after 9/11—books that associated travel with danger were viewed as especially out-of-step with national sentiment. For example, the newest book in its Worst Case series, Chronicle Books' *Worst Case Scenario: Travel* (2001), was released just prior to September 11 but promotions were quickly cancelled (Milliot, Zeitchik, & Baker, 2001) In contrast, armchair travel books by authors such as Bill Bryson, Peter Hopkirk, and Mary Taylor Simeti outsold books on international travel in the months after the attacks (Wells, 2001).

In the realm of children's literature, story hours at local bookstores found increased attendance in the weeks after 9/11. Perhaps seeking an alternative to television—which repeatedly replayed the attacks—parents and children alike found solace in the familiar activity of being read to. A wide range of children's books were popular during those weeks, from "nonthreatening, cheery books" to "books on grieving, loss, and coping" (Roback & Britton, 2001, p. 33). *When Dinosaurs Die* (1996) and *What's Heaven* (1999), both of which address death in a general way, sold well during the weeks after the attacks, while *One April Morning* (2000)—a children's book about the Oklahoma City bombing—and *A Terrible Thing Happened* (2000) offered parents and teachers more specific narratives through which to talk about violence and trauma with their children. Patriotic books celebrating the United States and its heroes were also widely read by and to children, including *A is for America* (2001), *A Day in the Life of a Firefighter* (1981), *The Flag We Love* (1996), and *My New York* (1993) (Lodge, 2001; Roback & Britton, 2001).

Sports-related books also found new readership in the weeks after 9/11. As Rolf Zettersten of Warner Faith publishing stated: "I believe people are yearning for decency, values, and spirituality. The ugliness and horror of the terrorist attacks and impending war will cause people to seek noble themes. I think athletes who are known for leading selfless and honorable lives will be appealing for readers" (McEvoy, 2001, p. 31). In this vein, books like *The Ballpark Book: A Journey through the Field of Baseball Magic* (2000) and *Take Me Out to the Ballpark: An Illustrated Tour of Baseball Parks Past and Present* (2000) gave readers a welcome relief from their current realities by celebrating America's favorite pastime. Sport stories focused on overcoming adversity—such as Lance Armstrong's fight against cancer chronicled in *It's Not about the Bike: My Journey Back to Life* (2000)—or the underdog who perseveres only to succeed—as in the example of racehorse Seabiscuit—stood as clear metaphors for the country's challenges and its need to believe.

By October 21, 2001, best-seller lists already reflected a new post-9/11 era in popular reading. Seeking solace in the familiar, *The Best-Loved Poems of Jacqueline Kennedy Onassis* (2001) debuted at number four on the *New York Times Book Review* best-seller list. At least seven nonfiction best sellers were new to the list since September 11, and the topics reflected the nation's longing to understand the changes the country was facing. Books like *The New Jackals* (1999), *War in a Time of Peace* (2001), and *Germs* (2001) recorded the nation's anxiety about safety at home and abroad.

BEST SELLERS, OCTOBER 21, 2001

The Best-Loved Poems of Jacqueline Kennedy Onassis, selected by Caroline Kennedy
Germs—Judith Miller, Stephen Engelberg, and William Broad
Fire—Sebastian Junger
War in a Time of Peace—David Halberstam
Crossing Over—John Edward
Twin Towers—Angus Kress
An Open Heart—Dalai Lama
Living a Life That Matters—Harold S. Kushner
The New Jackals—Simon Reeve

—compiled by Sara E. Quay

Reference

Bestsellers. (2001, October 21). Book review desk. *The New York Times Book Review*, p. 34.

Twin Towers (1999), a history of the World Trade Center first published in 1999, rose to number eight on the list, while *Fire* (2002), which focused on individuals who risk their lives to save others, was number five. Reassuring books such as the Dalai Lama's *An Open Heart* and Harold Kushner's *Living a Life That Matters* (2001), registered the country's reflective tone. That both books were written by recognized spiritual leaders is not surprising as readers looked to figures they could trust and believe in to guide them through the difficult time. Other popular books after September 11 included *The Corrections* (2001), *The Greatest Generation* (1998), and *Bowling Alone* (2000).

By late November, books focused on spirituality, Nostradamus, and personal reflection fell in popularity while sales of "cookbooks, craft books, quilting, nesting and all manner of stay-at-home activity books" rose (Danford, 2001; Nawotka, 2001a, p. 16). Of special interest was *Windows on the World Complete Wine Course* (1995)—a title published about the Windows on the World restaurant that had once stood at the top of the North Tower of the World Trade Center (Danford, 2001). The next month, more titles related to the 9/11 attacks appeared on the list—*Bin Laden: The Man Who Declared War on America* (2001); *Taliban: Militant Islam, Oil and Fundamentalism in Central Asia* (2001); *The Battle for God* (2001); and *Jihad vs. McWorld* (1996) all met readers' interest in the information associated with the attacks.

Books about 9/11

Relatively soon after the attacks, the publishing industry released new books that met, and piqued, readers' interest. Some books took September 11 as their focus, chronicling in pictures and words the day's events. Others aimed to help readers cope with the tragedy and its aftermath. Not wanting to appear to be capitalizing on the tragedy, many of the first books published were marketed with the promise that a percentage of the sales would be donated. Authors of books like *Financial Security in Troubled Times* (2001) and *Where Is God When It Hurts* (2001)—both aimed at helping readers adapt to life post-9/11—donated their advances and/or royalties. Commemorative titles such as *September 11, 2001: New York Attacked* (2001) donated percentages of every sale, while authors of more generally inspirational and patriotic books such as *One Nation* (2001) and *America the Beautiful* (2001) donated their proceeds themselves. In December, 2001, Andrea Patel's *On That Day: A Book of Hope for Children* (2001), was published with a portion of the proceeds being dedicated September 11 scholarship programs (Zeitchik, 2001).

Photographic books were also especially popular in the aftermath of 9/11 and were frequently printed by companies known for publishing magazines or newspapers. *One Nation: America Remembers September 11, 2001* (2001), for example, was issued by *Life* magazine editors, while *September 11, 2001: A Record of Tragedy, Heroism and Hope* (2001), by the editors of *New York Magazine*, provided memorials to the World Trade Center and to those who died there. *New York September 11* (2001) was printed by Magnum Photographers. Some commemorative books of photography, such as

In the Line of Duty (2001), focused specifically on the rescue workers. Still others took the World Trade Center as their subject: *Men of Steel: The Story of the Family That Built the World Trade Center* (2002) gave the history of the site, while *A New World Trade Center: Design Proposals from the World's Leading Architects* (2002) charted the way for the future.

Books were also published specifically to help young readers understand the September 11 events. *911: The Book of Help* (2002) and *Understanding September 11th* (2002) were released in summer 2002 for readers ages 12 years and up. Books geared for younger children appeared in bookstores within the year, including, *The Day America Cried* (2002), *This Place I Know: Poems of Comfort* (2002), and *There's a Big Beautiful World Out There* (2002). *September 11, 2001: The Day That Changed America* (2002)—part of the War on Terrorism series by ABDO Publishing—chronicled the events with photos and a narrative chronology, while *The Day That Was Different* (2001), also published before the end of the year, offered teachers, parents, and counselors a workbook full of activities to help children understand more about the day.

A year after 9/11, more than 300 books—including approximately 25 best sellers—had been published about the attacks. According to *Publishers Weekly*, this was a record for books about a specific event (Maryles, 2001, p. 16). The books took a range of forms. Commemorative books—*A Nation Challenged: A Visual History of 9/11 and Its Aftermath* (2002), *So Others Might Live: A History of New York's Bravest* (2002), and *Stepping through the Ashes* (2002)—offered readers visual images of the heroes, victims, and events of the day. Eyewitness accounts of 9/11 gave readers personal stories of the harrowing day. *At Ground Zero: 25 Stories from Young Reporters* (2002); *What We Saw: The Events of September 11, 2001, in Words, Pictures, and Video;* and *Report from Ground Zero* (2002) provided details not found in the more visually appealing picture books. Oral histories were collected under the titles of *Never Forget: An Oral History of September 11, 2001* (2002) and *September 11: An Oral History* (2002), both which gather the stories of people who escaped from the Twin Towers and the Pentagon, where *Tower Stories: An Oral History of 9/11* (2004) took New Yorkers specifically as its subject. Other top-selling books a year after 9/11 included *Let Freedom Ring* (2002), *Longitudes and Attitudes* (2002), and *What Went Wrong?* (2001) (Minzesheimer, 2002).

Books focused on the heroes and victims of 9/11, including Lisa Beamer's *Let's Roll* (2002) and *Among the Heroes: United Flight 93 and the Passengers and Crew Who Fought Back* (2002), focused on those individuals who died in the attacks. Most notable of these, perhaps, was *Portraits of 9/11/01: The Collected "Portraits of Grief" from the New York Times*, which was released in 2002. From September 15, 2001, through February 5, 2002, the *New York Times* printed portraits of those who lost their lives on 9/11 in the paper's "A Nation Challenged" section. Accompanying the photos were what the paper's executive editor Howell Raines described as "snapshots of lives interrupted as they were being actively lived" ("Portraits," 2002, p. vii).

In the year following 9/11 the nation pondered the impact the attacks would have on personal and national security. Books interested in these topics explored how the

United States had—or possibly would—change in light of terrorism in its own borders. *It's a Free Country: Personal Freedom in America after September 11* (2002) collected essays by a wide range of contributors, while *Terrorism and the Constitution: Sacrificing Civil Liberties in the Name of National Security* (2002) examined the 2001 Patriot Act. As it had in the first months after 9/11, patriotism remained a popular topic a year later, including titles such as *The American Creed: A Spiritual and Patriotic Primer* (2002), and *My America: What My Country Means to Me: By 150 Americans from All Walks of Life* (2002). At the same time, interest in the Middle East also continued with books on Pakistan—*Pakistan: The Eye of the Storm* (2002) and *Pakistan: In the Shadow of Jihad Afghanistan* (2002)—and other Middle Eastern countries.

Analysis of the events leading to 9/11 eventually became available to readers. *War of Words: Language, Politics and 9/11* (2004); *The Cell: Inside the 9/11 Plot and Why the FBI and CIA Failed to Stop It* (2002); and *Breakdown: How America's Intelligence Failures Led to September 11* (2002) each provided new information, or new perspectives, on the attacks. At the same time, books declaring a range of conspiracy theories about 9/11 found an interested reading audience. *Conspiracies, Conspiracy Theories, and the Secrets of 9/11* (2006) by Mathias Broeckers, and *Debunking 9/11 Myths: Why Conspiracy Theories Can't Stand Up to the Facts* (2006) by the editors of *Popular Mechanics* were released the same year, underscoring the controversy that, in some circles, swirled around what actually happened on that clear fall day.

Educational books for use in schools were released within the year. *Understanding September 11th: Answering Questions about the Attacks on America* (2002) included maps, photos, and a glossary of terms. The *New York Times*, in collaboration with Scholastic, printed a young readers' edition of *A Nation Challenged* (2002), which organized September 11 into easy-to-understand categories: September 11, 2001; The Days After; Meeting the Challenge Abroad; and Meeting the Challenge at Home.

As the years after 2001 unfolded, new books offered readers information about the national, international, and political events that led up to September 11. For example, John Miller's *The Cell: Inside the 9/11 Plot, and Why the FBI Failed to Stop It* (2002) and Quintan Wiktorowicz's *Global Jihad: Understanding September 11* (2008) explored the events and beliefs that allowed 9/11 to happen. *Out of the Blue: The Narrative of September 11, 2001* (2002) was one of the first books to attempt to construct a comprehensive narrative of the day. It was not until 2004, however, with the release of *The 9/11 Commission Report* that an official record of the events leading up to, and following, the September attacks was available. Understanding the events that occurred before and on September 11 was important to readers after 9/11, but so was examining how the day had changed the country. Books like Steven Brill's *After: How America Confronted the September 12 Era* (2003), Thomas Friedman's *Longitudes and Attitudes: Exploring the World After September 11* (2002), and Jericho and LeMahieu's *Ground Zero and the Human Soul: The Search for the New Ordinary Life* (2002) examined the reshaped landscape of life after 9/11. Susan Faludi's *The Terror Dream: Fear and Fantasy in Post-9/11 America* (2007) argued that the media's images of meek women and heroic men reinforced traditional gender roles in post-9/11 U.S. life.

Accounts of 9/11 in Poems, Plays, and Comics

In contrast to the nonfiction writing that focused on facts, details, and personal accounts of 9/11, creative writing offered new ways to think through, understand, and integrate the attacks into the national consciousness. Poetry was among the first form of creative written responses to 9/11. As Dennis Loy Johnson and Valerie Merians (2002) describe:

> There were, in the immediate aftermath, poems everywhere. Walking around the city you would see them—stuck on light posts and phone stalls, plastered on the shelters at bus stops and the walls of subway stations. In neighborhood newspapers the letters-to-the-editor pages were full of them. Downtown, people scrawled poems in the ash that covered everything. And on the brick walls of police stations and firehouses, behind mountains of flowers and between photos of the dead, poetry dominated. . . . There was something more to be said that only poetry could say. Everybody, apparently, knew this. (p. ix)

By its nature personal, expressive, and relatively short, poetry became an outlet for those in and around the World Trade Center, a way to put into words—in even a temporary way—the overwhelming fear, grief, anger, and disbelief that people were feeling. The use of poetry to capture the immediate experience of 9/11 extended beyond the streets of New York City, however. Poems circulated on the Internet, were posted on Web sites, and eventually gathered in anthologies such as Cohen and Matson's *An Eye for an Eye Makes the Whole World Blind: Poets on 9/11* (2002) and *September 11, 2001: America Writers Respond* (2002).

Established authors were also called on to share their feelings about the attacks in various publications, and collections of short pieces—personal reflections, poems, essays—were among the first books to be published with 9/11 in the title. For example, Johnson and Merians's *Poetry after 9/11: An Anthology of New York Poets* (2002) recorded poems that tried "to sum up the nation's sense of loss" after the attacks (p. 67), as did collections such as *110 Stories: New York Writes after September 11th* (2002), *September 11: West Coast Writers Approach Ground Zero* (2002), and *September 11, 2001: American Writers Respond* (2002). Poems by acclaimed poets Stephen Dunn ("The Insistence of Beauty"), Galway Kinnell ("When the Towers Fell"), Alicia Ostriker ("the window, at the moment of flame"), and Robert Pinsky ("9/11") were among the many to lend their voice to the written responses.

Plays about 9/11 were written and produced relatively quickly. Anne Nelson's *The Guys*, for example, was written in the first months after the attacks and performed in December 2001. The play, which starred Sigourney Weaver, focuses on the experience of a New York fire captain and writer who work together in the painful process of writing eulogies the captain must give for the firefighters he lost in the Twin Towers. *The Guys* was later produced as a film also with Weaver in the lead female role. *The Mercy Seat*, written by Neil LaBute, opened a year after *The Guys* in December 2002. Set on September 12, the play's plot centers on Ben and Abby, both workers in the

Twin Towers who, on the morning of the attack are engaged in an adulterous affair rather than in their office. Ben, who assumes his wife and children believe he died in the Towers, considers whether to take advantage of the situation, let his family go one believing he is dead, and start a new life. Other 9/11-related plays written after the attacks include Charles Evered's *Adopt a Sailor*, which premiered in September 2002 at New York City Hall; Theresa Rebeck's *Omnium Gatherum* (2003); Craig Wright's *Recent Tragic Events* (2003); and Deborah Zoe Laufer's *End Days*, a 2007 play focused on a father who survived the attacks and the long-term implications the trauma has for him and his family.

In contrast to poems and plays, works of fiction took longer to be written, published, and made available to readers. The first narratives focused on the attacks themselves, attempting to make sense of—literally to narrate—the day and its impact. They tended to do so with narrative forms which, like the day itself, broke the bounds of the expected. From nonlinear story lines to minute-by-minute chronicles, the fiction about 9/11 wrestled with its subject in visible ways. Book covers used images and shapes that mimicked the shape of the Twin Towers, or, alternatively, registered the nation's distress with covers that were plain and black.

Among the earliest works of fiction to be published about 9/11, Frédéric Beigbeder's *Windows on the World* (2004) tells the story of people trapped at the top of the North Tower in the Windows on the World restaurant. While there are no actual records of what occurred on the 110th floor of the North Tower after the plane hit, other than phone calls and e-mails sent by those who died there, Beigbeder's story offers readers a novel organized around each minute of the day—from the first chapter titled "8:30 a.m." (just prior to the first plan crashing into the North Tower) to the last chapter, 102 minutes later, titled "10:29 a.m.," just 1 minute after the North Tower collapsed. Where *Windows on the World* narrates the story minute by minute, Jonathan Safran Foer's *Extremely Loud and Incredibly Close* (2005) shifts time between the main character's present (a period shortly after the attacks) and his grandparents' past. The story of Oskar, whose father died in the North Tower, the book tells the tale of confusion, loss, and longing from the perspective of a nine-year-old child.

BOOK COVERS

Covers of books about 9/11 often relied on visual images and colors to represent their content. Many of them—such as *110 Stories, Tower Stories, Eleven, Extremely Loud and Incredible Close*, and the first edition of *Falling Man*—use pictures and/or words to create images of the Twin Towers. Others, like *In the Shadow of No Towers* and *Spider-Man #36*—use a solid black background to symbolize death and loss. Still others, including the *New Yorker* magazine and *In the Shadow of No Towers*, contrast shades of black so that an outline or shadow of the Twin Towers is just visible.

—*Sara E. Quay*

In later novels, 9/11 is a precipitating, background, or contextual event that might motivate the characters to act but is not the central topic of the narrative. Books like Don DeLillo's *Falling Man* (2006), Wendy Wasserstein's *Elements of Style* (2006), Colson Whitehead's *The Colossus of New York* (2003), Ian McEwan's *Saturday* (2005), and Lynne Sharon Schwartz's *The Writing on the Wall* (2005) explore characters who have been touched by September 11—some more directly than others—and whose lives have been changed as a result. Capturing a moralistic tone, Karen Kingsbury's *One Tuesday Morning* (2003) and Charlotte Vale Allen's *Sudden Moves* (2005) also use 9/11 as plot point, one which changes the fate of the main characters by forcing them to move closer to God, family, or self. Standing in contrast to the stark, raw emotion of the earliest poems and essays written after and about 9/11, these most recent works of fiction register the fact that time has distanced writers and readers alike from the day's events. Here, 9/11 stands as a metaphor, a symbol, for loss, pain, and sometimes renewal quite distinct from the earlier words that recorded raw emotion, shock, and awe.

Illustrated forms of writing, such as comic books, comix, and graphic novels, made a unique contribution to post-9/11 writing. David Rees's satiric graphic novel, *Get Your War On* (2002), began as an Internet comic posted online on October 12, 2001. Composed "entirely of computer clip art depicting offer workers bantering about the war on terror ... [the site] drew millions of visitors" and was eventually published as a book (Nawotka, 2001b, p. 22). Art Spiegelman won the Pulitzer Prize

---

AMERICAN WIDOW

American Widow (2008) is a graphic novel memoir that documents a calendar year in the life of 9/11 widow, Alissa Torres. Her husband, Luis Eduardo Torres, was a Colombian citizen who died in the North Tower of the World Trade Center on September 11, 2001. It was his second day of work at Cantor Fitzgerald, and Torres was seven and one-half months pregnant. Torres describes her book as a "9/11 victims' history," structuring it so that as the story moves slowly forward through the density of grief, each chapter explores a specific theme that the 9/11 families confronted. These themes include: therapeutic and spiritual support, charitable relief, the 9/11 Federal Victims Compensation Fund, and the future of Ground Zero, among others. And while Torres focuses on the small private details of her life and that of her husband, she also includes "cameo" appearances of those well known to the "9/11 story," such as Cantor Fitzgerald CEO Howard Lutnick, Special Master of the 9/11 Victims Compensation Fund Kenneth Feinberg, and Chief Medical Examiner Dr. Charles Hirsch. Overall, Torres strips off the glorification of the 9/11 victims and their families by revealing her own true and sometimes unflattering story.

—*Alissa Torres*

Reference

Torres, A. (2008). *American widow*. New York: Villard.

for his graphic novel, *In the Shadow of No Towers* (2004), Spiegelman's personal tale of watching the attacks from his neighborhood in lower Manhattan. In 2006, *The 9/11 Report: A Graphic Adaptation* was released, and, several years later, Alissa Torres—a 9/11 widow whose husband died in the North Tower—used the graphic novel form to tell her painstaking, personal story in *American Widow* (2008).

Comic books also found ways to address the attacks. Spider-Man writer J. Michael Stracynski took on the challenge of doing so in *Spider-Man #36* (2001), a black cover special edition of the Spider-Man series in which Spider-Man—like his readers—is forced simply to witness the attacks. Unable to save the Towers, the superhero is only able to help ordinary people, rescue workers, and children. Other comic book responses to 9/11 focus on children, who, in their innocence and inability to fully comprehend the

---

COMICS AFTER 9/11

After the superheroes of Marvel Comics mourned over September 11, 2001, readers were ready for the old story lines of yesterday: good guys fighting the bad guys in usually clearly defined roles. That hasn't been the case, however. The Marvel universe has been reconfigured by several meta-events that tie into the U.S. national narrative in the wake of 9/11. These events seem to have long-lasting implications for the Marvel universe and reinvent or tap into the politics surrounding 9/11 and its aftermath. Additionally, the language used in the naming of these continuity-wide events demands close examination.

The House of M (Bendis, 2005) takes place in the actual Marvel universe. Reality has been reoriented into a world where mutants dominate and humans are second-class citizens. The House of M leads this new world with its patriarch, Magneto, the world's most powerful terrorist in the "normal" world. Within the Marvel universe, Magneto has held a place comparable to bin Laden in that he has been both an ally and an enemy to the United States. He has led terrorist groups and split the world according to his polarizing ideology of mutant superiority; much akin to bin Laden's belief in Islamic superiority.

Following this, the *Civil War* (Millar, 2006) speaks to the domestic stress underlying the United States. Undeniably, the U.S. public grappled with the Bush administration's decisions, which continually invoked 9/11 while leading the country into the questionable territory of preemptive war, rendition, the alien status of Guantanamo detainees and wiretapping. This division became evident even in the 2004 election, which was only won by a slim majority. In the end—at least for the comics, this resulted in the death of patriotism (Captain America)—albeit temporarily.

Finally, in the storyline *World War Hulk* (Pak, 2007), the Hulk reveals the true nature of the world's most iconic superhero leaders, showing a darker and more Machiavellian nature to these protectors and thus leaving the world in an even more dubious position.

—*Lance Eaton*

References

Bendis, B. M. (2005). *The house of M*. New York: Marvel Comics.
Millar, M. (2006). *Civil war*. New York: Marvel Comics.
Pak, G. (2007). *World war Hulk*. New York: Marvel Comics.

day's events register a national feeling of innocence lost and disbelief. Comic books, such as Marvel Comics' *Heroes* (2001), *9–11-Artists Respond, 9/11: Emergency Relief* (2002), and *A Moment of Silence* (2002), similarly wrestled with reconciling the imaginary world of superheroes—so often set in Gotham City—with the reality that had changed the literal and figurative landscape of readers (Cooper & Atkinson, 2008).

Trends in Books Post-9/11

As the first decade of the twenty-first century progressed, books about 9/11 continued to be written, published, and read. While not necessarily reaching the top of the best-seller lists as they did during the first year or so after the attacks, writing about 9/11 remained popular. As Donahue (2006) of *Publishers Weekly* states: "any book that presents either new concrete information or a new way of looking at the tragedy will most certainly find a receptive audience" (p. 22).

Topics of more recent 9/11 books fall into several distinct categories. The 9/11 widows, as they were called by the media, published their own accounts of losing loves ones and fighting for their rights as survivors. In September 2005, Marian Fontana published *A Widow's Walk: A Memoir of 9/11* (2006), a personal account of losing her husband, a firefighter, on September 11 and the weeks and months that followed. Other narratives of 9/11 widows include *Love You, Mean It* (2006)—written by four women who lost husbands in the attacks—and *Wake-Up Call: The Political Education of a 9/11 Widow* (2006), Kristin Breitweiser's tale of moving from grief to activism aimed at learning the truth about September 11. Tapping into the success of the graphic novel as a form for telling the 9/11 story, Alissa Torres chronicles her own journey of loss through the pages of *American Widow* (2008).

By 2006, first-hand accounts of 9/11 had been more or less replaced by an onslaught of "untold" stories said to give readers the truth about the day, the events, and the people who acted in the crisis. William Keegan's *Closure: The Untold Story of the Ground Zero Recovery Mission* (2006) narrates the rescue and recovery mission, while David Friend's *Watching the World Change: The Stories behind the Images of 9/11* (2006) gives readers insight to what photographers were thinking as they snapped shots of the day. Tom Murphy's *Reclaiming the Sky: 9/11 and the Untold Story of the Men and Women Who Kept America Flying* (2007) focuses on the men and women who work in the air travel industry and the challenges 9/11 presented to them, both personally and professionally. On a related topic, in *Touching History: The Untold Story of the Drama That Unfolded in the Skies over America on 9/11* (2008) Lynn Spencer, a commercial airline pilot, describes the collaborative efforts made between civil and military aviation groups on September 11. Similarly, *Aftermath: The World Trade Center Archive* (2006) presents readers with previously unseen photos of the vast recovery effort, along with text by photographer Joel Meyerowitz who was allowed unmatched access to the site after the attacks.

As the post-9/11 world took shape, new trends in creative writing could be seen. Graphic novels have a strong presence in 9/11 literature, suggesting that conventional

NARRATIVES ABOUT THE FALLING PERSONS OF 9/11

Exploring the construction of narrative is the natural purview of fiction, and a number of novelists have used the genre to examine and explore the ramifications of September 11. In the destruction of the Twin Towers, nearly 3,000 individuals died largely unseen. Few images exist of the interior of the building, beyond the lobby. This invisibility haunts us. What happened to those people that day? The question serves as the impetus for the nonfictional *102 Minutes* (Dwyer & Flynn 2004) and its fictional counterpart, Frédéric Beigbeder's *Windows on the World* (2004). It is the mystery that haunts Oskar in Jonathan Safran Foer's *Extremely Loud and Incredibly Close* (2005) and propels his quest to learn how his father died that day. And it is the trauma from which Don DeLillo's protagonist seeks to recover in *Falling Man* (2006). In each of these novels, falling persons are the emotional epicenter of the trauma.

But why the focus on the falling persons? First, they are the most salient and human representation of the suffering undergone that day. The final, private moments of these individuals "personalize" an event that is more often depicted as the destruction of iconic buildings in the most iconic of U.S. cities. Second, they are the only visible victims, if only so briefly. Their visibility becomes the anchor for the writer's imagination. Third, they are an existential reflection of our own fates and fears. The "unbearable vulnerability" (Butler, 2004, p. xi) exposed on that day was revealed most explicitly in their publicly viewed private despair. Finally, they embody the very definition of trauma as characterized by the inability to assimilate an event. It is only through art and fiction that we can afford to revisit the experience, on our own terms and controlling the manner in which we are assailed, unlike the victims.

Although created to provoke and illuminate, narratives of the falling people can also aggrieve and prolong suffering. The creation of art representing the falling bodies and the visceral responses to them reflect our conflicting responses to the trauma. Dori Laub (2003) observes, "We are still involved with the ongoing struggle between an imperative need to know what it is that has happened to us all . . . and an equally powerful urge not to know, a defensive wish to deny the nature of the tear in the fabric of our shared lives" (p. 204). The desire to create these works of literature and the corresponding desire to censor them are the two faces of trauma. The struggle to agree on the appropriate creation at the site of the Twin Towers is emblematic of this tension.

The representations of the falling persons—real as well as fictionalized—continue to disturb because they offer little redemption—they refuse to be incorporated into a soothing narrative. They remain that part of the day not counteracted by stories of heroism or good luck or divine intervention. But it is for this very reason that the representations gain their significance, they continue to communicate the pain that September 11, 2001, will forever hold.

—*Tim S. Gauthier*

References

Butler, J. (2004). *Precarious life: The powers of mourning and violence.* New York: Verso.

Laub, D. (2003). September 11, 2001—an event without a voice. In J. Greenberg (Ed.), *Trauma at home: After 9/11* (pp. 204–215). Lincoln and London: University of Nebraska Press.

narrative fails to capture something important about the experience. Other forms have also been shaped by the attacks. For example, Karen Springen (2008) writes that, as of 2008 "one of the hottest segments of children's literature is about surviving the end of the world" (para. 2). Series such as Books of Ember, books like *The Hunger Games* and *The End of Life as We Know It*, and *Wall-E* focus on apocalyptic topics. While the tales seem especially dark for the genre of children's literature, they reflect a world changed since 9/11, including important messages and lessons about the world, and "tend to end on a positive, if not happy, note" (para. 3). Schoolbooks have also been impacted by 9/11. Since 9/11 the most common history textbooks used in middle and high schools have increased their emphasis on the Middle East and Islam, although critics suggest there remains work to be done in presenting nonbiased information (Manzo, 2008, p. 11).

Numerous popular novels—thrillers and mysteries in particular—have used September 11 as a backdrop or plot point. In Iain Banks's *Dead Air* (2002), for example, a novel about a radio personality, includes a chapter on the attacks, while Jeffrey Archer's thriller, *False Impression* (2006), takes place concurrently with September 11 and its aftermath. John Updike's novel, *Terrorist* (2006), looks at life after 9/11 through the eyes of a radical Muslim, while Philip Roth's novel, *Everyman* (2006), follows the experience of a man who leaves New York City for the Jersey Shore in fear after the attacks. Tom Robbins's *Villa Incognito* (2003), Arthur Neresian's *Unlubricated* (2004), Jess Walter's *The Zero* (2006), David Llewllyn's *Eleven* (2007), and Stephen King's *Song of Susannah* (2006) each take September 11 as their starting point or as an event in the novel that motivates the characters and/or the plot. In contrast, some post-9/11 novels begin before September 11 or just on the verge of the attacks. Andre Dubus's *In the Garden of Last Days* (2008), for example, evokes the activities of the real terrorists through its focus on the fictional character of Bassam, a Muslim who is depicted in the novel taking flying lessons in Florida during the days just prior to September 11.

Conclusion

Initial writings focused on representing and witnessing the attacks. As time went by, the need to record shifted to the need to understand, to analyze, even to question and synthesize the events that shook the nation on that fall day in 2001. From poetry and novels to comics and nonfiction, books engaged with 9/11. They serve as a "cultural response to national wounds that are sustained intimately, by ordinary citizens" (Keniston & Quinn, 2008, p. 285).

—*Sara E. Quay*

References

Abbott, C. (2001, September 24). Readers turn to new titles after September 11. *Publishers Weekly, 248*(39), 12–13.

Baer, U. (Ed.). (2002). *110 stories: New York writes after September 11.* New York: New York University Press.

Cooper, S., & Atkinson, P. (2008). Graphic implosion: Politics, time, and value in post-9/11 comics. In A. Keniston & J. F. Quinn (Eds.), *Literature after 9/11* (pp. 60–81). New York: Routledge.

Danforth, N. (2001, December 3). The way to a nation's heart. *Publishers Weekly, 238*(49), 19–20.

DeLillo, D. (2001, December). In the ruins of the future. *Harper's Magazine, 303,* 33–40.

Donahue, D. (2006, August 21). Remembering 9/11 on the page. *Publishers Weekly, 253*(33), 22–23.

Fitch, S. (2001, October 29). Armageddon sells. *Forbes, 168*(11), 28.

Ford, M. (2001, October 15). The good book in bad times. *Publishers Weekly, 248*(42), 37.

Glasner, J. (2004, September 20). Free content still sells. *Wired.com.* Retrieved from http://www.wired.com

Johnson, D. L., & Merians, V. (2002). *Poetry after 9/11: An anthology of New York poets.* Hoboken, NJ: Melville House.

Keniston, A., & Quinn, J. F. (Eds.). (2008). *Literature after 9/11.* New York: Routledge.

Lodge, S. (2001, December 17). Checking in with children's booksellers. *Publishers Weekly, 248*(51), 50–51.

Manzo, K. K. (2008, June 11). Review criticizes textbooks' take on Middle East, Islam. *Education Week,* p. 11.

Maryles, D. (2001, November 12). Behind the bestsellers. *Publishers Weekly, 248*(46), 16.

McEvoy, D. (2001, October 22). Sports books in a somber time. *Publishers Weekly, 248*(43), 31–33.

Milliot, J., Zeitchik, S., & Baker, J. F. (2001, September 24). After the attack. *Publishers Weekly, 248*(39), 10.

Minzesheimer, B. (2002, September 8). 9/11 lives on the best-seller list. *USA Today.* Retrieved from http://www.usatoday.com

Mutter, J., Howell, K., & Nawotka, W. (2001, November 12). Bookselling since 9/11. *Publishers Weekly, 248*(46), 17–18.

Nawotka, E. (2001a, November 26). Ingram sizes up the holidays. *Publishers Weekly, 248*(48), 18–19.

Nawotka, E. (2001b, November 18). Two edgy looks at 9/11. *Publishers Weekly, 249*(46), 22–23.

Portraits 9/11/01: The collected "Portraits of Grief" from the New York Times (2003). New York: Henry Holt.

Roback, D., & Britton, J. (2001, October 8). In the aftermath. *Publishers Weekly, 248*(41), 33.

Springen, K. (2008, July 21). Unhappily ever after. *Newsweek, 152*(3), 58.

Wells, D. (2001, December 17). Travel bookstores: Endangered species? *Publishers Weekly, 248*(51), 21–22.

Zeitchik, S. (2001, November 12). Donation claims for 9/11 books a slippery concept. *Publishers Weekly, 248*(46), 15.

SPOTLIGHT ESSAY/BOOKS: *THE 9/11 COMMISSION REPORT* AND THE GRAPHIC NOVEL

In 2004, *The 9/11 Commission Report* was released in bookstores as well as online. The lengthy (more than 500 pages) volume was an immediate best seller (Glasner, 2004). The fact that the *Report* was produced at all was in part a result of the persistent demands of a group of women—popularly known as the Jersey Girls—whose husbands had died in the attacks. Their insistence that a federal investigation in the September 11 attacks be pursued, and that the findings be released to the public, led to the publication of *The 9/11 Commission Report* (Breitweiser, 2006).

The largely text-based *9/11 Commission Report* was rightly praised for its literary merit and readability, something that was important to the Commission (Posner, 2004; Yagoda, 2004). The chair and vice-chair of the Commission stated that their goal was "to tell the story of 9/11 in a way that the American people could read and understand" and to make it "accessible to all" (Kean & Hamilton, 2006, p. ix). However, the length of the report is not conducive to quick reading; the volume appears intimidatingly large even in paperback. Five years after the events of September 11, 2009, two collaborators translated the 9/11 Commission's 2004 report into a graphic version with the expressed interest of making the lengthy report more readable for the general public (Jacobson & Colón, 2006).

Sid Jacobson and Ernie Colón's graphic adaptation of *The 9/11 Commission Report* was intended to more clearly and immediately convey the report's information (Turner, 2006). They accomplished this in part by tightening the narrative; while most of the text was taken directly from the original report, it was condensed from an unwieldy 567 pages into 117. This made the narrative accessible to a broad audience that may not have the time or inclination to read a lengthy government report. This is not because comics are "easier" to read, but rather because the use of two communication media, both text and image, enables a shorter but more densely packed information space.

The facts of the day's events are made more immediate by virtue of the visual format. This is evident from the first chapter; the comic conveys the account of the four flights more fully than the original text by presenting the events of each in a visual timeline (Jacobson & Colón, 2006, p. 6). The four flight accounts are depicted stacked on top of each other, the timeline printed on a long, folded piece of paper that enables it to be read clearly. This is an easier process than reading 16 pages of text and flipping those pages back and forth to get a sense of simultaneous events (National Commission, 2004, pp. 1–14, 32–33). In the graphic version, it is immediately clear to the reader that United Flight 93 was cleared for takeoff 23 minutes after the first messages were received that American Flight 11 had been hijacked. The following account of the awareness and response of federal agencies to each of the four hijackings is also broken into a visual timeline. The only graphics in the 46 pages of the original report's first chapter are four maps depicting the four flight paths, and two maps showing the locations of FAA centers, the North American Aerospace Defense Command (NORAD) headquarters, and the Northeast Air Defense Sector (NEADS) sectors. The comic's graphic presentations convey the simultaneous context of the events in the space of just nine pages.

Throughout the work, Jacobson and Colón combine the text and diagrams of the original report with compelling illustrations of the events. This creates a feeling of immediacy, of not simply conveying information about the events, but also immersing the reader in them. Likewise, some illustrations provide emotional overtones not present in the text alone. The original report states that Khalid Shaikh Mohammed "speculated about striking the World Trade Center and CIA headquarters as early as 1995" and mentions additional targets on the following page (National Commission, 2004, pp. 153–154). The graphic adaptation punctuates this text with illustrations of the U.S. Capitol Building, CIA Headquarters, the World Trade Center, and the White House overlaid with red crosshairs (Jacobson & Colón, 2006, p. 37). This silent, symbolic addition immediately conveys a devastating impression of these locations as targets of violence.

Specific facts are more evident in the graphic adaptation, particularly for visually oriented readers. For example, a simple illustration of the Twin Towers of the World Trade Center with the impact zones highlighted transforms mere numbers (the 94th to 98th floors of the North Tower and 78th to 84th floors of the South Tower) into concrete, visible depictions (Jacobson & Colón, 2006, p. 80). The immediate scope of the impact is evident with a single glance, as is the large area above those zones that proved so difficult to evacuate.

The graphic adaption closes with a report card grading action taken on the Commission's recommendations. This report card was originally made public in December of 2005 by the 10 original commissioners, through the 9/11 Public Discourse project they initiated (9/11 Public Discourse Project, 2005). While the text for the report is the same as the original, the graphic version enhances readability by depicting only the "grades" of C and below in red, causing them to stand out from the A and B grades (Jacobson & Colón, 2006, p. 115). This provides a sobering postscript to the document.

The purpose of Jacobson and Colón's graphic adaptation of *The 9/11 Commission Report* was to convey unbiased information in a clearer, more digestible format. Their adaptation not only made an important document accessible and meaningful for all Americans, but also used its medium's unique potential to more effectively convey its message.

—*Starr Hoffman*

References

Breitweiser, K. (2006). *Wake-up call: The political education of a 9/11 widow*. Boston: Grand Central.

Glasner, J. (2004, September 20). Free content still sells. *Wired*. Retrieved from http://www.wired.com

Jacobson, S., & Colón, E. (2006). *The 9/11 report: A graphic adaptation*. New York: Hill & Wang.

Kean, T. H., & Hamilton, L. H. (2006). Foreword. In S. Jacobson & E. Colón, *The 9/11 report: A graphic adaptation* (pp. ix–x). New York: Hill & Wang.

National Commission on Terrorist Acts upon the United States (National Commission). (2004). *The 9/11 commission report: Final report of the national commission on terrorist acts upon the United States*. New York: W.W. Norton.

9/11 Public Discourse Project. (2005). One page summary of grades. *9/11 Public Discourse Project*, retrieved June 30, 2009, from http://www.9-11pdp.org/press/2005-12-05_summary.pdf

Posner, R. A. (2004, August 29). The 9/11 report: A dissent. *The New York Times*. Retrieved from http://www.nytimes.com

Turner, J. (2006, September 10). The trouble with drawing Dick Cheney: Ernie Colón and Sid Jacobson, the comic-book vets behind the 9/11 report: A graphic adaptation. *Slate*, Retrieved from http://www.slate.com

Yagoda, B. (2004, November 8). The 9/11 Commission Report: How a government committee made a piece of literature. *Slate*. Retrieved from http://www.slate.com

SPOTLIGHT ESSAY/BOOKS: CHILDREN'S LITERATURE AND 9/11

In the years following 9/11, a number of children's books were written and published about the day and its events. Some were available to readers within months, while others were released several years later. The purpose of such books changed as time went on, revealing not only changes in how Americans viewed September 11, but how the day—as a moment in U.S. history—would be passed on to children in the form of books.

The first children's books to be published about September 11 were notable in two ways: They were directly tied to the field of education, and they were visibly endorsed by experts—whether organizations or individuals—in working with children. Andrea Patel's book, *On That Day: A Book of Hope for Children* was published in December 2001 as part of public television's acclaimed *Reading Rainbow* program. Patel, a veteran teacher, tells the story of 9/11 in general terms appropriate to young readers. She writes, "[O]ne day a terrible thing happened. The world, which had been blue and green and bright and very big and really round and pretty peaceful, got badly hurt" (p. 3). While a few of the collage images in the book feature the Twin Towers, fire, and smoke, most of the book answers the question "Is there anything we can do to make the world right again?" (p. 6). Indeed, this book—published so quickly after 9/11—is targeted at children who may have experienced the actual day and reassures them that "There will always be good things in the world" (p. 12).

Published shortly afterward in 2002, *September 12th: We Knew Everything Would Be All Right* serves a similar function to *On That Day*. Published by Scholastic, Inc., one of the country's leading producers of children's books, *September 12th* was written and illustrated by first graders from Missouri. The book describes all of the daily activities and events that were the same after 9/11 as before. In contrast to *On That Day*, however, *September 12th* contains several children's drawings of planes flying into tall buildings and firefighters working to rescue people.

The Day America Cried (2002) is a similar book in that it aims to recount, and reassure, young readers after 9/11. The book is also vested with authority through the author—Dr. Teri Schwartz—whose biography reveals that she is a clinical psychologist in New York City who works with children. Aimed at a slightly older audience, the book nonetheless fits into the first generation of children's books about 9/11 because of its descriptive focus of what happened and its efforts to reassure children that they are safe.

A second generation of children's books about September 11 appeared in 2003. In contrast to previous books, which told the literal story of 9/11 and reassured children after it had happened, this group contextualized 9/11 and/or the Twin Towers through a range of larger narratives. *The Little Chapel That Stood* (2003), for example, tells the story of St. Paul's Chapel, which stood next to the Twin Towers and, because it was not damaged, served as a place of refuge for rescue workers and volunteers. Playing on the title of the popular children's book *The Little Engine That Could*—a tale that uses the metaphor of a train to celebrate American perseverance during hard times—*The Little Chapel That Stood* uses St. Paul's Chapel to remind readers that the United States and its people can survive the tragedy of 9/11. As the author writes, "We raised up the flag from the dust and the pain. Freedom that's lost must be won again" (p. 21). Rather than being the focus of the story itself, September 11 becomes an event in the larger story of this national landmark.

In a similar way, *The Man Who Walked Between the Towers* (2003) tells the story of September 11 through the tale of a real man, Philippe Petit, who walked on a tightrope between the Twin Towers during the 1970s. The book memorializes the Twin Towers through its words and images, both which emphasize the dramatic, unique height of the towers and their place in Manhattan's skyline. The towers are in fact a character in the book, as is apparent in the description of Petit's walk between them: "Out to the very middle he walked, as if he were walking on the air itself. Many winds whirled up from between the towers, and he swayed with them. He could feel the towers breathing" (n.p.). Images in the book of people looking up to the top of the Towers at Petit are reminiscent of those taken of people on the streets of Manhattan on September 11, watching in disbelief as the planes struck the buildings. In *The Man Who Walked Between the Towers*, however, they look up in wonder "A quarter mile up in the sky someone was dancing" (n.p.). As the book closes it reminds readers that, "Now the towers are gone. But in memory, as if imprinted on the sky, the towers are still there. And part of that memory is the joyful morning, August 7, 1974, when Philippe Petit walked between them in the air" (n.p.).

Two other children's books use a similar strategy for telling the story of 9/11. *September Roses* (Winter, 2004) is about two sisters from South Africa who, traveling to New York City on September 11 to show their roses at the flower show, find a city in chaos, shock, and grief. Unsure of what to do with their beautiful roses, the sisters end up at Union Square where they use the flowers to create visual memorials of the Twin Towers. In *T. Bear's Tale: Hugs across America* (2004) domestic kindness shapes the narrative. Instead of roses, teddy bears are the vehicle for expressing feelings of concern and care to the children of New York and the nation.

Initially, children's literature attempted to reassure the nation's youth that the world was safe, despite the tragedy of September 11. As time went on, new books appeared which memorialized the towers and integrated them into U.S. culture and history for young readers. Reflected in this transition is the country's shift from shock and disbelief to acceptance and integration, necessary steps to moving forward.

—Sara E. Quay

References

Curtiss, A. B. (2003). *The little chapel that stood.* Escondido, CA: Old Castle.

Gerstein, M. (2003). *The man who walked between the towers.* New York: Holtzbrinck.

Lucarelli, S. (2004). *T. Bear's tale: Hugs across America.* Escondido, CA: Old Castle.

Patel, A. (2001). *On that day: A book of hope for children.* Berkeley, CA: Tricycle Press.

Scholastic. (2002). *September 12th: We knew everything would be all right.* New York: Scholastic.

Schwartz, T. J. (2002). *The day America cried.* New York: Enduring Freedom Press.

Winter, J. (2004). *September roses.* New York: Frances Foster Books.

SPOTLIGHT ESSAY/BOOKS: COMIC BOOKS

Despite their fictional premise, superhero comics still push to make their characters, plots, and settings as realistic as possible. September 11, however, reinforced a long-standing dilemma for the superhero universes of Marvel Comics and DC Comics. Can a fictional universe address real-world events in a genuine fashion that does not contradict their fictitious nature? That is, if both DC and Marvel want their readers to buy into the realistic elements of their narratives, then how do they account for the events of September 11 within their mutual universes? These two universes overflow with superhero characters of all shapes, sizes, and abilities, yet the publishers chose not to let their superheroes prevent 9/11 in their fictional universes out of respect for, but also fear of, forsaking their readership. That leaves the question of how the DC and Marvel universes dealt with or integrated 9/11 into their narratives.

Historically, tragic worldly events have proved problematic for superhero comics. The superheroes' fictional existence means that they cannot actually engage or prevent tragic events, but the writers still feel the need to address these historical moments or else fear losing touch with their readers. Often in World War II, superheroes were sent abroad to fight in battles that may have severe consequences if the enemy won, but were inconsequential to the war as a whole if the superheroes won. For those superheroes that stayed home from the war, the engagement with the enemy entailed routing out spies and foreign plots to destroy the United States. While the cover to the *Captain America #1* in 1941 featured the patriotic superhero punching out Hitler, the story line and subsequent story lines could never actually do it.

DC Comics responded to 9/11 by a self-reflexive admission of Superman about his own fictitious nature in a short two-page comic in the dedicated anthology, *9–11: September 11, 2001: Stories to Remember, Volume 2*, published in January, 2002. In the short piece, "Unreal," Superman flies through the universe saving a colliding spaceship and satellite while explaining to the reader that while he can do great things such as "defy the laws of gravity . . . ignore the principles of physics . . . breathe in the vacuum of space" he cannot "break free from the fictional pages" (pp. 15–16). As the panel pulls back, the reader sees that this Superman is part of a comic book within the story that a child is reading as he is rescued by a firefighter, presumably in one of the Twin Towers. The last panel silhouettes the firefighter holding a U.S. flag while a page of the comic book is opened to reveal Superman saluting and saying, "A world, fortunately, protected by heroes of its own" (p. 16). In this sense, DC Comics simply identifies that it genuinely has no legitimate means of justifying or engaging the tragic events. At least for the immediate future, DC Comics acknowledged that they were not capable of incorporating the tragic event but instead would pay homage to those who had assisted, survived, and died.

Marvel Comics tackled 9/11 directly, by pulling it into its fictional universe as a "real event" to which its characters would need to respond. In December 2001, *Amazing Spider-Man #36* halted its ongoing story line for a single issue in which readers witness the travesty of 9/11 through Spider-Man's eyes. The story mainly plays as an internal monologue of Spider-Man's as he comes to terms with what has happened. After the introductory pages, readers find Spider-Man in a double-page display, clutching his head and uttering "God" (p. 2) as he sees the destruction, flame, and smoke of the fallen towers. In the following pages, he is confronted by bystanders who ask—"How could you let this happen?" (p. 4)—to which he can offer no valid response for his (and other superheroes') inability to prevent it. He continues, "How do you say we [the superhero community] didn't know? We couldn't know. We couldn't imagine. Only madmen could contain the thought, execute the act, fly the planes. The sane world will always be vulnerable to madmen because we cannot go where they go to conceive of such things" (p. 4). From there, Spider-Man explains that although they couldn't prevent it, the superheroes were helping in the recovery efforts. As the story cuts to Ground Zero, readers see several identifiable Marvel characters using their powers to help dig out the survivors.

Most interesting, several super-villains of Marvel Comics are presented in the scenes that follow, including Dr. Doom, the Kingpin, and Magneto—all of who have attempted similar heinous acts in their fictional lives. Here, these villains shed their past hate and violence to participate in the recovery because, according to Spider-Man, "even the worst of us, however scarred, are still human" (p. 9). From there, the comic returns to applauding the efforts of firefighters, police, and others who helped out. Spider-Man briefly addresses Captain America, emphasizing this was his second time experiencing such a tragedy, the first being Pearl Harbor. The story concludes by recognizing the diversity of U.S. culture that has been unified by the terrorist acts.

In their initial responses, both publishers recognize the event of September 11, but seemed to disengage or sacrifice their narratives' legitimacy in order to respond. DC Comics chose to break what is known as "the fourth wall" and directly address the reader. DC admits to the shortcomings of a fictional universe, while Marvel simply positions its superheroes as just as fragile and subject to the whims of humankind.

It took several years before the publishers could grapple with 9/11 in a narrative sense. In 2002, *Amazing Spider-Man Vol 2.: Revelations* and *9-11 Emergency Relief* were published. Perhaps the most dynamic approach to 9/11 came from the publication of the series Ex Machina in 2004 by Wildstorm, one of DC's publishing lines. The premise centers on Mitchell Hundred, the new fictional mayor of New York City in 2002.

As the story continues, readers learn that Hundred has superpowers and had prevented the second tower from being hit on 9/11. In this way, the publishers met readers halfway, giving them the reality of the strike, but the opportunity for their readers to see the superheroes directly respond to the tragic event.

—*Lance Eaton*

References

Hastings, J. (2002). *Untitled.* In J. Mason (Ed.), *9–11 emergency relief.* Gainesville, FL: Alternative Comics.

9–11: September 11, 2001: Stories to remember. Vol. 2. (2002). New York: DC Comics.

Straczynski, J. M., Romita, Jr., J., & Hanna, S. (2001). *Amazing Spider-Man #36.* New York: Marvel Comics.

Straczynski, J. M., Romita Jr., J., & Hanna, S. (2002). *Amazing Spider-Man: Vol. 2. Revelations.* New York: Marvel Comics.

SPOTLIGHT ESSAY/BOOKS: *EXTREMELY LOUD AND INCREDIBLY CLOSE* BY JONATHAN SAFRAN FOER

Published in 2005, *Extremely Loud and Incredibly Close* was one of the first and most widely recognized novels to address the terrorist attacks of September 11. Its popularity was due, in part, to its high visibility as Jonathan Safran Foer's first novel after his acclaimed debut, *Everything is Illuminated* (2003). There are many factors that put *Extremely Loud and Incredibly Close* in a class of its own simply as a novel—from the authenticity of Foer's offbeat characters to his thought-provoking and hermeneutically challenging incorporation of images. The novel is a graceful mechanism of diverse overlapping and interlocking parts—so much so that it is hard to focus on one part without having to examine them all. But the central cog that makes *Extremely Loud and Incredibly Close* stand out as a 9/11 novel, in particular, is the way in which the peculiar nature of the protagonist and his journey allows Foer to engage the terrorist attacks in a way that is whimsical, intellectual, funny, heart-wrenchingly bittersweet, always meaningful, and never maudlin.

With many layers and unconventional techniques, *Extremely Loud and Incredibly Close* defies easy and comprehensive summary. At its core, it is a quest narrative. It is a story about a search—a search for meaning, like numerous other 9/11 novels, but also a literal search. Nine-year-old New Yorker Oskar Schell's journey begins after September 11 when he finds a mysterious key left behind by his father, who died at the World Trade Center. It becomes Oskar's mission to find the lock that the key fits, a search that covers all five boroughs and fosters new relationships for the young boy. While Foer's novel encompasses more than just this simple premise and is temporally unconventional, jumping nimbly and almost unnoticeably across time and story lines, it is Oskar's clever accumulation of clues that primarily drives the story forward and delivers its message.

Oskar Schell is possibly one of the most endearing, memorable, and vibrant characters in contemporary fiction, reminiscent of John Irving's titular hero Owen Meany. Precocious is too small a word for Oskar. Hyper-verbal, prolific in his generation of original ideas, and voracious in his accumulation of knowledge, Oskar naturally functions on the same level as adults—sometimes even above them. He sets the standard for intellectual daring and uses his imagination as a way to reconfigure unpleasant realities rather than escape them. When Oskar's mind is unquiet, it turns to hypothetical inventions that allow him to redirect potentially negative thoughts to be more positive and productive. Some inventions are geared toward minimizing uncertainty, mitigating sadness, and changing the past—a scrolling marquee for ambulances to broadcast their occupant's well-being, a reservoir for the tears of New Yorkers to measure their grief, and birdseed shirts for those trapped in the Twin Towers so that birds could have carried them down to safety. Through such inventions, Oskar is not escaping reality by entering some imaginary world; he is using an imaginary world to have a better grasp on reality, exactly what novelists like Foer do for their readers and encourage their readers to do. Oskar is an exemplar of one who does not retreat from the world but instead chooses to see it differently. Although frequently frustrated and negative, he is the epitome of someone who, to borrow from George Bernard Shaw, dreams things that never were and asks why not. In this way, Oskar is the key to what makes *Extremely Loud and Incredibly Close* a different kind of 9/11 novel. With the perspicacity of an adult and the wonder of a child, his approach to the world encourages readers to learn to look for possibilities they might have otherwise thought impossible, rather than to puzzle over why unimaginable realities have come to be.

Oskar's quest can be considered symbolic of the public's search for meaning in the post-9/11 era. That it is shown to be quirky and humorous makes it seem somehow less daunting and unpleasant. Furthermore, while his search may be a consequence of 9/11, it is not a direct response to it. 9/11 shadows Oskar on his journey but it is rarely at the forefront. Indeed, the search for the lock that fits the key his father left behind is not terribly different from other cerebral scavenger hunts his father designed for him while still alive. Oskar has always enjoyed acquiring clues and searching for meaning—a cornerstone of his relationship with his father. In this way, Oskar's quest derives a certain purity; he searches because it is natural to him—because it is, in his words, his ultimate *raison d'être*. Oskar does not know what he is looking to find—literally or figuratively. He simply revels in the process of searching and pursuing symbols that happen to have acquired new meaning after 9/11. What is of paramount importance and makes the novel stand out is that Oskar does so in a way that allows him to find beauty and connections where none existed before, rather than being haunted by beauty and connections that once were and are now gone.

Oskar's ongoing quest is given added philosophical weight by an adjacent narrative told through the letters of his immigrant grandparents, which speak to their traumas and struggles in the wake of their own life-changing tragedy: the firebombing of Dresden. Foer also used a parallel ancestral story line in his first novel, but what this technique allows him to do here is to keep Oskar's story as light and innocent as possible while still grappling with the gravity of death and destruction. By doing both—bluntly confronting tragedy in one story line and gingerly dancing with it in another—the novel sets itself apart from others that largely do only the former. In this merger, Oskar's quest can be lighthearted without being glib and can maintain meaning without sacrificing its quirkiness. Indeed, the two story lines eventually and dramatically converge, bringing tragic past and optimistic future together. This convergence is made even more powerful by the final pages óf the novel, which provide a virtual flipbook of an actual image of a human figure falling from one of the Twin Towers. In this case, however, as the reader flips through, the body ascends rather than plummets. Time cannot be turned back, we know, but we still needn't surrender the childlike faith that tragedy can be turned around and, maybe, even become uplifting.

Extremely Loud and Incredibly Close is exceptional as a genuinely joyful story brought out by intrinsically devastating events. Like Oskar's quest, the novel is not always an easy read but it is a fun one and, by its ending, Foer has impressed a tricky but surprisingly simple notion in his readers' minds. To return to the words of George Bernard Shaw, and words Oskar's father might just as easily have said to him: "Life is not meant to be easy, my child; but take courage—it can be delightful."

—*Kathryn Palmer*

Reference

Foer, J. S. (2005). *Extremely loud and incredibly close*. New York: Houghton Mifflin.

SPOTLIGHT ESSAY/BOOKS: *FALLING MAN* BY DON DELILLO

No U.S. author seemed better suited to write the definitive 9/11 novel than Don DeLillo. His previous work, with its emphasis on terrorism, the power of the media, and the machinations of government, presaged the event and its aftermath. Just as 9/11 was said to resemble a disaster film, many aspects of that day had already appeared somewhere in DeLillo's oeuvre. Even the cover of *Underworld* (1997), the novel considered his masterpiece, depicts the Twin Towers, their upper floors shrouded in clouds. No doubt DeLillo himself was aware of these readerly expectations. This may have been cause for some ambivalence and trepidation on the author's part. It comes as no surprise, then, that *Falling Man* (2007) is a very self-conscious and frequently metafictional text that focuses on survival, but also on the question of representation in the shadow of trauma.

DeLillo gives some indication of the novel he might write in a piece published in *Harper's* in December 2001. The essay, "In the ruins of the future," depicts a destabilized community looking for meaning—a way of making sense of the events—and DeLillo outlines the narratives constructed by the media and the government, while underlining their inherent insufficiencies. He then delineates the writer's role in relation to this national trauma: "The writer begins in the towers, trying to imagine the moment desperately. Before politics, before history and religion, there is primal terror. People falling from the towers hand in hand. This is part of the counternarrative, hands and spirits joining, human beauty in the crush of meshed steel" (p. 39). Here DeLillo first broaches the topic of the falling people as a way of invoking the "primal terror" of that day. He wonders how these victims might contribute to the construction of a counternarrative, an alternative to over-mediated and government-endorsed images of 9/11. Six years later, *Falling Man* is his answer to that question.

Falling Man returns the reader to the world evoked in the article beginning with its protagonist, Keith Neudecker, emerging bloodied from the rubble of the World Trade Center. He stumbles to the apartment of his estranged wife, Lianne. In muted fashion, replicating the shock that follows trauma, the novel catalogs a series of responses to the event. Keith begins an affair with a fellow survivor, eventually turning to the sureties of tournament poker. Lianne exercises her anger by assaulting a neighbor who plays "Middle Eastern" music too loudly. Their son spends time with his friends scanning the skyline for more attacks from "Bill Lawton," the name they hear when people around them talk about bin Laden. As one character observes, "Everything now is measured by after" (p. 138). It may be too early to know what the new narratives are, the novel suggests, but we strive to create them nonetheless.

One significant obstacle is that our sense-making abilities have suffered as a result of this trauma, and DeLillo hints subtly at the repressed portions of Keith's psyche. Throughout the novel, thoughts of Rumsey, Keith's friend and co-worker, intrude upon the narrative (in the final pages we learn of Rumsey's death in the tower and Keith's futile attempts to save him). And in the interactions between Keith and his fellow-survivor, Florence, we are afforded glimpses of lingering effects: "If I live to be a hundred I'll still be on the stairs," she observes (p. 57). The text effectively communicates the repetitive aspects of trauma and the shock that incapacitates the victim's ability to compartmentalize the experience. As Cathy Caruth (1996) notes, "the trauma consists not only in having confronted death but *in having survived, precisely, without knowing it.* What one returns to in the flashback is not the incomprehensibility of one's near death, but the very incomprehensibility of one's own survival" (p. 64). The novel's conclusion reveals the loop in Keith's mind. We return with him to the moment when the plane strikes the tower, the ensuing chaos, and Rumsey's death. We learn how closely linked Keith's traumatized state is to the fate of the falling people. Having failed to save his friend, he looks out the office window and sees a man "falling sideways, arm out and up, like pointed up, like why am I here instead of there" (p. 244). Earlier intimations of Keith's experience are concretized in a conclusion highlighting the recursive nature of trauma while making the meaning of the novel's title clear.

But the title also refers to a performance artist named Falling Man, whose presence in the novel reflects a preoccupation with the falling people of September 11, and with the inherent limitations of any representation of those horrors. The character of David Janiak emphasizes the inevitable shortcomings of any representation of trauma, but also the desire to represent that is an inherent component of trauma. Falling Man leaps from buildings adopting stylized poses that re-create the images of the falling persons, briefly presented by the media on 9/11 then quickly repressed. The performance artist engages in an act of empathy as he strives to connect with the experiences of the falling people. His obituary alludes to the fact that he intended to perform his final jump without a harness. At the same time, the act is aggressive; his goal is to cause onlookers to relive those moments of "traumatized spectatorship" (Lurie, 2006, p. 46). So the performances work on two levels: on the spectators who relive the event as still-life, and on the artist himself who strives to connect with the most painful, and most human, element of the destruction of the World Trade Center.

Although no justification is ever provided for the performances, there remains a sense that Janiak is contributing to a counternarrative, another way of looking at the event. One onlooker stares up at Falling Man, "seeing something elaborately different from what he encountered step by step in the ordinary run of hours. He had to learn how to see it correctly, find a crack in the world where it might fit" (DeLillo, 2007, p. 168). The same thing would be said about the events of September 11; we were all forced to reconfigure our narratives. Falling Man, suspended in mid-air, after the deadening jolt, provides an opportunity to try to "see it correctly." The scene is a microcosm of what DeLillo (2001) calls "the massive spectacle that continues to seem unmanageable, too powerful a thing to set in our frame of practiced response" (p. 35).

But does this revisiting of horror serve a purpose? Is this catharsis or retraumatization? Choosing the falling people as a focus of his novel, DeLillo reveals a desire to touch the awful truth through them. The narratives constructed after September 11—whether patriotic, political, or therapeutic—emphasize certain elements (those that help us cope and survive)—often to the exclusion of others (those that trouble). The images of the falling people (real as well as fictionalized) disturb because they offer no redemption, *and* because they resist incorporation into a soothing narrative. They are the most explicit example of trauma's resistance to metaphor and simile. As such, DeLillo's own novel attests to the limitations of any counternarrative. The return to trauma at the conclusion of *Falling Man* makes clear that the intervening years (and all the coping strategies contained therein) are only marginally successful in keeping memory at bay. Falling Man's presence speaks to our ongoing need to speak of and represent the horror, while acknowledging our inability to truly palliate the pain.

—*Tim S. Gauthier*

References

Caruth, C. (1996). *Unclaimed experience: Trauma, narrative, and history.* Baltimore: Johns Hopkins University Press.

DeLillo, D. (2007). *Falling man.* New York: Scribner.

DeLillo, D. (2001, December). In the ruins of the future: Reflections on terror and loss in the shadow of September. *Harper's, 303,* 33–40.

Lurie, S. (2006). Falling persons and national embodiment: The reconstruction of safe spectatorship in the photographic record of 9/11. In D. J. Sherman & T. Nardin (Eds.), *Terror, culture, politics: Rethinking 9/11* (pp. 44–68). Bloomington: Indiana University Press.

SPOTLIGHT ESSAY/BOOKS: FICTION AND 9/11

Novelists immediately responded to the events of September 11, but not in their usual medium. In the days after the attacks and for years afterward, writers questioned the adequacy of fiction to express the incomprehensibility of the attacks. Like Julia Alvarez (2005), they asked, "In a world of such horrors, what does a novel have to offer?" (p. BW10). This is a question of imagination: How do writers reclaim the power to create worlds in the shadow of those who imagined and made real the attacks? And how is fiction suited to depict an event "outside imagining even as it happened" (DeLillo, 2001, p. 39)? In response to the overwhelming sense of unreality engendered by both the event itself and its coverage in the media, authors moved to ground the events of September 11 in the real and the everyday, focusing on the lives of individuals directly affected by the attacks and those adjusting to a new world in the aftermath.

The first to respond to the event were authors of genre fiction, particularly Christian fiction and mystery writers. Typically these novels address the most immediate question following 9/11—"How could this happen?"—by attempting to reckon the injustice of the attack with a belief either in God or in one's ability to protect family and country. Karen Kingsbury's *One Tuesday Morning* (2003), for example, blends elements of the romance, detective, and Christian genres to explore issues of memory, loss of identity, and altered personal relationships.

According to Julia Glass (2006), "serious fiction" about 9/11 did not appear until 2004 (p. 20). Some novels, including Jonathan Safran Foer's *Extremely Loud and Incredibly Close* (2005) and Don DeLillo's *Falling Man* (2007), take September 11 as their central and controlling event precisely because the working-through of trauma requires characters to revisit the event in memory, image, and action. Other writers choose to consider how the attacks were eventually absorbed into routine existence. 9/11 does directly impact many of these characters, but it nonetheless moves from the center to the background of daily life. In Hugh Nissenson's *The Days of Awe* (2005), 9/11 becomes yet another source of danger and disrupted routine among the many distressing surprises of old age. Nissenson's omniscient narration and changing point of view allow the reader to remain with characters until their moment of death, be it from illness or the attacks. Guy Stewart, whose choices are to "jump [from] or burn [in]" (p. 151) the Trade Center, speeds through first memories and final fears as he falls, thinking, "The sidewalk's coming up at me so fast!" (p. 152) at the moment of impact. Joanna, who dies of a heart attack unrelated to the event, has a similar experience of death. Nissenson's work thus dwells as much on the typicality as the uniqueness of the loss of life on September 11.

Another novel addressing personal life in the wake of 9/11 is Ken Kalfus's *A Disorder Peculiar to the Country* (2006), which uses the experience of divorce as a means of understanding terrorism. Like Nissenson's, these characters are directly affected by the attacks: Marshall escapes from the Trade Center, and Joyce was supposed to be on one of their planes. Kalfus also touches on aspects of memory and trauma in the depictions of their children, who obsessively jump from a porch, reenacting the falls of the jumpers. However, the novel focuses on the increasingly destructive divorce of Joyce and Marshall as a means of imagining the roots of violence. Humiliated by Joyce, Marshall thinks of their lives in terms normally applied to suicide bombers: "Deep within the moist, throbbing folds of Marshall's brain tissue, something turned over: their crappy, disordered existences, these shameful skirmishes, this soiled money, this debasement, this cruelty, this insensitivity, this impiety had become intolerable to God" (p. 185). This revelation leads Marshall to a failed attempt to build a bomb that would destroy his family. Although Kalfus touches all of these scenes with light comedy, his novel's disintegrating marriage allows for a serious consideration of the ways in which small, personal indignities explode into previously unthinkable acts of terror.

Later fiction examines the cultural conflicts, especially those of race, that have surfaced in the years since the attacks. Left adrift in the city after his wife and child flee to London following the attacks, Hans, the Dutch-born protagonist of Joseph O'Neill's *Netherland* (2008), meets Chuck Ramkissoon, an immigrant with aspirations of uniting America's Dutch past with its West Indian immigrant future through the game of cricket. At stake here is the ability to create an identity in the United States that does justice to both one's homeland and one's adopted land. Implicitly, the intensification of xenophobia after 9/11 complicates this issue, as does the United States' sense of disconnect from its own history. Lacking is that one common element that would draw together past and present, native and foreigner. While cricket does allow Hans to unite his conflicting identities so that he can "hit the ball in the air like an American cricketer . . . without injury" to his sense of self (p. 176), Chuck's vision "of a stadium, and black and brown and even a few white faces crowded in bleachers" (p. 176) never comes to fruition, thus reinforcing the notion of a United States further divided along lines of race and national identity in the years following September 11.

Also of interest are those novels-in-progress that were interrupted by and therefore required to change in response to the attacks. Claire Messud's *The Emperor's Children* (2006), for example, takes place primarily in New York City between March and November 2001. Marina and Bootie, cousins with literary dreams and a desire "'to do something important'" (p. 73), look longingly at the historic events of the 1960s and wonder when their generation's 1968 will occur. The reader, of course, already knows. When the attacks finally happen, the characters, despite being New Yorkers, experience it as most of the rest of the world did: through television. Likewise, they are mainly unaffected by the immediate loss of life. Bootie, inspired by the attacks as a profound act of imagination-turned-reality, allows his family to think he has died while temping downtown, allowing for his reinvention as Ulrich New, someone who would one day return to "take them by surprise" (p. 479). Messud thus considers 9/11 within the larger context of cultural angst, personal rebellion, and the power of the imagination to remake the world.

Other works that take 9/11 as their topic include *The Last Days of Mohamed Atta* (2006) by Martin Amis, *Windows on the World* (2003) by Frédéric Beigbeder, *Eleven* (2006) by David Lllewellyn, *The Usual Rules* (2003) by Joyce Maynard, *The*

Good Life (2006) by Jay McInerney, *The Good Priest's Son* (2005) by Reynolds Price, and *A Day at the Beach* (2007) by Helen Schulman.

Fiction after September 11 works to address issues of memory, trauma, and identity particular to the survivors and their families; it also examines how the event impacts the lives of those far from its epicenter through its treatment of personal problems and cultural contexts.

—*Lee Ann Glowzenski*

References

Alvarez, J. (2005, September 11). The writing life. *The Washington Post*, p. BW10.

DeLillo, D. (2001, December). In the ruins of the future. *Harper's Magazine, 303*, 33–40.

DeLillo, D. (2007). *Falling man*. New York: Scribner.

Foer, J. S. (2005). *Extremely loud and incredibly close*. New York: Houghton Mifflin.

Glass, J. (2006, August 21). In the dust that refuses to settle: Writing fiction after 9/11. *Publishers Weekly, 253:* 20–21.

Kalfus, K. (2006). *A disorder peculiar to the country*. New York: Ecco.

Kingsbury, K. (2003). *One Tuesday morning*. Grand Rapids, MI: Zondervan.

Messud, C. (2006). *The emperor's children*. New York: Knopf.

Nissenson, H. (2005). *The days of awe*. Naperville, IL: Sourcebooks Landmark.

O'Neill, J. (2008). *Netherland*. New York: Pantheon Books.

SPOTLIGHT ESSAY/BOOKS: *IN THE SHADOW OF NO TOWERS* BY ART SPIEGELMAN

Awarded a 1992 Pulitzer Prize, *Maus* (1986), Art Spiegelman's two-volume comic book on the Holocaust established comics as serious art. Spiegelman himself referred to the medium as "comix," underscoring the sophisticated ways comic book art juxtaposes (literally, co-mixes or mingles) image and text to make meaning. In its own complex verbal and visual interweaving of past and present, *Maus* follows Artie Spiegelman as he interviews his father about the latter's experiences during World War II, up to and including imprisonment in Auschwitz. With the exception of each volume's front and back covers, the work is drawn and lettered entirely in a black and white. Despite its use of "funny animals," Spiegelman's serious and relentless commitment to historical accuracy is well known. Moreover, as Thomas Doherty (1996) notes, while the imagery in *Maus* is not always understated, "the language and tone of Spiegelman's comic book work is tempered and austere" (p. 78).

In the Shadow of No Towers (2004), Spiegelman's first graphic book project since *Maus*, is, conversely, anything but "tempered and austere." The severity of its critique of the Bush administration's response to 9/11 kept U.S. mainstream presses from publishing the work until 2003, when, as Spiegelman notes with some bitterness, "vigorous criticism [of the current administration] . . . could be contained as part of our business as usual" (Spiegelman, 2004, "Introduction," n.p.). The work's bold aesthetics match its outspoken and outraged content: On opening the huge—even looming—hardback pages, the reader faces an onslaught of primary colors, outsized images, and competing comic strips. Moreover, rather than carefully distinguishing a more serious notion of "comix" from the work of the Sunday funnies, *In the Shadow of No Towers* reinforces those associations, with Spiegelman casting himself in the role of several late nineteenth- and early twentieth-century comic strip characters, and even including seven color-plate reproductions of these turn-of-the-century strips at the end of the work. In fact, *In the Shadow of No Towers* showcases the fundamental elements of comics in order to underscore the unexpected, yet oddly appropriate, ways this apparently un-serious medium enables readers to confront traumatic history. Spiegelman's use of two such elements—namely, space and color—offer a particularly fitting way of approaching the events of September 11.

Readers of *In the Shadow of No Towers* must contend with the undeniable physicality of the work. Composed of 21 hardback pages, which each measure 10 inches by 14-1/2 inches, the book is heavy to pick up and awkward to read. With its black on black covers, it is a dark, imposing, boxlike (even towering) structure. Despite approximating the shape (if not the thickness) of an early twentieth-century broadsheet newspaper, the hardback pages cannot be folded back on themselves to make handling and reading the work easier. Rather than being able to fold the work back at its crease, for example, in order to focus on just one of the several crisscrossing panel sequences on the page, readers are confronted, at least in the first instance, with the whole teeming, 20-inch surface. As a result, the reader contends first, not with words or particular narrative threads, but rather with exploding shapes and colors.

In a move that only comics could accomplish, Spiegelman underscores his own unremitting sense of alarm by embedding huge, if oblique, exclamation points within the tapestry of the page as a whole. Just as in *Maus*, when Spiegelman used the shape of the swastika and the Star of David as a literal backdrop to communicate Anja and Vladek's ideological entrapment in Nazi-controlled Poland, so too does he here use shape to create another layer of meaning through the seemingly chance arrangement of oblong boxes and circles. On first glance, for example, of page one of *In the Shadow of No Towers*, the reader faces an onslaught of rectangles, with one large circle taking up more than a third of the bottom half of the page. If one follows the two central columns of rectangles down instead of across (as the narrative logic of the panel sequences demands) the eye ends at the circle, and a huge exclamation point thus becomes the central, underlying motif. A second, smaller exclamation point presides over the top left corner of the page, with the slightly angled uppercase "I" hovering over the only other circle on the page. And finally, by aligning the slightly askew rectangle in the top right corner with the big circle at the bottom of the page, the reader collaborates with Spiegelman to construct the third exclamation point. Given Spiegelman's interest in encouraging the public to remain alarmed by September 11, rather than sinking back into life as usual, it is telling that he thus involves the reader in the construction of alarm.

In keeping with Spiegelman's call for alarm is his use of color. On the same opening page of the work, we encounter the deep, flat blue of the sky enclosed in television-shaped panels; the canary yellow of the underlying captions invoking the sensationalist reporting of early twentieth-century "yellow journalism"; and finally the dotted orange and red of Spiegelman's computer-generated image of the burning, and here seemingly teetering, North Tower. In the circle at the bottom of the page, we find the colors of what Scott McCloud in *Understanding Comics* (1993) refers to as the "bright primary colors" of a "bright primary world" (p. 187): It would appear to be a page out of a superhero comic book. In offering a brief history of the comic book industry, McCloud notes the introduction of color, commenting: "Color comics hit the newspaper industry like an atomic bomb" (187). Spiegelman's use of arresting colors, on the first page and following, suggests his interest in assaulting the reader with color. In *Maus II* (1992), when Artie's father has died, and he finds himself further alienated from Vladek's history, Artie asks his psychiatrist, a Holocaust survivor, what it felt like to be in Auschwitz. The psychiatrist thinks, and then says suddenly, "BOO!" In using bold colors, Spiegelman doesn't undercut the gravity of September 11; rather, he uses the techniques of comics to enact the experience of alarm to his readers.

What Spiegelman does not want is a world that succumbs to what McCloud refers to as "the dulling effects of newsprint," or, business as usual (p. 188). Thus, in the book's only black and white sequence, we find the following scenario:

"I was walking back to my place on Avenue C last night," a woman at a Tribeca party begins.

"Some guy came from behind me and pulled a knife!"

"He slammed me against a brick wall, grabbed my handbag and ran off!"

"I was, like, soooo relieved! Things are finally getting back to normal!" (Spiegelman, p. 9)

Through a careful and deliberate use of the comic book strategies of shape and color, *No Towers* works hard to keep readers from "getting back to normal."

—*Davida Pines*

References

Doherty, T. (1996). Art Spiegelman's *Maus*: Graphic art and the Holocaust. *American Literature* *68*(1), 69–84.

McCloud, S. (1993). *Understanding comics: The invisible art* . New York: Harper Perennial.

Spiegelman, A. (1986). *Maus: A survivor's tale*. New York: Pantheon Books.

Spiegelman, A. (2004). *In the shadow of no towers*. New York: Viking.

SPOTLIGHT ESSAY/BOOKS: *THE INSISTENCE OF BEAUTY* BY STEPHEN DUNN

Shortly after 9/11, a number of books appeared comprised of writers responding to the tragedy. These included *110 Stories: New York Writes after September 11* (Baer, 2002) and *September 11, 2001: American Writers Respond* (Heyen, 2002). In *Poetry after 9/11: An Anthology of New York Poets* (Johnson & Merians, 2002), Pulitzer Prize winner Stephen Dunn (2004) published the poem "Grudges," a villanelle with a repeating line (and variations of it), that describes men who acted differently than they had felt for years. The "men" Dunn refers to are the terrorists, and the poem is a way of trying to understand the motives behind the attack and the way the terrorist could work on plans of violence for years while seemingly going about a normal life. To make it clear he is referencing 9/11, Dunn mentions Ground Zero early in the poem. Despite what is an apparent sense of bewilderment on the part of the speaker who calls the terrorists men who took flight without any intention of landing, the poem also rhetorically asks who is innocent of holding a grudge or a secret (p. 40). Thus "Grudges" turns back on the speaker and his reader, and we are forced to acknowledge our own irrational fears or prejudices. The poem evokes the complex mixture of emotions that rippled across the country after 9/11, from anger and grief to questions of why the event occurred and what is it that differentiates us from the terrorists.

Despite the power of "Grudges," it was not this poem that became the title piece of Dunn's next book, although it was reprinted there. Instead, the book is named after "The Insistence of Beauty," and this is the superior poem, both aesthetically and philosophically. The poem begins on the day before 9/11, with the speaker oddly admiring what he paradoxically calls the "beauty" of long strands of smoke coming from an industrial site in Newark, New Jersey (p. 86). In this way the speaker initiates what will be, among other things, a meditation on forms of beauty by calling attention to the negative effects of U.S. industrialism (the pollution) while also surprisingly finding beauty within it. The speaker thereby positions himself early on as a critical observer of the United States, but also a lover of it.

The speaker's recognition of the strange beauty of the smoke leads him in the second stanza to look at the attacks on the World Trade Center from the perspective of the terrorists and their supporters. He notes that people from another part of the globe witnessed what they likely considered "gorgeous," an image of the fiery end of the towers that signaled the achievement of their cause (p. 86). Lest the reader assume he sympathizes with the terrorists, however, the speaker follows in the next stanza by speaking of the pull of "revenge" that welled up inside him on watching the broadcasts for hours in a trance (p. 86). In the following stanza he comments on how he came to appreciate what he considers is either the "intensity" or perhaps the "coldness" of the vision of the photographers who produced the pictures that appeared the day after 9/11 (p. 87). Here, Dunn's discussion has moved from the experience of the event itself to an examination of how the event is represented. For the poet this becomes a question of aesthetics and an artist's relationship to, and distance from, his or her subject. Does he himself look at the event with an "intensity" to be admired, or is it rather a cold, clinical point of view?

Deciding what it is that interests him about the photographs leads the speaker to reflect that for years he has resisted clichéd forms of beauty in his work such as images of mountains, the sunset, or the face of a beautiful and famous woman, and yet he now concludes that even those clichés, when viewed properly, might be seen to assume an "edgy place" in our minds (p. 87). Thinking about the representations by the media of 9/11 soon after the event forces the poet to reconsider his relationship to beauty itself, and it is significantly those standard images of beauty often recycled in popular culture (the sunset, etc.) that bring about his reexamination of his art. The speaker decides that the sentimental, which he describes as "sloppy cousin" to beauty, deserves reconsideration; he rhetorically asks whether even a tear fails to merit closer scrutiny (p. 87).

To illustrate the newfound appreciation for the sentimental he has acquired, the speaker relates how, after the event, he repeated a story about Ground Zero to everyone he encountered. In the story, a firefighter hid in the rubble of the World Trade Center so that his dog, who was "dispirited" at not finding anyone, could at least aid him (p. 87). About retelling this story, the speaker admits that rather than do this for the sake of community or beauty, he did it for himself, and yet very quickly it took on a "rhythm" and what he terms a "frame" (p. 87). The honesty here, that the speaker concedes he was trying to console himself more than making an altruistic attempt to comfort those around him, is remarkable. The repetition of the story about the dog, despite the speaker's original intentions, produces art. It is thus impossible for the speaker not to turn his experience, and therefore his understanding of the world as he comprehends it through popular culture, into an aesthetic object, presumably a poem in that it had a "rhythm" and a form that produced its "frame." "The Insistence of Beauty" ends here, and the reader realizes that the poem operates as a critique of itself and its poet's relationship to 9/11 in his desire to render the event as an art object.

But, this is a choice the speaker clearly makes self-consciously. Slavoj Žižek (1990), in his widely influential book, *The Sublime Object of Ideology*, revises Marx's famous dictum that ideology can be defined as, we do not perceive it, but we are doing it (p. 28). Žižek says that in our age the point is rather, we know what we are doing, but we are doing it anyway (p. 33). Žižek notes that although we may use cynicism in an attempt to distance ourselves from our complicity in the machinery of ideology, we are still participating nevertheless (p. 33). The speaker of Dunn's poem recognizes that he is part of a larger political system and that forms of beauty are culturally rooted. His ability to identify beauty in the smokestacks of Newark is offset by the recognition that those same smokestacks might look like symbols of U.S. industrial might and political hegemony to the terrorists. This of course does not excuse for the speaker the violent actions of the terrorists, but he does what he can to make something positive come out of the tragedy by allowing it to compel him to reconsider nothing less than his relationship to art and the world around him.

—*Joe Moffett*

References

Baer, U. (2002). *110 stories: New York writes after September 11*. New York: New York University Press.

Dunn, S. (2004). *The insistence of beauty.* New York: W.W. Norton.

Heyen, W. (Ed.). (2002). *September 11, 2001: American writers respond.* Silver Springs, MD: Etruscan Press.

Johnson, D. L., & Merians, V. (Eds.). (2002). *Poetry after 9/11: An anthology of New York poets.*
        Hoboken, NJ: Melville House.
Žižek, S. (1990). *The sublime object of ideology.* London: Verso.

SPOTLIGHT ESSAY/BOOKS: MEMORIAL TEXTS

In the days after September 11, the popular press, magazines, newspapers, and the daily television news were dominated by photos of the events, of horrific images of falling individuals, victims endeavoring an escape, rescue workers digging through the wreckage, and the suffering survivors reeling from the experience.

Relatively quickly, these images were collected in books aimed at memorializing the attacks, including the Twin Towers, the victims on all three planes, the crash sites, and the rescue and recovery efforts. Such books raised contradictory responses in readers. They offered a way to remember, understand, commemorate, and memorialize the trauma of September 11. At the same time, however, the shock and brusque reality of the images seemed somehow inappropriate, as if the reader was "looking on" as an observer of the suffering and horror. As Marianne Hirsch (2002) describes it, the photograph has emerged as "the most evocative medium in our attempts to deal with the aftermath of September 11" (p. 1).

Among the plethora of memorial texts published in the wake of September 11, a handful became widely recognized visual records of the events: *One Nation: America Remembers September 11, 2001* (Life Magazine, 2001); *New York September 11* (Halberstam, 2001); *America's Heroes* (Sports, 2001); *September 11, 2001: A Record of Tragedy, Heroism and Hope* (New York Magazine, 2001); *September 11: A Testimony* (Reuters, 2001); and *Here is New York: A Democracy of Photographs* (Peress, Shuland, Traub, & George, 2002). Frequently produced through collaborations between photographers and magazine publishers, the 9/11 memorial books offer a unique contribution to the literature of September 11.

One of the most popular memorial books, *One Nation: America Remembers September 11, 2001*, opens with an introduction by then New York City Mayor Rudolph Giuliani. Edited and distributed by *Life* magazine, the text is peppered with individual stories as well as poignant photographs of the fallen and the survivors. More specifically, the book follows an evacuee of the Trade Centers on his way to safety out of the danger of the towers giving readers a narrative of escape to follow through the book's pages.

New York September 11 was released by Magnum Photographers and author David Halberstam. Vacillating between black-and-white and vivid color photography, esteemed Magnum photographers provide a more aesthetic view of the traumatic occurrences that took place on 9/11. Critics and reviewers have called the "beauty" of the pictures a "haunting tribute" to the day, alluding, in their comments, to the complex sentiments surrounding the creation of art based on tragedy ("Nonfiction Notes," para. 8).

America's Heroes begins its focus around the individual remembrance of the heroes of both the Twin Towers and also United Flight 93, which crashed in Shanksville, Pennsylvania. The book emphasizes the modern day, post-9/11 hero who was embodied in the firefighters, police officers, rescue workers, and regular citizens who helped to save countless would-be casualties on September 11. Brimful with pictures, the book calls itself a tribute to those who risked and gave their lives to save those of others.

Two books—*September 11, 2001: A Record of Tragedy, Heroism and Hope*, by the editors of *New York Magazine*, and *September 11: A Testimony*, by the staff of Reuters—began as compilations of photographs reproduced to document different perspectives of the events. The books ultimately emerged as photojournalistic accounts with charitable intentions, advertising their texts as sponsoring several nonprofit organizations dedicated to the victims and their families.

Finally, *Here is New York: A Democracy of Photographs* is a record of an exhibition held outside of an empty store in SoHo close to Ground Zero. *New Yorker* photographer Gilles Peress and fellow collaborator, Michael Shulan, joined forces to create a living exhibition out of the photographs submitted by ordinary citizens. The exhibition gained fame and acclaim, eventually leading to the collection of the photos in a hard copy book.

Perhaps in an attempt to address the controversy surrounding the publication of photographs that documented the horrific events of September 11, some publishing houses, such as Norton, offered a lump sum donation after the attacks for works sold in connection to the tragedy, while other houses, such as Abrams, donated $8 for each copy of *September 11, 2001: New York Attacked* to charitable causes. Little, Brown donated all 10 percent of its profit from *One Nation: America Remembers September 11, 2001*. However, in the face of a struggling economy, publishing donations gradually waned along with their impending profit margins (Kerwin, 2001).

Several other genres of memorial texts were published after September 11. Books such as *Fireboat* (2005), by Maira Kalman, and *New York's Bravest* (2002), by Mary Pope Osborne, both commemorate 9/11 and help teachers to explain a difficult topic to children. Likewise, the Library of Congress began collecting more than five terabytes of 9/11 content, including photographic memorials, textual accounts, and information, on a web archive of September 11 with the focus on information and education. In a similar vein, the American Folklife Center sponsored "The September 11, 2001, Documentary Project," engendering a national video-audio response to the events. While the experience of looking at images of September 11 could be emotional, readers found solace, understanding, and an opportunity to remember in the range of memorial texts published after the attacks.

—*Elizabeth Spies*

References

Editors of New York Magazine. (2001). *September 11, 2001: A record of tragedy, heroism, and hope*. New York: Harry N. Abrams.

Halberstam, D. (2001). *New York September 11*. New York: powerHouse Books.

Hirsch, M. (2002, January 25). The day time stopped. *Chronicle Review*, p. B11.

Kerwin, A. M. (2001, September 17). Print proves mettle. *Advertising Age.* Retrieved from
    http://adage.com

Life Magazine. (2001). *One nation: America remembers September 11.* Boston: Little, Brown
    and Company.

Nonfiction Notes. (2001, December 17). *Publishers Weekly.* Retrieved from http://
    stage.publishersweekly.com

Peress, G., Shulan, M., Traub, C., & George, A. R. (Eds.). (2002). *Here is New York: A democ-
    racy of photographs.* Zurich: Scalo.

Sports Publishing, Inc. (2001). *America's heroes.* Champaign, IL: Author.

Staff of Reuters. (2001). *September 11: A testimony.* New York: Reuters Prentice Hall.

SPOTLIGHT ESSAY/BOOKS: *THE TERROR DREAM* BY SUSAN FALUDI

In *The Terror Dream: Fear and Fantasy in Post-9/11 America*, cultural commentator
Susan Faludi (2007) examines the U.S. response to the terrorist attacks on September 11.
In her analysis, Faludi suggests that the way Americans, and the American media,
responded to 9/11 provides insight into deep cultural beliefs about U.S. ideology,
government, and the roles of men and women. In the first part of the book, Faludi
examines media relevant to 9/11 itself, specifically how September 11 and its aftermath
were characterized in ways that reflect certain ideas about U.S. life. In part two, Faludi
argues the narratives present in media coverage about 9/11 emerge from historical
precedent in two-and-a-half centuries of captivity narratives and rescue myths created
in response to threats on the safety of the nation's citizens.

In her analysis of how the story of 9/11 was told in prominent media outlets
by government officials, pundits, and journalists, Faludi argues that a myth of
September 11—a myth of a heroic battle of strong men fighting for meek women
against the ominous threat of Al Qaeda—eclipses the myriad stories that actually took
place on that day and afterward. Throughout the book, Faludi targets the media coverage of 9/11 and post-9/11 related content. She argues, for example, that the media
framed September 11 as a time of grieving widows and courageous firefighters and
points out that such gender representations did not hold up in real life. Many of the
9/11 widows became powerful advocates for political action after the attacks. The
"Jersey Girls," a group of women whose husbands had died in the Twin Towers, played
a pivotal role in the 9/11 Commission that investigated, and reported on, the events
surrounding the attacks. Moreover, it was not just men who participated in the search
and recovery effort at Ground Zero. Women firefighters, police officers, and rescue
workers were also present. Despite these facts, women "heroes" were not the focus of
9/11 media coverage. Instead, Faludi claims, women were cast in traditional female roles
as wives and mothers who longed to give up their careers, nest at home, and procreate.

The Terror Dream is filled with facts about contemporary culture as well as historical
accounts of captivity narratives, and Faludi offers many examples—from early America
to Tom Cruise's movie *War of the Worlds* (2005)—to support her argument. More

specifically, *The Terror Dream* considers how Thomas Burnett, Jeremy Glick, and Mark Bingham became the heroes of Flight 93, how Jessica Lynch's story was manipulated as army propaganda, and what the historical examples of Mary Rowlandson, the Salem witch trials, and Cynthia Ann Parker have in common with these 9/11 narratives. For Faludi, the treatment of Cora and Alice Monroe by James Fenimore Cooper in *The Last of the Mohicans* (1826) is as shocking as Ann Coulter calling the Jersey Girls, a group of activist widows who were essentially responsible for creating the 9/11 commission, "'self-obsessed women' who were 'reveling in their status as celebrities' ... 'witches' and 'harpies' who were 'enjoying their husbands' deaths" (p. 113).

Faludi also argues that a particular characterization of September 11 persisted in years following the attacks. She states, "By mid-2007, long after the nation had passed the five-year-anniversary mark of the attacks, we were still sleepwalking. Virtually no film, television drama, play, or novel on 9/11 had begun to plumb what the trauma meant for our national psyche" (p. 2). Faludi's ultimate point is that instead of recognizing our vulnerability as a nation, fiction and nonfiction alike has sought to cover our weaknesses with the infallible tale of America as masculine savior. "In the aftermath of the attacks," she writes, "the cultural troika of media, entertainment, and advertising declared the post-9/11 age an era of neo-fifties nuclear family 'togetherness,' re-domesticated femininity, and reconstituted Cold Warrior manhood" (p. 3). Rather than focus on the fact that the country's financial (World Trade Center) and military (Pentagon) power centers had been directly attacked by the terrorists, the media created a narrative focused on a different story all together: One in which the ultimate victims of the attacks were female—epitomized by the image of the 9/11 widows—and the saviors were male—as captured in the image of the iconic firefighters.

In *The Terror Dream*, Susan Faludi is skeptical of the direction U.S. culture moved in after September 11, but is hopeful that, through an uncovering of the invincibility myth we will find agency as citizens and look beyond gender as the paradigm for how to live in a post-9/11 world. Recognizing the cultural trends that reinforce that myth is just the first step in awakening from what she calls "the terror dream."

—*Julia Kaziewicz*

Reference

Faludi, S. (2007). *The terror dream: Fear and fantasy in post-9/11 America*. New York: Metropolitan Books.

SPOTLIGHT ESSAY/BOOKS: *WINDOWS ON THE WORLD* BY FRÉDÉRIC BEIGBEDER

Frédéric Beigbeder's *Windows on the World* (2004) is currently the only fiction text that attempts to reproduce the actual experiences of those who were trapped inside the World Trade Center on the morning of September 11, 2001. Written in 2004 by a French author who acts as one of the novel's two narrators, *Windows on the World* juxtaposes the story of Beigbeder himself attempting to write a novel about 9/11 with a fictional character, Carthew Yorston, who is stuck in the restaurant Windows on the World with his two sons on the morning that the Twin Towers were attacked. Beigbeder simulates the Americans' experience of dining at Windows on the World atop the North Tower by eating breakfast every morning at the top of the Tour Montparnasse in Paris.

As the reader becomes thoroughly engaged with Carthew's story, Beigbeder also personally connects himself to the narrative with his claim that "Carthew Yourston was my grandmother's family name. Take out a 'u' and you have Carthew Yorston, a fictional character" (p. 299). One may question why Beigbeder made this choice in name for his brother narrator. It is a small yet significant detail that aligns Beigbeder with the victims of 9/11, and, perhaps, gives him a certain right to tell the story that he feels is so necessary to tell. Toward the end of his novel, he furthers his claim: "If you go back eight generations, all white Americans are Europeans. We are the same: even if we are not all Americans, our problems are theirs, and theirs are ours" (p. 296).

Windows on the World is unique in its format as well its narrative. It begins with, essentially, the end. Beigbeder writes as his first line: "You know how it ends: Everybody dies" (p. 1). This immediate declaration from the narrator accomplishes two things: First, it upsets the temporality of the novel from the very beginning. Second, it creates a sort of intimacy between the reader and the narrator by this shared secret—this knowledge—that Carthew lacks. These ideas of intimacy and temporality are interwoven throughout the novel and never allow the reader to forget that this is a novel about a specific time, a specific event, an event with which we should be intimately acquainted. He furthers this by writing "it is more appalling still to allow you to imagine what became of them [the victims]" (p. 272). Beigbeder's allowance to his readers is also a chance for their own agency (to imagine), an allowance that creates a new type of intimacy that is no longer based on what is shared but what is not shared. This intimacy with the events of 9/11 also occurs on a corporeal level with the exchange of bodily fluids, as Beigbeder states "New Yorkers of every age, creed, race, and social class waited patiently in a line that stretched four blocks just to make an appointment to donate blood" (p. 272).

To perhaps further the credibility of his novel, Beigbeder also takes advantage of the post-9/11 obsession with "real time." The chapter titles in *Windows on the World* are consecutive minutes, from 8:30 to 10:29 a.m. Describing the experience within the towers, Beigbeder states: "Hell lasts an hour and three quarters. As does this book" (p. 6). This temporal progression forbids the reader to remain comfortable within the text. After nearly every page, there is a shift plot, setting, and/or narrator. As the novel advances, Beigbeder transcends time by taking a Concorde flight from Paris to New York City; the author literally travels through time by landing in New York before leaving France. He uses this as an escape mechanism: His girlfriend has broken up with him, but in taking the Concorde he lands in New York before his heart has been broken. Yet just as we cannot turn back the clock to prevent 9/11, it is too late for Carthew to decide not to take his sons to Windows on the World. The author puts himself in a position of power by overcoming the one force that no other characters (or, for that matter, Americans) can.

The reader of *Windows on the World* does not always know from the outset of a chapter who, where, or when the narrator is. Within each chapter, both narrators vacillate between their present moment and flashbacks. For Beigbeder, these flashbacks are remembrances; for Carthew, they are forays into his glory days and shameful past. These flashbacks allow the reader to create identities for the characters in the novel. Those trapped inside the Windows on the World restaurant are often referred to merely by their appearances ("the woman in the Ralph Lauren suit") to perhaps dichotomous ends. It could first be an attempt to "everyman-ize" the events of 9/11. But these descriptions could also be a statement as to what has become salient to our identity formation.

Windows on the World blurs the line between fiction and nonfiction. Beigbeder even tells of his visit to Paul Virilio's exhibit *Unknown Quantity*, an exhibit that actually took place. The novel also comments on the U.S. obsession with visual culture: "It is a recent phenomenon: we call it globalization, but its real name is television" (p. 111). In an interview, Beigbeder claims that his "role is not to embellish reality." He states: "My goal in writing . . . was to humanize, to return to something human inside that simulacrum . . . we need someone to denounce the simulacrum but we also need sometimes to humanize it. And that is the novelist's role" (Beigbeder, 2006). Beigbeder's reflection makes clear his intent in writing *Windows on the World*—to bring readers into the real (corporal, human) post-9/11 world.

—Justine Lutzel

References

Beigbeder, F. (2004). *Windows on the world*. New York: Miramax Books.
Beigbeder, F. (2006, December). Interview with Alain-Philippe Durand. Paris.

SPOTLIGHT ESSAY/BOOKS: *THE WRITING ON THE WALL* BY LYNNE SHARON SCHWARTZ

Lynne Sharon Schwartz's 2005 novel, *The Writing on the Wall*, is but one example of how literature has been employed as a vehicle for understanding the philosophical questions raised by 9/11. Schwartz's novel is among other fictional stories that use 9/11 as a starting point and then make meaning of the terrorist attacks and their consequences through their own narrative trajectories. As forms of commentary, novels are particularly useful in that they provide imaginings through which we can understand our own reality. Moreover, the primacy of the written word in literature gives a novelist the room to explore and develop complex ideas and provides the reader with time to pause in order to grasp their complexity. As an existential meditation on 9/11, Lynne Sharon Schwartz's novel capitalizes on and exemplifies such creative advantages.

The Writing on the Wall takes up two central issues, which are communicated in two opening quotations that frame the novel and speak to its philosophical purpose: to emphasize the importance of personal history and expose the breakdown of language in the context of 9/11. First, Schwartz uses her protagonist's history to demonstrate the significance of one's past in experiencing one's present. Second, her protagonist's personal struggle to find the right words with which to understand 9/11 is, essentially, Schwartz's own rumination on the problematic nature of language in the wake of tragedy. Not only does Schwartz explore these issues through a fictional story line, but she also takes advantage of the novel's form to, ironically, use her words to delve more deeply into why words fail.

The novel's general function is communicated by way of a quote from Celia Streng, which is an expression of anxiety over the presumption that the way individuals experienced 9/11 was fairly uniform. The task Schwartz takes on is to craft a complex individual experience to show that, as Streng put it, "the people who endured the transforming effects of that day were not blank slates ready to be imprinted with the same images. They brought to that moment all the events of their lives until then, and the new events, by their very force, called forth earlier shocks and reconfigured them in a new context" (Melnick, 2009). Schwartz gives shape to Streng's words by inventing the story of Renata, an intentionally emotionally isolated New York City linguist obsessed with language. The story line follows Renata from the morning of September 11, 2001, and into the months that followed. Through her process of coping, Renata eventually moves forward in unexpected and uncharacteristic ways. The primary way she resolves her questions about how to proceed with her life is to make human connections she was loathe to make before 9/11 because of her difficult history—involving abuse, unwanted pregnancy, and the loss of her twin sister. Formerly terrified of needing others because of her past, 9/11 prompts Renata to resolve her past by entering into deeper relationships, forging new ones, and resolving old ones. Renata's is, at its heart, an unlikely story of personal progress prompted, not hindered, by 9/11.

Schwartz explores how individual histories produce a multitude of diverse 9/11 experiences by constantly delving into Renata's past through a series of flashbacks throughout the book. The linear story line is frequently interrupted by flashbacks that jump throughout time to give insight into why Renata experiences 9/11 as she does. In this way, Schwartz implicitly makes a philosophical case that the past is part of the present by enmeshing Renata's history in the present narrative. In addition, she does so in ways that show how intimately her past experiences are connected to her current one. Specifically, the exploration into Renata's tumultuous childhood and early adult years explains her personal limitations and makes her ability to overcome them as a result of 9/11 nothing short of miraculous. By showing how Renata came to be the person she was on 9/11, and how her past colored her experience that day and her life thereafter, Schwartz reminds us how psychologically influential personal histories are.

The second quote that opens the novel is used more symbolically to establish its central theme: language. Several lines selected from *American Ground*, William Langewiesche's book documenting the cleanup efforts at Ground Zero, draw attention to the literal importance of paper as part of the destruction of the World Trade Center. By Langewiesche's account, paper, a once innocuous entity, was a culprit in fueling the fires that caused the towers to collapse. In this way, as a symbol, paper acquired new meaning in the wake of 9/11. In *The Writing on the Wall*, this is shown to be true of language as well. That paper and words are often counterparts allows for a link between Langewiesche's testimony and Schwartz's message; just as the events of 9/11 transformed the meaning and function paper, so did they alter the meaning and function of words. As evidenced by its title and plot, the novel primarily engages the relationship between language and 9/11. The term "paperwork" in the opening quote can be read as being symbolic of language—a once taken for granted resource that has been given new significance. With this framework in place, the novel proceeds to engage the transformation and complexities of language in the face of tragedy and uncertainty.

Mastering language is both Renata's livelihood and obsessive hobby. As a translator, she is constantly negotiating the origins of words and the inconsistencies of their meanings across languages. She is also a collector of words, jotting things down that she finds meaningful and cataloguing them in great detail. But, in the wake of 9/11, words become her necessary tool for understanding the attacks and *The Writing on the Wall* shows them to be much more difficult to employ in this new context. Words are necessary, the novel tells us through Renata's struggle to use them, but hard to find—perpetuating the "there are no words" sentiment expressed by many, beginning with disbelieving journalists' live reports of the collapse of the Towers. What Renata discovers during the course of the novel is that 9/11 rendered language unstable and problematic, making her accumulation and examination of words all the more compulsive and frustrating—and all the more important.

Renata's attitude toward and treatment of language show her to literally be attempting to decipher the meaning of words in order to understand the meaning of her post-9/11 life, assuming that meaning exists somewhere but is yet to be discovered. Similarly, creative works in popular culture—this novel included—attempt to do symbolically through fictional stories. The difference, however, is that the very nature of *creative* works in popular culture indicates that they use language and stories to *make* meaning, with the assumption that it is *not* preexisting nor waiting to be found.

The person Renata has become on September 11, 2001, is one who attempts to cope through finding "the right words." But it is through accessing her preexisting past that she forms human bonds that will allow her to move forward. Her unsuccessful search for words may be interpreted as a way of saying that it is through our own history and connections with others, not language, that we cope with tragedy—in this case, 9/11.

—*Kathryn Palmer*

References

Melnick, J. (2009). *9/11 Culture*. West Sussex: Wiley-Blackwell, p. 154.
Schwartz, L. A. (2005). *The writing on the wall*. New York: Counterpoint.

Chapter 4

TELEVISION

INTRODUCTION: TELEVISION AND SEPTEMBER 11, 2001

For many people, the September 11 attacks took place on TV. People who were in the middle of watching the network morning shows found the programs interrupted by reports of a plane crashing into one of the Twin Towers. People driving to work, who heard reports on the radio, arrived at their destination and gathered with others around whatever television was available. As one woman remembers about that morning, "Someone brought a small TV out of a car—it seemed to come out of nowhere—and it was balanced above a few cubicles. We gathered around to watch as events unfolded" (Dera, 2007, para. 6). As the morning went on, Americans as well as people around the world remained glued to their TV at work, home, schools, restaurants, and any other place a television was available.

The close connection between September 11 and television is not surprising. Since its inception, TV has served as a gathering place during difficult historic moments, including the assassination of President John F. Kennedy, the explosion of the Space Shuttle *Challenger*, the shootings at Columbine or the bombing of the Oklahoma City Federal Building. Television is not just a medium through which real, historic events are watched, however. It is also a powerful medium that shapes the way viewers understand those moments. As soon as the 9/11 attacks started, TV reporters began to shape narratives that would eventually tell a common story about what took place on that tragic day. Television viewers would learn that narrative, but they would also find that TV became a medium through which they could engage in understanding how the nation changed after 9/11.

Television programming addresses aspects of our lives and culture in its fictional narratives, documentaries, and talk shows. In its unique role in American life, television mirrors—and challenges—aspects of our cultural norms, politics, and societal practice. Through its programming, television provides an outlet for viewers to engage in processing the hopes, issues, fears, and dreams of the nation. As a result, significant events that impact our nation, such as the attacks on September 11, alter the television landscape and shape the way we understand such events. From early televised 9/11 benefit programs, to TV documentaries and specials, the repercussions of the attacks gradually began to appear in all kinds of TV programming. Eventually, new types of television shows would appear on network and cable channels across the country registering a post-9/11 world in both fact and fiction.

Television's Initial Response

Within minutes of the terrorist attacks on September 11, 2001, cable and network channels provided nonstop television news coverage of the unfolding events in a commercial-free format. Regularly scheduled television shows were quickly suspended while news gatherers and reporters took over the programming on most channels. Responding in part to viewers' need to know what had happened and how the country was reacting, television offered a way for people around the world to obtain information, see images, and begin to process the shocking events.

Partly because of viewer fatigue from the sobering images in New York, Washington, D.C., and Pennsylvania, and partly in an effort to return to a sense of normalcy, within a week the networks began to transition back to their regular broadcast schedules. There were some notable alterations, however. Similar to the choices made by Hollywood executives regarding the release of certain films, television executives also cancelled planned television airings of movies deemed insensitive in the wake of the terrorist attacks. For example, the terrorist film, *The Siege* (1998), the violent movie, *Lethal Weapon* (1987), and the New York City destroyer film, *King Kong* (1933), were replaced with films considered less disturbing to audiences, such as *Look Who's Talking* (2005), *Grease* (1978), and *Jaws* (1975) (Spigel, 2004). A made-for-TV terrorist movie, originally titled *Ground Zero* and slated to air in the fall of 2001, was shelved by NBC until 2003 and released under the name *Critical Assembly* (Erickson, 2003). In addition, a scene with an exploding airplane was edited out of an episode of Fox's *24* (2001–2010); an episode of CBS's *The Agency* (2001–2003), which featured an anthrax attack was cancelled; and NBC's *UC: Undercover* (2001–2002) eliminated a script with a terrorist plot (Spigel, 2004). In general, the television industry hoped to provide light, escapist entertainment as an alternative to the aftermath of the terrorist attacks being covered on news programming (Jones & Dionisopoulos, 2004).

Despite these programming changes and the apparent need among audiences for lighter fare, television comedy immediately began to reflect the new post-9/11 environment. In general, out of respect for the victims, survivors, and rescue workers still in the heartbreaking process of recovering and identifying those who had been lost in the attacks, it was not seen as appropriate to make jokes, laugh, or find humor in the face of such tragedy. Late-night television comedy shows stopped airing the day of the attacks and cautiously resumed about a week later. One of the first late-night talk shows to start up again, *Late Night with David Letterman* began with Letterman's emotional speech praising New York City Mayor Rudolph Giuliani and reflecting

---

WORLD WRESTLING ENTERTAINMENT'S *SMACKDOWN*

World Wrestling Entertainment (WWE)'s *SmackDown*'s scheduled September 11 program was canceled after the attacks. It aired instead on Thursday, September 13 (WWE, 2001) and began with a patriotic speech given by Vince McMahon to what he described as "the first public assembly of its size since the tragedy of Tuesday." Throughout the newly scripted program, wrestlers voiced their reactions to the attack. More than 12,000 spectators attended the special live event, which was held in Houston.

—*Amy M. Damico*

Reference

WWE *SmackDown* (WWE). (2001, September 13). [Television program]. Clip retrieved from YouTube, June 9, 2009, from http://www.youtube.com/watch?v=XFU0kehteWE

---

on the terrible circumstances with which New Yorkers were currently faced. Other comedic talk show hosts followed suit, replacing their opening monologues with serious, heartfelt speeches. In a similar way, the first broadcast of *Saturday Night Live* (*SNL*) after the attacks aired on September 29 and featured members of the New York City Fire Department (FDNY) and Mayor Giuliani. Directly acknowledging the difficulties of embracing comedy in the wake of tragedy, *SNL* producer Lorne Michaels asked the Mayor if it was okay to be funny. Giuliani replied, "Why start now," suggesting that yes, it was okay to laugh (McCarthy-Miller, 2001). When comedians ventured into humorous presentations, initial jokes were "benign, non-hostile, and solidarity-building" (Kuipers, 2005, p. 74).

Celebrity appearances on television also reflected the somber state of the nation and celebrity participation in the first televised events after September 11 focused on themes of national unity rather than the usual emphasis on self-promotion or gossip. For example, on September 21, 2001, the major television networks collaborated to broadcast *America: A Tribute to Heroes* (2001), a two-hour telethon where celebrities raised money for victims' families. This special was telecast live from New York City, Los Angeles, and London on more than 320 national broadcast stations and was one of the most watched programs of the year (Spigel, 2004). *America* featured a wide variety of celebrities including musicians, singers, actors, and athletes both performing and answering phones. In between performances, celebrities would share stories of those who died or risked their lives on September 11. The following month, a number of musicians participated in The Concert for New York, a live 9/11 charity performance at Madison Square Garden that was broadcast on VH-1 and featured a number of rescue workers who reflected on lost loved ones and introduced the musical performances.

While celebrities would play a role in other fundraising and memorial events, the 53rd Annual Emmy Awards ceremony, usually an anticipated event in Hollywood and on the networks, was canceled twice because Hollywood was reluctant to flaunt its usual star-studded glamour during such a difficult time. The ceremony finally aired on November 4 with a theme of national unity prominently displayed through images of the U.S. flag, the Statue of Liberty, and historic footage of events such as the Civil Rights movement. Themes of patriotism were apparent throughout the show, from Ellen DeGeneres's monologue to a montage of celebrities entertaining U.S. troops during wartime (Spigel, 2004).

The other widely viewed awards program, *The 2002 Academy Awards*, carried on as planned in March. During the ceremony actor and writer Woody Allen, whose films are known for their celebration of New York City and who had never before accepted an invitation to the Academy Awards, performed a comedy routine and then introduced a montage of film clips from films shot in New York City. Allen's presence and participation helped mark, and begin to memorialize, the World Trade Center attacks ("Oscar-Shy Allen's NY Tribute," 2002). Later in the program, actor Kevin Spacey invited people to stand in silence for those who died on September 11. However, despite these program additions, the nation may have still been reluctant to view the Hollywood spectacle; viewership of the awards show was the lowest since 1997 ("Disappointing U.S. Oscar Ratings," 2002).

Initial Integration of September 11 into Television Narratives

When television networks returned to their regularly scheduled entertainment programming, a number of shows had undergone changes to reflect the post-9/11 environment, including the altered New York City landscape. The initial changes made by some producers were simple, such as removing the images of the World Trade Center towers from the opening of HBO's hit series *Sex and the City* (1998–2004). Other responses were more involved such as the special episode of *The West Wing* (1999–2006), written and produced within three weeks of the attacks. Like filmmakers, television producers were challenged with how to address the terrorist attacks in their programs, particularly those programs that took place in New York.

For one program, the terrorist attacks were purposefully and quickly integrated into the story narratives. The rescue worker drama *Third Watch* (1999–2005), which took place in New York City, made quick alterations to its content. Such changes were made, at least in part, because many rescue workers who participated in the production of *Third Watch*—in minor speaking roles, as extras, or as technical advisors— were killed in the attacks (Collins, 2001). *Third Watch*'s most immediate response to 9/11 was to edit two of the five episodes set to air for the fall 2001 season to eliminate a story line focusing on an Arab American store keeper who shoots and kills an African American shoplifter (Owen, 2001).

In addition to these changes, three new episodes of the show were crafted to address the World Trade Center disaster specifically. The first episode was a two-hour tribute that highlighted the work of firefighters, police officers, and EMTs through interviews and news footage. This documentary episode, titled "In Their Own Words," progressed chronologically through the hours of September 11 using images and witness accounts that are gritty and unpolished. The second specially produced *Third Watch* episode, titled "September 10," depicts the lives of *Third Watch* characters on the day before the tragedy, while the third episode, "After Time," focuses on the characters days after the attacks. Reviews for the programs were positive, highlighting how well *Third Watch* dealt with and explored the psychological and emotional effects of trauma (James, 2001). The executive producer of *Third Watch*, John Wells, acknowledged at the time that it was difficult to remain true to the program's premise while not exploiting program content. Wells hoped that the three-episode arc of *Third Watch* would highlight the courage and dedication of rescue workers (Owen, 2001).

In the weeks and months following the attacks, other television programs began to integrate references to subject matter related to September 11, including the newly created Department of Homeland Security, terrorism, rescue workers, and loss into their narratives. For example, *N.Y.P.D. Blue* (1993–2005) added two newly written scenes into an existing script, and the PAX drama *Doc* (2001–2004) crafted an episode about a firefighter who made it out of the World Trade Center with survivor's guilt (James, 2001). Additionally, *South Park*'s (1997 to present) November 2001 episode titled "Osama bin Laden Has Farty Pants" is an ironic satire where the South Park characters visit Afghanistan, meet Afghan children, and eventually kill bin Laden. Special episodes of programs also began to address the events of September 11 head on. An *Ally McBeal* (1997–2002) episode, for example, referred to two lawyers killed in the terrorist attacks; a legal case tried on *Judging Amy* (1999–2005) addressed the question of custody over a child whose mother died in the World Trade Center; and *Without a Trace* (2002–2009) produced three episodes that centered their missing person cases around September 11-oriented narratives. As television adjusted to post-9/11 life, September 11 was woven into the experiences of television characters, rather than being the focus of stand-alone episodes.

Television about 9/11: Memorials, Tributes, and Documentaries

After the attacks, network and cable television producers began producing memorials, tributes, and documentaries that addressed aspects of September 11. These nonfiction programs included footage of the day's events, interviews with rescue workers, survivors and victims' families, and overviews of historical events leading up to the attacks. While some programs focused on one particular theme, for example the actions of rescue workers on September 11, other programs discussed September 11 from several perspectives: rescue workers at the attack sites, timeline of events, interviews with witnesses, and memorializing the lives of the missing.

One of the first nonfiction television shows to be aired after September 11 was *World Trade Center: In Memoriam* (2001), which was released in October 2001. This piece, part of the History Channel's *Modern Marvels* series, explored the construction of the World Trade Center and had just been completed when the towers were attacked. Originally scheduled to air in December 2001, History Channel Executive Vice President Abbe Raven moved up the air date with a few conditions: There would be no commercials during its broadcast, no scenes of the World Trade Center (WTC) destruction would be added, and family members of those interviewed in the program who were missing would be informed about the show's release (Salamon, 2001). Minor edits were made to the program to acknowledge the current state of the site. *World Trade Center* was one of the network's highest rated programs, attracting 2.8 million viewers and suggesting that Americans wanted to learn about the Twin Towers' history and reflect upon its significance in American culture.

By the first anniversary of September 11, many television tributes, memorials, and documentaries had been produced; a number of them aired on or around September 11, 2002. For example, HBO produced a documentary titled *In Memoriam—New York City 9/11/01* (2002), which memorialized those killed in the attacks and gave an overview of the day's events; CNN crafted *CNN Tribute: America Remembers* (2002), which intersperses journalists' recollections of 9/11 with footage of the events; and PBS's *Frontline* series created a program titled "Faith and Doubt at Ground Zero" (2002), which examined how the events of September 11 impacted people's beliefs. The History Channel produced *Ground Zero America* (2002) about news coverage of the events, and *First Response* (2002) about the successes and failures of emergency procedures.

On September 11, 2002, ABC, NBC, CBS, and FOX altered their daytime schedules to provide all-day, limited commercial coverage of memorial events taking place in New York, Washington D.C., and Pennsylvania. Evening programs also focused on the anniversary. The FOX documentary *9/11: The Day America Changed* (2002), for example, aired without commercials; CBS produced a special episode of *60 Minutes* that was followed by the film *9/11* (2002); NBC broadcast *Concert for America* (2002) that featured a variety of musical artists offering a performance program as an alternative to more sober programming; and ABC produced *Report from Ground Zero* (2002), which featured interviews with rescuers, survivors, and witnesses (McDonough, 2002). A number of cable networks produced special programs as well. For example, the Discovery Channel's *Portraits of Grief* (2002) offered viewers a television version of the *New York Times'* profiles of people killed in the attacks; home movies and photos were used in the program to celebrate the lives of several individuals who died on September 11.

In the months and years following the attacks, as more research was completed and made available, a number of television documentaries were produced, aired, and made available for purchase on commercial Web sites. In addition to those aired, a number of documentaries and memorials were produced directly for the DVD market. Some documentaries, such as *The Road to 9/11* (2006) and *Inside 9/11* (2006), provide overall narratives of events leading up to and briefly following the attacks on September 11. Information for these documentaries was culled from *The 9/11 Commission Report*, government documents, and interviews with officials, and families of victims. Other documentaries integrated citizen-generated content. *102 Minutes That*

Changed America (2008), for example, a narrative of New York after the first plane hit the World Trade Center, is told through real images New Yorkers captured with their cameras, cell phones, and video recording devices on the day of the attacks.

Other television programs, such as *New York Firefighters: The Brotherhood of 9/11* (2002), *Fireboats of 9/11* (2003), and *Brothers in Blue* (2003), focused on 9/11 rescue efforts and operations. A number of documentaries such as *The World Trade Center: The Rise and Fall of an American Icon* (2002), *Why the Towers Fell* (2002), *Building on Ground Zero* (2006), and *What Really Happened: Inside the Twin Towers* (2006) told the story of the World Trade Center towers and why and how they collapsed. Documentaries such as *War on Terror: A Year in Review* (2002), *Portrait of a Terrorist: Mohamed Atta* (2002), *Terror Tech: Defending the High Rise* (2003), and *Suicide Bombers* (2003) explored terrorism in the pre and post-9/11 world. Still other documentaries concentrating on specific aspects of September 11 and its aftermath emerged as well. For example, *The 9/11 Commission Report* (2004)—based on the government-published book by the same name—provided an explanation and exploration of the government investigation and publication. *The Pentagon* (2005) examined the history of the Pentagon up through the attacks and aftermath of September 11, *Metal of Honor* (2006) presented the perspectives of structural iron workers who assisted with the cleanup at the World Trade Center site, and *Deadly Dust* (2007) explored the heath impact working at the Ground Zero site had on cleanup and rescue workers. The History Channel also produced many of these documentaries, about three a year since the attacks in 2001.

Television Dramas and 9/11: Mini-Series and Movies

The first television dramas about 9/11 emerged within two years of the attacks. Showtime's *DC 9/11: Time of Crisis* (2003), about President Bush and the government's pursuit of Al Qaeda, was a docudrama that re-created the government's response to the terrorist attacks. USA's *The Rudy Giuliani Story* (2003) chronicled the life of the New York City mayor, including aspects of his personal life, his evolving career, and his actions on September 11 in New York. Britain's television special, *The Hamburg Cell* (2004; released in the United States in 2005), fictionalized the stories of the September 11 hijackers. The film was written based on research that included interviews, *The 9/11 Commission Report*, and unpublished documents. NBC's docudrama, *Homeland Security* (2004), originally intended to be a new series pilot, aired solely as a television movie about the problems in interagency communication prior to the terrorist attacks and the resulting establishment of the Department of Homeland Security. Two programs specifically examined what took place on United Flight 93, which crashed in Shanksville, Pennsylvania. The docudrama, *The Flight That Fought Back* (2005), dramatized the story of the passengers of United 93 with integrated voiceovers and clips from victims' families who provided emotional commentary about their loved ones, while *Flight 93* (2006) dramatized the story of United 93 in television movie format.

THE FLIGHT THAT FOUGHT BACK AND FLIGHT 93

The Flight That Fought Back (2005) offers a documentary account of the events aboard United Airlines Flight 93 based on the small amount of available information. Scenes mixed reenactments of what took place aboard the plane, and the experiences of passengers' families on the ground, with interviews of family members and voice recordings drawn from cell-phone conversations (Craig & Goodison, 2005). Directed by Bruce Goodison and using no well-known actors, the film first aired on September 8, 2005, on the Discovery Channel, and takes a more general approach to the topic, chronicling the hijacking and the passengers' response without focusing too closely on any specific individuals.

Flight 93 (2006) offers a more fully dramatized account of the events aboard Flight 93, using recognizable actors (including Jeffrey Nordling as Tom Burnett, Brennan Elliott as Todd Beamer, Ty Olsson as Mark Bingham, Colin Glazer as Jeremy Glick, and Kendall Cross as Deena Burnett) to portray the passengers and family members on the ground, while also augmenting the narrative with use of the cell-phone voice recordings (Gerber & Markle, 2006). Directed by Peter Markle, the film first aired on January 30, 2006, on A&E, and centers on the purported revolt effort led by Burnett, Beamer, Bingham, and Glick.

—Lloyd Isaac Vayo

References

Craig, P. (Producer), & Goodison, B. (Director). (2005). *The Flight That Fought Back* [Motion picture]. United States: Brook Lapping Productions.

Gerber, D. (Producer), & Markle, P. (Director). (2006). *Flight 93* [Motion picture]. United States: A&E.

After *The 9/11 Commission Report* was released, both ABC and NBC began production on miniseries that would dramatize aspects of the Report. While NBC cancelled production of its miniseries plans in June 2005, stating the project was too expensive ("Report," 2005), ABC's miniseries, *The Path to 9/11* (2006) told the story of government officials who have been tracking Osama bin Laden for the majority of their careers, notably John P. O'Neill (played by Harvey Keitel) who was killed in the World Trade Center attacks. The five-hour docudrama hones in on the 1993 World Trade Center bombing and identifies the events that led to the attacks on September 11, 2001. The series also highlights bureaucratic battles within the government, particularly between the CIA and FBI, and is critical of the Clinton administration. Although its narrative was culled from *The 9/11 Commission Report* and a variety of government interviews, many of the scenes are fictitious, and members of the 9/11 Commission were critical of what they labeled distortions in the program (Atkins, 2008). Given the controversy around inaccuracies surrounding the docudrama before it was released, the producers reedited a fictional scene in the film where the CIA had the chance to capture bin Laden in 1998 but instead aborted the mission (Stanley, 2006).

Although a fictional story, the backdrop for the made-for-TV Disney Channel movie *Tiger Cruise* (2004), starring Hayden Panettiere and Bill Pullman, begins before the terrorist attacks happened and was inspired by events that took place on the aircraft carrier the USS *Constellation* in the days after 9/11. For the first time in history, this naval ship went into full combat alert mode with civilians on board. In *Tiger Cruise*, a film targeted for younger audiences, daughter Maddie Dolan joins her father, Captain Gary Dolan, in Operation Tiger, a weeklong naval tour for families aimed at showing civilians what their family members do in the military. The movie opens with Maddie determined to convince her father to give up his military career, but when the September 11 attacks take place and the ship has to go into combat mode, she understands the value of his service.

Entertainment TV: Militainment and Counterterrorism Programming

The earliest responses made by entertainment programming to the events of September 11 were plots with a renewed focus on terrorism and counterterrorism in existing military and law-enforcement dramas, often referred to as "militainment." According to Seelye (2002), the Pentagon views "militainment" as an effective way to communicate with the public about military policies and procedures. Still shaken by the attacks on 9/11, the viewing public was receptive to TV that depicted competent and heroic actions by the U.S. government (Seelye, 2002; Stanley, 2004).

Militainment was also evident in existing programs that modified their plots to reflect the state of the nation after the attacks; viewers' preferences for some of these programs increased. For example, the Navy-focused *JAG* (1995–2005) was ranked the tenth most popular prime-time program by March of 2002, up from a rank of 28 the year before (Seelye, 2002). In April 2002, *JAG* aired an episode where a leader of a terrorist network is on trial for plotting the September 11 attacks. The program gained news attention because of the Pentagon's cooperation in assisting with research for this episode, as well as program creator and Executive Producer Donald Bellisario's belief that military tribunals were the best way to deal with terrorists. Given that television cameras are excluded from real-life military tribunals, *JAG* offered the public a visual version of what a military tribunal might look like. Writers for *JAG* were made aware of the details of conducting military tribunals from the Pentagon before they were released to the public. The relationship between *JAG* and the Pentagon was in place prior to September 11: Although they may not have had editorial control, contacts at the Pentagon reviewed scripts and provided feedback (Seelye, 2002). In addition, several other post-9/11 military-themed programs were crafted with Pentagon cooperation such as CBS's *AFP: American Fighter Pilot* (2002), ABC's *Profiles from the Front Line* (2003), and VH1's documentary, *Military Diaries* (2002). Part of the post-9/11 entertainment landscape, military-focused programming increased after the terrorist attacks and during the wars in Afghanistan and Iraq.

PENTAGON PARTICIPATION

In the post-9/11 world, the relationship between the Pentagon and entertainment programming can be viewed from a variety of perspectives. Given that many people get their news and understanding of world events from entertainment programming, it is important for television programs to accurately display information. At the same time, television script writers are not obligated to provide the same critical eye as journalists when making sense of the information and the government can have control over content. For example, in the case of *Homeland Security USA* (2009), an ABC reality program created with the help of the Department of Homeland Security, the government must approve content before it is aired (Lyke, 2005).

—*Amy M. Damico*

Reference

Lyke, M. L. (2005, July 26). Military dramas. *Seattle Post Intelligencer.* Retrieved from http://www.seattlepi.com

A few years after the attacks, post-9/11 existence emerged as a plot on a number of television programs. The first new program to appear was *Threat Matrix* (2003), a government drama centered on a government team of terrorist fighters, who work in the newly created Department of Homeland Security and report directly to the president. Plots deal with terrorist threats ranging from biological chemical weapons to suicide bombers. At the time of the show's premiere, Executive Producer Daniel Voll pointed out that viewers were interested in stories about the men and women who keep them and the country safe. Voll compared *Threat Matrix* to the hospital drama, *ER*, by saying "*ER* figured out how to give us characters and stories that made us say 'I sure would like to have those people on our side'"(Albiniak, 2003, p. 22). *Threat Matrix* producers also relied on government insight in crafting accurate displays of government procedures; consultants to the program included a former National Security Agency (NSA) director, a former FBI agent, informed Congress members, ex-CIA agents, former military intelligence officers, and members of the Department of Defense (Albiniak, 2003). *Threat Matrix* lasted just a year, possibly because, although viewers wanted programs displaying the best of the U.S. government's skills, the show's portrayal of the smooth relationship between the CIA and FBI may have had too little credibility (Stanley, 2004).

In addition to militainment, counterterrorism dramas dominated the television landscape in the years following the attacks. Shows already in production, such as *24* (2001–2010) and *Alias* (2001–2006), enjoyed respectable ratings and integrated terrorist plots into their narratives that were representative of the current climate. For example, *24* integrated threats from Middle Eastern terrorists into its narratives, while *Alias* incorporated minor references to the Department of Homeland Security

---

MUSLIM TERRORISTS ON *24*

After 9/11, many Middle Easterners were concerned that they would be unfairly associated with the terrorists who orchestrated and participated in the September 11
attacks. As a result, they made an effort to raise awareness around problematic and
stereotypical depictions of people from the Middle East. In 2005, Islamist groups protested the portrayal of Muslims on the hit television show *24* (2001–2010), a drama
about terrorism threats against the United States. Season four of *24* focused primarily
on planned terrorist attacks on the United States by a number of terrorist cells led by
Middle Easterners, and protesters were concerned that, given *24*'s portrayals in the aftermath of the attacks on September 11, Americans would only associate Muslims with
both terrorists and the Middle East. However, according to Stephen Prothero (2007),
author of *Religious Literacy*, the American Muslim population is growing and currently
an estimated three to six million people practice Islam in the United States. Prothero
points out that Islam is usually associated with Middle Eastern people, but the majority
of Muslims do not live in Middle Eastern countries. Indonesia has the most Muslims,
followed by Pakistan, Bangladesh, and India.

After meeting with the Council of American-Islamic Relations (CAIR) based in
Washington, D.C., FOX responded to the criticism of their portrayal by broadcasting
a short clip where Keifer Sutherland reminded *24*'s viewers that the Muslim characters
were not representative of all Muslims before the program started. Three years later, in
2007, *24* was briefly in the news again because of continuing protests that the program was portraying Middle Eastern people as ruthless terrorists.

—*Amy M. Damico*

Reference

Prothero, S. (2007). *Religious literacy: What every American needs to know—and doesn't.*
       San Francisco: Harper Collins.

---

as a new entity with which to engage in operations. New programs were also introduced. In 2004, TNT's new series, *The Grid* (2004), debuted as a terrorism action
drama that examined the stories of government terrorism fighters as well as the stories
of terrorists. *The Grid* was coproduced by the BBC and featured a lead character, Max
Canary (played by Dylan McDermott), who lost his best friend in the World Trade
Center attacks.

The Showtime miniseries, *Sleeper Cell* (2005–2006), focuses on displaying counterterrorism from the terrorists' perspectives. While trying to communicate terrorist
ideology to viewers, *Sleeper Cell*'s narrative examines the inner workings of a terrorist
cell in California. In season one, a devout Islamic undercover FBI agent penetrates a
terrorist cell, works with, and ultimately thwarts plans made by a group of Islamic
fundamentalists for massive terrorist attacks in several major cities. In season two,
the undercover agent joins a new cell and works again to undo plans for a nuclear
attack. The focus of *Sleeper Cell* is not just to expose the inner workings of terrorist

cells; interpretations of Islam are repeatedly integrated into the narrative. Considerable time is spent explaining Islam and showing rituals of prayer. Characters who are devout to Allah in opposing ways, those waging a jihad against the infidels in the United States and those who are opposed to the fundamentalist approach to their religion, demonstrate to viewers how Muslims are divided. The September 11 terrorist attacks are frequently referred to in both seasons, and as the narrative unfolds, the program integrates aspects of post-9/11 military policy including references to Guantanamo Bay, treatment of detainees, torture, and rendition.

Television programming outside of the United States also took counterterrorism as its topic. The BBC spy drama, *MI-5* (called *Spooks* in the United Kingdom) (2002 to present), for example, centers on the counterterrorism unit of the British secret service. The program began airing in the United States on A&E and some PBS stations in 2003, and *New York Times* critic Caryn James (2004) described it as "so swift in its action, so pointed about post 9/11 threats, that it is easily the best suspense show around" (para. 1). The show provides audiences with a British perspective on the war on terror fight. In its multiple seasons, *MI-5* has presented complicated terrorism narratives contextualized in international politics, and September 11 is often mentioned in its character dialogue.

Post-9/11 Television Trends

As the years passed, the post-9/11 environment became part of the television landscape. Criminal procedural programs such as *Law and Order* (1990 to present), *Law and Order: Criminal Intent* (2001 to present), and *The Closer* (2005 to present) integrated references to the terrorist attacks in character dialogue. Aspects of the post-9/11 climate such as increased security measures and references to *The 9/11 Commission Report* became part of the television entertainment landscape. Several programs debuted that specifically used the events of 9/11 as a central plot point. Most notable, perhaps, is *Rescue Me* (2004 to present), an FX drama about New York firefighters suffering from posttraumatic stress disorder after September 11. The show's lead character, Tommy Gavin, played by Denis Leary, lost his best friend and cousin in the terrorist attacks, and all the characters in the firehouse struggle to deal with working in New York City after 9/11. The attacks are also the motivating plot point for the opening season of *Brothers and Sisters* (2006 to present), as Kitty Walker returns to Los Angeles to be with her family after living through September 11 and its aftermath in New York.

Television programs also integrated specific references to September 11 that stood alone as markers of contemporary history in the post-9/11 television landscape. For example, the "earth history" montage at the end of *Star Trek: Enterprise*'s "Storm Front: Part II" (2004) depicts an image of the burning World Trade Center towers. A 2007 episode of the NBC sitcom, *30 Rock* (2006 to present), shows the character Liz Lemon (Tina Fey) watching the NBC "Salute to Fireworks" display that

New Yorkers were not told about. As the explosions occur and smoke rises in New York, the camera pans to Lemon and her friends watching the program and she says "that's going to scare a lot of people." The episode gently pokes fun at the post-9/11 tension seen during an event that took place at a real NBC 2002 anniversary special where the studio audience was frightened by fireworks explosions (James, 2007). In "Gnothi Seauton," (2008), an episode in *Terminator: The Sarah Connor Chronicles* (2008 to present), Sarah Connor travels in time to 2007 and learns about the terrorist attacks on September 11. The first season of BBC's drama, *Mistresses* (2009), develops a story line in which one of the four heroines is mourning the loss of her husband, who she believes died in one of the Twin Towers, only to discover that he has faked his death in order to run off with his mistress. The 2009 season finale of *Fringe* (2008 to present) shows lead character, Olivia Dunham (Anna Torv), in the upper floors of one of the World Trade Center towers, and references to the standing World Trade Center towers in a parallel universe continue in the following season. The season premiere of *V* (2009) asks viewers to recall where they were when 9/11 happened.

Other television programs seemed to reflect a uniquely post-9/11 mood. Although absent any explicit references to the terrorist attacks, these programs register a post-9/11 zeitgeist of loss, uncertainty, fear, and needs for closure, justice, and revenge. For example, *Lost* (2004–2010) has been described as a metaphoric example of the post-9/11 world, a world of uncertainty, doubt, and terror (Gilmore, 2007). *Heroes* (2006 to present) is a comic book-themed drama about a number of individuals who discover, mutate, and use supernatural powers to prevent destruction of a city. *Battlestar Galactica* (2003–2008) has been dubbed a "funhouse mirror for American post 9/11 cultural anxieties" and has addressed contemporary issues of torture, military occupation, religious freedom, and war crimes (Rogers, 2008, para. 4). Still other programs addressed issues the country was grappling with after September 11 in their narratives. For example, *24* brought forth issues of torture and civil liberties, and military dramas such as *The Unit* (2006–2009) focused on the stresses military families face in war time while their loved ones valiantly protect the United States.

Conclusion

On television, quick alterations of program content eventually were replaced with an integration of the post-9/11 environment into entertainment programming. In response to the terrorist attacks, some programs made minor alterations to their content while others purposefully integrated content related to September 11 into their programming. Over time, existing television programs reflected the post-9/11 environment by altering their scripts to incorporate new aspects of life after 9/11. Newly conceived television programs addressed life after September 11 with a focus on the military, counterterrorism units, and characters who find themselves in uncertain times.

—Amy M. Damico

References

Albiniak, P. (2003, October 13). Post-9/11 becomes a television plot. *Broadcasting and Cable, 22.*

Atkins, S. (Ed.) (2008). *The 9/11 encyclopedia*. Westport, CT: Greenwood Press.

Collins, G. (2001, October 15). And now, we return to scheduled programs; TV production quickly rebounds, with New York City as a backdrop. *The New York Times*, p. C8.

Dera, D. (2007, September 5). Where were you on September 11, 2001? *Associated Content*. Retrieved from http://www.associatedcontent.com

"Disappointing US Oscar ratings." (2002, March 26). BBC News. Retrieved from http://www.news.bbc.co.uk

Erickson, H. (2003). Critical assembly: Review summary. *The New York Times*. Retrieved from http://www.nytimes.com

Gilmore, M. (2007, May 31). Get lost. *Rolling Stone, 1027*(44).

James, C. (2001, October 29). Critic's notebook: Dramatic events that rewrite the script. *The New York Times*. Retrieved from http://www.nytimes.com

James, C. (2004, January 11). Television; On *MI-5*, the special relationship is sibling rivalry. *The New York Times*. Retrieved from http://www.nytimes.com

James, C. (2007, May 13). No one says "9/11." No one needs to. *The New York Times*. Retrieved from http://www.nytimes.com

Jones, R., & Dionisopoulos, G. (2004). Scripting a tragedy: The "Isaac and Ishmael" episode of the *West Wing* as parable. *Popular Communication, 2(1)*, 21–40.

Kuipers, G. (2005). "Where was King Kong when we needed him?" Public discourse, digital disaster jokes and the functions of laughter after 9/11. *Journal of American Culture, 28*(1), 70–84.

McCarthy-Miller, B. (Director). (2001, September 29). *Saturday Night Live* [Television broadcast]. New York: NBC.

McDonough, K. (2002, September 8). Cover story; 9/11/02; Not a time for business as usual. *The New York Times*. Retrieved from http://www.nytimes.com

Oscar-Shy Allen's NY tribute. (2002, March 25). BBC News. Retrieved from http://news.bbc.co.uk

Owen, R. (2001, October 15). *Third Watch* weaves terrorism into premiere. *Post-gazette.com*. Retrieved November 25, 2008, from http://www.Post-gazette.com

Rogers, T. (2008, April 2). Everything you were afraid to ask about Battlestar Galactica. Salon.com. Retrieved from http://www.salon.com

Salamon, J. (2001, November 13). Critic's notebook; Trying to keep up with history on the run. *The New York Times*. Retrieved from http://www.nytimes.com

Seelye, K. (2002, March 31). A nation challenged: Public relations; Pentagon plays a role in fictional terror drama. *The New York Times*. Retrieved from http://www.nytimes.com

Spigel, L. (2004). Entertainment wars: Television culture after 9/11. *American Quarterly, 56*(2), 235–270.

Stanley, A. (2004, July). Television review; battling terrorism in the grid, clouded by moral complexities. *The New York Times*. Retrieved from http://www.nytimes.com

Stanley, A. (2006, September 8). Laying the blame and passing the buck, dramatized. *The New York Times*. Retrieved from http://www.nytimes.com

30 Rock citation: Fey, T., Finkel, D. and Baer, B. (writers) and McCarthy-Miller, B. (director). (2007). Fireworks [Television series episode]. In T. Fey (producer) 30 Rock. New York: National Broadcasting Company.

SPOTLIGHT ESSAY/TELEVISION: *24*

Since the terrorist attacks on New York and Washington on September 11, 2001, nations have struggled to develop the correct military, political, and legal responses to the event. The balancing act required to respond effectively while retaining the values of democracy, freedom, and the rule of law has challenged the leaders and citizenry of each concerned nation and sparked intense debate and often grievous discord. Unsurprisingly, many television series have incorporated these debates and issues into their plots, but one series has had a particularly significant role in the thoughts, beliefs, and discourse of American legal, political, and military leaders. *24* (2001–2010), the intense spy thriller featuring Jack Bauer and the other members of the Counter Terrorist Unit (CTU) Los Angeles, has caused powerful leaders facing perhaps the most difficult questions of these times to ask in their discussions and dialogues, "What would Jack Bauer do?" Given that the series is premised on the "ticking time bomb" scenario, which rarely occurs in reality, *24* represents a specific response to the anxiety around terrorism that followed the September 11 attacks.

As millions of viewers know, Jack's actions occur against a constant background of "ticking bombs." Conceived of as a real-time presentation of 24 hours in the life of Jack Bauer, every episode involves a scenario in which time is running out to save the American public from a terrorist attack: A bomb is about to explode; a devastating virus is about to be released into a public space; or worse, Jack's family member or friend is being held hostage and about to be murdered unless Jack helps the terrorists. In innumerable sequences over the show's lengthy run, Jack can only save his country or his family by forcing information from a suspected terrorist. He has only minutes, or even seconds, to get the information. Jack employs any means necessary, including torture, to extract this information and, over and over again, he is shown to have made the right choice in resorting to these illegal tactics. The message, in other words, is that in the face of such extreme threats, torture is justified and even necessary.

In reality, the ticking time bomb scenario almost never happens. One of the show's creators, Bob Cochran, has acknowledged as much. In an interview with the *New Yorker*, he commented on the disparity between his show and real life: "Most terrorism experts will tell you that the 'ticking time bomb' situation never occurs in real life, or very rarely. But on our show it happens every week" ("Whatever It Takes," 2007, para. 4).

Despite this fictional background, Jack Bauer's approach to counterterrorism has received explicit approval from an array of American leaders. At a recent judicial conference, U.S. Supreme Court Justice Antonin Scalia debated the ticking time bomb scenario with Mr. Justice Richard Mosley of the Federal Court of Canada. Mr. Justice Mosley, after listening to a presentation on the proper role of criminal law in circumstances of chaos and war, commented "Thankfully, security agencies in

all our countries do not subscribe to the mantra 'What would Jack Bauer do?'"
("What Would Jack Bauer Do," 2007, p. A9). Mr. Justice Scalia disagreed:

> Jack Bauer saved Los Angeles . . . He saved hundreds of thousands of lives . . . Are you
> going to convict Jack Bauer? Say the criminal law is against him? "You have the right
> to a jury trial?" I don't think so . . . so the question is really whether we believe in these
> absolutes. And ought we believe in these absolutes. ("What Would Jack Bauer Do,"
> 2007, p. A9)

This exchange between dueling jurists is fascinating as an example of how popular
culture not only provides the metaphors for, but actually informs, sophisticated
international debates. The fact that the judges framed their debate in terms of *24*
demonstrates just how deeply the show has infiltrated the public consciousness. That
one of the country's highest legal officers points to Bauer—a TV character who is constantly breaching his own agency's protocols on acceptable levels of torture—as an
example of appropriate action in the face of terrorism suggests that *24* has truly captured the imagination of Americans faced with post-9/11 feelings of helplessness
and fear.

Other American leaders have also cited Jack Bauer when arguing against the use of
torture, finding that in a world where popular culture portrays Bauer as always right
and almost always effective, it is necessary to differentiate the real world from the
world of *24* in order to convincingly argue against Jack Bauer-type methods of
interrogation. For example, former President Bill Clinton changed his own view
on the ticking time bomb scenario from accepting that the president should be
able to grant emergency dispensations from legal requirements to a view that
torture should never be permitted. In arguing that the United States should oppose
torture on the basis that torture may result in false information, lower the
international perception of the United States, and make U.S. citizens vulnerable to
torture, Mr. Clinton noted that the "Jack Bauer situation," rarely happens in reality
(*Meet the Press*, 2007).

Similarly, U.S. Army Brigadier General Patrick Finnegan, disturbed by the effect
that *24* was having on future soldiers, traveled to California in 2006 to meet with
the producers, hoping to persuade them to consider the consequences of their
portrayal of Jack Bauer and the constant success of his barbaric techniques. Instead,
he hoped to see a story line where torture backfires, because the unfailing success of
Jack's methods was encouraging support from U.S. soldiers for the use of torture
("Whatever It Takes," 2007).

Clearly, *24* has impacted the post-9/11 debate on torture in the United States significantly. It has tapped into a common fear and shown a morally ambiguous protagonist
who is nevertheless consistently proven to be right in choosing violence and torture in
the face of the ticking time bomb. In fact, *24*'s underlying suggestion that the ticking
time bomb is all pervasive has arguably increased fears that further acts of terrorism
are imminent and nearly unstoppable. Whether in support of, or opposition to, the
fictional hero's approach, the question, "What would Jack Bauer do?" has moved from

popular culture to become an essential element of the debate in legal, political and military contexts.

—*Sharon Sutherland and Sarah Swan*

References

Meet the Press. (2007, September 30). [Transcript]. Retrieved March 24, 2008, from http://www.msnbc.msn.com/id/21065954/

What would Jack Bauer do? (2007, June 16). *The Globe and Mail*, p. A9.

Whatever it takes: The politics of the man behind *24*, (2007, February 19). *The New Yorker*. Retrieved from http://www.newyorker.com

SPOTLIGHT ESSAY/TELEVISION: *AMERICA: A TRIBUTE TO HEROES*

On September 21, 2001, "America: A Tribute to Heroes" (McCarthey-Miller & Gallen, 2001) aired commercial free on more than 30 network and cable channels and as many as 200 networks worldwide. In addition to the musical artists and actors featured on the show, Tom Hanks, who was the first to speak, defined the telethon as being purely philanthropic, saying he and his fellow celebrities were there to entertain and raise money for victims' families, but were not national or spiritual leaders. Raising more than $150 million, the telethon certainly fulfilled its duty; but it did much more. Despite Hanks's claim, the celebrities who participated *did* take on the roles of national and spiritual leaders. Their musical performances and short speeches did more than help raise money—they brought people together into a national family, created a strong bond within that family, and allowed the nation to collectively mourn its fellow Americans. More of a funeral than fundraiser, the telethon's setting and structure created a national memorial service. With its candle-lit stage, somber mood, and its alternating between musical performances and commentary, "America: A Tribute to Heroes" turned the stage into a national place of worship, popular songs into hymns, and words spoken by celebrities into eulogies. It was, in short, an unusually successful merger of entertainment, nationalism, and religious faith.

The musical program of the telethon was both patriotic and spiritual. It opened with Bruce Springsteen's modest and sparse performance of his pre-9/11 song, "My City of Ruins." Introducing the song as "a prayer for our fallen brothers and sisters," Springsteen immediately set the national and religious tone of the telethon by portraying it as a familial and funereal event. Essentially a prayer to recover from a shared trauma, symbolized by the "city of ruins," Springsteen's song becomes an anthem of strength. Like the overall telethon itself, "My City of Ruins" builds to a call for renewal, a literal call to "rise up," replete with a sense of national unity and religious invocations.

It is this mood and this message that laid the telethon's foundation. As was the case in "My City of Ruins," backup singers reminiscent of a church choir are a frequent feature throughout. Also like "My City of Ruins," many of the songs fit the context in tone and lyrics even though many of them were written before 9/11. Songs were selected that typically involved lyrics that moved from sadness and loss to resilience, heroism, and love—the very lineup of performers reflected this evolution. Some were classic examples of comfort music, such as Neil Young's rendition of "Imagine," Paul Simon's "Bridge Over Troubled Water," and Tom Petty's defiant "Won't Back Down." In other cases, songs were pointedly religious by appealing to a higher power and bestowing blessings upon the people. One example is Faith Hill's "There Will Come a Day," which also included a choir echoing the phrase "amazing grace" and an organ. Wyclef Jean was one performer who merged religion and patriotism, wearing a U.S. flag shirt, praising New York and the United States, and blessing the country in his version of Bob Marley's "Redemption Song."

The messages implied by many of the songs were also delivered by celebrities, who eulogized and philosophized between the musical interludes. In the majority of cases, they simply told the story of individual victims, whether it was of their noble lives or their noble deaths. Given the national context of the event, these stories did not only extend to friends and family as they would in a church, but included the U.S. public by treating the fallen as family members. By making personal stories public, these eulogies placed viewers in the larger national 9/11 narrative and encouraged the audience to mourn perfect strangers as they would loved ones.

The telethon, however, was also not without political messages meant to help the public make sense of their shared traumatic experience and find the right direction in which to move forward. In one presentation meant to guide the public's response to the terrorist attacks, a montage was shown of Muslim American children voicing their post-9/11 fears and anxieties in their own country. This was followed by commentary from Muhammad Ali, an American icon and a Muslim, who, with heroic effort, conveyed that it would be "un-American" to respond to the attacks with vengeance and suspicion toward our fellow citizens.

In most cases, other connections were made through historical reference to earlier times of strife and recovery through the words of iconic figures such as John F. Kennedy, Franklin Roosevelt, Winston Churchill, and Anne Frank. By creating these associations, speakers crafted a certain ethos for Americans. In keeping with this, allusions to World War II were frequent, being perhaps the most common and comforting comparison Americans were able to make at the time. One of the most obvious and recurrent allusions was to Franklin Roosevelt's "War Message" delivered after the bombing of Pearl Harbor—further establishing 9/11's symbolic link to that attack and paving way for the "just" war that would result. At the conclusion of the telethon, it was Roosevelt's "War Message" that was used to begin and end Clint Eastwood's closing monologue. Eastwood took on the persona of a national leader by addressing the public in the style and words of a lauded wartime president. To draw the mourning to a proper end, Eastwood concluded by encouraging the American people to get back up and move forward "to win through the ultimate triumph, so help us God."

The telethon brought together a diverse array of entertainers who effectively brought the American people together to collectively mourn members of a national family and recover from shared loss. Looking specifically at the selection of entertainers who had key roles in the telethon—Hanks, Springsteen, Eastwood, and Willie Nelson, who led all the celebrities in singing "America the Beautiful" after Eastwood's speech—shows it to be decidedly American. Hanks, the common man of U.S. history; Springsteen, the everyman and champion of the justice; Eastwood, the emblem of America's unique Wild West mythology and the righteous and uncompromising lawman; and Nelson, America's cowboy, the symbol of a national spirit possessed by no other nation. Taken as a whole, these entertainers, their songs, and their words reveal that the work of national mourning does not only happen at the podium and the pulpit; it happens on what we might call a new kind of national stage.

—*Kathryn Palmer*

Reference

McCarthey-Miller, B., & Gallen, J. (Directors). (2001). *America: A tribute to heroes* [Telethon broadcast]. United States: Warner Brothers.

SPOTLIGHT ESSAY/TELEVISION: *BATTLESTAR GALACTICA* AND *STARGATE SG-1*

As a genre, science fiction allows creators and audiences to intellectually grapple with real-world problems through the protective presence of escapist fantasy. Two television science fiction shows that accomplish this after September 11 are *Battlestar Galactica* (2003–2009) and *Stargate SG-1* (1997–2007). Both shows offer an important glimpse into the United States after one of its darkest days, providing fictional representations of the complex topics of religious fundamentalism, unilateral tactics, and a debatable joining of politics and military power. The programs have been described as ones that address post-9/11 topics of military power, human rights, and fear.

Shot in the aftermath of 9/11, *Battlestar Galactica* revels in the anxieties of twenty-first-century United States. Emotionally charged representations of power abuse frame a fictional reworking of the disruptive effects of terrorism on culture, offering a "space for critical self-reflection" (Potter & Marshall, 2008, p. 12). Reflecting the real images that were seen on 9/11, the series included images of terror coming from the sky, suggesting a state of emergency that ultimately reshapes both politics and society.

In *Stargate SG-1*, the main character, SG-1, believes that the Earth is under threat of an alien attack, whereas *Battlestar Galactica* opens with an airborne nuclear assault against humans perpetrated by a race of beings called the Cylons. Indistinguishable from men, Cylons embody the "enemy aliens" referred to by U.S. immigration policies as well as the anonymous hijackers who carried out the attacks. Their amorphous presence explains *Battlestar Galactica*'s constant references to inspection, quarantine, and isolation, stirring a state of paranoia that, echoed by *Stargate SG-1*, justifies recourse to corruption and state violence.

Also as in the post-9/11 United States, social unrest follows these fictional crises, demanding renewed declarations of national belonging and a redefinition of the boundaries of the community in reactionary and religious terms. The appearance of Senator Kinsey in *Stargate SG-1* is a case in point. A television series spun off from the 1994 film *Stargate* in 1997, *Stargate SG-1* presents a commentary on the neoconservative movement in the United States. When told by SG-1 that the aliens, if they make it to Earth, will enslave humans and force them to worship the aliens as gods, Kinsey responds that "There is only ONE God, sir! And I do not believe for one moment that he will allow what you're trying to tell me come to pass, we are after all, one nation, under God" (Wright, 1998). Kinsey's religious views are mentioned again in the episode "2010" (Wright, 2001), and the story line continues in ways that perhaps parallel the political movements by Christian conservatives in the United States. While Kinsey represents the perceived post-9/11 government corruption, *Stargate*'s SG-1 reflects the American desire to have an inherently just administration. As a result, the heroic President senses Kinsey's treacherous nature and forces him to step down (Wright, 2004).

Similarly, *Battlestar Galactica* characters react to their attack by exercising unconstitutional powers through an unprecedented joining of civil and military quarters. The show displays a dictatorship that, disguised as democratic government, polices community boundaries by way of general pleas for freedom and "humanity." Acts of tyrannical rule such as torture and illegal detention remind post-9/11 viewers of the situations of Abu Ghraib and Guantanamo Bay. In the episode "Flash and Bone," for example, Lieutenant Thrace confronts a character who protests against her violent methods of interrogation by saying "There [are] no limits to the tactics I can use" (Graphia, 2005), a scene that refers directly to discussions of interrogation tactics and torture in the United States after September 11. It could be argued that *Battlestar Galactica*'s quest for human preservation is a fictional extension of the Bush administration's international abuses in the name of Western protection (Johnson-Lewis, 2008).

Through their narratives, *Battlestar Galactica* and *Stargate SG-1* suggest that exceptional rules, even in times of despair, are dangerous to society. By placing their characters in situations that force them to deal with democratic ideals in the face of current turmoil, these shows offer an interesting analysis of post-9/11 United States. By engaging with the effects of the War on Terror, in their fictionalization of a paranoid society populated by invisible enemies, the shows provide a multilayered representation of post-9/11 anxieties, addressing national trauma as a platform for the use of "improvised" power. *Battlestar Galactica* and *Stargate SG-1* present the moral compromises inherent in the notions of freedom and democracy invoked by the Bush administration to justify its policies.

—Enrica Picarelli and Nicholas Yanes

References

Graphia, T. (Writer), & Turner, B. (Director). (2005, 25 February). Flesh and bone. [Television series episode]. In R. Moore and D. Eick. (producers) *Battlestar Galactica*. New York: Sci-Fi Channel.

Johnson-Lewis, E. (2008). Torture, terrorism, and other aspects of human nature. In T. Potter & C. W. Marshall (Eds.), *Critical studies in Battlestar Galactica* (pp. 27–39). New York: Continuum.

Potter, T., & Marshall, C. W. (2008). "I see the patterns": *Battlestar Galactica* and the things that matter. In T. Potter & C. W. Marshall (Eds.), *Critical studies in Battlestar Galactica* (pp. 1–10). New York: Continuum.

Wright, B. (Writer), & Wood, M. (Director). (1998, February 27). Politics [Television series episode]. In W. Brad (producer), Los Angeles, CA. *Stargate SG-1*. MGM Studios.

Wright, B. (Writer), & Mikita, A. (Director). (2001, January 12). 2010 [Television series episode]. In W. Brad (producer), Los Angeles, CA. *Stargate SG-1*. MGM Studios.

Wright, B. (Writer), Cooper, R. C. (Writer), & Wood, Martin (Director). (2004, March 19). Lost City Pt. 2 [Television series episode]. In W. Brad (producer), Los Angeles, CA. *Stargate SG-1*. MGM Studios.

SPOTLIGHT ESSAY/TELEVISION: *CROSSING OVER WITH JOHN EDWARD*

In the months following the September 11 attacks, celebrated television psychic John Edward proposed a new theme for his popular TV series, *Crossing Over with John Edward* (Edward, 1999–2004). This was to be, in his words, "about death and dying . . . how can I not deal with the biggest incident of death—especially when it's in my own backyard?" (Edward, 2001, p. 279). Specifically, these new *Crossing Over* episodes were to be based on the experiences of the victims of September 11, and as Edward explains, marked a shift in how his program was to operate:

> I want to start doing readings for 9/11 families on a limited basis. I want the producers to *randomly* select people from the many, many letters and calls that have been coming in . . . I don't want to do them in the studio. Instead I want to go to people's homes, with minimal crews and equipment. (p. 278)

Positioning *Crossing Over's* successful ratings alongside a recent national tragedy offered to increase the show's popularity even more. Not only were viewers already familiar with the show's format, but they were now positioned to connect that format to the collectively experienced trauma of September 11. Airing Edward's psychic communication with the ghosts of 9/11 (as opposed to other, "random" ghosts) would tap into the emphasis on healing and memory already present across the country at large.

As word of Edward's program circulated the broadcasting networks of the country, however, a mounting resistance ensued. A memorandum sent through the daily

Broadcasting and Cable TV Fax that the shows were taking place resulted in a speedy backlash. The program was censored—deemed a coarse exploitation of September 11 for commercial gain—and Edward was pitted as a callous abuser of a global trauma— a "media medium" (by his own self-titling) gone crooked (Edward, 2001, p. xv). Headlines in TV tabloid columns indicated the raw public nerve that Edward's proposed program touched on, variously positioning him as a "tomb reader," "medium rare," and "hustler" of the bereaved who exploits emotions for commercial profits (Gliatto & Stoynoff, 2002; Nickell, 2001; Wolk, 2001). The conflicting responses to the 9/11-themed episodes reflected a larger cultural concern with creating an appropriate or "correct" national memory of 9/11, as well as defining who is to be remembered, by whom, and how.

Crossing Over's ability to tap into these cultural issues arose from the show's hybrid form, which draws on a mixture of twenty-first-century viewing trends including talk shows, game shows, and trauma TV. The show also feeds audience's interests in the occult, enlightenment-era mystics, and technology. In *Crossing Over*'s format, a live studio audience is fed data "sent" from the deceased. This data is communicated by Edward in symbols—letters, numbers, and descriptions of death. The studio audience responds to Edward's symbols with affirmations of recognition that slowly build to become complete stories: narratives of pain that publicly recollect the very private nature of loss. The process is watched by millions of home viewers who both celebrate the wonder of Edward's alleged psychic ability and express various forms of vicarious despair often bolstered by what sociologist Laura Grindstaff (2002) calls reality TV's money shot—the moment when a reality TV participant is prompted to break into emotional revelation, which is usually tears.

While *Crossing Over* enables viewers to reflect upon and construct a sense of collective identity through stories of grief and trauma, the censorship of the 9/11 episodes removes certain kinds of "ghosts" from being watched in this way. The fact that Edward's 9/11 spectres were deemed inappropriate exploitations of the event for commercial gain suggests that his construction of the 9/11 ghost conflicted with other sanctioned memorials of the time, including Ground Zero and the New York City Fire Department (FDNY) Memorial. The censorship, in fact, creates a hierarchy around what kind of ghosts the public is permitted to produce, and how they are permitted to mourn.

—*Bryoni Trezise*

References

Edward, J. (Executive Producer). (1999–2004). *Crossing over with John Edward* [Television series]. Los Angeles: NBC Universal.

Edward, J. (Executive Producer). (2001). *Crossing over: The stories behind the stories.* New York: Princess Books.

Gliatto, T., & Stoynoff, N. (2002, May 6). Medium rare. *People Weekly, 57*(17), 85–86.

Grindstaff, L. (2002). *The money shot: Trash, class and the making of TV talk shows.* Chicago: University of Chicago Press.

Nickell, J. (2001). John Edward: Hustling the bereaved. *Skeptical Inquirer, 25*(6). Retrieved from http://www.csicop.org

Wolk, J. (2001, September 14). Tomb reader. *Entertainment Weekly, 6*(14). Retrieved from http://www.ew.com

SPOTLIGHT ESSAY/TELEVISION: *DC 9/11: TIME OF CRISIS*

U.S. television docudrama sometimes found itself at the leading edge of politically charged revisionist accounts of 9/11, producing versions of the attacks that played to conservative interpretations of the wars that followed. The two-part docudrama on ABC, *The Path to 9/11* (2006), which first aired during the fifth anniversary of the attacks, dragged September 11 into the orbit of contemporary culture wars by alleging that it was Clinton, not Bush, who was responsible for 9/11, because his administration had ignored the threat from Al Qaeda during the 1990s. Less well known, but also controversial at the time of its release, was Showtime's docudrama *DC 9/11: Time of Crisis* (Chetwynd, 2003), a made-for-TV movie that first aired during the second anniversary of the attacks, six months after the invasion of Iraq. With a script written by well-known Hollywood conservative, Lionel Chetwynd, and what the *New York Times* referred to as "a sour, partisan undertone" (Stanley, 2003, para. 6), *DC 9/11* presents President Bush as a heavyweight statesman, doing God's work, redeeming U.S. history from mistakes made by the Clinton administrations in the 1990s.

From the opening scenes, *DC 9/11* tells the story of September 11 from a neoconservative perspective, presenting the Bush administration and its ideologies in a positive light. The script begins in the Pentagon on the morning of 9/11, with then Defense Secretary Donald Rumsfeld, arguing that the U.S. military must be transformed to meet the new threats of the twenty-first century. Moments later, American Airlines Flight 77 plows into the Pentagon, appearing to vindicate Rumsfeld's position. In another scene, Chetwynd rescripts the famous documentary footage from the Emma Booker Elementary School in Sarasota, Florida, where then President Bush was engaged in a photo opportunity on the morning of the attacks. In *Fahrenheit 9/11* (2004), Michael Moore would use the documentary footage from Emma Booker to depict Bush as an incompetent leader paralyzed by the day's events, a commander in chief unfit to defend the American people. In Chetwynd's "docudrama" rewrite, however, Bush is reconstructed as a charismatic father figure and accomplished leader to the "nation" of children grouped at his feet, his words reassuring, his actions decisive and resolute, his eyes showing a momentary spasm as he digests the news from New York and feels the pain of his people.

DC 9/11's conservative revisionism was pitched at political groupings in and around the Bush administration, notably neoconservatives and the Christian right, who the narrative brought together in the film. References to a nondenominational Christian practice are pervasive in *DC 9/11*. Bush consults the Old Testament *Book of Psalms* as he crafts the speech to be delivered to Congress on September 20;

Rumsfeld leads the war cabinet in prayer; and the giving of thanks to God punctuates the narrative at regular intervals. Religious references litter the soundtrack too, one recurring motif in the film's music being an unsettling, tuneless, otherworldly dirge, like a choir of angels in mourning or dread, usually heard over evocative images of carnage from Washington and New York. In a sequence where Bush leaves the National Cathedral in Washington and is shown flying to New York, the rendition of "The Battle Hymn of the Republic" ("his truth is marching on") bridges the two scenes on the soundtrack, so that as the president's plane comes in over Ground Zero, the music reaches a crescendo, and Bush is positioned centrally in a shot looking through the window at the devastation below.

Throughout *DC 9/11*, the script implied, the important stories were those of U.S. political elites, not those of ordinary citizens. In another clear echo of neoconservative ideology, the film's United States often resembles a classical republic governed by virtuous politicians who act, more or less independently of citizens, on their behalf. *DC 9/11* portrays "ordinary" Americans as mute children, or as victims in hospital beds begging Bush to "take care of us," or as emotional Ground Zero rescue workers crying for vengeance. In times of crisis, the film implies, "our" job is to do as we are told by the elites who know what is best for us, and the script repeatedly features Bush telling members of his administration that Americans must be "educated" before they can cope with 9/11. The film also suggests that it was time to start thinking in "unconventional" ways about civil liberties.

DC 9/11's neoconservative values seem reemphasized by its ending, which comes immediately after Bush's delivery of his speech to Congress on September 20. What Bush had to say about 9/11, the structure of the film implies, was all that needed to be said. When the president finished, the film finished, because from *DC 9/11*'s point of view there was nothing left to say.

—*David Holloway*

References

Chetwynd, L. (Writer). (2003). *DC 9/11: Time of crisis* [Motion picture]. United States: Showtime.

Stanley, A. (2003, September 5). Sept. 11, before and after. *The New York Times*. Retrieved from http://www.nytimes.com

---

SPOTLIGHT ESSAY/TELEVISION: *DEXTER*

One consequence of the terrorist attacks of September 11, 2001, was a rising sense of communal confusion regarding the meaning of "justice." Traditional American values of civil rights and due process clashed with a desire for vengeance. On television, this confusion provided the central conflict in numerous shows, most notably in criminal procedurals and spy thrillers where an ends-versus-means debate was so readily dramatized. Increasingly, television programs have presented morally ambiguous protagonists and fed a public fascination with the moral dilemma of committing evil acts as a means to bring about good results.

The Showtime original series *Dexter* (2006–2009) may well represent the most extreme and intentionally ironic expression of this post-9/11 trend: The hero is a blood-splatter analyst for the Miami police department, as well as a serial killer who kills other serial killers. Dexter believes that he is serving a social and moral purpose by meting out "justice" to murderers the law is unable to capture. As a young boy, Dexter learned from his foster father, police officer Harry Morgan, that killing people who killed others was justifiable, and this Code of Harry, as Dexter calls it, lies at the heart of Dexter's notions of morality. Through the responses of the other characters to the "Bay Harbor Butcher" (the name given to Dexter when the bodies of his victims are discovered), *Dexter* self-consciously explores the question: Does the average American believe that murder is justified if the victim is sufficiently evil? While *Dexter* presents a nuanced view of public reaction to these questions, the most broadly represented perspective in the series is the "law and order" view of the law enforcement professional. That perspective can be used as a lens through which to explore exploration of post-9/11 ambiguity in perceptions of evil.

From his first memories, Dexter was told that there are people who, by virtue of their evil deeds, do not deserve to live. While taking a life is normally immoral, Dexter has been taught by his foster father that some lives simply do not have the same value as others. In a flashback scene, Harry tells the teenaged Dexter: "Son, there are people out there who do really bad things. Terrible people. And the police can't catch them all. Do you understand what I'm saying?" Dexter responds with the apparently correct answer: "You're saying . . . they deserve it" (Colleton & Goldwyn, 2006). Three examples serve to demonstrate the most interesting of the law enforcement views on this Code: the experience of Sergeant James Doakes, the only member of the police force who finds Dexter creepy; the opinion of Dexter's sister, Deb; and the significant change in Harry's own perspective.

Doakes is a superb police officer with the singular instincts to recognize that Dexter is somehow dangerous. Committed as he is to enforcing the law, Doakes nonetheless executes a former Haitian military officer in retribution for war crimes the man committed 15 years previously (Colleton & Goldwyn, 2007). While Doakes claims it was an act of self-defense, there is no doubt in the viewer's mind that Doakes murdered the man. Doakes's commanding officer, Lieutenant Maria LaGuerta, effectively condones his crime: She tells him that if that man committed the acts Doakes describes, he deserved a lot worse than the death he received. Despite this obvious parallel, Doakes sees no connection between himself and the Bay Harbor Butcher he views as evil. It is no small irony that the second season concludes with Doakes carrying a mistaken identification as the "Bay Harbor Butcher" to his grave.

Dexter's sister, Deb, is a police officer with a very clear vision of good and evil. Unlike many of her colleagues, Deb never wavers from a belief that the Bay Harbor Butcher is evil and deserves to die just as much as his serial killing victims. She sees no contradiction in advocating for the public execution of the killer since she sees a clear dividing line between vigilantism and lawful execution by the state. That Deb is the most unambiguous in her feelings about the murderer produces oddly charged moments in her interactions with her brother: As Deb speaks of the need to see the killer dead, Dexter alone is aware of how completely Deb's world would be destroyed were that to happen.

While Deb's relationship with Dexter balances moments of irony with a fear of emotional catastrophe, perhaps the most poignant moments in the series arise when Dexter learns that Harry himself could not follow the Code through to its logical conclusion. Finding Dexter in the act of excitedly cutting up his first human kill—a deserving victim that Harry had pointed out to him—Harry cannot face the monster he has created and chooses to take his own life. In the end, even Dexter's mentor finds that the notion of deserving to die is not as simple as he had taught Dexter to believe.

The ambiguous messages that Doakes, Harry, and others on the police force send about the potential to use murder as a tool against murderers provides the canvas for *Dexter*'s exploration of post-9/11 public ambiguity regarding the notion that perhaps some people deserve to die and killing them might be good. In this context, it is not surprising that Dexter imagines crowds coming out to cheer him for his work if he is ever caught. In fact, Dexter does receive a form of support from the millions of weekly viewers who cheer for him to escape the consequences of his actions and continue with his murderous spree. Of course, enjoying *Dexter* is not the same as condoning the protagonist's moral code, but it does suggest a willingness to overlook some surprisingly large character flaws in our fictional heroes. Arguably the post-9/11 appeal of Dexter as a character suggests that the murders he commits are not wholly morally repugnant to the viewing audience: Perhaps we enjoy the flirtation with a code that suggests that some deserve to die because it speaks to fears of unstoppable serial killers and a desire for vengeance against the hidden evil in our midst. In the post-9/11 world, *Dexter* and its morally ambiguous hero allow us to indulge in a fantasy solution to the perceived inability of law enforcement to truly keep us safe from evil.

—Sharon Sutherland and Sarah Swan

References

Colleton, S., & Goldwyn, J. (Executive Producers). (2006). *Dexter*, season one [Television series]. New York: Showtime.

Colleton, S., & Goldwyn, J. (Executive Producers). (2007). *Dexter*, season two [Television series]. New York: Showtime.

SPOTLIGHT ESSAY/TELEVISION: *GENERATION KILL*

Military-themed television programs became especially significant after September 11. Those already in production increased in popularity and, in the years following the attacks, a number of new television programs focusing on the U.S. military aired on network and cable channels. Initially, such programs centered on plots related to terrorism and September 11. As the United States engaged in the Bush administration's global War on Terror, however, television programming encompassed and represented these changes. The post-9/11 landscape of military programming was no longer solely about men and women in uniform thwarting terrorist threats on the United States; it expanded to include the range of military actions the United States was involved in, including the war in Iraq.

Generation Kill (2008), is an HBO miniseries based on the book of the same name by *Rolling Stone* reporter, Evan Thomas. A reporter embedded with the Marines of Bravo Company, First Recon Battalion, examines the invasion of Iraq in 2003 through the stories of those Marines. Throughout the six-part series, the focus remains on the experience of the men, and what they saw and endured in combat, without straining to make political points. This is not to say that *Generation Kill* glosses over the realities of war: it shows incompetent commanders, poor planning, mistakes, and civilian casualties. Running through the series, however, is a constant thread of the humanity and professionalism of the Marines, particularly the noncommissioned officers, which is in particular demand when soldiers are faced with the difficult choices endemic to war. *Generation Kill* does not focus on the larger moral question of why the United States invaded Iraq in 2003, or on the course of U.S. foreign policy since the 9/11 attacks. Rather, it explores the military experience and the moral choices common to U.S. soldiers engaged in combat since the start of the Global War on Terror in 2001.

Although a television miniseries, *Generation Kill* sits squarely in the trend of films over the last 10 years that attempt to bring a new realism to depictions of combat, partly through attention to historical detail, and partly through the use of special effects. Following *Saving Private Ryan* (1998), famous for its initial graphic sequence depicting Omaha Beach on June 6, 1944, came *Blackhawk Down* (2001) and its depictions of combat in Mogadishu during September, 1993. *Band of Brothers* (2001), another HBO miniseries, examined similar themes by focusing on a single company in the 101st Airborne Division during World War II, from their training through Victory in Europe (V-E) Day. In these films and miniseries, realistic combat action is accompanied by attention to the soldiers' characters and their relationships.

In addition to the attempts to portray combat as realistically as possible on film, these films and miniseries also express the concept of primary group cohesion—the idea that soldiers are motivated to fight in battle by the bonds that they have formed with their comrades, rather than from more lofty ideals. "It's about the man next to you," one of the Delta operators succinctly stated in *Black Hawk Down*. *Generation Kill* provides viewers with soldiers who are funny, flawed, loyal, and dedicated to their country at a time when there is public disagreement around the Bush administration's military response to the terrorist attacks on September 11.

What is most striking in *Generation Kill* to viewers conditioned to see Americans committing atrocities in films such as *Apocalypse Now* (1979) or *Platoon* (1986), is the extent to which the Marines in *Generation Kill* go to minimize or prevent civilian casualties. They often fail, but seeing these failures depicted on screen is startling, because viewers may expect well-intentioned soldiers to succeed. The series shows a constant tension between the urge to restrain and the will to violence. In one scene, Lance Corporal Harold Trombley shoots two civilians in what has been declared, in effect, a free-fire zone. Although the character Trombley feels little remorse for his actions, other, more senior soldiers attend to the wounded civilians and attempt to secure medical care for them. In another scene, while maintaining a road block, Sergeant Brad Colbert attempts to use nonlethal force to stop oncoming vehicles by firing smoke grenades at them, attempting to balance the need to protect his Marines against potential car bombs, with the preference not to harm civilians unless absolutely necessary. Colbert's action is undercut when one of his Marines, Corporal Walt Hasser, fires on a vehicle that does not stop immediately after seeing the smoke grenade, killing one of the occupants of the vehicle. In a third, similar scene, a Marine attempts to use a smoke grenade to stop a vehicle, but the round ricochets off the ground and hits an Iraqi pedestrian in the head, killing him.

The "realism" of *Generation Kill* relies on more than attention to ensuring that the proper uniforms are shown on screen or that the special effects are gory enough or the explosions large enough to keep viewers' attention. The series also shows Marines dealing with costly mistakes, the friction of war, and trying to act morally in a world that offers no clean solutions, only awful choices. Unlike other post-9/11 military programming that depicts the uncertainty of the times, *Generation Kill* does not provide viewers with an easy view of the War on Terror. Throughout most of the series, the Marines are given a series of choices among miserable alternatives in which, as Sergeant Colbert puts it when, after ordering his driver not to hit a severed head in the middle of a road, the Humvee runs over the headless corpse, "You just can't fuckin' win" (Simon, 2008).

—Mitchell McNaylor

Reference

Simon, D. (Producer). (2008). *Generation kill* [Television mini-series]. New York: HBO.

SPOTLIGHT ESSAY/TELEVISION: "ISAAC AND ISHMAEL" AND *THE WEST WING*

When the terrorist attacks happened on September 11, 2001, few television series had begun their new fall seasons. Television shows slated to be broadcast were delayed as the networks adjusted to coverage of the attacks and their aftermath. Programs set to air in the fall of 2001 were essentially completed, giving series' creators little room for addressing the events of September 11 in their initial episodes. A few programs, however, were able to integrate content related to the terrorist attacks purposefully and quickly into fictional narratives. One notable example of this was a special episode of *The West Wing*, titled "Isaac and Ishmael" (Sorkin, 2001), that aired on October 3, 2001, less than a month after the attacks.

The West Wing (1999–2006), a drama about White House business, politics, and policy making, premiered in 1999 and focused on the fictional Bartlet administration. Subject matter on the program was dealt with seriously; and writer and producer Aaron Sorkin hired numerous consultants such as Dee Dee Meyers (former White House press secretary to President Clinton), Patrick Caddell (former strategist for President Carter), Frank Luntz (a Republican pollster), and Peggy Noonan (former speechwriter for President Reagan) to inform the program's narrative (Gans-Boriskin & Tisinger, 2005). After the terrorist attacks, Sorkin wrote and produced "Isaac and Ishmael" within three weeks, an extremely fast accomplishment by Hollywood standards, and NBC announced that the third-season premiere of *The West Wing* would be delayed so that this special episode could air as a response to the events that were consuming the nation (Jones & Dionisopoulos, 2004). "Isaac and Ishmael" is a stand-alone episode in the series, and its narrative is separate from the end of season two or the beginning of season three.

The episode begins with a security breach resulting in a White House lockdown. Two story lines within this lockdown are pursued: Deputy Chief of Staff Josh Lyman, who is later joined by the other main characters on the program, discusses terrorism with a group of visiting high school students; and Chief of Staff Leo McGarry observes and participates in an interrogation of a White House staffer who is suspected of terrorism. Whereas the conversation with the students is informational, or pedagogical, in its presentation of a complicated issue, the interrogation of the White House staffer focuses on the irrationality, anger, and racism in McGarry's interactions with the suspect. For the purposes of this episode, the depiction of McGarry is not consistent with his character—normally, McGarry is presented as thoughtful and cool-headed; perhaps suggesting to viewers how fear and anger can alter a person's usually reserved ways.

The special episode drew unprecedented viewership (Jones & Dionisopoulos, 2004). At a time when the entertainment industry was editing or delaying the release of particular content deemed unsuitable so close to the attacks on the United States, the popularity of "Isaac and Ishmael" suggested that viewers were looking for a narrative response to events. Although the broadcast drew 25 million viewers (Shales, 2001), critics were mixed in their reviews of the episode. While some called it "articulate" ("West Wing," 2001) and "appropriate" (Levesque, 2001), others accused it of being "condescending" (Bianco, 2001, para. 1) and "preachy and self important" (James, 2001, p. E26). Despite these varying perspectives, "Isaac and Ishmael" stands out as one of the earliest attempts to react to and process the events of September 11 through an established network drama. In so doing, the show touched on topics such as the history of terrorism, racism, fear, civil liberties, and Islam, issues that were forefront in Americans' minds at the time.

As the third season of *The West Wing* progressed, the writers pursued narratives that were more representative of the post-9/11 world. Given that *The West Wing* takes place in a fictional current-day White House, the feeling among the program's creators was that it would have to address the situation (Carter, 2001). In season three, many episodes make mention of terrorism or terrorist activities. The impetus for discussion of terrorism within *The West Wing* was twofold. First, the fictional Qumar, a Middle Eastern country with a deplorable record on human rights and treatment of women, becomes part of the plot in several season-three episodes. Second, terrorist activities, both domestic and international, became central to episode narratives. Gans-Boriskin and Tisinger (2005) argue that, over time, *The West Wing*'s presentation of foreign policy after 9/11 was more hawkish than the Bush administration's, something important to evaluate given that presentation of politics in fiction may complicate how viewers think about world events.

—*Amy M. Damico*

References

Bianco, R. (2001, October 4). *West Wing* lectured more than entertained. *United States Today*. Retrieved from http://usatoday.com

Carter, B. (2001, September 22). *West Wing* rushes script keyed to attack. *The New York Times*, p. A22.

Gans-Boriskin, R., & Tisinger, R. (2005). The Bushlet administration: Terrorism and war on *The West Wing*. *Journal of American Culture, 28*(1), 100–113.

James, C. (2001, October 5). On *West Wing*, a twilight world where fact meets fiction. *The New York Times*, E26.

Jones, R., & Dionisopoulos, G. (2004). Scripting a tragedy: The "Isaac and Ishmael" episode of *The West Wing* as parable. *Popular Communication, 2*(1), 21–40.

Levesque, J. (2001, October 4). *West Wing* opener was sensitive, appropriate. *Seattle Post Intelligencer*. Retrieved from http://www.seatlepi.com

Shales, T. (2001, October 5). *The West Wing* assumes the role of moral compass. *The Washington Post*, C1. Retrieved from http://www.washingtonpost.com

Sorkin, A. (Writer). (2001) Isaac and Ishmael. [Television series episode]. In J. Wells (Executive Producer), *The West Wing*. Los Angeles: NBC.

West Wing terror show criticized. (2001, October 3). BBC News. Retrieved from http://news.bbc.co.uk

SPOTLIGHT ESSAY/TELEVISION: *JERICHO*

In the midst of a post-9/11 explosion of dramatic serial television dramas, CBS's *Jericho* (Barbee, 2006–2008) stands out for two reasons. The first relates to the show's resuscitation after season one. *Jericho* premiered in September 2006, ran for a first season, and, because of low ratings, ended with a cliffhanger finale in May 2007. After CBS cancelled *Jericho* that same month because of low ratings, the show's fans mounted an unprecedented online campaign to convince the network to revive the show. In a move that made television (and Internet) history, CBS acquiesced to viewers' online campaign, running seven episodes during the second season before shutting down the show (again, due to low ratings) on March 25, 2008. Despite CBS's decision, *Jericho* continues to have resonance beyond its limited run, on blogs, fan sites, and in popular cultural and political analysis. The reason is simple—post-9/11

U.S. television audiences looking for substantive and timely content would be hard pressed to imagine a more relevant show than CBS's *Jericho*. The show tackled some of the most pressing issues of the post-9/11 world in an intimate, engaging, and challenging way, and created compelling, complex, and conflicted characters without resorting to hackneyed stereotyping (like *24*) or the use of supernatural or *deux ex machina*-like plot-bending.

Jericho revolves around 11 characters in a small, rural Kansas farm town, whose lives are irrevocably changed when the United States comes under a mysterious nuclear attack, and 23 U.S. cities (including nearby Denver) are destroyed. With the support of his wife Gail, the town's aging but well-liked mayor, Johnston Green (a former U.S. soldier and avid hunter), contends with reorganizing a town almost completely cut off from the outside world. His two sons, meanwhile, cope with troubles of their own: Older son Eric struggles with a troubled marriage and an affair with a local barmaid, while younger son Jake returns home after a long-term absence just before the nuclear attacks begin. A few major themes prove surprisingly relevant to the post-9/11 world. Four of the most important are: nuclear war; terrorism, continuity of government (COG), and U.S. government conspiracies; post-peak oil living; and unveiled corporate power, including "disaster capitalism."

In real life, the U.S. government possesses approximately 10,000 nuclear weapons (Arms Control Association, 2007), and nuclear proliferation has never been more of a hot-button issue, especially with "rogue states" such as Iran and North Korea developing nuclear programs. In *Jericho*, occasional "official" news sources blame Iran and North Korea for nuclear war, whereas the true nature and purpose of the apocalyptic attacks is gradually revealed as the story progressed.

Post-9/11 United States has seen the viral spread of so-called conspiracy theories about the nature and purpose of the "terrorist" attacks. These run rampant on the Internet, in films, and in books. *Jericho* tackles conspiratorial concerns head on by creating a mysterious character named Robert Hawkins, who arrives in Jericho with his family just prior to the attacks. Viewers quickly learn that Hawkins is a CIA operative who appears to have been involved in planning the nuclear attacks, but decided to go "rogue" and blow the whistle. *Jericho* also explores continuity of government (COG) possibilities. COG refers to how the U.S. government (since 2002) has structured contingency plans for perpetuating itself in the face of a nuclear strike, natural disaster, or "terrorist" attack, when normal Constitutional law is suspended and martial law declared. In a country where very few Americans know anything about real-life COG plans, *Jericho*'s characters referenced the plan in the show's script.

What happens in a twenty-first-century United States when the more than 20-million barrels of oil our civilization depends on stops its reliable flow? How might we rapidly relocalize food and energy needs in the face of what observers call an emerging "peak oil" dilemma? Twenty-first-century scholars, including Richard Heinberg, Colin Campbell, Michael Klare, Matthew Simmons, and David Goodstein have all explored this question in numerous books, articles, and interviews. One of *Jericho*'s most pressing themes involves the town's struggle to suddenly reorient itself in the wake of disaster, while confronting hostile townspeople, desperate survivors from major urban areas struck by atomic radiation, vigilantes from neighboring towns, and the new and much more violent remnants of the U.S. government and its military machine.

In her book, *The Shock Doctrine: The Rise of Disaster Capitalism*, Canadian journalist Naomi Klein (2007) chronicled the various ways in which corporations and governments work together to privatize publicly owned assets in the wake of wars, natural disasters, terrorist attacks, and other acts of God. In real life, the U.S. government has come under intense international scrutiny for its brokering of private no-bid contracts with multinational corporations like Halliburton, and its hiring of private security corporations like Blackwater to fight foreign wars and conduct domestic "relief" efforts in the wake of Hurricane Katrina and other domestic disasters. *Jericho* features the appearance of Ravenwood, a group of mercenaries managed by a large and mysterious corporation called Jennings and Rall, which also manages to control the antidote to a mysterious Hudson River virus, dispensing it only to those survivors who toe the company line.

In its two seasons, *Jericho* explored some unfolding themes in contemporary twenty-first-century U.S. life. Television programming has historically reflected and influenced aspects of the times. What specifically identifies *Jericho* as a post-9/11 drama is its attention to characters placed in a situation where the walls of "normal" civilization as we know it came tumbling down.

—*Rob Williams*

References

Arms Control Association. (2007). Nuclear weapons: Who has what at a glance. *Strategic Arms Control and Policy Fact Sheet*. Retrieved July 31, 2009, from http://www.armscontrol .org/factsheets/Nuclearweaponswhohaswhat

Barbee, C. (Executive Producer). (2006–2008). *Jericho* [Television series]. Los Angeles: CBS.

Klein, N. (2007). *The shock doctrine: The rise of disaster capitalism*. New York: Metropolitan Books.

SPOTLIGHT ESSAY/TELEVISION: *LOST*

If corporate commercial broadcast industry executives wanted to invent a popular television show that somehow channeled the U.S. public's complete sense of helplessness after the horrific events of 9/11, they could not do much better than *Lost* (Abrams, 2004–2010). With an average of 16 million *Lost* watchers tuning in each week during the show's first season (2004), U.S. television viewers seemed to agree. Since it first aired, the show has garnered numerous awards since, including a 2005 Emmy (Outstanding Drama Series), a 2006 Golden Globe (Best Drama), and a Screen Actors Guild Award.

The premise of *Lost* seems simple on the surface. A transcontinental aircraft crashed on the beach of a remote and seemingly deserted island, and the survivors must tend to their most immediate basic needs, while figuring out how to get back to civilization. The airplane crash, the show's frightening and defining touchstone event, which calls to mind the planes that crashed on September 11, represents each character's disconnection to the twenty-first-century world. With no way of even contacting anyone "off island," *Lost's* characters are plunged into a disorienting new reality that feels very much beyond their control, much like the collective sense expressed by Americans after the tragedy of the 9/11 attacks.

Yet this description does little to describe *Lost's* genre-defying acrobatics—equal parts mystery, thriller, drama, science fiction, and adventure, and, post-9/11 political zeitgeist. *Lost* succeeded because it reflected the nation's collective sense of disorientation after September 11, as well as the frustrated desire to understand how seemingly random events fit together and make sense. Everything is connected in *Lost;* the problem is that no one, not even the show's producers, can say exactly how.

As its title suggests, *Lost* is all about the experience of being disoriented. For example, *Lost's* setting—a seemingly deserted island—is populated by unexplained forces: mean-spirited wild boar, a spooky black mist, an elaborate but mysterious underground "hatch" full of the latest high-tech gadgetry, and a strange group of "Others," whose identities are gradually revealed as the seasons unfold. Strangely enough, surveillance cameras also become a focal point of *Lost's* story, mimicking the rise of a post-9/11 surveillance state.

It is *Lost's* seemingly random narrative structure, however, that most dramatically enhances a viewer's sense of disorientation. Each 42-minute episode unpacks the "back story" of a particular character through a series of flashbacks (and, beginning in season 5, "flashes sideways") that unfold concurrently with the main action taking place on the island. Unlike programs that are relentlessly linear, *Lost* is exactly the opposite— viewers literally have no idea where the show is going, from moment to moment and episode to episode, and the "not knowing" keeps viewers coming back for more.

Viewers may find hope, however, through the ways in which *Lost* represents its multiracial cast in a post-9/11 climate of fear. The program features the trials of an Arab Iraqi character who is smart, capable, and handsome; the story of a young Korean couple's troubled marriage; and a tale of a Nigerian warlord-turned-priest. These narratives unfold with nuanced attention and sympathetic treatment. *Lost* also created female characters like Kate Austen (played by Evangeline Lilly), who emerge on the island as physically capable, emotionally tough, and brainy leaders.

This is the promise, albeit a tenuous one, of *Lost*. While we live in a post-9/11 world in which fear, disorientation, and anger drive our political culture, *Lost* suggests that strangers struggling to work together to "get off the island" might actually come to understand one another better, despite the hardship and pain of their own personal circumstances, in the midst of a larger situation very much beyond their collective control.

—*Rob Williams*

Reference

Abrams, J. (Executive Producer) (2004–2010). *Lost* [Television series]. Los Angeles: ABC.

SPOTLIGHT ESSAY/TELEVISION: *RESCUE ME*

In the three years following the terrorist attacks of 9/11, only single episodes of popular television series dealt with the consequences of the attacks. The emergence of the HBO-drama series *Rescue Me* in 2004, however, marked a new direction in the relationship between TV and September 11. A program that was created as a direct result of the events, *Rescue Me* (2004 to present) tells the story of traumatized firefighters in post-9/11 New York City. Created by actor/comedian Denis Leary and Peter Tolan, the show focuses on the story of Tommy Gavin (played by Leary), a professional firefighter still affected by the repercussions of 9/11. The series is set around the fictional firehouse Ladder 62 in New York City and begins approximately three years after the attacks with the protagonist still suffering from posttraumatic stress, drinking heavily, and even hallucinating about his cousin and best friend Jimmy Keefe who died on September 11. Explicit references to September 11 were especially prevalent in the first two seasons of the program and helped underscore the fact that *Rescue Me* concentrates on the psychological consequences of the characters' jobs rather than on heroic rescue missions. In 2005, it was the most successful television series on U.S. television.

In their audio commentary of the pilot episode titled "Guts," Leary and Tolan emphasize that they want to deliberately distance themselves from the stereotypical glorification of the rescue workers who had been constructed as indestructible heroes by the media and politicians in the wake of the September 11 attacks. The protagonists of *Rescue Me*, the firefighters of Ladder 62, do not want to be called heroes, as becomes evident in a speech Gavin gives in front of young recruits of the FDNY:

> I've been in the middle of shit that would make you piss your pants right now. . . . There ain't no medals on my chest, assholes, 'cos I ain't no hero! I'm a fireman. We're not in the business of making heroes here! . . . I knew sixty men who gave their lives at Ground Zero. Sixty! Four of them from my house. . . . These four men were better human beings and better firefighters than any of you will ever be. (Leary & Tolan, 2004)

The program makes it evident that the surviving men do not see themselves as heroes. Instead, attention is drawn to the four deceased members of Gavin's crew. The distinction between the surviving and the deceased firefighters serves to illustrate the almost cult-like glorification of the "dead heroes of 9/11," while at the same time rejecting the idea that the survivors are entitled to be called "heroes."

Early on in the pilot it becomes evident that the protagonist is suffering from severe posttraumatic stress disorder, culminating in his hallucinations of his dead cousin who died on September 11. By the visual staging of Gavin's hallucinations and daydreams, the series stresses the protagonist's problems: After his speech to the recruits, Keefe is already waiting for him in his car, congratulating, but also teasing him: "Those probies wouldn't think you were such a tough guy if they knew you were talking to a dead guy" (Leary & Tolan, 2004). Not only is Gavin hallucinating, but he is also interacting and communicating with his dead cousin. Moreover, his dreams frequently take him back to Ground Zero—where he is looking for his friends in the rubble—or to the still-standing Twin Towers where his cousin heads off to climb the stairs where he ultimately dies. This compulsive reliving of the traumatic memory in flashbacks is one of the symptoms of posttraumatic stress disorder described by trauma theory (Caruth, 1996). Although Gavin seems aware that he is having problems, he is unable to seek help and withdraws to his house where he spends his nights drinking and talking to Keefe.

While criticizing the general glorification of New York's firefighters on the one hand, the series, on the other hand, stresses the exceptional position of the rescue workers by touching on another very sensitive subject: Who has the right to call oneself traumatized? Thus, the series challenges the popular notion of a collective American trauma that has been evoked by the terrorist attacks (Alexander, 2004; Greenberg, 2003; Kaplan, 2005; Smelser, 2004). Afraid of being ridiculed by his colleagues, Lieutenant Shea, one of Gavin's co-workers, turns to a self-help group for people suffering from posttraumatic stress disorder after 9/11 in the episode titled "Revenge." After sharing one of his poems he learns that none of the other participants in the group was in downtown Manhattan (or even close) on September 11 or lost somebody in the attacks. Shea gets angry and starts to abuse the others because in his opinion only people who suffered directly from the consequences of 9/11 are entitled to be traumatized. The idea of a collective American trauma as well as that of an oblique trauma is rebutted strongly in the series.

Rescue Me does not merely deal with the firefighters' problems in the wake of the attacks; it also sheds light on the difficulties the men's families are facing. Due to Gavin's inability and unwillingness to confront his psychological issues and his ensuing substance abuse problems, in the episode "Gay," his wife has left him and considers leaving New York with their three children in order to protect them, as she explains to her husband:

> I need to get away from this. . . . Every other house on the block has a dead hero dad, every other kid at school has lost a father or an uncle. And you know what's worse than all the guys that died that day? The rest of you left behind, walking around like everything's fine, when you're dead inside. (Leary & Tolan, 2004)

The program emphasizes that it is not only the firefighters who have to come to terms with the effects of 9/11, but that their families and friends are similarly affected by the changes.

Rescue Me does not deal with the instantaneous consequences of 9/11, but rather concentrates on the medium- and long-term repercussions of the attacks. It renegotiates the image of the glorious firefighter who fights fearlessly against evil, no matter what. *Rescue Me* raises questions of how to cope with posttraumatic stress disorder brought on by 9/11, not only for the firefighters but also for their families. By its depiction of the lives of firefighters in post-9/11 New York, the concept of a collective American trauma is strongly rebuffed and even ridiculed. The difficult situation many

firefighters are still facing is the recurring theme of *Rescue Me*, reminding viewers that
the effects of 9/11 are still being felt.

—*Stefanie Hoth*

References

Alexander, J. (2004). Toward a theory of cultural trauma. In J. Alexander, R. Eyerman,
      B. Giesen, N. Smelser, & P. Sztompka (Eds.), *Cultural trauma and collective identity*
      (pp. 1–30). Berkeley: University of California Press.
Caruth, C. (1996). *Unclaimed experience: Trauma, narrative, and history.* Baltimore: Johns
      Hopkins University Press.
Greenberg, J. (Ed.). (2003). *Trauma at home: After 9/11.* Lincoln and London: University of
      Nebraska Press.
Kaplan, E. A. (2005). *Trauma culture: The politics of terror and loss in media and literature.* New
      Brunswick, NJ: Rutgers University Press.
Leary, D., & Tolan, P. (Creators) (2004–present). *Rescue Me* [Television series]. Los Angeles:
      Fox Cable Networks
Smelser, N. (2004). September 11, 2001 as cultural trauma. In J. Alexander, R. Eyerman,
      B. Giesen, N. Smelser, & P. Sztompka (Eds.), *Cultural trauma and collective identity*
      (pp. 164–182). Berkeley: University of California Press.

SPOTLIGHT ESSAY/TELEVISION: *SEX AND THE CITY*

Sex and the City (*SATC*) (1998–2004) presents an intriguing case of how a fictional
series deals with, and can be read through, a traumatic event. While none of the episodes of *SATC* produced after September 11, 2001, ever refer directly to the events of
9/11, they can be understood as reflecting those events or being influenced by them.
Specifically, by working within the already established formula of *SATC*, these episodes celebrate the city of New York—the center of the September 11 attacks—in
highly romantic ways, laden with doses of comedy and irony. The stories emphasize
fractures in the protagonist Carrie's life, but they often end with the strengthening
of ties between Carrie, her friends, and the city of New York. These plots of fracture
and subsequent union helped to create a sense of hope which many viewers, especially
New Yorkers, found appealing in the months following 9/11.

Throughout the highly popular series, New York City is often referred to by
the *SATC* actresses and writers (all New Yorkers themselves) as the fifth character on
the show, the "fifth lady." *SATC* was in a mid-season hiatus when the attacks on
September 11, 2001, occurred, and several previously produced episodes began airing
on January 6, 2002. The final episode of the season, "I Heart New York," was seen by
many viewers as a direct response to the events of 9/11, even though the program was
produced before the terrorist attacks took place. In this episode Carrie's ex-boyfriend,
Mr. Big, moves away from New York to Napa, California. The episode takes place
at the beginning of the fall (when 9/11 happened), unusual for a show which, as

writers have noted, seems to take place in a kind of perpetual spring and summer (King, 2003).

In "I Heart New York," Carrie tells Big, "You can't leave New York! You're the Chrysler Building! The Chrysler Building would be all wrong in a vineyard!" For Carrie, Big is a fixture of the city, so his absence for her would be like the New York skyline without the Chrysler Building; a building that can be understood as a fixture in Carrie's life as well. Both the absence of the man and the building would change her life in incalculable ways. In a similar way, New Yorkers' experiences of the physical city after 9/11 were changed radically. Many, including Sarah Jessica Parker herself, spoke about the city feeling fundamentally different, not only because of 9/11 but also because of the changed skyline ("Manhattan Rhapsody," 2002, p. 237). Calling Big the Chrysler Building takes on a richer meaning in post-9/11 New York, evoking the literal loss of the Twin Towers, which marked the skyline so vividly before their fall. His departure also recalls the impulse of many New Yorkers, in the wake of 9/11, to leave the city for greener and safer pastures (Williams, 2001, p. 35).

In response to Big's decision to leave New York, Carrie decides they "have to do it up right. A proper goodbye. You, me, New York." She plans a nostalgic evening in which the city is celebrated as the landscape where their romance occurred. Indeed, their romantic carriage ride through Central Park is interrupted by Miranda's call that she is in labor. The following morning, after attending to Miranda at the hospital, Carrie returns to Big's apartment to find it empty, save for a Henry Mancini record—one which includes the classic *Breakfast at Tiffany's* tune "Moon River," both which have been long associated with Manhattan—and a plane ticket she can use for a trip to California. The final monologue of the show, even thought it was written prior to the attacks, seems to refer directly to 9/11:

> Maybe our mistakes are what make our fate. Without them what would shape our lives? Perhaps if we never veered off course we wouldn't fall in love, or have babies, or be who we are. *After all seasons change . . . so do cities.* [italics added] People come into your life and people go. But it's comforting to know the ones you love are always in your heart and if you're very lucky a plane ride away. (King, 1998–2004)

This episode begins with a rupture, but ends with a renewed sense of Carrie's union with her friends and New York, as do many episodes of the show. Critical reviews often comment on the prescience of this episode and its resonance and poignancy after 9/11 (Rosenberg, 2002).

Very few television shows knew how to deal with the events of 9/11, and many—even those set in New York—ignored the tragedy. *SATC*, however, had already been interpreted through the events of 9/11 because of its own unique relationship to New York, as a series filmed on location. In an effort to continue this subtle acknowledgment, the first episode written after 9/11, "Anchors Away," is a nostalgic tribute to patriotism and contains references to the classic New York film, *On the Town* (1949). The episode makes humorous references to the patriotic duty of shopping and attending a Fleet Week party, and jokingly refers to an ex-boyfriend as "manthrax."

Here the most direct references to 9/11 are made in the familiar terms of the show: shopping and men.

In episodes filmed both before and after 9/11, *SATC* not only celebrated New York, but seemed to reflect the city's problems in the protagonists' narratives. Both the city and the *SATC* characters are depicted as wounded but recovering and moving on with their lives. *SATC* managed to respond to the events of 9/11 by maintaining its own formula and style. Episodes filmed before the event were powerful because they celebrated the city while maintaining a sense of irony and comedy. Episodes made both before and after 9/11 displayed characters whose lives had been ruptured like the city, through breakups, but who were finding ways of repairing. In the case of Carrie, this repair involved a deepened commitment between her and her city. New York takes on a new meaning in these episodes because of the events of 9/11, but so do the lives of the characters in *SATC*.

—Victoria Pass

References

King, M. P. (Producer and Writer). (1998–2004). *Sex and the city* [Television series]. New York: HBO.

King, M. P. (Producer and Writer). (2003). *Sex and the City: The complete fourth season* [DVD commentary]. New York: HBO Video.

Manhattan Rhapsody. (2002). *Vogue, 192*(2), 232–237.

Rosenberg, H. (2002, January 4). A love note to New York. *Los Angeles Times*, p. F-1.

Williams, A. (2001). Should we stay or should we go. *New York, 34*(38), 34–39, 74.

SPOTLIGHT ESSAY/TELEVISION: *SUPERVOLCANO*

Shortly after September 11, 2001, Karl Rove and a White House team met with Hollywood executives to set the terms by which that day could be cinematically represented (Sterritt, 2004, p. 65). Years later, however, mainstream TV movies and films that explicitly and directly portray the attacks are scarce. Instead, representations of the attacks are made using metaphor and allusion, as is apparent in *Supervolcano* (Gabler, 2005), a two-part, made-for-television project, one movie and the other documentary, about what would happen if the "supervolcano" under Yellowstone National Park erupted.

Supervolcano is a three-hour Discovery Channel/BBC television event narrated by Tom Brokaw. It aired in the spring of 2005, having been scheduled for earlier release but postponed after the Indian Ocean tsunami in December 2004. The first two hours of *Supervolcano* are a dramatic reenactment of a hypothetical supereruption at Yellowstone, structured as a retrospective documentary depicting attendant personal and scientific dramas through the story of Rick Lieberman, the fictional government scientist in charge of monitoring the volcano there. The story line has the "supereruption" lasting for seven days, destroying the U.S. West and Midwest, bringing the rest of the nation to a standstill, killing hundreds of thousands of people, and drastically altering the global climate. Once fictional Yellowstone is tranquil again, the final hour provides a scientific explanation of the geophysical events just depicted, in which the real-life equivalents of the film's characters alternate between assuring audiences that there is nothing to worry about and encouraging them to prepare for the worst. Such commentary echoes the contradictory post-9/11 advice given to ordinary Americans as they absorbed the shock of the attacks.

Indeed, despite its ostensible subject, *Supervolcano* is actually about America in a frightening new post-9/11 world, one which appears neat and tidy by talking about national trauma while dodging difficult questions of causation. The film accomplishes this feat by removing existential threats to the United States from the intricacies of geopolitics, and focusing instead on a thoroughly natural disaster, a catastrophe by which all Americans are affected and for which all Americans are blameless. Here, the natural features of the "homeland" acquire new meaning and importance. This ascription is particularly easy for a place like Yellowstone. The United States' first national park is an "idealized and conspicuously nonviolence space" in the American imagination (Germic, 2001, p. 79), conveniently located in the American West, the region that often symbolizes the "real" America and the only part of the country with volcanic features (Alexander, 1993, p. 105). Yellowstone's location and geothermal dynamism thus make it a logical setting for a post-9/11 apocalyptic scene.

Supervolcano frames this allegory first through its characters. Lieberman's vow that the volcano will not erupt again "on my watch" cites an oft-repeated promise by former President George W. Bush. In the movie, the character, Lieberman, works closely with the fictional Federal Emergency Management Agency (FEMA) director, Wendy Reiss, and their coordination of federal disaster response positions them as analogues to Bush and Condoleezza Rice. The courage of the U.S. Geological Survey (USGS) team serves to remind viewers of the self-sacrifice of military personnel and first responders, while FEMA, the Office of Homeland Security, and other federal agencies are omnipresent, and the nameless thousands of casualties become a crucial rhetorical and political touchstone.

Verbal and visual narrative details construct these comparisons as well. A real FEMA employee says that a post-supereruption rescue effort would be hundreds of times larger than their biggest (pre-Katrina) responsibility to date, the Ground Zero cleanup. "Red" and "yellow" alerts warn the public about subterranean volcanic activity and calibrate the threat of eruption. Aerial shots of Chicago going dark in a blackout index the attacks on New York City. A montage of global news reports (including one that looks like Al Jazeera) echoes the "worldwide synchronization of attention" (Debatin, 2002, p. 165) that followed 9/11. Fictional satellite images of the eruption recall the lore that the fires at the World Trade Center were visible from space. Similarly, the posteruption emergency air traffic ground stoppage, visualized through standard stock footage of airport closures, invokes the transportation situation after September 11.

All of this reminds us that a supereruption at Yellowstone would have disastrous consequences for the entire nation and, in fact, the world. The national impact of such a calamity would be concrete; Yellowstone's proximity to the nation's major agricultural region, for example, underscores the threat of post-supereruption starvation. Alternately, the film visualizes the global relevance of a Yellowstone supereruption with maps simulating the movement of the ash cloud, ash fall, and toxic gasses, "news" broadcasts, and computer-generated images. The supereruption causes a nearly instantaneous 15-degree drop in the temperature of the Northern hemisphere and results in monsoon and thus crop failure in the South. And yet, although the supereruption imperils the whole world, the film also suggests that the real tragedy would be distinctly American.

The documentary that concludes *Supervolcano* tends toward fatalism, encouraging viewers both to consider the possibility of their own fiery demise, and to "come and see" for themselves the hydrothermal majesty of Yellowstone. This is a call to vigilance similar to that which followed 9/11, couched in an invitation to return, insofar as Yellowstone is the very essence of America, to an uncomplicated patriotism. The final image of *Supervolcano* is a quintessential American ritual: a throng of tourists cheering at the sight of Old Faithful erupting punctually and predictably in a controlled and entertaining release of devastating force. This, it seems, is the "natural" harmony to which the film aspires.

—Rebecca A. Adelman

References

Alexander, D. (1993). *Natural disasters*. New York: Chapman & Hall.

Debatin, B. (2002). "Plane wreck with spectators": The semiotics of terror. In B. S. Greenberg (Ed.), *Communication and terrorism: Public and media responses to 9/11* (pp. 163–174). Cresskill, NJ: Hampton Press.

Gabler, D. (Executive Producer). (2005). *Supervolcano* [Docudrama/documentary]. United States: Discovery Channel.

Germic, S. (2001). *American green: Class, crisis, and the deployment of nature in Central Park, Yosemite, and Yellowstone*. Lanham, MD: Lexington Books.

Sterritt, D. (2004). Representing atrocity: From the Holocaust to September 11. In W. Winston Dixon (Ed.), *Film and television after 9/11* (63–78). Carbondale: Southern Illinois University Press.

SPOTLIGHT ESSAY/TELEVISION: *THE UNIT*

In the years following September 11, military-oriented programming became dominant in the entertainment landscape. *The Unit* (2006–2009; "About *The Unit*," n.d.) was a prime-time program on the CBS network that first aired in the spring of 2006, and recently concluded its fourth and final season in May 2009. Based on the book *Inside Delta Force: The Story of America's Elite Counterterrorist Unit* (Haney, 2002), written by former Delta Force member and show producer Eric L. Haney, episodes of *The Unit* were executive-produced by David Mamet and Shawn Ryan. The show follows the activities of "a covert team of Special Forces operatives as they risk their lives on undercover missions around the globe, while their families maintain the home front, protecting their husbands' secrets" ("About *The Unit*," n.d). Operating under the guise of the 303rd Logistical Studies Group, the team is composed of six members: team-leader Sergeant Major Jonas Blane (aka "Snake Doctor," played by Dennis Haysbert), Colonel Tom Ryan (aka "Blue Iguana," played by Robert Patrick), Master Sergeant Mack Gerhardt (aka "Dirt Diver," played by Max Martini), Sergeant First Class Charles Grey (aka "Betty Blue," played by Michael Irby), Sergeant First Class Hector Williams (aka "Hammerhead," played by Delmore Barnes), and Sergeant First Class Bob Brown (aka "Cool Breeze," played by Scott Foley).

Blane, Gerhardt, and Brown are accompanied by their wives, who must negotiate the difficulties of base life and the secretive existence necessitated by the nature of the team's activities. Their silence is crucial, as any slip of the tongue regarding their husbands' occupation will lead to immediate expulsion from the team, as well as additional damage to their careers and possible compromise of the team's mission, which could lead to termination of the team itself. Blane's wife, Molly, "is the base matriarch who comforts and counsels the other wives as they cope with the fear and uncertainty they experience when their husbands leave home" ("About *The Unit*," n.d.), while Gerhardt's wife Tiffy hides an affair with Colonel Ryan, and Brown's wife Kim adjusts to her new life while managing a pregnancy.

Over the span of its four seasons, *The Unit* addresses a multitude of national security scenarios, some drawn from Haney's own Special Forces experiences, and others reflective of the threat environment that exists in the wake of 9/11. Among these scenarios are the sale of nuclear materials to Iran ("Security," season 1, episode 6), the use of torture ("SERE," season 1, episode 8), the use of biological weapons ("Change of Station," season 2, episode 1), intervention in a hurricane zone ("Force Majeure," season 2, episode 5), consultation on the problem of suicide bombers in Israel ("Two Coins," season 2, episode 18), and a hostage situation in a school ("In Loco Parentis," season 2, episode 20).

Episodes frequently resonate with past or ongoing security threats, with the aforementioned episodes addressing Iranian President Mahmoud Ahmadinejad's statements regarding Iran's nuclear program, the debate over torture and its use in Abu Ghraib and Guantanamo Bay, the threat of weapons of mass destruction (WMD) and their stated importance to the decision to intervene in Iraq, the cultural and political fallout after Hurricane Katrina, the ongoing dispute between Israel and Palestine, and the seizure of a school in Beslan by Chechen separatists under the command of Shamil Basayev.

One episode in particular, the pilot episode entitled "First Responders," which aired on March 7, 2006, comments directly on 9/11 in its portrayal of the team's intervention in an attempted hijacking. After a plane is hijacked by an anonymous, unaffiliated group of Middle Eastern men and directed to Wyndham Regional Airport in rural Idaho, the team is called in to diffuse a hostage situation where a reporter at the scene notes that it is "abundantly clear that these terrorists have a well-conceived plan to take the life of one hostage every hour" (Mamet & Guggenheim, 2006). On evaluating the situation, team leader Jonas Blane concludes that "[t]hey [the hijackers] don't care about the businessmen. They want to kill the first responders" (Mamet &

Guggenheim, 2006), recalling the significant losses taken by the New York fire and police departments on 9/11. The team devises a plan that involves killing a terrorist lookout in the surrounding woods, then using his walkie-talkie to lure the hijackers into opening the plane's entry door, enabling the team to storm the cabin. They execute it flawlessly, killing the hijackers before they may detonate a bomb and sparing the lives of the passengers. Because of the secrecy surrounding the team, their efforts cannot be recognized, and are instead called "one hell of an operation by the National Guard" by Colonel Ryan and "a perfect example of coordinated interagency cooperation" by the president (Mamet & Guggenheim, 2006), referring to the very lack of readiness and interagency confusion evident on 9/11.

The team's capacity for just this sort of swift, decisive action is seen in Blane's terse aside to FBI agents in the early stages of assault planning: "You, you, and you, panic. The rest of you come with me" (Mamet & Guggenheim, 2006). The hijacking scenario in this episode revised the particulars of 9/11, replacing the suicide attack with a hostage situation, ineffectual agency response with swift action, and vulnerability with security. Although military shows as a genre predate 9/11, *The Unit*'s particular attention to notions of family and team, in "First Responders" and throughout its many episodes, reflects the post-9/11 need for the togetherness and protection offered by groups in the wake of a trauma. It also provides the sense that, when governments fail, there is someone there to take the necessary actions to ensure the safety of the United States.

—*Lloyd Isaac Vayo*

References

About *The Unit*. (n.d.). CBS. Retrieved from http://www.cbs.com/primetime/the_unit/About

Haney, E. (2002). *Inside Delta Force: The story of America's elite counterterrorist unit*. New York: Delacorte Press.

Mamet, D. (Writer), & Guggeneheim, D. (Director). (2006). First responders [Television series episode]. In D. Mamet & S. Ryan (Producers), *The Unit*. Chicago: David Mamet Chicago.

On the six-month anniversary of the attacks, two columns of light were projected into the sky over New York City visually marking where the Twin Towers had once stood. (Denise Gould, Department of Defense)

The passengers on United 93 were called heroes for their courageous efforts in fighting the hijackers. Flag at United 93 Memorial, Shanksville, PA. (Sara Quay)

Firefighters became the most celebrated heroes of 9/11 and those who had lost their lives trying to save people in the Twin Towers were especially honored. A dedication set up for Fire Department of New York Ten House (FDNY Ten House) at the site of the World Trade Center. (Michael Rieger, old.911digitalarchive.org)

Many 9/11 memorials—such as the one in Shanksville, PA—list the name of each person who was lost in the attacks. Angels at the United 93 Memorial. (Sara Quay)

Many Americans found themselves tied to the television as they watched the 9/11 attacks and their aftermath unfold. "Can't stop watching tv" by Marie Blanchard (from Exit Art). (Marie Blanchard, Library of Congress)

New words—such as Ground Zero—entered the national vocabulary after September 11, 2001. September 12, 2001, "New Vocabulary" by Liz Johnson (from Exit Art). (Liz Johnson, Library of Congress)

September 12, 2001

NEW VOCABULARY:

Ground Zero
The Pile
suicide hijackers
Missing
The Office of Homeland Security
Heightened state of alert
Security checkpoints
Anthrax
Bioterrorism
Cipro
Stockpiling supplies
Military tribunals
Sky marshals
Covert operations
Patriotic shopping
Sir Rudy Giuliani

The destruction of the Twin Towers, whose presence had distinctly marked the New York skyline, was mourned by people around the world. Graffiti "WTX, RIP, 9 11 2001" on a sidewalk in response to the September 11 terrorist attack on the World Trade Center. (Library of Congress, Prints & Photographs Division, photograph by David Finn. See http://www.loc.gov/rr/print/res/310_finn.html for info re: public domain of Mr Finn's photos, Library of Congress.)

The radio tower that once stood at the top of the North Tower is now on display in the 9/11 Gallery at the Newseum in Washington, D.C. Newseum 9/11 Gallery. (Sam Kittner newseum)

Fritz Koenig's statue, *The Sphere*, which originally stood between the Twin Towers, was recovered from the wreckage and relocated to Battery Park as a 9/11 memorial. *The Sphere* and Eternal Flame at Battery Park. (Sara Quay)

Posters of people missing after the attacks were hung by loved ones around New York City. Notices and pictures of missing persons posted on a city mailbox following the September 11 terrorist attack on the World Trade Center. (Library of Congress, Prints & Photographs Division, photograph by David Finn, Library of Congress.)

One of the first 9/11 memorials to be unveiled was the FDNY Memorial Wall located at Engine Company 10-Ladder Company 10 adjacent to Ground Zero. FDNY Memorial Wall. (Sara Quay)

Spontaneous memorials—made of candles, flowers, photos, and mementoes—sprang up across the country after the attacks. Memorial for the victims of the September 11 terrorist attack on the World Trade Center, New York City. (David Finn, Library of Congress)

After the attacks, sales of flags increased dramatically as Americans sought ways to express their patriotism. Flag seller. (Kevin Bubriski, Library of Congress)

Artists created a range of memorial images that represent patriotism: the Twin Towers, the Pentagon, and the four planes involved in the attacks. In memory 9/11/01. (Brian Niemann, Library of Congress)

In the years following 2001, memorials were erected at all three of the crash sites, including the Pentagon. A memorial inscribed on a piece of limestone, from the original quarry used in the building, is at the reconstruction site at the Pentagon. (Jocelyn Augustino, old.911digitalarchive.org)

J. Seward Johnson's bronze statue, *Double Check*, was recovered from the rubble at Ground Zero and now stands as a 9/11 memorial in nearby Liberty Park. (Sara Quay)

Chapter 5

FILM

INTRODUCTION: FILM AND SEPTEMBER 11, 2001

When the planes crashed into the Twin Towers on September 11, 2001, it looked—for a moment at least—like something out of a movie. Long the focal point of action films containing dramatic, extravagant scenes of destruction, New York City had been attacked on the big screen so often that the images of such attacks were oddly familiar. As the facts about what was actually happening in New York became clear, however, it was quickly and frighteningly apparent that the attacks were not the result of special effects, stunt artists, or Hollywood's imagination. This time, the city—along with Washington, D.C.—was under attack for real.

The close relationship between New York City and Hollywood movies made the film industry's response to 9/11 especially interesting. Since their origins in the 1920s, moving pictures, as they were once called, have reflected a culture's concerns, beliefs, uncertainties, and ideals. At the same time, films have shaped the way members of a culture understand and interpret the events, ideas, and changes that inevitably change during a given time. After September 11, filmmakers across the board were unsure how to proceed. Would audiences seek escape in movie entertainment? What types of entertainment were appropriate? Would new forms of movies draw viewers' attention in the aftermath of the attacks?

The answers to such questions unfolded in the weeks, months, and years after September 11. Changes to films in production were immediately made. Images of the Twin Towers or scenes of death and destruction were eliminated to respect the nation's understandable sensitivity to such imagery. Release schedules were altered so that films deemed possibly upsetting to audiences were held, and more comforting lighthearted movies were distributed. In light of both the attacks on U.S. soil, and the military response to those attacks in Afghanistan and Iraq, films with themes of patriotism were encouraged by the Bush administration, and Hollywood responded.

Films focused on 9/11 emerged gradually, as the industry considered how to address the attacks on the big screen. Documentary films provided firsthand accounts of the day and its aftermath from multiple perspectives. Others offered a political critique of the events leading up to 9/11 and the government's response. Eventually, Hollywood produced dramatized versions of the events surrounding the attacks, focusing specifically on the victims and rescue workers who were hailed as heroes. Over time, the tragic events of the day would become plot points in films focused on other issues. Regardless of the role September 11 played in individual films, the events would influence the industry for years to come.

Hollywood's Initial Response

Hollywood initially responded to the events of 9/11 by changing a number of its filmic productions out of concern that audiences would not be receptive to certain imagery soon after the attacks. At least 45 films were cancelled, altered, or delayed. Of particular concern were images of the Twin Towers, which were commonly included in films set in New York City. After the attacks, the Twin Towers were quickly edited out of comedies such as *Zoolander* (2001), *Serendipity* (2001), and *Kissing Jessica Stein* (2001) (Germain, 2002). Similarly, *Men in Black II*'s (2002) ending was reshot to include the Chrysler Building in the final sequence rather than the Twin Towers (Bell-Metereau, 2004). Some filmmakers elected to leave the Twin Towers in their films but made different choices about where and when in the film the images would appear. For example, the *Spider-Man* (2001) trailer contained an action scene in which a helicopter is captured in Spider-Man's web—a web that is woven and hung between the Twin Towers. Both the trailer and the action scene in the film were pulled after the attacks. However, scenes of the Twin Towers were not entirely edited out of the movie and remained part of the scenic backdrop of the film.

In addition to changes made to images of the Twin Towers, films with terrorism plots were also put on hold for release. For example, the Schwarzenegger terrorist action-film, *Collateral Damage* (2002), initially slated for a fall 2001 opening, was delayed until April 2002, and the film's Web site was edited to omit the games Web site visitors could play, which included tracking of terrorists (Horrmann, 2002). *Big Trouble* (2002) was also postponed until April 2002 because the plot included a bomb on an airplane. Even films that were set in New York's historical past were withheld from distribution after 9/11. As director Martin Scorsese and producer Harvey Weinstein explained, they would delay the release of *Gangs of New York* (2002) because "[i]n light of the ever changing current events, we've decided to err on the side of sensitivity and postpone the wide release of the film until 2002" ("Scorsese's Gangs Has Release Date Pushed Back," 2001, para. 2).

Other film releases scheduled for September were deferred for a few weeks, rather than months. For example, *Training Day* (2001) was delayed until early October when the producers thought audiences would be more in the frame of mind to watch a police drama, and *Sidewalks of New York* (2001) was postponed until November because distributors were unsure audiences would be ready, so soon after the attacks, for a romantic comedy set in New York (Lyman, 2001a). At the same time, the releases of *Behind Enemy Lines* (2001) and *Black Hawk Down* (2001), both military movies with unfettered patriotic themes, were moved forward and opened before the end of 2001 (Markovitz, 2004).

The period after 9/11 was new to producers and audiences alike; the attacks left Hollywood in uncharted territory with no precedent for how to make decisions. Film producers and distributors tried to identify which films would perform well at the box office and which ones would be seen as offensive or unpalatable so soon after the tragedy. When explaining their choices to change film timetables or edit out images of the Twin Towers, publicists and representatives from film production companies claimed they did not want to appear insensitive, to offend viewers, or to depress audiences (Schneider, 2004). Miramax Co-Chairperson Harvey Weinstein summed up the general sentiment, stating he did not believe Americans wanted to be reminded of the tragedy they had just experienced while watching their escapist, entertainment media (Pulver, 2001).

Hollywood and the Military Response to 9/11

The terrorist attacks were not the only events Hollywood had to wrestle with in the fall of 2001. The government's choice to launch a military "war on terrorism" in response to September 11 also placed the industry in an unusual position. According to CNN, then President Bush asked his advisors to meet with top Hollywood representatives to see how they could help with the war effort and whether films could provide "patriotic escape" to the nation's viewers ("Uncle Sam," 2001). In accordance with this request, in November 2001 then Senior White House Advisor Karl Rove led a group of senior officials to Hollywood to meet with studio executives as part of a series of meetings. CNN reported that Rove was concerned that a poor filmic image of the United States could negatively influence international support for the war, and the administration hoped that moviemakers would make films in line with the campaign against terrorism ("Uncle Sam," 2001).

According to the *New York Times*, at the meeting Rove made suggestions to executives that Hollywood could help clarify the war was on terrorism and not Islam; encourage volunteerism across the country; and organize entertainment and support for U.S. troops and the families (Lyman, 2001b). Documented tangible outcomes of the Rove-Hollywood talks were: United Service Organizations (USO) tours, where first-run films were sent on DVD and videocassette to troops abroad; public service announcements (PSAs), which used celebrities to promote USO tours or convey supportive messages to service people; PSAs that were used to emphasize the war was against terrorism rather than Arabs or Islamic peoples; and PSAs that were used to encourage tolerance of Arab Americans (Chambers, 2002).

Although both Hollywood and the Bush administration conveyed the message that the aforementioned actions were voluntary and that the government was not dictating Hollywood content, the marketing and distribution of certain films in the year following 9/11 nonetheless changed. For example, as the country began to witness a war in

Afghanistan and a possible war in Iraq, Hollywood became concerned that certain films would be viewed as un-American. After September 11, *The Quiet American* (2001) was a source of such concern because it was unclear whether audiences would interpret the film as unpatriotic. Other films with distribution plans that were altered in response to the war on terror included the military comedy, *Buffalo Soldiers* (2001), and the holocaust film, *The Grey Zone* (2001) (Thompson, 2002).

Films about 9/11

Within a year of the terrorist attacks, two of the first films about the events were produced. The documentary, *7 Days in September* (2002), offered viewers images of lower Manhattan—from the time of the attacks through one week later—from the perspectives of more than two dozen filmmakers. The documentary, which was released in New York and California theaters and then later aired on the A&E television network, captured the emotional spirit of New York from a variety of viewpoints. Created by both professional and amateur filmmakers, each segment includes a voice-over by the individual who filmed the segment, and the film is naturalistic in its approach and tone. Some of the segments are interview-driven while others focus on the changing visuals of the area around Ground Zero. All of the segments document live reactions of grief and resolve in the week following the attacks. In its limited release, the film earned positive reviews for its ability to capture the days following 9/11 from divergent vantage points. Reviewer Norm Schrager (2002) pointed out that the film records changes in lower Manhattan the week following the attacks, while also recognizing and giving voice to the emotion of those witnessing the crisis and its aftermath.

September 11 (2002), also titled *11/09/01*, similarly displays a variety of perspectives on the terrorist attacks. Released in local theaters and at film festivals, the work is a compilation of 11 different films, which are each 11 minutes, 9 seconds, and 1 frame in length, a representation of the 9/11/2001 date in European fashion. Reflecting the fact that the filmmakers hailed from different countries—including Mexico, Bosnia, Egypt, Japan, and the United States—each of the 11 films presents a different reflective piece on 9/11 or the aftermath. Whereas *7 Days in September* (2002)—as well as many of the documentaries and films about 9/11 present a New York or American view of the attacks—*11/09/01* offers a range of international viewpoints on the day.

Since 2001, other films about 9/11 have been produced. Described as an accidental product, the documentary *9/11* (2002) is perhaps the most accurate account of what happened in New York on September 11, 2001. At the time, brothers Jules and Gedeon Naudet were in the city filming a documentary about a New York City firefighter. On the morning of September 11, both brothers were filming in different locations and turned their attention to the attacks, rescue operations, and reactions of the firefighters as the situation unfolded. With the help of New York City firefighter, James Hanlon, the footage was edited into a documentary (Atkins, 2008).

Most documentaries about the event were created for or aired on television, but a few independent films were released in theaters, particularly in New York City. For example, the documentaries, *The First 24 Hours* (2002) and *Collateral Damages* (2004), both

---

9/11

9/11 (2002) was filmed and directed by French filmmakers Jules and Gedeon Naudet and codirected by New York City firefighter James Hanlon. One of the reasons the documentary is so well regarded is because of the access the Naudet brothers had to the World Trade Center and firefighter operations and reactions. This access, and the resulting documentary, was a result of circumstance: The Naudet brothers were initially in New York filming a documentary about a rookie firefighter when the attack happened. The filmmakers immediately shifted their focus and as a result collected some of the most extensive footage of the attacks and their aftermath.

Because of their proximity to the firefighters, specifically Engine 7, Ladder 1 Company of the New York City Fire Department (FDNY), the Naudets were able to record aspects of the terrorist attacks that unfolded as the attacks were happening. For example, footage of American Airlines Flight 11's crash into the World Trade Center North Tower was captured by Jules Naudet while he was checking out a gas leak with Chief Joseph Pfeifer. The reaction and initial response of firefighters was filmed by Gedeon Naudet who was at the firehouse when the attacks were made known (Atkins, 2008). With permission from the FDNY, the Naudets kept their cameras rolling and were able to capture almost three hours of footage, including scenes that the filmmakers later decided should not be included in their final product out of respect for the victims and their families. The documentary aired several times on network television and was not edited for profanity. A federal order temporarily halted the Federal Communication Commission's indecency rules given the unique circumstances.

—Amy M. Damico

Reference

Naudet, G., Naudet, J., Klug, R., & Hanlon, J. (Directors). (2002). *9/11* [Documentary]. United States: Columbia Broadcasting Company.

---

films that hone in on memories of the day and follow the process of clearing the rubble from Ground Zero, were shown in New York City theaters. *Saint of 9/11* (2006), a memorial film about the Reverend Mychal Judge, a priest who died while trying to assist firefighters at the World Trade Center, also played in New York. The release of such films in New York suggests that at least some New York audiences were receptive to films that memorialize components of the attacks, identify the stories of individuals, and document the process of rebuilding.

A number of conspiracy-oriented films surfaced in the following years. Although not released in mainstream movie theaters, many of these films were widely viewed on the Internet or via for-purchase DVDs. The Internet film, *Loose Change* (2005), in particular, was extremely popular and widely distributed. Conspiracy films, in general, echoed the content documented on the many conspiracy-oriented Web sites and put forth concerns by prominent conspiracy groups such as the 9/11 Truth movement—maintaining that Americans have not been told the full story about the terrorist attacks and that lies and misconceptions have been perpetuated by the U.S. government.

One of the most notable and popular films to be released about 9/11 was Michael Moore's *Fahrenheit 9/11* (2004). Moore, known for his prior movies, *Roger and Me* (1989) and *Bowling for Columbine* (2002), uses documentary filmmaking as a tool to raise issues, pose questions, criticize the government, share documented information, entertain, and make people laugh. Moore won an Academy Award for his 2002 film, *Bowling for Columbine*, and generated significant press for *Fahrenheit 9/11* in advance of its release, stating that he hoped it would impact the upcoming presidential elections (Higgins, 2004). *Fahrenheit 9/11*, with a title that conjures up the Ray Bradbury science-fiction novel, *Fahrenheit 451*, about a dysfunctional society, is a critical documentary that questions then President George W. Bush and his administration's foreign policy, reaction to the events of 9/11, and decision to go to war. Moore argues in the film that the terrorist attacks were unfairly and dishonestly used by the Bush administration to justify and garner support for a war in Iraq.

In its first weekend of release, *Fahrenheit 9/11* was number one at the box office, and in its first month earned more than $100 million, an amount never seen before for a nonfiction film (Toplin, 2006). Considerable controversy surrounded the film and Moore's somewhat unique approach to documentary filmmaking. When *Fahrenheit 9/11* was released in 2004, George W. Bush was running for reelection, the United States was fighting wars in Afghanistan and Iraq, and there was considerable public debate about the Iraq war. The film impacted national politics and prompted a number of responses from politicians, pundits, film critics, and scholars. Much of the controversy surrounding *Fahrenheit 9/11* were heated debates over whether or not it was a true documentary; a label many felt was disingenuous to the partisan perspective offered in the film (Toplin, 2006).

Dramatizing 9/11 in Film

Perhaps the first film to dramatize aspects of 9/11 was *The Guys* (2002), which focused on the experience of a New York fire captain, Nick, as he writes eulogies for the eight firefighters he lost on 9/11. To facilitate this difficult process, Nick connects with an editor who shares Nick's painful journey of remembering and recording the lives that were lost. Based on the real experiences of journalist Anne Nelson, *The Guys* was first written as a play that was performed in New York's off-Broadway Flea Theater in December, 2001. The film version, starring Sigourney Weaver, was released at the Toronto Film Festival on September 11, 2002.

More mainstream Hollywood films about 9/11 were eventually produced. In 2006, two films that dramatized aspects of 9/11 were released. *United 93* (2006), by British director Paul Greengrass, centers on the passengers aboard United Airlines Flight 93 who thwarted the hijackers' plans to fly the plane into buildings in Washington, D.C. The plane ultimately crashed in a field in Shanksville, Pennsylvania. In *United 93*, Greengrass focuses on the inside of the hijacked plane, providing audiences with a view of how passengers, as total strangers, ultimately collaborated to attempt to take the plane away from the hijackers. Although the film is a dramatic account, absent is the usual character development and dialogue that is present in films, a choice that perhaps emphasizes the reality of what happened on that day.

A very different dramatization of the September 11 attacks appeared in the Oliver Stone film, *World Trade Center* (2006). Where *United 93* focuses on the experience of passengers on a hijacked plan, *World Trade Center* tells the story of two New York Port Authority police officers who were caught in the rubble of the Twin Towers. In doing so, it became the first Hollywood film to dramatize events that took place in New York City on that day. Like the creators of *United 93*, Stone and his colleagues worked with families and New York City officials to ensure that the depiction of the police officers' stories was as accurate as possible. While most of the film was shot on location in New York City, the action scenes were largely shot in Los Angeles on sound stages so as to not re-create the disaster scenes in New York (Associated Press, 2005). Although there was minor controversy about the accuracy of some of the film's assertions (Liss, 2006), overall *World Trade Center* was well received, perhaps in part because it told the story from a perspective Americans were eager to hear about after the attacks: a story of survival.

New York as a Filmic Backdrop

New York City and its familiar skyline have long been either the backdrop, or the focal point, of films. Given this history, the city's presence in films after 9/11 was significant. One group of films released after the attacks—including *25th Hour* (2003), *Great New Wonderful* (2005), and *Cloverfield* (2008)—depicts the damaged New York City as the setting of the story. Other films—such as *Gangs of New York* (2002) and *I Am Legend* (2007)—are set in New York City during different time periods and implicitly call the New York City skyline to the viewer's attention.

One of the first films set in New York City after 9/11 was *25th Hour* (2003). Based on the book by the same name published prior to the attacks, the film and its director, Spike Lee, acknowledges the city's post-9/11 environment. In one sweeping scene, the New York skyline is punctuated by the two columns of light that became an iconic representation of the Twin Towers after their fall. In another scene, characters engage in conversation in an apartment located above Ground Zero. Although the events of 9/11 are not explicitly part of the *25th Hour* narrative, the imagery of the former site of the Twin Towers implicitly contributes to the gritty feel of the film. Additionally, a noted rant by the main character Monty, who yells about Osama bin Laden and Al Qaeda, represented some of the post-9/11 anger many were feeling.

Released two years after *25th Hour*, *Great New Wonderful* (2005) does not explicitly mention the fact that its story is set in New York City after the terrorist attacks. However, in one scene the bells that ring on the first anniversary of the attacks can be heard. In addition, director Danny Leiner explained that many of the characters' actions and emotions are the result of living and processing life in New York City one year later (Hill, 2005). The film also contains numerous references to the day of the attacks, as in the moments when characters use the phrase "that day" in conversation.

Also set in New York City, *Reign Over Me* (2007) was the first fictional film to use a main character's loss of his family on 9/11 (in this case the loss of his wife and daughters) as the impetus for a dramatic story line. Other story lines with characters related in some way to the events of September 11 followed. For example, *Julie and Julia* (2009) features a lead character who works for the Lower Manhattan Development Corporation, an organization formed after 9/11 to plan the reconstruction of, and distribute money related to, rebuilding lower Manhattan.

New York City under Attack in Film

Hollywood films have regularly depicted scenes in which cities are obliterated, and New York City has been a favorite target of such destruction. The interest in New York lies, at least in part, in the fact that the diverse, active city contains recognizable symbols of U.S. strength and power—including Wall Street, the Empire State Building and, until 2001, the Twin Towers. The destruction of those symbols—and the city itself—contributes to dramatic film narrative (Salamone, 2008). Beginning as early as 1933, New York was submerged by a tidal wave in *Deluge*. In years prior to the terrorist attacks, the city was attacked and/or destroyed in blockbuster films such as *Independence Day* (1996), *Mars Attacks* (1996), *Armageddon* (1998), *Deep Impact* (1998), *Godzilla* (1998), and *Artificial Intelligence: A.I.* (2001).

The September 11 attacks on the Twin Towers seemed, at first, to replicate the filmic destruction of New York City so familiar to movie goers. The destruction, however, was not fictional. The images that had once been created for, and contained by, the big screen were all too real in their impact on lower Manhattan. The question for filmmakers, then, was when would it once again be acceptable for films to make New York City the focus of attacks and destruction?

Within a few years, this question was answered as newly released films featured attacks on New York. Such films were perhaps deliberately fantastic so as to maintain some distance from both the real events of 9/11 and more representative 9/11 films such as *World Trade Center*. In *The Day after Tomorrow* (2004), for example, New York is largely destroyed by first a tidal wave and then a new Ice Age as a result of global warming. *King Kong* (2005) re-creates a 1930s New York terrorized by the now iconic beast, another example of New York under attack. *I Am Legend* (2007) projects New York into the year 2012 where a lone scientist works in the destroyed city to cure a disease that transformed some people into terrifying mutants and killed many others. Most notably perhaps, *Cloverfield* (2008) depicts Manhattan under attack by a monster. The film's visuals can be read as references to the attacks: The streets are cloudy and smoky; the Chrysler Building collapses; reams of paper fall from the sky; and the head of the Statue of Liberty falls into the city streets.

The first films to return to the familiar images of New York City under attack were well received. According to the Internet Movie Database, *The Day after Tomorrow* and *I Am Legend* both made the list of the top 10 grossing movies for the years they were released: *The Day after Tomorrow* grossed more than $186 million, and *I Am Legend* grossed more than $256 million. Such figures suggest that, despite the reality of what occurred on 9/11, mainstream audiences were comfortable with seeing the city's destruction in fictionalized settings.

Trends in Film Post-9/11

Historically, film scholars have looked at the popularity of films and film narratives as indicators of what—in a particular historic moment—audiences are receptive to and what the concerns, tone, mood, or zeitgeist, of the time is. Lists of top grossing movies for any given year highlight which films were the most favorably received by viewing audiences. The most popular films, however, are not always those that earn critical acclaim, as evidenced by overwhelming positive reviews, award nominations, and/or award wins. Lists of top grossing movies obtained from the Internet Movie Data Base for the years following 2001 show that the top selling movies fell into identifiable categories: novel adaptations (such as four Harry Potter films in 2002, 2004, 2005, 2007; *The Lord of the Rings: The Two Towers* in 2002, and *The Return of the King* in 2003; *The Chronicles of Narnia: The Lion, the Witch and the Wardrobe* in 2005); family films (such as *Ice Age* in 2002, *Finding Nemo* and *Elf* in 2003, *Shark Tale* in 2004, and *Happy Feet* in 2006); blockbuster sequels (such as *Terminator 3: Rise of the Machines; Star Wars: Episode III—Revenge of the Sith* in 2005; and *National Treasure: Book of Secrets* in 2007); and superhero movies.

Most notable, perhaps, was the increased production and popularity of superhero films after September 11, including: *Spider-Man* (2002), *Spider-Man 2* (2004), *X2* (2003), *X-Men the Last Stand* (2006), *Batman Begins* (2005), and *Superman Returns* (2006). The superhero trend began prior to 9/11 (*X-Men* was released in 2000, and *Spider-Man* was in production when the 9/11 attacks occurred), but the subsequent proliferation of superhero movies since 2001 suggests that viewers embraced this genre after the attacks. When released, *The Dark Knight* (2008) (the latest Batman movie) became the top grossing movie in the United States and was widely regarding as superior filmmaking.

A close relation to superhero films, action-hero films also graced the top 10 money-making film lists in the years following 2001, including the films in the Bourne series—*The Bourne Supremacy* (2004) and *The Bourne Ultimatum* (2007)—as well as the James Bond film, *Casino Royale* (2006). Although they did not earn as much as the aforementioned titles, several other superhero and action films were also made in the years following the attacks on the World Trade Center, for example, *The Fantastic Four* (2005) and *The Hulk* (2003). The popularity of these kinds of films can be understood from a number of perspectives relevant to post-9/11 life: an assertion of traditional masculinity; the idea that Americans want to be "saved" by superior, although flawed, heroes; an escape from grim reality; or a fanciful quest for stories that allow viewers to explore the complexities of good and evil through entertainment.

Although not always superior box-office hits, other types of films were released that reflected the mindset of the post-9/11 climate. Dramas, comedies, and specific genre films integrated post-9/11 themes into their narratives and, while some of these replicated the conflicts present in superhero films, others introduced new characterizations

---

TOP 10 GROSSING SUPERHERO MOVIES
BEFORE AND AFTER 2001

Note: The year noted indicates the year the film was released.

Superhero Films 1995–2001   Superhero Films 2002–2008
Batman Forever (1995)   *Spider-Man* (2002)
X-Men (2000)   *X2* (2003)
                                              Spider-Man 2 (2004)
                                              Batman Begins (2005)
                                              X-Men: The Last Stand (2006)
                                              Superman Returns (2006)
                                              Spider-Man 3 (2007)
                                              The Dark Knight (2008)
                                              Ironman (2008)
                                              Hancock (2008)

—Amy M. Damico

Reference

Internet Movie Data Base. [Data file]. Available from http://www.imdb.com/

---

of the world after 9/11. Some of these characteristics were explicit. For example, both *Flight Plan* (2005) and *Red Eye* (2005) have stories that are set on planes and—reflecting a post-9/11 anxiety about flying as well as new airline security policies—the films feature federal agents whose presence on the planes is to protect passengers. The opening narration of *Love Actually* (2003) features a reflective line about the place of love in times of distress and specifically refers to the planes hitting New York as an example. *I Am Legend* (2007) uses the now-common phrase "Ground Zero" to refer to destroyed parts of the city. A number of films refer to 9/11 in passing so as to place the film in a specific timeframe.

Other films such as *Civic Duty* (2006), *Shooter* (2007), *Vantage Point* (2008), and *Lions and Lambs* (2007) provide commentary about key aspects of the post-9/11 culture in the United States such as the Patriot Act, the Department of Homeland Security, the wars in Afghanistan and Iraq, and *The 9/11 Commission Report* within their narratives. Films with terrorist-oriented plots are situated in, and made reference to, the post-9/11 culture. For example, the docudrama, *Strange Culture* (2007), tells the story of a man incorrectly detained as a bioterrorist; *The Kingdom* (2007) looks at terrorist bombings against Western interests; and the action film, *Live Free or Die Hard* (2007), references aspects of security in a post-9/11 world.

Other films addressed the post-9/11 culture metaphorically. *New York Times* critic Stephen Farber (2005) noted that by 2005 a number of apolitical films focussing on grief, anger, and profound sadness, were on the horizon. Films such as *Hide*

THE DARK KNIGHT

One of the movie posters for *The Dark Knight* (2008) features Batman standing in front of a burning building; the area burning in the shape of the familiar bat icon. This image does not appear in the film and some identified this marketing approach as a way to tie the events of September 11, particularly terrorism, to the film. The copy on the movie poster reads "Welcome to a world without rules," a characterization that is often used when describing terrorist strategy. The poster was distributed through a viral marketing game connected to the movie.

The Dark Knight itself was widely interpreted as reflecting aspects of September 11 within its narrative. As what one critic calls "New York's alter ego" (Dawson, 2008, para. 1), Gotham City is under attack by the terrorist, the Joker. Images of firefighters, destruction, and citizen-fear pervade the film, and ideas of good and evil dominate the narrative. *The Dark Knight* has been described as a "post 9/11 allegory" (Stevens, 2008, para. 3), a film with a "heavy handed, wearisome 9/11 connection" (Landesman, 2008, para. 2), and a film that addresses 9/11 through "inference and ideas" (Dargis, 2008, para. 8).

—Amy M. Damico

References

Dargis, M. (2008, July 18). Showdown in Gotham town. *The New York Times*. Retrieved from http://www.nytimes.com

Dawson, J. (2008, June 20). Has the new Batman plundered its plot from 9/11? *TimesOnline*. Retrieved from http://www.timesonline.co.uk

Landesman, C. (2008, July 27). *The Dark Knight* [Review of the motion picture]. *TimesOnline*. Retrieved from http://www.timesonline.co.uk

Stevens, D. (2008, July 18). No joke: *The Dark Knight*, reviewed. *Slate*. Retrieved from http://www.slate.com

and Seek (2005), *Fear X* (2003), *Winter Solstice* (2004), *Bereft* (2004), *Imaginary Heroes* (2004), and *The Upside of Anger* (2005) all contained characters who suffered immeasurable, long-standing grief after a traumatic event, perhaps representing the post-9/11 zeitgeist of a nation still trying to come to terms with loss.

Other post-9/11 trends included thought-provoking or issue-driven films as representative of life after September 11. Jason Solomons (2005) of the British newspaper, *The Guardian*, drew a parallel between a group of complex Hollywood films released in 2005 and the release of thoughtful and provocative films in the 1970s, a time when the United States was dealing with the unpopular Vietnam War and the Watergate scandal. To make his argument, Solomons pointed to a number of critically acclaimed and successful films that required audiences to consider global-scale issues and reflect upon their own participation or nonparticipation in the current sociopolitical climate. His list includes *Crash* (2005), *A History of Violence* (2005), *The Constant Gardener* (2005), *Good Night and Good Luck* (2005), *Brokeback Mountain* (2005), *Munich* (2005), *Thank You for Smoking* (2005), and *Lord of War* (2005).

CHARLIE WILSON'S WAR

Charlie Wilson's War (2007) tells the story of Texas Congressman Charles Wilson's involvement in Operation Cyclone, an operation designed to assist Afghanistan in fighting the Soviet occupation in the 1980s. The film explores how Wilson successfully worked with CIA operative Gust Avrakotos to assist Afghans in reclaiming their land. Although specific references to the events of September 11 are not a component of the film, the message is clearly conveyed by Wilson and Avrakotos that the United States did not do enough in the 1990s to assist Afghans in repairing their war-torn country, perhaps then setting the stage for Osama bin Laden to gain power and support for a jihad.

—*Amy M. Damico*

Reference

Nichols, M. (Director). (2007). *Charlie Wilson's War* [Motion picture]. United States: Universal Pictures.

FILMS WITH POST-9/11 TERRORIST-ORIENTED PLOTS

Team America: World Police (2004)
The War Within (2005)
Paradise Now (2005)
Civic Duty (2006)
Next (2007)
The Kingdom (2007)

Live Free or Die Hard (2007)
A Mighty Heart (2007)
Rendition (2007)
Vantage Point (2008)
Body of Lies (2008)
Traitor (2008)

New York Times critic Caryn James also pointed to a number of issue-driven films that surfaced in the years after 9/11, claiming that dramas focusing on social issues were part of the post-9/11 landscape. Four years after 9/11, James (2005) pointed out that Hollywood films reflected a cultural atmosphere of a "world in turmoil" (para. 2). Her list is similar to Solomons's with the addition of *North Country* (2005), *All the King's Men* (2006), and *Syriana* (2005). All of these films, whether or not they take place in current day, address complicated issues and call attention to grim outcomes that can result from certain choices. For example, although *Good Night and Good Luck* is a period film of the McCarthy years, the concern about news content is represented today in debates over corporate-media ownership. Although *Brokeback Mountain* is set in the 1960s, same-sex marriage is a current debate. *Syriana*, a film set in the Middle East post-9/11, hones in on the global oil industry.

Not all films after 9/11 were weighty, however. Lists of top grossing films in the years after 9/11 show that family oriented films continued to be popular among audiences, suggesting that viewers were interested in what lighthearted, frequently animated, movies had to offer.

Comedies about the political world post-9/11 were scarce but for a few notable exceptions. *Team America: World Police* (2004) was one of the first satiric looks at the world after 9/11. Created by Matt Stone and Trey Parker of TV's *South Park* series, this animated film focuses on the invasion of Iraq and U.S. politics. Other films such as *American Dreamz* (2006) and *Harold and Kumar Escape from Guantanamo Bay* (2008) also poke fun at the U.S. government's actions after 9/11. More germane to humanizing the lives of Middle Eastern people during a time when there is noted cultural misunderstanding is *Looking for Comedy in the Muslim World* (2006), a film by Albert Brooks that follows a character who is on a government-appointed mission to investigate what Middle Easterners find funny.

America at War in Post-9/11 Film

After the terrorist attacks, a number of war-oriented films made their way to the big screen. Some of the initial war films were finished prior to 9/11 while others were in production. In the years since 2001, a crop of war-themed films were released. Many of these films present war-related issues, while others focus on a plot whose impetus was a documented event that had taken place in Afghanistan or Iraq. For example, *Redacted* (2007) tells the story of an Iraqi family who is persecuted by an Army squad; *Stop Loss* (2008) depicts a soldier who rejects an order to report back for duty because he has finished his service requirements; *In the Valley of Elah* (2007) dramatizes the real murder of a U.S. soldier at a Georgia bar; *Grace is Gone* (2007) addresses the grief a widower and his daughters face when a wife and mother is killed in the line of duty; *Lions for Lambs* (2007) debates issues around politics, war and media representation; and *Battle for Haditha* (2007) is based on a series of events that led to the killing of 24 Iraqi civilians.

Despite the increase in war-oriented films, however, by Hollywood standards these films did not perform well at the box office (Patterson, 2008). Additionally, to date none were awarded Academy Award nominations or wins. Even films with significant star power such as *Lions for Lambs* (featuring Tom Cruise, Meryl Streep, and Robert Redford) and *The Kingdom* (2007) (starring Jamie Foxx, Chris Cooper, and Jennifer Garner) did not draw large audiences, suggesting that, despite their topical nature, the subject matter was not as appealing to post-9/11 audiences as other types of films.

Conclusion

After the attacks on September 11, the film industry first reacted by altering release dates of films and editing or reshooting imagery of the World Trade Center towers. Within a few years, films about 9/11 were released, and films that were reflective of the post-9/11 zeitgeist of uncertainty, mourning, anger, and fear became part of the cinematic landscape. Different types of military-oriented films surfaced, and

Hollywood eventually returned to producing its standard fare of violent films where cities and people were under attack. A number of prominent directors addressed the events of September 11 directly or metaphorically in their work as the years passed.

—*Amy M. Damico*

References

Associated Press. (2005, November 2). Oliver Stone shoots Sept. 11 movie in New York. *USA Today*. Retrieved from http://www.usatoday.com

Atkins, S. (Ed.) (2008). *The 9/11 encyclopedia*. Westport, CT: Greenwood Press.

Bell-Metereau, R. (2004). The how-to manual, the prequel, and the sequel in post 9/11 cinema. In W. Dixon (Ed.), *Film and television after 9/11* (pp. 142–162). Carbondale: Southern Illinois University Press.

Chambers, D. (2002). Will Hollywood go to war? *Transnational Broadcasting Studies*, 8. Retrieved from http://www.tbsjournal.com

Farber, S. (2005, March 13). 9/11 is sneaking onto a screen near you. *The New York Times*. Retrieved from http:///www.nytimes.com

Germain, D. (2002, April 20). Images of trade center preserved in fresh films shot before September 11th. *The Associated Press*. Retrieved from http://www.berkleydailyplanet.com

Higgins, C. (2004, May 17). *Fahrenheit 9/11* could light a fire under Bush. *The Guardian*. Retrieved from http://www.guardian.co.uk

Hill, L. (2005, April 11). The first great 9/11 film? *New York Magazine*. Retrieved from http://www.nymag.com

Horrmann, N. (2002, February 1). "Damage" control. *Entertainment Weekly*. Retrieved from http://www.ew.com

James, C. (2005, October 11). The trouble with films that try to think. *The New York Times*. Retrieved from http://www.nytimes.com

Liss, R. (2006, August 9). Oliver Stone's World Trade Center fiction: How the rescue really happened. *Slate*. Retrieved July 15, 2008, from http://www.slate.com

Lyman, R. (2001a, September 28). At the movies: Hollywood soul searching. *The New York Times*. Retrieved from http:///www.nytimes.com

Lyman, R. (2001b, November 12). A nation challenged: The entertainment industry; Hollywood discusses role in war effort. *The New York Times*. Retrieved from http:///www.nytimes.com

Markovitz, J. (2004). Reel terror post 9/11. In W. Dixon (Ed.), *Film and television after 9/11* (pp. 201–225). Carbondale: Southern Illinois University Press.

Patterson, J. (2008, May 9). The home front. *The Guardian*. Retrieved from http://www.guardian.co.uk

Pulver, A. (2001, September 28). I'm back so watch out. *The Guardian*. Retrieved July 17, 2008, from http://www.guardian.co.uk

Salamone, G. (2008, January 9). Filmmakers view New York as a disaster waiting to happen. *New York Daily News*. Retrieved from http://www.nydailynews.com.

Schneider, S. (2004). Architectural nostalgia and the New York City skyline on film. In W. Dixon (Ed.), *Film and television after 9/11* (pp 29–42). Carbondale: Southern Illinois University Press.

Schrager, N. (2002). 7 days in September. *Filmcritic.com*. Retrieved July 15, 2008, from http://www.filmcritic.com

Scorsese's *Gangs* has release date pushed back. (2001, October 8). *The Guardian*. Retrieved July 17, 2008, from http://www.guardian.co.uk

Solomons, J. (2005, September 25). Do be serious. *The Guardian*. Retrieved from http://www.guardian.co.uk

Thompson, A. (2002, October 17). Films with war themes are victims of bad timing. *The New York Times*. Retrieved from http:///www.nytimes.com

Toplin, R. (2006). *Michael Moore's* Fahrenheit 9/11: *How one film divided a nation*. Lawrence: University Press of Kansas.

Uncle Sam wants Hollywood. (2001, November 9). *CNN*. Retrieved from http://www.cnn.com

SPOTLIGHT ESSAY/FILM: *BLACK HAWK DOWN* AND *KINGDOM OF HEAVEN*

After September 11, 2001, public memory of the attacks in the United States became inseparable from political rhetoric about "rogue" and "failed" states that was used to justify the wars that followed in Afghanistan and Iraq. Popular culture also played a role in circulating these ideas. In Hollywood, for example, filmmakers often fell back on well-established traditions portraying Arab, Islamic, and African cultures as failed, chaotic, backward, and dangerous to the West. Painting these "Oriental" cultures as inferior meant that filmmakers could depict Western military violence waged against them as spectacular, beautiful, cathartic, and redemptive, in films that made little attempt to debate the rights and wrongs, or the causes and consequences, of contemporary U.S. wars. Making military violence beautiful, and pleasurable, has always been part of Hollywood film, but after 9/11 the combination of new digital technologies, multiple-theater warfare, and hyper-patriotic forms of U.S. nationalism, produced movies that took the vicarious thrills of screen combat to spectacular new heights. One key figure is Hollywood director Ridley Scott, whose movies *Black Hawk Down* (2001) and *Kingdom of Heaven* (2005) constructed an aesthetic of redemptive, beautiful, perpetual war that depicted non-Western societies as overtly inferior, which was the closest the post-9/11 period came to a fully realized neoconservative style in American mass culture.

Black Hawk Down (2001), Scott's account of the disastrous "humanitarian" military intervention in Somalia by U.S. military forces in 1993, was substantially finished before September 11, then rushed through postproduction to capitalize on the political climate created by the attacks and the war in Afghanistan (Quenqua, 2002). *Black Hawk Down* was a study in American victimhood and spectacular military violence, which began with a caption describing perpetual war as a universal truth intrinsic to human beings. "Only the dead," the film's epigraph from Plato promised audiences, "have seen the end of war." The film's visual style elaborated on this premise in a combat sequence that spans most of the film, making spectacular use of computer-generated imaging (CGI), minutely detailed digital sound-tracking, and camera positions that place audiences in combat roles with a spectacular, visceral realism. Just as important were the uses to which Scott put these thrills, celebrating military sacrifice and immersion in war as profound human truths, in camerawork that lingered lovingly on American wounds, and a plot that anchored viewers' attention to the crash sites of downed Black Hawk helicopters, with the story returning repeatedly to these sites of American trauma. *Black Hawk Down* became to neocons and fellow travellers what *The Passion of the Christ* (2004) was to the contemporary religious right. President Bush let it be known that *Black Hawk Down* was one of the films he turned to for inspiration after 9/11 (Borger, 2004), while Vice President Cheney and Defense Secretary Rumsfeld attended a gala presentation of the film in Washington, D.C.

Scott's epic film about the twelfth-century Crusades, *Kingdom of Heaven* (2005), did not generate the same sense of profound immersion in war as *Black Hawk Down*, partly because the script also incorporated several familiar elements of the Hollywood "blockbuster" that competed with the film's spectacular combat sequences for the attention of the viewer. (In addition to combat, for example, *Kingdom of Heaven* featured a central love story and several subplots about troubled or tense family relationships. It also had more established Hollywood stars than *Black Hawk Down*.) Although a lesser film aesthetically because of this, *Kingdom of Heaven* managed to extend and develop *Black Hawk Down*'s cultural politics by celebrating the compatibility of militarism and liberty, an argument that plugged directly into contemporary anxiety about the effects of "empire" abroad on democratic values at home. The emphasis Scott placed on individual conscience in Balian, the hero, and his knightly quest, and the film's repeated assertions that anyone could become a knight if he mustered his talents appropriately, offered a focused rejoinder to the contemporary claim that militarism and empire would be the undoing of democratic values. As if to illustrate the point, in a stock Hollywood narrative Balian enjoys a fairy-tale rise through the ranks to become a respected and influential Crusader and leader of men; but when there is hard labor to be done in the desert he still works, with his sleeves rolled up, side by side with the rest. Not even Hollywood could fully erase the class-bound character of the Crusades, but Scott did his best in *Kingdom of Heaven*.

In *Kingdom of Heaven*, military violence was again routinely beautiful to watch, listen to, and *feel*, in Scott's loving, slow-motion shots of punctured flesh and spouts of blood and bodies slick with battlefield gore. One reason militarism could be so pleasurable in *Kingdom of Heaven* was that it was redemptive, allowing Balian to atone for the sins that sent him to the Crusades at the start of the film, and thence to come home with a new wife, Sybilla, at the end. The closing sequence shows Balian and Sybilla, together on horseback, riding across a bountiful spring landscape that contrasts voluptuously with the dust and desert to which we have become accustomed through most of the movie, and with the flurries of winter snow that fall in the opening scenes. In *Kingdom of Heaven* it is militarism, and a cathartic immersion in perpetual war ("Nearly a thousand years later," a closing caption observes, "peace in the Kingdom of Heaven remains elusive") that make this return to a conventionally Romantic "homeland" possible.

Like *Black Hawk Down, Kingdom of Heaven* was also a narrative of benevolent Western "progress" brought to bear militarily on an "East" unable to better itself. Under Balian's Western guidance wells are dug, water flows, the desert dust turns green. *Kingdom of Heaven* gives us the holy Western Crusader as "improver," a classic justification of Euro-American imperialist violence and colonialism from the eighteenth century to the present day. At one point Sybilla says to Balian, "You've been given a patch of dirt and it seems you will build a new Jerusalem here." "It is my land," Balian replies, "Where would I be if I did not try to make it better?" The casting of military conquest as "improvement" is Western modernity's archetypal ideology of empire. Its glib reiteration at the heart of a conventional Hollywood blockbuster like *Kingdom of Heaven* offered depressing evidence of the banality of imperialist "just war" imagery in American popular culture after 9/11.

—*David Holloway*

References

Borger, J. (2004, June 4). The best perk in the White House. *The Guardian*. Retrieved from http://www.guardian.co.uk

Quenqua, D. (2002, January 21). Pentagon lends unofficial support to new army flick. *PR Week*. Retrieved from http://www.prweekus.com

Scott, R. (Director). (2001). *Black hawk down*. [Motion picture]. United States: Sony Pictures.

Scott, R. (Director). (2005). *Kingdom of heaven* [Motion picture]. United States: Twentieth Century Fox.

SPOTLIGHT ESSAY/FILM: THE *BOURNE* FILMS

American films often illustrate ideas already well established in American society; the Hollywood depiction of the so-called Global War on Terror following the September 11, 2001, terrorist attacks is no exception. The years since 9/11 spawned a series of films sharply critical of the U.S. government, including *Rendition* (2007) and *Lions for Lambs* (2007), both of which challenge the War on Terror in relatively clear terms. Offering another perspective are the Jason Bourne films, starring Matt Damon: *The Bourne Identity* (2002), *The Bourne Supremacy* (2004), and *The Bourne Ultimatum* (2007). Submerged within all three films is a critique of the post-9/11 U.S. government as one that contains rogue elements willing to commit morally questionable and illegal acts in the name of national security. Indeed, the entire series of films is premised on the notion that the United States has created a supersecret group of assassins able to undertake clandestine assassination missions without the killings being traced to anyone, certainly not the U.S. government.

All three Bourne narratives are briskly paced with carefully choreographed and entertaining fight scenes. The films do require a certain suspension of disbelief for many reasons, not the least of which is the fact that despite enduring numerous beatings, falls, and even being shot, Mr. Bourne never seems to stop for a few days of physical therapy and a spot of hydrocodone. In the Bourne world, U.S. bureaucrats are not the only ones without respect for the law: In the course of three films, Bourne himself raises aggressive driving from the level of moving violation to crime against humanity. Although, in a scene near the end of *The Bourne Supremacy*, Bourne does express remorse for some of his intentional killings, he never shows remorse for his collateral damage: the trail of dead, maimed, or injured individuals left on the streets of Paris, Moscow, and New York, who merely appeared in the wrong place at the wrong time.

The third film in the series, *The Bourne Ultimatum*, is the most fully developed critique of the U.S. government's counterterrorism establishment since 9/11. Reflecting a number of controversial post-9/11 issues, *The Bourne Ultimatum* has everything it needs to terrify the liberal and the civil-libertarian American: waterboarding, data-mining, warrantless surveillance, and extrajudicial killings, in addition to a creative and creepy ability of U.S. officials to view, in real time, the feeds from all of the surveillance cameras in London's Waterloo station. In the film, U.S. counterterrorism official Noah Vosen repeatedly attempts to have U.S. citizen Jason Bourne killed, on U.S. soil and elsewhere around the globe, without due process of law. Some might see this as running afoul of the Fifth Amendment of the U.S. Constitution, but Vosen appears more concerned with defending a certain idea of America, without concerning himself too particularly about the contents of the Constitution. Likewise, a journalist investigating U.S. counterterrorist efforts is assassinated by an agent of Vosen's, and the film suggests that the corrupt official has taken similar action, all in the pursuit of national security by extremely Machiavellian means. The film's hero is arguably Pamela Landy, Vosen's subordinate, who eventually releases evidence of Vosen's crimes to the press. Anyone who views Daniel Ellsberg, the man who leaked the *Pentagon Papers* to the *New York Times*, as a hero of the Vietnam Era will be quite comfortable with this conclusion.

As action films that feature riveting action sequences, the Bourne films are at the top of their genre. No one should mistake these films, however, for a reasoned, cogent critique of U.S. foreign policy since 2001. The films depict visually a current of distrust of the U.S. government present in some segments of U.S. society. For a more thorough understanding of that critique of the United States, and for reasoned responses to it, there is no substitute for reading.

—Mitchell McNaylor

References

Greengrass, P. (Director). (2004). *The Bourne supremacy* [Motion picture]. United States: Universal Pictures.

Greengrass, P. (Director). (2007). *The Bourne ultimatum* [Motion picture]. United States: Universal Pictures.

Liman, D. (Director). (2002). *The Bourne identity* [Motion picture]. United States: Universal Pictures.

Mayer, J. (2008). *The dark side: The inside story of how the war on terror turned into a war on American ideals.* New York: Doubleday.

SPOTLIGHT ESSAY/FILM: CONSPIRACY FILMS: *LOOSE CHANGE* AND *ZEITGEIST*

About 20 minutes into the October 19, 2007, show of the popular HBO program, *Real Time with Bill Maher,* some audience members began shouting, "What happened to Building 7, Bill?" and "We are being lied to in this country!" Maher then angrily ran into the audience and helped security remove the individuals who caused the disturbance (Maher, Carter, & Griffiths, 2007). A number of fringe beliefs have arisen in recent years. Some insist that what happened on 9/11 was a false flag operation (defined as a covert operation by government designed to appear as if it was carried out by others) and urge the public to search for the "truth behind 9/11."

These arguments have largely been made by members of the 9/11 Truth movement, a loosely organized group that exists to challenge the official account of what occurred on September 11. Two widely viewed documentaries, *Loose Change* (2007) and *Zeitgeist* (2007), both available for free on Google Video and YouTube, provide concise overviews of the major arguments put forth by those challenging the official position. Brian Keeley's (1999) fourfold framework for understanding what he has termed "unwarranted conspiracy theories" (UCTs) can be used to shed light on the views put forth by the films. A UCT is, according to Keeley (1999), a "class of explanations to which we should not assent, *by definition*" (Emphasis is in the original, p. 111). In other words, these conspiracies are too "out there" to even be worthy of serious debate (Bale, 2007; Clarke, 2002).

The first characteristic of UCTs, according to Keeley is that they run "counter to some received, official, or 'obvious' account" (pp. 116–117). *Loose Change* was made on a home computer by Dylan Avery and Korey Rowe and begins with the question, "was September 11th a surprise attack on America by 19 Islamic terrorists or something else entirely?" (Avery, 2007). *Zeitgeist,* divided into three parts, the first dealing with Christianity, the second with September 11, and the third with the Federal Reserve Bank, also purports to be challenging the official position.

Second, UCTs tend to argue that "the true intentions behind the conspiracy are invariably nefarious" (Keeley, 1999, p. 117). *Loose Change,* for example, states that the wing of the Pentagon that was hit contained "important budget information" (Avery, 2007). More nefarious intentions are thought to exist behind the collapse of Building 7, which evidently housed offices for agencies such as the Securities and Exchange Commission and the Internal Revenue Service. With so many governmental offices losing their records, the film states that "numerous cases would be closed" (Avery, 2007). Thus, elements within the Bush administration destroyed the building so that evidence of any corrupt activities would collectively disappear. Presumably, Building 7 did not have any paper shredders. The orchestration of 9/11 would additionally help to "authorize the doctrines and funds needed for a new level of imperial mobilization" such as the invasions of Afghanistan, Iraq and, possibly, Iran (Avery, 2007).

Third, UCTs "typically seek to tie together seemingly unrelated events" (Keeley 1999, p. 117). When discussing why, on 9/11, fighter jets were nowhere near New York or Washington, D.C., *Loose Change* points out a slew of occurrences: A simulation exercise known as Vigilant Guardian was in its second day on September 11. Another drill, known as Northern Vigilance, moved fighter jets to Canada and Alaska. Three F16s from Andrews Airforce Base, located close to the Pentagon, were moved to North Carolina for a training operation. Both films argue that by initiating a handful of drills (that were eerily similar to what actually occurred) on the same day that the government was planning its attack on the World Trade Center, NORAD could be delayed, and the danger of fighter jets interfering in their plans would be eliminated.

Fourth, proponents of UCTs argue that the real truth of the matter is a well-guarded secret (Keeley 1999, p. 117). The largest section of *Loose Change* provides numerous eyewitness testimonies from disoriented individuals after the attack stating that the noises they heard were "like a bomb going off." A firefighter states, for example, that the elevator shaft exploded and he could not understand why since the "plane is up there." When discussing Flight 93, which crashed into the ground in Shanksville, Pennsylvania, *Loose Change* again shows interviews with witnesses and cleanup crews stating that no large debris had been found. One individual states that "there is nothing that you could distinguish that a plane had crashed there" (Avery, 2007). Most members of the 9/11 Truth movement will argue that the plane was shot down by a fighter jet and that the Bush government is keeping this a secret.

Another secret exists regarding the plane that crashed into the Pentagon. Both films note that, according to his instructors, Hani Hanjour, the lead hijacker of Flight 77, was a horrible pilot. If he wanted to injure as many people as possible, he should have simply maintained his trajectory and crashed into the roof of the Pentagon. Instead, this unskilled pilot performed an expert 330-degree turn and managed "to hit the only section that was reinforced to withstand a terrorist attack" (Avery 2007). Both films question whether the Pentagon was hit by a plane or a government cruise missile.

A mixture of cunningly placed eyewitness testimony, crafty editing, and well-timed sarcastic and rhetorical questions make the viewer feel as if he or she is bearing witness to some secret being revealed. As one stops to think, however, it becomes clear that very few answers are provided—only well-placed questions and testimonies from disoriented individuals leaving the scene of the tragedy. If no plane hit the Pentagon, for example, where is Flight 77 and its occupants? Were they, to be facetious, taken underground to see the flying saucer that crashed at Roswell? It is simple questions like these that vast conspiracy theories tend to ignore.

—Amarnath Amarasingam

References

Avery, D. (Director). (2007). *Loose change: Final cut* [Motion picture]. United States: Louder Than Words.

Bale, J. M. (2007). Political paranoia v. political realism: On distinguishing between bogus conspiracy theories and genuine conspiratorial politics. *Patterns of Prejudice, 41*(1), 45–60.

Clarke, S. (2002). Conspiracy theories and conspiracy theorizing. *Philosophy of the Social Sciences, 32*(2), 131–150.

Joseph, P. (Director). (2007). *Zeitgeist: The movie* [Motion picture]. United States: Author.

Keeley, B. L. (1999). Of conspiracy theories. *Journal of Philosophy, 96*(3), 109–126.

Maher, B. (Host & Executive Producer), Carter S., & Griffiths, S. (Executive Producers). (2007, October 19). *Real Time with Bill Maher.* Los Angeles: Brad Grey.

SPOTLIGHT ESSAY/FILM: *THE KINGDOM*

The Kingdom (2007), directed by Peter Berg, attempts to reveal a realistic portrait of modern Arabic life through the eyes of a team of FBI agents investigating a terrorist bombing. Most Hollywood films that have attempted to do so have failed to be fair in their portrayal of Arabs; *The Kingdom* is no different. Jack G. Shaheen (2001), a noted expert on representations of Arab filmic imagery, has documented at length in his books and articles that Arabs in film are "the cultural other" (p. 2) and, as "seen through Hollywood's distorted lenses, Arabs look different and threatening. Projected along racial and religious lines, the stereotypes are deeply ingrained in American cinema" (p. 2). He also notes, "*The Kingdom* is Hollywood's most anti-Arab post-9/11 film" (Shaheen, 2008, p. 127).

Initially, the director offers a general overview of the historic relationship between the United States and Saudi Arabia, giving the appearance that Berg takes seriously his responsibility to fairly depict a culture that has been under intense scrutiny since 9/11. However, this sense of fairness is immediately dispelled. The first scenes are devoted to Arab jihadists bombing a softball game where U.S. families are gathered. The first Arab characters portrayed in the film are terrorists; the first Americans are victims. The next American character introduced is an FBI agent portrayed by Jamie Foxx, the film's star. He is seen interacting with his son in a loving and positive way.

Foxx's character provides the lens through which the audience views the Middle East. He leads an FBI team to investigate the terrorist bombing of Americans within the Saudi "kingdom." The most striking element of this fictional bombing investigation is the idea that the local Saudi government is portrayed as incapable of investigating the attack. It seems that the only way to ensure justice in a post-9/11 world is to leave it in the hands of the United States. This leads *Seattle Times* movie critic John Hart (2007) to write: "[Saudi Arabia's] citizens are presented mostly as rabid killers who can be defeated only by American know-how. Since most of the [September] 11 hijackers were Saudis, the movie could be called Hollywood's long-delayed revenge" (p. 1). Not only is this message of Saudi incompetence voiced as an American prejudice by the FBI team, but it is shown as fact by the filmmaker. The Saudi lead, portrayed by Ashraf Barhom, is introduced in a scene that reveals an innocent man being tortured as part of an interrogation about the bombing. Barhom's character condemns the torture, but it appears to be standard procedure for criminal investigation.

The dynamic between the Foxx and Barhom characters could have made for a compelling story, offering an opportunity for Berg to present a multidimensional look at Middle Eastern culture. Two men of color are the leads in the film, yet they come from cultures that are deeply suspicious of each other. Foxx's character, as an African American man, should be particularly sensitive to prejudice based on generalizations. Yet, he is quick to judge the Arab policeman as slow and inept without making any attempt to understand the culture, the bureaucracy, or the religion of Saudi Arabia. Foxx and his FBI team act impulsively and recklessly in their investigation while Barhom can only try to keep them out of trouble. Gradually, the American and the Arab come to understand one another.

The audience is allowed to see inside the family life of two Arab characters, including the loving family life of Barhom. A montage reveals these men in their home lives and they are given a dimension that is otherwise lacking in the film. Outside of this montage, however, portrayals of Arabs are far less well-rounded. Berg uses a female FBI agent played by Jennifer Garner to reveal stereotypical Arab attitudes. Barhom's policeman takes the team to their shared lodging when they arrive. He mentions that he could not find a "pink screen" to shield Garner's sleeping area from her colleagues, and, as a result, he initially wanted to house her in the bathroom. Although the character claims that he was merely joking, this dialogue conveys a stereotypical Middle Eastern attitude.

According to Shaheen (2008), most of the children in the film are portrayed as "terrorists" (p. 131). Children play videogames in an arcade owned by a reformed terrorist, and the FBI agents raid a terrorist cell consisting of teenaged boys. The climax of the film uses Garner's feminine point of view to reveal that Arab children are being used as pawns for the jihadists. At this point, the terrorist mastermind is revealed as the children's grandfather. His teenaged grandson shoots Barhom's Saudi policeman, the one honorable and law-abiding Arab depicted in the film. The terrorist whispers his dying words to his younger grandson; the boy reveals these words to be, "We are going to kill them all" immediately, "the camera presents an extreme close-up of the boy's threatening eyes" (p. 131). This scene only makes it more likely that Western viewers will fail to mourn the deaths of innocent Arab children who are gunned down or blown up in the Middle East (p. 131).

In the end, *The Kingdom* serves only to reinforce clichés about Arab culture, government, and religion, despite the fact that Berg hired a Saudi consultant to offer script revisions. In an article entitled, "Peter Berg is the Unlikely Ruler of *The Kingdom*," Scott Bowles (2007) writes: "Berg says ultimately his intention is to 'entertain' " (p. 1). Nevertheless, film is a powerful medium, one with the opportunity to show multiple perspectives and use humanity to dispel stereotypes. This film simply followed a good versus evil plotline by presenting Americans as good and Arabs as almost exclusively evil. *The Kingdom* is a missed opportunity.

—*Yvonne D. Sims*

References

Berg, P. (Director). (2007). *The kingdom* [Motion picture]. United States: Universal Pictures.

Bowles, S. (2007, September 25). Peter Berg is unlikely ruler of *The Kingdom*. *USA Today*. Retrieved from http://www.usatoday.com

Shaheen, J. G. (2001). *Reel bad Arabs: How Hollywood vilifies a people*. New York: Olive Branch Press.

Shaheen, J. G. (2008). *Guilty: Hollywood's verdict on Arabs after 9/11*. New York: Olive Branch Press.

SPOTLIGHT ESSAY/FILM: *THE PACIFIER*

When terrorists attacked the United States on September 11, 2001, the nation was left feeling shocked, wounded, and vulnerable. The masculine ideals of self-defense and invincibility had been challenged, and the aftermath of the 9/11 attack and the ensuing War on Terror produced scores of images of reinvigorated masculinity. Amidst the chaos, death, and debilitating destruction of the terrorist attacks, heroic firefighters and police officers valiantly went about the business of rescuing victims, often risking their lives to do so. Despite the fact that rescue workers included both men and women, the heroic acts became tied to masculinity. As Michael Kimmel (2006) points out, "even those few writers and pundits who managed to notice that there were female firefighters, police, and rescue workers among the heroes of 9/11 trumpeted the revival of traditional masculinity" (p. 249). The U.S. actions in Iraq reflected a "my way or the highway" approach to foreign policy, and although the war has not always been popular, it has produced a steady stream of images of military heroes. Brave, strong, and protecting their country, these men (and the images are usually of men) provided a model for proving masculinity in a time when masculinity seemed to be in crisis.

Another cultural response to 9/11 was an emphasis on domesticity, as Americans turned away from the traumas outside to focus on the family home, leading to what Susan Faludi (2007) refers to as the "nesting nation." This trend intersected with the valorization of heroic masculinity in the portrayal of the war on terror as occurring in our own back yards. The outrage that followed 9/11 repeatedly focused on the fact that the attacks took place on U.S. soil, and immediately turned "homeland security" into a national obsession. President Bush (2006) emphasized this in his speech on the fifth anniversary of the attack when he said, "We face an enemy determined to bring death and suffering into our homes" (p. 659). Protection of the nation became everyone's responsibility, not just that of the soldiers fighting overseas. This has led to the awkward pairing of military machismo with domestic concerns, as the government has suggested that the war on terror will, in many ways, be fought at home.

The Pacifier (2005) dramatizes the awkward transformation of military masculinity into domestic masculinity after 9/11 The film tells the story of Lt. Shane Wolfe (Vin Diesel), a Navy SEAL who is assigned to protect the family of a recently murdered Defense Department security expert. The government believes that the man was killed because of a nuclear defense program he was working on, and they are concerned that enemies may harm his family in an attempt to find out more information about the program. Shane is sent to the suburbs to live with this family, protect them from potential enemies, and search for any evidence of the missing defense program.

Initially, Shane's version of masculinity seems completely out of place in the suburban domestic sphere. The physical strength and aggressive demeanor that make him a good Navy SEAL are useless when it comes to changing diapers and feeding babies. This mismatch is a primary source of comedy within the film, and Shane initially has difficulty adjusting to his new surroundings. But just after the family's oldest daughter tells Shane that the kids all hate him and do not need him, two people dressed as ninjas crash through the window to attack the family. Shane fends off the attackers with his bare hands, brute strength, and the help of some household objects like baby powder and a broom. Incorporating the trappings of domesticity into his violent display of masculinity, Shane is able to protect the family and save the day, which he will do multiple times before the film's conclusion.

Although the early scenes question the role of violent masculinity in suburban spaces, Shane is able to prove that his tough-guy persona does, in fact, serve an important function—but only based on the internal logic of the film. After all, it takes a comically exaggerated threat—masked ninjas who crash into the house through a second-story window—to justify Shane's presence. The suspension of disbelief that makes the suburban ninjas seem plausible is also required to make Shane's violent masculinity seem appropriate. Situated within its post-9/11 context, the film offers a striking parallel to the actions of the Bush administration, which not only stepped up military force to fight an official war overseas, but also bolstered a military presence and warlike atmosphere at home. The emphasis on homeland security has often been justified by reminding people that terrorists are living within our borders, potentially "in our backyard." Critics of the War on Terror have argued that the Bush administration exaggerated the threat posed by Middle Eastern terrorists in order to justify a violent response overseas and increased "security" (in the form of surveillance and suspicion of foreigners) at home. This military might, like Shane's hypermasculinity, depends on an audience willing to believe in the threat as it is presented to them.

On the surface, *The Pacifier* suggests that heroic masculinity can be transferred to domestic concerns with desirable results. However, in order for the film to reach this conclusion and provide the tidy closure and happy ending expected of the family comedy/action film, it must suppress the absurdity of hypermasculinity in the domestic realm. It does this by constructing threats to the home that are even more absurd (ninja neighbors), to make the violent, masculine response seem justified. In this way *The Pacifier* reveals the kind of work required to justify many of the domestic policies of the post-9/11 Bush administration, as well as the ongoing work required to maintain the dominance of hegemonic masculinity.

—*David Coon*

References

Bush, G. W. (2006). The fifth anniversary of September 11, 2001. *Vital Speeches of the Day, 72*(24), 658–661.

Faludi, S. (2007). *The terror dream: Fear and fantasy in post-9/11 America.* New York: Metropolitan Books.

Kimmel, M. S. (2006). *Manhood in America: A cultural history* (2nd ed.). New York: Oxford University Press.

Shankman, A. (Director). (2005). *The pacifier* [Motion picture]. United States: Walt Disney Pictures.

SPOTLIGHT ESSAY/FILM: *THE QUIET AMERICAN*

On the evening of September 10, 2001, a day after its Vietnam-based production received an extensive write-up in the *New York Times* (Mydans, 2001, sec. 2, p. 43), approximately a dozen people sat down in a private venue in New Jersey for the first American test screening of *The Quiet American* (2002), a film adaptation of Graham Greene's celebrated 1955 novel. The audience response was reportedly positive. Miramax, which had acquired the domestic distribution rights to the film, planned on a winter release. But just several hours later, and not too far away, American life came to a grinding halt. With the horrific attacks on the East Coast, the United States now found itself embarking upon what George W. Bush gravely designated a "monumental struggle of good versus evil" (Bush, 2003, p. 1101). In this struggle there was no room for nuanced understandings of the American present or past. *The Quiet American* thus found itself being quietly killed, morphing from what one critic called a "hot Oscar prospect" into a "problem child." What had been intended by Miramax as "a romance set against the backdrop of early American involvement in Vietnam," the critic suggested, "now could be seen as a searing critique of United States imperialism" (Thompson, 2002, p. E1). In the context of Bush's "monumental struggle," such notions were strictly verboten. The Vietnam War—unless it was rewritten as a World War II narrative like *We Were Soldiers* (2002)—was off-limits.

This was not the first time that a screen version of *The Quiet American* had become entangled in the politics of U.S. foreign relations. A 1958 adaptation of Greene's novel by the award-winning director Joseph Mankiewicz famously reimaged, with the assistance of CIA-operative Edward Lansdale, what had been a literary indictment of U.S. meddling in Southeast Asia into an unrestrained celebration of U.S. political intervention. In the 1958 production, unlike in Greene's novel, the Viet Minh, the revolutionary forces who sought to expel the French, engineered a terrorist bombing in a Saigon square that killed "at least 50" innocent civilians. In the most recent film, however, responsibility for the bombing was more properly laid at the feet of Alden Pyle, the "quiet American."

On September 10, an allusion to this tragic event in Vietnamese history may not have seemed especially controversial. But when, the following day, Americans became terrorism's victims, not its sponsors, this flashback to the early years of the Vietnam War raised too many uncomfortable questions. The implications were apparent. "[Y]ou needed to have your head examined if you thought this was a time for questioning America," claimed Miramax Co-Chairman Harvey Weinstein (Hochman, 2002, sec. 2, p. 17). Some test audiences apparently agreed. "Are you out of your mind?" Weinstein says he was told by members of his staff and others to whom he showed the film. "You can't release this now; it's unpatriotic. America has to be cohesive, and band together" (Thompson, 2002, p. E1). The conundrum for Miramax was spelled out by the film's director, Phillip Noyce. "Like Graham Greene's novel, the audience has to accept that the American character should be executed for crimes against humanity because he's a sponsor of terrorism," said Noyce in referring to Pyle's death at the hands of the Viet Minh. "That's a big leap right now" (Maddox, 2002, p. 14). Miramax thus quashed the project, with Noyce's calls to Weinstein going unanswered for months (Thompson, 2002, p. E1).

Had it not been for the incessant lobbying of Noyce, producer Sydney Pollack, and, especially, the film's star, Michael Caine, *The Quiet American* may never have been released. Yet their advocacy led Miramax to agree to retest the production in September 2002 at the Toronto International Film Festival. The audience loved it, with one critic, Richard Corliss of *Time* magazine, imploring "Oscar-minded Miramax" to release the film by year's end, for Caine's outstanding screen performance was "guaranteed a nomination" (Corliss, 2002, p. 25). Given the positive response, Miramax agreed to a limited November release in New York, Los Angeles, and the United Kingdom that would qualify the actor for the Academy Awards. Yet the subsequent marketing of the film, noted the industry journal *Variety*, took a curious turn: "Miramax's campaign seems to be framed this way: 'Michael Caine is great in a movie that's about, well, don't ask what it's about. He's just great in it'" (Higgins, 2002, sec. 2, p. 75).

Caine did indeed secure his nomination (although Adrien Brody ultimately received the Oscar) and *The Quiet American* did eventually go into wider release. It opened on the art-house circuit in February 2003 amidst the Bush administration's fervent mobilization for war with Iraq. The timing, disclosed scriptwriter Christopher Hampton, "made Miramax really nervous." Yet the impending Iraq campaign was precisely the reason the film "should be released now," Hampton argued. "It's a way of saying, 'Think twice before getting involved in a foreign country you know very little about'" (Gritten, 2002, p. 23). In the end, as the subsequent U.S. invasion would reveal, too many Americans failed to think twice.

In both its content and its handling, *The Quiet American* represented Hollywood's first post-September 11 encounter with the sordid history of U.S. imperialism. The past recounted in Noyce's film was, in most important respects, neither inaccurate nor unimportant. But in the context of an imagined American innocence, it was simply inconvenient. Americans could not be the sponsors of international terror; they were its unalloyed victims. The film thus had to be killed. That *The Quiet American* did finally see the light of day owes not so much to the loosening of a constrictive political culture as it does to a studio's accession to star power and the encouraging potential for financial returns. It may be years before scholars learn of the projects that were never made because they lacked a Michael Caine behind them.

—*Scott Laderman*

References

Bush, G. W. (2003). Remarks following a meeting with the national security team, September 12, 2001. *Public Papers of the Presidents of the United States: George W. Bush, 2001, Book II*. Washington, DC: U.S. Government Printing Office.

Corliss, R. (2002, September 23). Toronto, A year later. *Time*, p. 25.

Gritten, D. (2002, November 26). The film that scared a studio. *Daily Telegraph* [London], p. 23.

Higgins, B. (2002, December 9). "Quiet" campaign is getting a bit louder. *Daily Variety*, sec. 2, p. 75.

Hochman, D. (2002, November 24). From popcorn movies to a diet of salty politics. *New York Times*, sec. 2, p. 17.

Maddox, G. (2002, August 8). All quiet on the U.S. front for Noyce. *Sydney Morning Herald*, p. 14.

Mydans, S. (2001, September 9). Backward to when the road to Vietnam was paved. *New York Times*, sec. 2, p. 43.

Noyce, P. (Director). (2001). *The quiet American* [Motion picture]. United States: Miramax.

Thompson, A. (2002, October 17). Films with war themes are victims of bad timing. *The New York Times*, p. E1.

SPOTLIGHT ESSAY/FILM: *STRANGE CULTURE*

In 2004, Steven Kurtz, a tenured art professor at State University of New York at Buffalo (SUNY Buffalo) and founder of the Critical Art Ensemble (CAE), prepared an interactive exhibit for the Massachusetts Museum of Contemporary Art on genetically modified foods. On May 11, he awoke to find that his wife of 27 years, Hope, had died of heart failure in her sleep. Distraught, Kurtz dialed 911 and the police arrived, only to be distracted by his art installation in progress, in turn alerting the FBI to their discovery: Petri dishes full of bacteria, laboratory equipment, an invitation with Arabic writing on a living room table. Government paranoia led to spectacle, as later agents in hazmat suits arrived at Kurtz home, confiscating his exhibit materials as well as his books, computer, his cat, and most tragically, the body of his wife, who was autopsied multiple times. Disturbingly, the FBI's offered explanation was that this was "procedure post-9/11"; however, Kurtz was detained illegally for 22 hours and suspected of harming his wife as well as bioterrorism. Today, along with scientist-collaborator Robert Ferrell, Kurtz awaits a trial on reduced charges of mail and wire fraud, which under the USA Patriot Act put into place after the September 11 terrorist attacks, could result in up to 20 years of imprisonment.

Reflecting changes in U.S. life after 9/11, Kurtz's example also begs the question: How does the work of an artist come to this? Did the Joint Terrorism Task Force believe Kurtz and the CAE wanted to overthrow the government, or were they more concerned about what his bio-art would reveal about government's connection to corporate interests and deceptive, misleading food practices? The urgency of these questions and their greater implications for artists' freedom of expression after 9/11 drove Lynn Hershman Leeson to make *Strange Culture* (2007) a hybrid, experimental documentary using illustrations, dramatic reenactments, news footage, testimony, and commentary by both Kurtz and the actors, all of which highlight his horrifying and ongoing ordeal. *Strange Culture* serves to draw attention to Kurtz's plight and mis-treatment, but in doing so proves that the USA Patriot Act has not only affected Kurtz but Leeson as she presents activist art, shaping the content and style of her film as well as its exhibition and distribution. In *Strange Culture*, art is both restrained by the post-9/11 Patriot Act and created in response to it.

Aside from its content, the film's experimental, self-reflexive structure fractures our viewing practice, echoing Kurtz's disruptive and traumatic experience. Leeson's dramatic reenactments of Kurtz's colleague in the classroom hint at the historical responses and their collision with art and politics. Josh Kornbluth (as "Phil") asks his class if they are familiar with Joe McCarthy, evoking the Cold War era, and the House Un-American Activities Committee (HUAC). Later Kornbluth stands in front of a 1930s Diego Rivera mural, extolling the virtues of the days when the Works Progress Administration (WPA) supported and encouraged artistic expression. Rivera, however, was also attacked for art that often revealed his political affiliations, such as the famous mural commissioned and later destroyed by the Rockefellers for its inclusion of a por-trait of Lenin. Here, Leeson's inclusion of historical censorship of the artist on political grounds points out that history repeats, as her film's not so subtle reenactments compares the "Red Scare" with post-9/11 paranoia in the name of the war on terrorism.

While these examples hint at the film's reflexive capabilities, it's important to remember why they are included. Kurtz has been prohibited by his lawyers from speaking about the events of "5/11," as he has dubbed May 11, 2001, and thus legal restraint has guided how Leeson must present Kurtz's story. Viewers may be jarred when two people (Thomas Jay Ryan and Kurtz) in subsequent scenes introduce them-selves as "Steven Kurtz, a founding member of the Critical Art Ensemble," but this duality serves to emphasize not only of the restrictions of Kurtz' civil liberties but also that there is more than one narrative thread here—the story the FBI tells through speculation, imagination, and paranoia, and the one that Kurtz and Leeson tell through *Strange Culture*. John Knechtel (2006) in the *Alphabet City, Suspect* magazine, notes "[The idea of] Suspicion . . . tells a story in an instant, a story that is scripted in imagination before anything can be known of the reality" (p. 21).

Strange Culture illuminates the FBI's vivid imagination at work, while documenting how they fail to conduct a closer examination of the CAE's history. In the first

10 minutes of the film, we learn that the CAE has been creating installations and publishing books for more than 15 years, with a goal to, as Liese (2004) cites "create semiotic shocks that contribute to the negation of the rising intensity of authoritarian culture" (p. 292). Their engagement with science and technology and its problematic intersection with government practices and policies has been central to the CAE, and various arts institutions and universities have supported these efforts. Why did the Joint Terrorism Task Force omit this research from their investigation? It's been argued that the government's political agenda and the critical content of CAE's work is the root of such paranoia. Fellow artist Claire Pentecost (2007) notes "In the arts, where expectations for the most part have not included responsible decision-making—being passionate, personal and opinionated are assets, but being political is considered the end of creativity" (p. 6).

While being political has actually marked the beginning for Leeson's creativity and desire to create *Strange Culture* (with no budget in under a year), its politics have been a roadblock in getting her film seen widely. Despite praise from dozens of critics and acclaim at festivals, the film had only a limited theatrical release and was distributed on DVD by Docurama/New Video, a small specialty company. On such, Leeson (2008) proclaims, "the film seems too politically charged for large companies to take on" (personal communication, February 23, 2008). Thus the cycle of censorship continues as the War on Terror devolves into the war on liberal values, creative expression, and political freedom. When artists are censored, they respond in kind—with art that interrogates the very thing that limits their creative and often political expression. Moving beyond the events of "5/11," Kurtz's story has inspired many other artists, in addition to Leeson, to make activist art that fights for the return of an artist's civil liberties in the post-September 11 world.

—*Rachel Thibault*

References

Beer, S., & Leeson, L. (Directors). (2007). *Strange culture* [Motion picture docudrama]. United States: Docurama New Video.

Knechtel, J. (Ed.). (2006). *Alphabet city 10: Suspect*. Cambridge: MIT Press.

Liese, J. (2004). United States vs. Steven Kurtz. *Artforum*. Retrieved from http://www.artforum.com

Pentecost, C. (2007). When art becomes life: Artist-researchers and biotechnology. *Transform eipcpnet*. Retrieved from http://transform.eipcp.net

SPOTLIGHT ESSAY/FILM: THE TWIN TOWERS IN FILM

In the years since September 11, 2001, a handful of narrative features—and a slew of documentary films—have taken up some aspect of that sad and terrible day. With relatively few exceptions, however, U.S. filmmakers have shied away from incorporating visual references of the Twin Towers in their stories. Three post-9/11 films demonstrate how images of the Twin Towers are inscribed with and accumulate meaning over time: a fact lost neither on the architects and perpetrators of the attacks—whose targets were potent symbols of American economic and military power—nor on the filmmakers whose stories of loss, retribution and redemption offer a way to make sense of those seemingly incomprehensible crimes.

Gangs of New York (2002), Martin Scorsese's historical epic of mid-nineteenth-century New York City, opens with a bravura street fight between the Irish immigrant Dead Rabbits, led by Priest Vallon (Liam Neeson) and the anti-immigrant nativists, headed by Bill the Butcher (Daniel Day-Lewis). When Bill vanquishes the Priest, the nativists assume control of the infamous slum known as the Five Points of Lower Manhattan—the year is 1846. Sixteen years later—amid waves of Irish immigrants who are summarily abused by nativists, courted by the city's political machine, and drafted into the Union Army—Priest Vallon's son, Amsterdam, (Leonardo DiCaprio) returns to the Five Points, infiltrates Bill's inner circle, and sets about avenging his father's death.

At the film's climax, Amsterdam defeats Bill as the city succumbs to the violence and mayhem of the 1863 draft riots. The final image, a time-lapse shot of lower Manhattan taken from the vantage point of a Brooklyn graveyard, chronicles the city's growth from the Civil War to September 10, 2001. Viewers are left with an indelible image of the Twin Towers—fixed in place, frozen in time—as U2's post-9/11 anthem "The Hands That Built America" plays during the credit sequence. As the song fades out, police sirens and fire alarms are heard: the unmistakable sounds of the city's first responders to the terrorist attacks.

The presence of the towers at the conclusion of *Gangs* accentuates the film's historical subtext. Throughout, Scorsese likens this period of New York's history to a crucible out of which a modern metropolis will one day emerge. Over the final image, Amsterdam says: "My father told me we was all born of blood and tribulation. And so then too, was our great city." By way of an otherwise conventional revenge story, *Gangs* chronicles a traumatic and decisive moment in the city's history. And through it's evocation of the Twin Towers, the film reminds us that the city has seen—and survived—great turmoil and tragedy.

Steven Spielberg's *Munich* (2005) likewise concludes with an image of the Twin Towers. Whereas Scorsese's film evokes the towers to provide historical perspective, Spielberg's purpose is to punctuate his cautionary tale of vengeance with an unambiguous reference to post-9/11 United States. *Munich* tells the story of a team of Israeli assassins, led by Avner Kaufmann (Eric Bana), charged with hunting down members of Black September, the Palestinian terrorist organization responsible for killing 11 Israeli athletes at the 1972 Olympic games. Equal parts political thriller and unflinching character study, *Munich* unfolds a geography of global terror and retribution steeped in moral ambiguity and existential dread.

In the person of Avner Kaufman, *Munich* suggests that the cycle of violence that characterizes Israeli-Palestinian relations does little to promote individual, let alone collective, security on either side of the conflict. When we first meet Avner, he is a loving husband, a dutiful son, and a fastidious, albeit low-level Israeli intelligence officer. Over the course of the film, Avner's loses his moral compass, and as the body count rises he is thoroughly dehumanized. By the film's end, Avner is reduced to a cipher: a man racked with guilt, alienated from his family, and disavowed by the government that enlisted him for its vengeful mission.

The film's final scene—a chilling exchange between the assassin and his aloof and single-minded handler, Ephraim (Geoffrey Rush)—takes place along the Brooklyn waterfront. There, the two men debate the ethics, and efficacy, of retribution. "Did we accomplish anything at all?" Avner asks. "Every man we killed has been replaced by worse," he suggests. Ephraim responds coolly: "Why cut my fingernails, they'll grow back."

As the two men go their separate ways, the camera pulls back to reveal lower Manhattan—the Twin Towers clearly discernable in the distance. *Munich*'s powerful, poignant final image speaks eloquently to the futility of vengeful reprisal and, by inference, the chimera of peace and security offered by Bush's War on Terror.

Unlike *Gangs of New York* or *Munich*, Spike Lee's *25th Hour* (2002) takes place in the immediate aftermath of 9/11. Whereas the other films (re)assert the towers' presence, *25th Hour* is haunted by their absence. According to Mr. Lee, "It was just an honest way of dealing with being a New Yorker afterwards, trying to represent a battered but still-standing NYC. What else could I do? Pretend it hadn't happened?" ("Ghosts of New York," 2003). To that end, the film's credit sequence begins with abstract patterns of light and shadow—Terence Blanchard's mournful score accentuates the disorienting perspectives—only to reveal the Tribute in Light, the Twin Towers memorial, observed from different vantage points across the city.

This sequence sets the tone for the story of heroin dealer Monty Brogan's (Edward Norton) last day of freedom before he goes to prison for seven years. The film follows Monty as he says goodbye to family and friends—and attempts to discover who among them might have ratted him out to the cops. Throughout, Lee evokes the raw vulnerability of post-9/11 New York.

Nowhere is this more evident than in a brilliantly rendered scene in which Monty confronts himself in a mirror—the words "Fuck You" scrawled beneath his reflection. Speaking directly to the camera, Monty unleashes an invective against New York, its inhabitants, and those who have desecrated his city. Monty's diatribe is exhaustive if not all-inclusive. Emotionally drained, Monty stops himself and acknowledges that he alone bears responsibility for his plight. It is a stark and unsettling moment of pathos rare in contemporary American cinema—a perverse love letter to New York City fueled by self-recrimination and despair.

The film concludes with a fantasy sequence that finds Monty fleeing prison to lead an anonymous counter-life in the American West. Driving his son to Otisville penitentiary, Monty's father (Brian Cox) imagines his son's flight from New York City, and the law, and his subsequent reinvention as a hardworking family man. In an improbably rhapsodic monologue, Monty's dad tells him: "This life was so close to never happening." The scene is cathartic—a crystallization of the enormous sense of loss associated with September 11, 2001.

In their own distinctive fashion, each of these films evokes the Twin Towers—their presence as well as their absence—to place 9/11 in historical perspective; to warn against the perils of vengeful retribution; and to lament countless lives that might have been.

—*Kevin Howley*

References

Ghosts of New York. (2003, April 11). *The Guardian*. Retrieved from http://film.guardian.co.uk

Lee, S. (Director). (2002). *25th hour* [Motion picture]. United States: 40 Acres and a Mule.

Scorsese, M. (Director). (2002). *Gangs of New York* [Motion picture]. United States: Miramax.

Spielberg, S. (Director). (2005). *Munich* [Motion picture]. United States: Dreamworks.

SPOTLIGHT ESSAY/FILM: *UNITED 93*

It took several years for Hollywood to release films that dramatized the very serious and traumatic events of September 11. The first nationally released mainstream film, *United 93* (2006) focuses on the people aboard the United Airlines flight that ultimately crashed in Shanksville, Pennsylvania. A group of passengers confronted the hijackers of the plane, resulting in the diversion of the hijackers' plans to crash the aircraft into the nation's capital. The film was directed by Paul Greengrass, a British director whose choices regarding how to present this story were met with high regard from film critics.

United 93 is unique for several reasons. The film was shot in a way that places viewers in the position of passengers on the plane, making audiences feel they are witnessing the actions of the men and women who experienced the hijacking. In an attempt to emphasize the fact that ordinary people were the victims and heroes of Flight 93, there is no character development of the passengers and no extended dialogue between them. Similarly, the director and producers elected to use relatively unknown actors to dramatize the events as a tragic story of everyday Americans. The film was also significant because of the outreach to victim's families. According to the Associated Press (2006), the producer sought out and worked with families of *United 93* victims when creating the film; the reconstructions of phone calls from the plane to families assisted Greengrass in crafting how events and the passengers' understanding of what was happening unfolded in the air. Other important aspects of the film included the way the shots cut back and forth between the interior of the plane and air traffic stations, control stations, and military command rooms. Many of the officials in these sites are played by the actual men and women who were working in these organizations on 9/11, or by those who work in similar jobs.

United 93 was not without controversy. In April of 2006 theaters began running previews of the film and some audiences, particularly in New York, were upset by its content. Some theaters pulled the trailer while others showed a promotional spot about the making of *United 93* in its place (Associated Press, 2006). Overall, however, the film received positive reviews. Critics from across the country described the film as "powerful," "as accurate as possible," "sobering," "non exploitive," and "a memorial" (see e.g., Turan, 2006; Burr, 2006; Ebert, 2006). In addition, 40 film critics cited the film as one of the top 10 movies in 2006 ("Metacritic: 2006," 2006).

Despite the serious nature of the film, the emphasis on characteristics Americans tend to value as a nation—the willingness to fight, the ability to work together in times of crisis, perseverance, and sacrifice—gave the film's narrative a hopeful strain. *United 93* also highlights the heroic deeds of those unprepared for the events that unfolded on that day in ways that are displayed by citizens' actions rather than by accompanying dramatic music. *United 93* did well at the box office. It was on the list of the top 10 grossing films for five weeks ("Box Office," 2007) and was nominated for two Academy Awards (Best Directing and Best Editing). A percentage of the box-office revenue was given to the Flight 93 memorial.

The movie was released on DVD in September of 2006. In keeping with the tone set by Greengrass's direction, the film commentary (authored primarily by Greengrass) highlights how collected evidence, conversations with family members, and discussions with on-the-ground air-control personnel assisted in writing and filming scenes. In addition, the DVD features excerpts of victims' family members meeting the actors who portrayed their loved ones in the film and a series of memorial-oriented content.

—*Amy M. Damico*

References

Associated Press. (2006, April 4). NY theater pulls United 93 trailer. *MSNBC*. Retrieved from http://www.msnbc.com

Box office. United 93. (2007) Retrieved on July 11, 2008 from http://www.rottentomatoes.com

Burr, T. (2006, April 28). Terror, in real time. *The Boston Globe*, weekend, p. N5.

Ebert, R. (2006, April 28). United 93. *Chicago Sun Times*. Retrieved from http://rogerebert.suntimes.com/

Greengrass, P. (Director) (2006). *United 93* [Motion picture]. United States: Universal Studios.

Metacritic: 2006 Film Critic Top Ten Lists. (2006). *Metacritic*. Retrieved from http://www.metacritic.com

Turan, S. (2006, April 28). Movie review: United 93. *The LA Times*. Retrieved from http://www.latimes.com

SPOTLIGHT ESSAY/FILM: OLIVER STONE'S *WORLD TRADE CENTER*

In August 2006, director Oliver Stone's *World Trade Center* was released to the general public. Like other 9/11 films, its initial production inspired skepticism because of its political significance and, more specifically, its director's political reputation. However, the film turned out not to be a propagandistic manipulation, nor was it a revisionist history lesson. Ultimately, because of the uncharacteristically objective approach taken by Stone, the film turned out to be a well received and respectable historical representation.

Although he is often seen as more a conspiracy theorist than a dispassionate film-maker, Oliver Stone was more interested in capturing the consequences of the attacks on September 11, 2001, than examining their causes. Stone effectively bracketed his political views, describing his opinions as those of "John Q. Citizen," and expressed his autonomy from the potential political motives of others, explaining: "This is the film I wanted to make. . . . No one tells me how to cut my films" (Pearlman, 2006, p. 12D). The film Stone wanted to make proved to be more contemplative than some of his other more politicized films, such as *JFK* and *Nixon*.

Stone's goal was to "narrow [the story] down to two men and feel their fear, their strength and their courage" in order to make the film about resilience. As he put it: "I thought this was a fresh way to purge our systems of this tragedy" (Pearlman, 2006, p. 12D). As such, the film does not tell the broader story of the attack on the World Trade Center. It is, by and large, the story of John McLoughlin (Nicolas Cage) and Will Jimeno (Jay Hernandez), two members of the Port Authority Police Department (PAPD) who were trapped in the rubble of Tower 2 before they could leave the underground concourse to begin their rescue effort. The film opens in a manner typical of the World Trade Center's story—with New Yorkers beginning an ordinary day made extraordinary only by the noticeably nice weather. As events unfold, the audience discovers what is going on through the perspective of a range of individuals. The hub of the film is the interaction between McLoughlin and Jimeno as they lay trapped in the rubble, and it is their rescue that concludes the narrative.

The dominant McLoughlin-Jimeno story line does extend to include their families, allowing the narrative to span from those trapped below 20 feet of twisted steel and concrete to suburban family homes. Within each of these story lines are a number of flashbacks to life before the attacks. Also, complementary to them, is the story of former U.S. Marine, Dave Kearns, who left his workplace in Connecticut to assist in the rescue efforts at what would soon be known as Ground Zero. Kearns's presence infuses the film with a sense of overlapping patriotic and religious loyalty and, taken together, all three story lines exhibit the courage and faith exhibited that day.

The result is a film that has both limitations and new contributions. First, Stone limited the scope of what could be portrayed because he narrowed the narrative to tell the story of two men rather than two towers. Some elements simply could not be included, given the narrative requirements and the length and structure of a feature film. Consequently, a number of components of the attacks are not present, such as what happened inside the World Trade Center above ground level, the heroism of the FDNY, New York Police Department (NYPD) (as well as office workers who helped each other out of the buildings), and the experience and response of government officials. Other portrayals, such as visual images of the attacks themselves, were deliberately left out, given that they went beyond the perspective of the characters and also because Stone did not wish to assault his audience with sensational images with which they were already familiar.

Despite what it excludes, *World Trade Center* reaffirms some of the most common elements of the broader 9/11 story, such as: the sense of normalcy earlier that morning, the role of the news media, the profound disbelief and confusion, the courage of rescue workers, and the anxiety of families, particularly women and children. In this regard, *World Trade Center*'s main contribution is its confirmation of a palpable sense of kinship and national unity that emerged that day. Moreover, the three main story lines place emphasis on the importance of faith in coping with and surviving tragedy. The strong sense of Judeo-Christian values after 9/11 is at play in *World Trade Center*, with continual affirmations of faith throughout the film—ranging from simple prayers to visions of salvation—making religion another prime component in the 9/11 narrative.

The film also gives publicity to some less-recognized elements of what happened at the World Trade Center. For one, it tells the story of PAPD officers, stepping away from the usual focus on the FDNY. In using their perspective, the film takes the audience to places that the broader narrative about 9/11 generally does not. The audience experiences the initial mobilization, the arrival at the site, the chilling sound of jumpers landing in the Plaza, the interaction of officials in the concourse before and during the collapse of Tower 2, and the first glimpses of Ground Zero. Through the PAPD officers' experience, the film also illuminates the men's initial unpreparedness, their confusion, their fear, and their physical weakness. The inclusion of these factors might seem unflattering to their story and that of other rescue workers. However, it actually enhances their bravery by casting the officers as human heroes rather than superheroes, thus making their selflessness and sacrifices all the more courageous.

New Yorkers who saw *World Trade Center* the day it opened were drawn to it for several reasons: Stone's reputation, their personal experiences of 9/11, or the film's historical focus. These are the three qualities that distinguish *World Trade Center*. It is an incomparable director's use of individual stories to contribute to collective history—a story of resilience and faith rather than destruction and loss that attests to humanity's ability to emerge from one of the most inhumane acts imaginable, as Stone intended.

—*Kathryn Palmer*

References

Pearlman, C. (2006, August 6). Stone hits home. *Chicago Sun-Times*, p. 12D.

Stone, O. (Director). (2006). *World Trade Center* [Motion picture]. United States: Paramount Pictures.

SPOTLIGHT ESSAY/FILM: *WORLD TRADE CENTER* AND *UNITED 93* MOVIE POSTERS

The release of the films *United 93* (2006) and *World Trade Center* (2006), defied the logic that preexisted their distribution: the erasure of images of the World Trade Center towers and the planes that struck them from popular-culture media. The films directly position 9/11 in the realm of entertainment, where an audience must choose to bear witness in the same cinematic space where they witnessed numerous disaster movies under the auspices of enjoyment. An audience had to be built that was willing to see the "unthinkable" once again, and it is through the potent single image of the film poster where the selling of 9/11 as experience takes place.

In general, film posters are everywhere and are not site-specific: They are in newspapers, magazines, cinemas; on billboards; and adorn bus-stops. The film "spills its contents into the stream of everyday life" through advertising (Burgin, 2004, p. 12). The posters demand casual consumption and are often viewed without warning or context. They are destined to be replaced by other posters and are situated in a quick cycle of promotion that is the antithesis of cultural understandings of 9/11—that this event could not possibly be replaced in collective consciousness. The way in which the films were sold to their potential audiences was through the recalling of mythic images, put together through representations of both the monuments that were destroyed and the personal lives under attack. These are the symbols with which an audience is supposed to identify the profound impact of 9/11. While public memorials may be erected in the place of buildings as a collective sign of triumph, the domestic sphere is also called upon to help interpret these events and to demonstrate resilience.

New York is the geographic center of the representation of 9/11 in the film posters. Despite United Airlines Flight 93 not crashing in New York, the personal and collective center of the attacks and the following resilience is framed as belonging to Manhattan. The posters for *World Trade Center* predictably revolve around a myriad of depictions of the towers; however, the individual is also used to help interpret 9/11. Perhaps the most iconic poster for *World Trade Center* (*World Trade Center* poster, 2006c)—two men walking toward a light in the middle of two black pillars—demonstrates this junction between the personal and the monument; the private and the public. The black towers appear as commemorative columns, which allow for ascension to the sky. In another poster, the firefighters appear above the World Trade Center towers in the New York skyline, the U.S. flag flying behind their troubled faces (*World Trade Center* poster, 2006d). The firefighter is synonymous with heroism in 9/11 as an extension of the nation state, encoded with duty and courage. However, firefighters also became emblematic of New York, and thus New York's spirit totemic for the remainder of the United States. Here, the firefighters are courageous and provide hope and a future, and the structures of the buildings (later to become public memorials) serve commemoratively. The firefighters are social structures that provide hope, similar to a memorial building.

United 93, however, is fraught by difficult representation. The plane was used as both a weapon and as a space for heroic actions. The two most common posters present two very different interpretations of the event. In one (*United 93* poster, 2006b), a plane heads toward the already ablaze World Trade Center towers, framed by the Statue of Liberty. This is the only direct representation of a plane *in action* in the posters across the two films. This poster demands that the events of *United 93* be read in context of what had happened in New York, and the temporal bounds of its depiction demonstrate that *United 93* takes place in a post-World Trade Center world, dictated by different rules. However, the narrative of *United 93* is also separated from the towers. Another poster presents a collage of images that provoke a democracy of grief, reminiscent of posters of the missing (*United 93* poster, 2006a). A collage of many squares showing the faces of individuals, the flight path, and the World Trade Center towers, ensure that the monument is treated equally in representation as the personal. Viewers are prompted to mourn the people and the buildings, the domestic and the ordered public. Both the loss of monuments and the loss of people are to be mourned, and each becomes synonymous with the other in recalling images of 9/11. They are two institutions that were directly under attack, the posters declare, but also two structures that provide hope for the future.

To view advertising as a type of memorial monument, there needs to be a willingness to see this cultural form as being imbued with multifaceted meaning. The film posters attempt to sell the experience of 9/11 to an audience that is grieving. To move the grieving and trauma into popular culture is an attempt to make sense of events that have left us haunted, and to situate the event in a document that survives the act of watching a film itself. The symbols that are called upon to interpret 9/11 appeal to an audience's memory of that day—and use images that are intended to draw an audience to choose to witness 9/11 again.

—*Kathleen Williams*

References

Burgin, V. (2004). *The remembered film*. London: Reaktion Books.

United 93 [Motion picture poster]. (2006a). Retrieved August 5, 2008, from http://impawards.com/2006/united_ninety_three_ver2.html

United 93 [Motion picture poster]. (2006b). Retrieved August 5, 2008, from http://impawards.com/2006/united_ninety_three.html

World Trade Center [Motion picture poster]. (2006c). Retrieved August 5, 2008, from http://impawards.com/2006/world_trade_center.html

World Trade Center [Motion picture poster]. (2006d). Retrieved August 5, 2008, from http://www.imdb.com/media/rm2035454464/tt0469641

SPOTLIGHT ESSAY/FILM: ZOMBIE FILMS

U.S. audiences have been interested in zombies as far back as the early twentieth century when voodoo became yet another imperialistic import of Central and South American cultures. Over the years, a zombie mythology has developed, helped in large part by filmmaker George A. Romero with his two most classic zombie films: *Night of the Living Dead* (1968) and *Dawn of the Dead* (1978).

While each zombie film often reconfigures elements of the zombie mythology (as happens with vampire and werewolf films), certain essentials are necessary for it to be identified as a zombie narrative. Zombies are originally human but have transitioned for some known or unknown reason. All zombies can infect humans, typically through biting or some bodily fluid exchange. The transition from being human to being a zombie, like the zombies' movements, is slow and prolonged. All zombies seek to consume human flesh (ultimately, the brain). Zombies are driven by endless hunger, but lack any real intelligence and, finally, the only way to stop or kill a zombie is decapitation or severe head damage.

Before 2001, only two particular eras for zombie films could be identified: pre-George A. Romero (all zombie films before *Night of the Living Dead*, 1968) and all zombie films since then. However, there has been a marked shift in the zombie narrative, which can only be described as a post-Romero paradigm or the Post-9/11 Zombie. By 2002, a new breed of zombie had appeared. This zombie is distinctly different. It is as aggressive as its predecessor is passive. It will not just pursue its victim in a slow stumbling gait, but sprint with athletic speed, hurdle obstacles, and manipulate objects (door handles, fixtures, and weapons) to get its prey. Once infected, humans take mere seconds to transition to a zombie state. This new zombie is best exemplified in movies such as *Resident Evil* (2002), *House of the Dead* (2003), *28 Days Later* (2003), *Dawn of the Dead* (2004), and *Resident Evil 2* (2004). Romero-esque zombie films have come out including Romero's own addition to his ongoing zombie series, *Land of the Dead* (2005), but few, if any of these have a wide theatrical release and do not make the kind of money that the post-Romero films do. The only one that garnered a bit more attention is *Shaun of the Dead* (2004), which was a satire of the zombie narrative.

It is interesting to see that the emergence of the new zombie transpired in the wake of September 11 and the beginnings of the War on Terror. September 11, 2001, put terrorism in America's own backyard; it was tangible. It created a moment in the national psyche when no one knew what was going on, and even the President was nowhere to be found—as close as total anarchy as most Americans have ever come. Religion, too, was also placed at the forefront as the terrorists were repeatedly identified by their religions more than any other factor.

The new zombie can be deconstructed in such a way to represent these branded concepts in American minds. When considering the speed and agility of the new zombies, it exemplifies the nearness of 9/11. Until this point, terrorists (zombies) were predominantly figures that existed elsewhere or were far enough from Americans that they would have little fear of them. They could escape. But these new terrorists can easily injure their prey. Here too, the zombie's presence and tenacity brings with it a sort of anarchy representing the absence of our most iconic leader at the moment of emergency. Quickly moving zombies and quick conversions leave no time to organize and cohesively respond.

While the United States does not have a state religion, it is hard to refute that its history has been predominantly influenced by Christianity. Considering that the zombie is an undead being, a person who has not ascended to Heaven, an easy translation can be made to read zombies as Islamic or at least non-Christian beings. This can also easily align with Western perceptions of the Islamic jihad, a kill-or-convert mentality that embodies the zombie. They either devour their enemy or convert them into zombies.

In briefly comparing the original *Dawn of the Dead* and the remake, some firm differences exist that correspond to these ideas. In the original, zombies are not the sole antagonist, but rather, the last third of the film deals with looters and marauders. People infected by zombies can taken hours or longer to change over. Additionally, the government is present and enacting a planned evacuation from the city; the opening setting for the original. However the remake situates itself in an idyllic suburban area which is struck without warning. The protagonists awaken one morning to find out the world has changed and been thrown into chaos and disorder—a morning that might closely resemble how people felt when they awoke on September 11, 2001. The new zombies remain the sole antagonist in the remake and conversion takes mere seconds.

This is not to say that audiences see zombies and think "Islamic terrorist," but rather the fear, anxiety, and excitement generated by this new zombie is derived from a media machine, which has stimulated similar fears in the minds of Americans over since 9/11. As horror films and amusement parks continue to reiterate, people enjoy experiencing fear in safe environments. The emotions that parallel those deeper genuine fears of a terrorist attack are experienced in the "safe" environment of the movie theater or home. Hence, it is no wonder why zombies can be used as metaphors to reflect an American narrative of terrorism in a post-September 11 mentality.

—Lance Eaton

Chapter 6

MUSIC

INTRODUCTION: MUSIC AND SEPTEMBER 11, 2001

After it became clear that the United States was being attacked on September 11, 2001, many radio stations stopped playing music in order to provide news coverage of the situation that was unfolding. But soon, regular broadcasts resumed and music took its place in the culture as a medium that helped people process their emotional reactions to the tragedy. Music is one of the oldest cultural forms practiced by people, and on a daily basis, people are exposed to a barrage of music from radios, computers, iPods, televisions, public events, and even elevators. Despite the trivial nature of some music, it is a potent force that exerts very strong influence on the emotions of people. The dynamic position of music in recent U.S. social and political history can be looked at in regards to musicians using their art to reflect upon, protest, and respond to national and international events.

An overview of popular music related to 9/11 provides a unique opportunity to explore the connections between music and the political world. There are many examples of music that supply different interpretations of 9/11 and the event's lasting impact on the United States. Through this lens, perhaps, lessons can be learned that will prove useful in understanding the impact of a major national crisis on popular music. Popular music supplied a variety of responses to 9/11; some were immediately evident, whereas others took more time to emerge. In the days after the terrorist attacks new releases, album art, and lyrics were delayed or changed. Benefit concerts, albums, and singles were produced to raise money for 9/11 victims. At the same time, the concert industry experienced tour cancellations from international performers. Long-term responses included a diverse collection of musical styles that interpreted and reflected on the consequences of the terrorist attacks and the world that emerged in its aftermath.

The Music Industry's Initial Response

In the immediate hours and days following the attacks, musicians and recording companies removed or altered artwork, lyrics, and songs that could be interpreted as symbolically suggestive of the attacks and could trigger despair, anxiety, or fear. Most of this self-censorship took place during a period of time when the nation was in a siege-like mentality, overwhelmed with raw emotions, and uncertain whether additional terrorist attacks were forthcoming. A number of changes were related to titles, song titles, and even musical group names that now seemed inappropriate in their initial forms. For example, the Dave Matthews Band decided not to release "When the World Ends" (2001) as a single. The Strokes dropped the song "New York City Cops" from the U.S. version of "Is This It" (2001), which necessitated a recall of the copies that had already been distributed. The band Bush changed the title of the single "Speed Kills" to "The People That We Love" (2001). An electronic group called, prior to the 9/11 attacks, I Am World Trade Center released an album whose track 11 was coincidently titled "September" (2001). As a result of allegations of exploiting the tragedy, even though the song and album were produced prior to the terrorist attacks, the group changed their name to I Am the World for a short period of time (Berlin, 2001).

The attacks prompted changes to music visuals as well. Imagery that once was seen as edgy or provocative now could be labeled insensitive, and in some cases, ironic. For example, the Cranberries recalled the video for their song "Analyse" (2001) because it contained images of an airplane flying over two skyscrapers. Album cover artwork produced prior to September 11 that depicted the World Trade Center in distress was recalled and replaced. The Coup changed the cover, originally designed in

---

BANNED SONGS

The world's largest radio network, Clear Channel, sent a memo to its radio stations soon after the attacks on September 11. In it, the network listed about 150 songs that were "recommended" to be eliminated from airplay because of assumptions that lyrics would be perceived as offensive or otherwise problematic ("America under Attack," 2001). The so-called "banned songs" list included titles such as Billy Joel's "Only the Good Die Young"(1977), AC/DC's "Safe in New York City" (2000), Drowning Pool's "Bodies" (2001), the Beatles' "Lucy in the Sky with Diamonds" (1967), and Dave Matthews Band's "Crash into Me"(1997). Reports about Clear Channel's memo are archived in the Library of Congress *September 11 Web Archive Collection.*

—*Amy M. Damico*

Reference

America under Attack, Banned Songs. (2001, September 21). *Chart Attack*. Retrieved from the Library of Congress September 11 Web Archive at http://memory.loc.gov/911/catalog/2512.html

May 2001, of their *Party Music* album, which featured an exploding World Trade Center. Similarly, the group Dream Theater's September 11, 2001, release of *Live Scenes from New York* was immediately recalled to change the cover image because it initially featured an image of the New York skyline, including the World Trade Center, in flames.

In addition to altering now-sensitive musical content, the music industry immediately engaged in widespread efforts to contribute to a national recovery effort. The music community was quick to take an active role in organizing and participating in benefit concerts to honor victims, recognize emergency response workers, and raise funds. Nine days after the terrorist attacks, the New York Philharmonic performed Brahms's *Ein Deutsches Requiem* (1868), a piece about mourning and sorrow, as a benefit concert for disaster relief. The music industry's first collective effort took place less than two weeks after the terrorist attacks as well. On September 21, 2001, *America: A Tribute to Heroes* was broadcast on more than 30 television networks and 8,000 radio stations. Organized by George Clooney and the four largest television networks, this concert telethon included performances by Bruce Springsteen, U2, Dixie Chicks, Dave Matthews Band, Faith Hill, Alicia Keyes, Neil Young, and many others to raise approximately $150 million.

Other large benefit concerts followed in the subsequent months, featuring a variety of well-known and established musicians. On October 2, 2001, at Radio City Music Hall, the previously scheduled *Come Together: A Night for John Lennon's Words and Music* expanded the focus of the concert for the additional purpose of marking the 9/11 attacks. Performers who participated in the concert included the Dave Matthews Band, Nelly Furtado, Moby, and Stone Temple Pilots. The *Concert for New York City*, organized by Paul McCartney, took place on October 20, 2001, at Madison Square Garden. The audience consisted of New York fire department and police personnel and their family members who listened to performers such as The Who, David Bowie, Five for Fighting, Jay Z, Elton John, Destiny's Child, Mick Jagger, Keith Richards, and others. On October 21, 2001, *United We Stand: What More Can I Give?* was staged at the Robert F. Kennedy Memorial Stadium (RFK Stadium) in Washington, D.C. It was taped for broadcast on the ABC television network and featured artists such as James Brown, America, Rod Stewart, Usher, Janet Jackson, and Pink. The classic rock concert *Volunteers for America* took place in Atlanta and Dallas from October 20 through 21, 2001, and it included appearances by Styx, Journey, REO Speedwagon, Peter Frampton, and Bad Company.

The onslaught of benefit concerts sharply contrasted with the reality of the dramatically altered live music business because of fears of large public gatherings and a deteriorating economic climate. On 9/11 and during the subsequent week, much of the United States came to a standstill: Concerts, along with professional sporting events, live theater, and other major entertainment events, were cancelled. In the following months a number of concert tours were canceled including that of Destiny's Child, who pulled out of their European tours, and Janet Jackson, who canceled all international concert dates because of concerns about the security of air travel security. The Sisters in the Spirit gospel national tour was also cancelled because of ongoing

---

THE CONCERT FOR NEW YORK CITY

On October 20, 2001, the *Concert for New York City* took place at Madison Square Garden and was televised across the country. The purpose of the concert was to raise money, entertain the public, and pay tribute to victims and survivors. While it certainly had its somber moments, it was far more of a joyous celebration. Not all performances were related to 9/11, and expressions of humor (and even anger) were added to expressions of loss, gratitude, and strength. More than anything, the concert was centered around New York City. Although it was broadcast nationally, the concert's true audience was its immediate audience—the heroes and citizens of New York City. The *Concert for New York City* was not a national celebration but an ode to the city and its citizens. In fact, among the variety of musicians, actors, directors, and politicians who participated, many portrayed themselves as New Yorkers, including those not native to the United States. New York City Fire Department (FDNY) and New York Police Department (NYPD) hats were also frequently donned by performers and presenters, placing added emphasis on rescue workers as those they were there to honor—the true heroes of 9/11.

An exemplar of the common tendency to perceive 9/11 as being New York City's tragedy in particular, the concert was more than a concert for the families of victims it was intended to financially benefit. It was a celebration of New York City as the greatest city in the world, New York City as the home of the brave, and New York City as a state of mind.

—Kathryn Palmer

security concerns and declining ticket sales (Collins, 2001). Even smaller concerts, in locations far distances from the attacks, were cancelled, such as the annual benefit concert for the Native American Scholarship Project that was to include Jackson Browne, Steve Earle, and Linda Ronstadt, scheduled for October 6, 2001, in Sedona, Arizona. The concert industry experienced additional challenges, such as not allowing concert goers to bring bags into venues, resulting from increased national security (Waddell, 2002). Immigration procedures grew much slower and unpredictable for foreign musicians, especially from the Middle East and North Africa, who applied for work visas in the United States. As a result, the overall number of international musicians touring in the United States declined after September 11, 2001 (LeBlanc, 2004).

As the first-year anniversary of September 11 approached, it became clear that the date took on symbolic importance in the music community, although recognition of the anniversary was not uniform among industry institutions and musicians. Some felt that attempts to sell products on the anniversary would be inappropriate; a recording company executive stated there would be no major releases on 9/11 and that silence was the best response from the industry (van Horn, 2002). Performers themselves had different opinions regarding whether to remain silent on the anniversary. Some musicians have avoided scheduling concerts on September 11 after 2001, whereas others, such as REM, made a conscious choice to perform in the belief that not doing so would amount to a surrender to the terrorist attacks (Ault, 2003).

AROUND-THE-WORLD REQUIEM

On the first anniversary of September 11, choirs around the world participated in a "Rolling Requiem." Beginning at the international date line, a series of Mozart requiems were performed at each time zone's 8:46 a.m., the time of the first attack on the World Trade Center. The performances followed the "sun around the world, providing 24 hours of musical unity, reflection and solace" (Bargreen, 2002, para 3). Choir members who participated donned heart badges marked with the name of a person who died in the attacks.

—Amy M. Damico

Reference

Bargreen, M. (2002, July 17). Around the world requiem will be performed Sept. 11. *The Seattle Times*. Retrieved from http://www.seattletimes.com

---

In implicit recognition of September 11, musicians like Toby Keith and Five for Fighting have performed for military personnel in the United States, Afghanistan, Iraq, and Guantanamo Bay over the years.

Although musicians were challenged with how to proceed in uncertain times, the value of the place music plays in the culture in periods of turmoil became increasingly evident. Contemplative classical selections were central at September 11 memorial concerts such as cellist Ha-Na Chang's performance of a Bach suite in Philadelphia (Sterns, 2002). In addition, musical organizations across the country put together special concerts to comfort listeners, pay tribute to those who lost their lives, and raise money for disaster relief (Waleson, 2001).

Benefit Recordings

After the terrorist attacks, the industry quickly packaged and released music with sales that would benefit September 11-oriented charities in the form of benefit singles and albums. Many of these musical compilations were well received by the public. The music industry also noted the public's displays of patriotism and responded accordingly. For example, *God Bless America* (2001) was an immediate Billboard chart topper album that contained an assortment of patriotic songs including a rendition of "God Bless America" by Celine Dion, Frank Sinatra's "America the Beautiful," and Pete Seeger's "This Land Is Your Land" (Moody, 2001). A live recording of *America: A Tribute to Heroes* sold 600,000 copies and the *Concert for New York City* live album had sales of 431,000 (Moss, 2002).

As the months passed, benefit albums with original compositions were produced as well. For example in November, a group of Latin artists released *El Ultimo Adios* (The Last Goodbye) (2001) dedicated to the families of September 11 victims and with sales that were donated to the American Red Cross and the United Way (Bonacich, 2001). In 2002, Suzanne Vega organized a benefit album titled *Vigil* featuring a collection of original songs about September 11 from artists from the Greenwich Village Songwriters Exchange. The album included songs such as "Ground Zero" by Jack Hardy, "Firehouse" by Christine Lavin, and "The Skyline" by Brian Rose. Proceeds from the sales were donated to the Windows on the World family fund. In addition, a group of Christian artists released *Let's Roll: Together in Unity, Faith and Hope* (2002) to benefit the Todd M. Beamer Foundation, an organization dedicated to helping children impacted by September 11.

In addition to the benefit albums, a number of individual singles were recorded or rerecorded and released to raise money for September 11-oriented charities. Patriotic singles were popular here as well. For example, proceeds from the sales of "Where the Stars and Stripes and the Eagle Fly" (2001) by Aaron Tippin were donated to the Red Cross and the rerelease of Whitney Houston's version of "The Star-Spangled Banner" (originally released in 1991) generated proceeds for firefighters and victims of the terrorist attacks. Other singles were rereleased, with musical additions or alterations, as charity singles. For example, "Never Too Far/Hero Medley" (2001) by Mariah Carey was released to benefit the Heroes Fund. A charity remake of Marvin Gaye's "What's Going On" (2001) was produced, recorded in nine different musical styles, and sold 228,000 copies (Moss, 2002). Although the remake was originally intended raise funds for AIDS, the project expanded to include 9/11 victims. Randy Travis's "America Will Always Stand" (2001) was released in October, and proceeds were donated to the American Red Cross. The song was also used in a Spirit of America public service announcement produced by the Foundation for a Better Life to commemorate the 9/11 attacks.

Music about 9/11

Many of the first songs to become popular after the terrorist attacks were not inspired by the day's events or even written after September 11 at all; they were previously written recordings that, in light of the nation's state of mind, gained new popularity

---

MICHAEL JACKSON AND FRIENDS: "WHAT MORE CAN I GIVE"

In response to the terrorist attacks on September 11, Michael Jackson gathered 35 stars in the music industry to record the single, "What More Can I Give." The song was performed at an October 2001 benefit concert. The recording and video features artists such as Celine Dion, Tom Petty, Mariah Carey, Aaron Carter, Reba McEntire, and Usher. Although intended to be released as a benefit single, the project was shelved for reasons that are unclear. Despite the lack of a commercial release, the song and video are widely available on the Internet.

—Amy M. Damico

as listeners used music to assist in dealing with their range of emotions. For example, new age singer Enya's calming song "Only Time"(2000) received significant airplay on radio stations in the weeks following the terrorist attacks, even though it was released a year prior to the attacks (Moody, 2001). Previously written songs were also reinterpreted given the events of the day. For example, Five for Fighting's "Superman" (2000) and Enrique Iglesias's "Hero" (2001) soared in popularity, perhaps reflecting the nation's new focus on ordinary people completing heroic tasks in the aftermath of the 9/11 attacks (Moody, 2001). Patriotic songs increased in popularity as well and were given airplay on mainstream radio stations. Finally, New York City was already an established theme in hundreds of songs, but after 9/11 songs about the qualities of the city became a symbol of the heroism that was displayed by firefighters and police, and radio stations integrated many New York-themed songs into their airplay in the days and weeks following the attacks.

As listeners were rediscovering the relevance of music created prior to September 11, musical artists were responding to the terrorist attacks by writing and composing. The 9/11 terrorist attacks inspired a great deal of music and continue to be a focal point for musical expression. Classical compositions were composed to honor the dead, while the many songs written about aspects of September 11, songs found in all genres of music, represent a variety of responses to the day and its aftermath. These responses are spiritual, patriotic, sad, angry, and vengeful. In a number of songs the artists assert and defend their role as storytellers to chronicle events in the world around them.

"NEW YORK, NEW YORK"

The popularity of Ryan Adams's CD titled *Gold* (2001), released two weeks after the terrorist attacks illustrates how music can take on different meanings to the listener. The first single from the album is titled "New York, New York," and although the song was written prior to the terrorist attacks after 9/11, listeners interpreted it as a renewed celebration of New York City. One line in the song, "I still love you New York," represented what many were feeling after the city was attacked. In an interview with the *New York Times*, while acknowledging that people were going to interpret songs in different ways, Adams explained the song was "a love song to a particular person, but in place of her name I just say 'New York'"(Lindgren, 2001, para. 6).

Additionally, the music video for the song was shot on September 7, 2001, and features the World Trade Center towers in the background of Adams's performance. The music video received more than average airplay on MTV after the attacks, and Adams performed "New York, New York" on *Saturday Night Live* on November 10, 2001.

—*Amy M. Damico*

Reference

Lindgren, H. (2001, November 4). The way we live now: 11–04–01: Questions for Ryan Adams: America rocks. *The New York Times*. Retrieved from http://www.nytimes.com

In the year following the attacks on September 11, a number of songs about aspects of the terrorist attacks emerged. Some of the first songs that were released were by established and well-known artists who, given their stature, would be listened to. For example, one of the first new songs specifically inspired by the attacks was "Freedom" (2001) by Paul McCartney. He first sang the song at the *Concert for New York*, and it was released as a single on November 13, 2001. The song depicted the terrorist attacks as an assault on freedom, but the single was not a commercial success; it sold fewer than 25,000 copies and reached no higher than 97 on the Billboard top 100 hot songs chart. After 2002, McCartney stopped performing the song because he believed that it had been inappropriately linked with support for a military response to the attacks (Dahlen, 2007). Around the same time, Neil Young, who was noted for antiwar, progressive stands since the 1960s, released "Let's Roll," (2001) a song performed with Booker T. and the MG's (later included on the *Are You Passionate* album). The song describes the events that were presumed to have taken place on United Airlines Flight 93 before it crashed in Pennsylvania. The phrase "let's roll" refers to what is believed to have been said before a group of passengers confronted and attempted to overpower the hijackers, causing United 93 to crash before it could reach its intended target. "Let's Roll" embodied the shared outrage at the monstrosity of attacking civilians and leading captive airline passengers to their death.

Other songs written about September 11 came from a variety of musical genres. Artist and songwriter Ani DiFranco wrote "Self Evident" (2001), a provocative reflection on the attacks, and the rock group Bon Jovi released "Undivided" (2002), a song about uniting after the tragedy of September 11. At times, songs about September 11 were popular outside of their musical genre. For example, country music singer Alan Jackson introduced the song "Where Were You When the World Stopped Turning/ Do You Remember" at the 2001 Country Music Association Awards. Due to the radio airplay the live version received on a variety of music stations, it was soon made available for purchase.

Wu-Tang Clan provided one of the earliest rap responses to 9/11 in the song "Rules" (2002), included on the *Iron Flag* LP. "Rules" is an angry and patriotic declaration about defending the United States, stating: "Who the fuck knocked our buildings down?/Who the man behind the World Trade massacres, step up now . . . America, together we stand, divided we fall/Mr. Bush sit down, I'm in charge of the war!" Other musical artists established themselves to respond to the terrorist attacks via song. The group My Chemical Romance formed after the lead singer saw the Twin Towers crash. The song "Skylines and Turnstiles" (2002) was the band's first song released from their LP *I Brought You My Bullets, You Brought Me Your Love*. The song vividly describes the devastated remains of the World Trade Center. In "Skylines and Turnstiles," the group acknowledges the pain caused by the attacks, yet hopes that the United States will not seek revenge and aim for a higher standard of behavior that could set an example for the rest of the world to follow. Commemorative music also addressed aspects of the attacks. The Pulitzer Prize-winning "On the Transmigration of Souls" (2002) a composition by John Adams, integrates lines from posters of the missing at Ground Zero and from the *New York Times* "Portraits of Grief" profiles into a 25-minute piece created in honor of the first anniversary of the attacks and performed by the New York Philharmonic Orchestra.

Over the years, many selections written by a number of musicians in diverse musical genres addressed various aspects of the terrorist attacks and components of the post-9/11 culture. For example, rapper Talib Kweli's "The Proud"(2002) is a 9/11-oriented tribute; composer William Basinski's "The Disintegration Loops I-IV" (2003) was produced as a reminder of those who lost their lives on September 11; pop punk band Yellowcard's "Believe" (2003) integrates pieces of news reports into its song about rescue workers; and the heavy metal group Iced Earth addresses the aftermath of 9/11 in "The Glorious Burden" (2003). Other examples that emphasize that all musical forms addressed and responded to the events on September 11 include alternative group Peroxwhy?gen's "September Day" (2003), Yi Chen's string-quartet composition, "Burning: Global Outrage: Denouncing Terrorist Attacks on 9/11/2001" (2004), hip-hop artist (and actor) Will Smith's "Tell Me Why" (2005) and thrash-metal band Slayer's "Jihad" (2006). In addition, music written and composed about September 11 was not confined to well-known professionals. A number of Web sites, such as the September 11th Tragedy: A Musical Gallery (http://www.kalvos.org/tragedy.html) served as portals for people to upload music and songs they had written in response to September 11.

In time, entire collections of songs were produced about September 11. Bruce Springsteen's *The Rising* (2002) was the number one album in 11 countries the week it was released. Many of the songs on the album were written after 9/11 and examined the attacks from a variety of individual perspectives; the album was hailed as the first significant cultural response to the events that took place on September 11. Given the subject matter and the popularity of the artist, the release was widely covered in the press. In addition to the expected reviews in publications such as *Rolling Stone*, the mainstream media honed in on Springsteen's and the E Street Band's collection of songs that mainly were written about working people who were personally impacted by the terrorist attacks. A *Time* magazine cover story describes the process Springsteen engaged in while working on the album, which included calling families of those killed in the attacks and hearing about their loved ones (Tyrangiel, 2002). A provocative track on the album called "Paradise" demonstrated Springsteen's willingness to probe the mindset of suicide bombers. Although some were uncomfortable that *The Rising* was marketed as a "September 11 record" and thus was potentially exploitative, the music was mainly critically acclaimed and positively received by the public.

Other compilations inspired by September 11 used music to examine the state of the world. Dolly Parton's *Halos and Horns* (2002) album was an introspective and spiritual examination of the consequences of the terrorist attacks. She wrote most of the tracks after 9/11, although she also included her cover of Led Zeppelin's "Stairway to Heaven" on the album. In "Hello God," Parton revealed some of the confusion and despair about the state of the world because of the conflict and hatred that seemed to be motivated by conflicting religions. Additionally, *Scarlet's Walk* (2002) by Tori Amos was an album devoted to contemplating the post-9/11 atmosphere of sadness, anger, and instability. Some songs in this collection directly refer to the attacks; for example,

"I Can't See New York" is a chilling piece of music where Amos describes circling over New York, unable to see the landmark World Trade Center. The benefit album *Vigil* (2002) also contains a number of individual songs that address aspects of September 11 and the aftermath.

Music and Post-9/11 Politics

Music has historically been a vehicle for political expression and a means for artists to both support and challenge government actions. After September 11, a number of songs emerged that addressed the U.S. government's response to the terrorist attacks. A few songs conveyed strong support for military action and retaliation by the U.S. government. For example, Toby Keith reached superstar status by writing the patriotic song, "Courtesy of the Red, White and Blue" (2002), which became his greatest hit and earned him the 2002 country music male artist award. "Courtesy of the Red, White and Blue" was aimed at an unnamed aggressor and conveyed anger and the desire for retaliation because "this nation that I love has fallen under attack/A mighty sucker punch came flying in from somewhere in the back."

Similarly, outrage and desire for retaliation were featured themes in Darryl Worley's release "Have You Forgotten?" (2003), which was dedicated to people serving in the military. The song was an emotional reminder of the horror of the attacks asking "Have you forgotten when those towers fell?/We had neighbors still inside going thru a living hell/And you say we shouldn't worry 'bout bin Laden/Have you forgotten?" At a certain level, Worley seemed to be speaking to those who argued that the causes of 9/11 were unlikely to be remedied by policies that were designed to avenge the attacks.

Many songs, however, challenged or protested the way the government handled September 11 and the aftermath. For example, Anti-Flag's "911 for Peace" (2002) was released as part of an album devoted to antigovernment activism. The song called for nonmilitary approaches to resolving international differences and included a recorded excerpt of Martin Luther King, Jr.'s "I Have a Dream" speech. Sleater-Kinney, an indie-punk group named the best rock band in the United States in *Time* magazine in July 2001, offered a striking commentary about 9/11 on their *One Beat* (2002) album. In several songs the trio criticized President Bush for his response to the attacks. In "Far Away," the band contrasted the President's behavior on 9/11, when he was secretly retreated across the country to find shelter in a secured underground bunker, with the bravery of the emergency responders who placed themselves at risk and suffered incredible losses of life. In "Combat Rock" they spoke to the pressures placed on musicians not to criticize or oppose the Bush administration's post-9/11 policies. The lyrics spoke of the need to challenge a political environment where "Dissent's not treason but they talk like it's the same/Those who disagree are afraid to show their face."

Interpreting September 11

Initially, some musical artists' interpretations of the events of September 11 included highlighting the responsibilities musicians felt the U.S. government had in the attacks. For example, Michael Franti and Spearhead, in "Bomb the World (Armageddon Version)" from the album *Everyone Deserves Music* (2003), voiced their belief that the underlying causes of the 9/11 terrorist attacks were partially attributable to U.S. foreign policies. The song described the political environment in the United States expressing skepticism about the need for a national consensus about a response to 9/11. In the song, Franti countered arguments that it was unpatriotic for him to fulfill his responsibility as a songwriter to document and evaluate historical events even if his observations ran counter to majority opinion. Immortal Technique with Mos Def touched upon hostilities against the United States in the song called "Bin Laden" (2005). The lyrics targeted U.S. foreign policy as a central cause of the 9/11 terrorist attacks because the government armed, trained, and funded Osama bin Laden during the Soviet Union's occupation of Afghanistan in the 1980s.

Concerns about direct government involvement in the terrorist attacks were also present. Conspiracy theories, already present in the culture, were sung about as well. The perennially controversial rapper Paris released *Sonic Jihad* containing the single "What Would You Do" (2003), where he addresses conspiracy theories about 9/11. Paris described the attacks as a ploy to manipulate the U.S. public with fear, and he proclaimed "So I'ma say it for the record we the ones that planned it/ Ain't no other country took a part or had they hand in." The song held back little in placing blame for 9/11 on the U.S. government. It also alleged that changes in the terrorist threat level seemed to be linked with fluctuations in public support for the Bush administration. Paris pushed the envelope even further with cover artwork featuring a large airplane flying directly toward the White House.

Other songs addressed economic issues related to the military response to September 11. The free download, "In a World Gone Mad" (2003), by the Beastie Boys voiced concerns about the influence of military suppliers and attacked the political process for its intertwined financial relationships with military suppliers. The song brushed with controversy, calling for "Peace to the Middle East peace to Islam/Now don't get us wrong 'cause we love America/But that's no reason to get hysterica." Using Arabic and wishing peace to Islam could have ignited a backlash, but the song pointed out that peace was not incompatible with patriotism.

Still other songs, written years after September 11, invited a broader interpretation of the tragedy while not diminishing its impact on the nation. For example, in "On That Day" (2006), Leonard Cohen, a highly acclaimed former poet laureate of Canada and vocalist, offered a haunting consideration of 9/11, referring to it as that day "they" wounded New York. Apart from Cohen's distinctive vocal style, the song is unique in the way it raises possible explanations for the attacks without reaching any conclusions.

Six-time Grammy winner Sheryl Crow's *Detours* (2008) album (nominated for the 2008 best vocal pop album Grammy award) contained a variety of interpretations of September 11. For example, "God Bless This Mess" linked 9/11 with the Gulf War, and "Shine over Babylon" described social and economic problems in the world and their impact on international relations. "Out of Our Heads" portrayed the powerful displays of courage displayed at the World Trade Center on 9/11. In the song Crow also took aim at President Bush's tearful words of comfort during his televised address to the nation on 9/11 and observed that in retrospect the president appeared manipulative and calculating. Interestingly, the video for "Out of Our Heads" promoted peace activism with a montage of antiwar protests from the 1960s and cameos of well-known historical figures from the past 60 years from different political backgrounds and many national origins. Despite the passing of seven years, *Detours* represented the continuing relevance of 9/11 as a subject matter for musicians.

Pressure on Musicians

Music is a form of communication that links together people and transcends the barriers of time and space. Music has always been a target of political and social criticism, and censorship has been the traditional tool to silence objectionable music. However, the influences on musicians to limit their expression or self-censor is subtle and originates from different sources. After September 11, as the nation tried to make sense of how to best deal with the aftermath and consider the government's response, a number of musicians were challenged on views that addressed government and law enforcement. For example, country-and-western music star Charlie Daniels had intended to introduce his song "This Ain't No Rag/It's a Flag" (2001) at a country concert in Nashville on October 21, 2001, but he declined to participate in the event after Clear Channel Entertainment and Country Music Television asked him to remove some lyrics from the song ("Country beat," 2001). At the June 2003, opening concert in New York City, Bruce Springsteen performed "American Skin (41 shots)" (2000), a song that obliquely criticizes the New York Police Department for shooting an unarmed man. Afterwards a New York Police Department chief ordered Springsteen's police security team removed. Springsteen did not perform "American Skin" at the following shows, and the security was restored for the final concert (Rush & Connor, 2003).

After the terrorist attacks, criticism of President Bush and U.S. national security policies increased over time as the president's popularity declined. Despite this shift, some musicians felt pressure to make changes to their work from those who believed the songs contained potentially inflammatory references about the terrorist attacks or the subsequent U.S. response to them. For example, Toby Keith was invited to participate in the ABC television special on the weekend of July 4, 2002, and perform his hit song "Courtesy of the Red, White and Blue." However, he was asked to change the lyrics or perform a different song. Keith refused both options and decided not to participate in the program. Michael Franti and Spearhead taped "Bomb the World" for the *Late Late Show* hosted by Craig Kilborn, but the song was not included during the regular broadcast of the program, and the incident was ultimately exposed only because of a report in *Billboard Magazine* (Gunderson, 2003). Six weeks after the premiere of Madonna's "American Life" video in 2003, it was withdrawn from broadcast because she believed it was widely misinterpreted as being anti-American and antimilitary (Wiederhorn, 2003).

An additional source of pressure on musicians and songwriters to curtail dissenting content can be found in the music awards environment. In the 2003 Grammy awards season several popular, but somewhat controversial, songs related to 9/11 such as Neil Young's "Let's Roll"; Toby Keith's "Courtesy of the Red, White and Blue (the Angry American)"; and Charlie Daniels's "This Ain't No Rag, It's a Flag" were not nominated. In contrast, songs that were more contemplative or spiritual were more successful. The best country song Grammy was won by Alan Jackson for "Where Were You (When the World Stopped Turning)," and Bruce Springsteen received several awards (Lewis, 2003).

Conclusion

Popular music has not shied away from 9/11 as the impetus for a variety of music. The range of music related to 9/11 covers many perspectives from a diverse style of musical approaches, suggesting that many musical artists recognize their responsibility to chronicle the world around them and to speak truth to power. Although the music industry is driven by economic impulses, if the public sentiment identifies with the perspectives found in music, then there will be an outlet for such songwriting and the impulse for self-censorship will be lessened. The music community can serve an important role in the interpretation of contemporary issues, and the musical responses since 9/11 highlight the complex relationship between popular culture, such as music, and political events. Taken together, music inspired by 9/11 provides an enduring, and even entertaining record of history that helps individuals interpret and cope with the world around them.

—*Chris McIntyre and Amy M. Damico*

References

Ault, S. (2003, September 13). Acts still skirt September 11 concerts. *Billboard*. Retrieved from http://www.billboard.biz/bbbiz/index.jsp

Beastie Boys. (2003). In a world gone mad. On *In a world gone mad* [http://www.beastieboys.com, Free download].

Berlin, M. (2001, November 30). Imagine: The music business in a post-9/11 world. *Austin Chronicle*. Retrieved from http://www.austinchronicle.com

Bonacich, D. (2001). El ultimo adios review. Retrieved August 28, 2009, from http://www.artistdirect.com/nad/store/artist/album/0,,1580379,00.html

Collins, L. (2001, November 17). In the spirit. *Billboard*. Retrieved from http://www.billboard.biz

Country Beat. (2001, October 29). *MTV News*. Retrieved from http://www.mtv.com/news

Dahlen, C. (2007, May 21). Interview with Sir Paul McCartney. *Pitchfork.com*. Retrieved from http:///www.pitchfork.com

Gundersen, E. (2003, March 10). Artists mount a chorus for peace. *Binghamton Press & Sun-Bulletin*. Retrieved from http://www.commondreams.org/

Keith, T. (2002). Courtesy of the red, white and blue. On *Unleashed*. [CD]. Nashville: Dreamworks.

LeBlanc, L. (2004, July 24). Acts face U.S. border bumps. *Billboard*. Retrieved from http://www.billboard.biz

Lewis, R. (2003, January 08). Reverberation of 9/11 heard in voters' nods. *Los Angeles Times.* Retrieved from http://articles.latimes.com

Moody, N. M. (2001, October 25). "God bless America" CD debuts at number one. *The Independent.* Retrieved from http://www.independent.co.uk

Moss, C. (2002, February 11). Post-9/11 tribute albums and singles: Big plans, not so big results: All-star remake of "what's going on," McCartney's "freedom," more suffer underwhelming sales. *CMT News.* Retrieved from http://www.cmt.com

Paris. (2003). What would you do. On *Sonic Jihad* [CD]. Danville, CA: Guerrilla Funk.

Pastorek, W. (2006, May 4). The Q & A: Pearl essence. *Entertainment Weekly.* Retrieved from http://www.ew.com

Rush, G., & Connor, T. (2003, October 8). Cop-out on Bruce NYPD pulled Boss' Shea escort after "41 Shots." *New York Daily News.* Retrieved from http://www.nydailynews.com

Sleater-Kinney. (2002). Combat rock. On *One Beat* [CD]. Seattle, WA: Kill Rock Stars.

Sterns, D. (2002, August 23). Post-Sept. 11, some musical styles just feel wrong. *The Philadelphia Inquirer.* Retrieved from Newspaper Source database (2W72386654847).

Tyrangiel, J. (2002, July 28). Bruce rising: An intimate look at how Springsteen turned 9/11 into a message of hope. *Time.* Retrieved from http://www.time.com

vanHorn, T. (2002, September 10). MTV artists debate releasing discs near 9/11 anniversary. Some ask why, while others ask, "Why not?" Retrieved from http://www.mtv.com

Waddell, R. (2002, September 21). Touring quarterly—playing it safe. *Billboard.* Retrieved from http://www.billboard.biz

Waleson, H. (2001, November 21). Ripple effect from September 11 seen in arts organizations across the United States. *Andante Magazine.* Retrieved from http://www.andante.com

Wiederhorn, J. (2003, March 31). Madonna yanks controversial "American Life" video. *MTV News.* Retrieved from http://www.mtv.com

Worley, D. (2003). Have you forgotten. On *Have You Forgotten* [CD]. Nashville: Dreamworks.

Wu-Tan Clan. (2002). Rules. On *Iron Flag* [CD]. New York City: Sony.

SPOTLIGHT ESSAY/MUSIC: CHRISTIAN ROCK AND 9/11

Songs from artists holding a myriad of views about the event and its meaning were inspired by the attacks on September 11, 2001. As is the case with public memorials that valorize and pay homage to victims of war and catastrophe, popular music can be used to create a space where memories and emotion are revisited. This form of expression is embraced by the masses, thus validated within the public eye. After September 11, a number of Christian musicians responded by incorporating themes of patriotism, faith, sorrow, and the post-9/11 world into their work.

After September 11, Christian artists contributed to the national gravitation toward music with patriotic themes. For example, DC Talk's "Let's Roll" (2002) honors U.S. troops and their families with Christian themes. The song references the U.S. flag, national unity (under God), commanding us to show the world what is right, as led by God. The song ends with the Lord's Prayer, perhaps indicating the group's desire for Americans to show forgiveness and to forgive. Aside from this, "Let's Roll" honors military service and the "American way" of life. Other contemporary Christian artists responded to the attacks by composing songs with patriotic themes as well. Michael W. Smith's "There She Stands" (2002) is a tribute to the U.S. flag's tenacity throughout history; he wrote this piece after former President George W. Bush asked him to create a song that responded to the terrorist attacks.

Other songs written about events related to 9/11 validate faith, recognize sorrow, and reinforce particular perceptions of divinity. For example, singer-songwriter Carrie Newcomer's "I Heard an Owl" (2002) dismisses the notion that hate or particular actions are part of God's will but rather, actions are the result of free will. In her song, Newcomer calls the listener to value courage and love above all else. Rachael Lampa's "Room" (2004) discusses the general presence of disaster and tragedy in the world, resolving that "God gets us through it" (Agee, 2005). Given Christian rock's implicit recognition of faith and hope in its lyrics, several musical groups were invited into mainstream music venues after the terrorist attacks. For example, the Newsboys performed at the Pentagon's sixth annual memorial service on September 11, 2007, honoring the people who gave their lives at the Pentagon and elsewhere on 9/11, and many Christian artists such as the group Petra performed at September 11-oriented benefit concerts.

Finally, many Christian rock artists composed songs that deal with the state of the world after 9/11. These artists view such happenings as part of a larger plan. Thus, songs can encourage, warn, express lament, proclaim, or enrage. For example, Buddy Miller's "Water When the Well Is Dry" (2002) considers the haunting reality of "a few thousand souls" that cannot be seen and admit the enemy cannot be fully known. Miller views the fight against this unknown enemy as one of resolve. Written several years after 9/11, "Antichrist Television Blues" (2007), by Arcade Fire, expresses continuing fear of urban areas and working in skyscrapers. The lead singer communicates trepidation about urban scenarios and the future of his daughter. The reference to God seems cathartic, expressing existential leaps to discern what God wishes for humanity and for his family.

Like musicians in other genres, Christian musicians responded to the terrorist attacks that took place on September 11 by composing songs that reflected the mood of the nation through the vantage point of their religious beliefs. At times, these songs and artists enjoyed listenership from mainstream audiences as people turned to music to assist them in processing their grief and making sense of such tragic events.

—*Shawn David Young*

Reference

Agee, L. (2005, February 14). Rachael Lampa interview: "No books or classrooms here." *About.com: Christian Music/Gospel Interviews*. Retrieved June 1, 2008 from http://www.about.com

SPOTLIGHT ESSAY/MUSIC: CONTROVERSY AND POST-9/11 MUSIC

As the United States engaged in war against Afghanistan and then Iraq, music began to reflect various reactions to the cultural differences among those living in the United States. Some of these songs contained a positive tone and were well received. For example, "An Open Letter to NYC" (2004) by the Beastie Boys spoke to New Yorkers and praised their resiliency in recovering from the destruction of the World Trade Center towers. The Beastie Boys also described New Yorkers' remarkable capacity to offer a receptive home to a large diverse multicultural population. However, during this time a number of songs emerged that were not widely regarded, and musicians faced criticism about their work in the mainstream media.

For example, Steve Earle stirred a great deal of controversy with "John Walker Blues" (2003), a song written about a young American who was captured in Afghanistan working alongside the Taliban and was sentenced to 20 years in federal prison. Controversy over Earle's song may have stemmed in part from the inclusion of an Arabic prayer and the reading of a passage from the Koran ("John Walker's Blues," 2003). In addition, the song was released soon after John Walker Lindh was sentenced; the attention devoted to the case may have primed the public for an angry response to songs that offered the appearance of justifying terrorism (Mansfield, 2002).

Other music caused considerable media coverage on its release because of its content. Prince's "Cinnamon Girl," from his *Musicology* (2004) album, focused on issues related to being a Muslim in the United States and the increasing violence against Muslims and people of Middle Eastern descent after 9/11: "Cinnamon Girl of mixed heritage/Never knew the meaning of color lines/911 turned that all around/When she got accused of this crime." Both the song and animated music video was a catalyst for a storm of controversy. The central character in the video reacts to her mistreatment by travelling to an airport and attempting a suicide bombing attack. Ultimately, she does not follow through with the bombing, but the video portrayed her imagining the devastation that her actions would cause. Reactions to "Cinnamon Girl" captured the intense scrutiny placed on popular music after 9/11. For example, the American-Arab Anti-Discrimination Committee commented on the video by stating:

> Prince's video may be misinterpreted by some as either rationalizing violence, or promoting dangerous stereotypes about Arabs and Arab Americans, but the artist should be credited with raising serious and difficult issues. Although a music video may not be the ideal format for exploring these sensitive and complex themes due to the time length, this video should be fairly clear to those who watch it carefully. ("Prince's," 2004, para. 4)

Michelle Malkin, a conservative political pundit, offered a different view writing in the right-wing blog Free Republic:

> Now, the artist formerly known as Prince has jumped into the murder-promoting, terror-sympathizing act. . . . What it is, is a washed-up pop star's crass exploitation of

post-9/11 race-card-playing by Arab-American apologists for terror. What it will do is further stoke the fires of the America-bashing MTV crowd. (Malkin, 2004, para. 1 & para. 10)

Disagreement among musicians themselves also emerged as some musical artists began expressing growing resentment at the exploitation of the powerful emotional responses and profound sacrifices that were caused by the 2001 attacks. Artists such as Paris, Beastie Boys, Sleater-Kinney, Michael Franti, and Sheryl Crow wrote songs that reflected their beliefs that the widespread public shock and tragedy experienced after the terrorist attacks was exploited by the Bush administration to pursue a number of policies, including, but not limited to, the Iraq War, that were unrelated to 9/11.

Upset with the military progress in Afghanistan and Iraq, other musicians produced work that specifically reflected this discontent. Pearl Jam's "World Wide Suicide" (2006) was the group's first number one hit since 1996. The song was about Pat Tillman, who quit the NFL's Phoenix Cardinals and enlisted in the army in response to the 9/11 attacks. Tragically, Tillman was killed in Afghanistan in a friendly fire incident that subsequently became mired in controversy because the U.S. military initially covered up the tragic circumstances of Tillman's death (White, 2005). Neil Young added to the political fray with an intensely political album called *Living with War* (2006). The album earned Young three Grammy award nominations including best rock album, best rock song, and best song. The well-regarded album contains "Let's Impeach the President," a straightforward criticism of President Bush relying on only a few lines: "Let's impeach the President for lying/And leading our country into war/Abusing the power we gave him" combined with clips of statements made by Bush since 9/11 with background chants of "flip-flop."

In the years following the terrorist attacks, musical artists used their talents and craft to respond to hot-button issues in the post-9/11 world. Although controversial on their release, many of these songs and albums enjoyed critical praise and commercial success, suggesting that listeners were interested in the perspectives musicians had to offer about such unsettled times.

—*Chris McIntyre*

References

American-Arab Anti-Discrimination Committee. (2004, October 24). Prince's cinnamon girl music video. Retrieved from http://www.adc.org

John Walker's blues' meets the boos. (2002, July 23). *CNN*. Retrieved from http// www.cnn.com

Malkin, M. (2004, October 8). Cinnamon girl: The latest martyrdom video (from Prince; blames US for terrorism). *Free Republic*. Retrieved from http://www .freerepublic.com

Mansfield, B. (2002, September 6). Country music, in 9/11 time. *United States Today*. Retrieved from http://www.usatoday.com

Prince. (2004). Cinnamon girl. On *Musicology* [CD]. New York City: Sony.

White, J. (2005, May 4). Army withheld details about Tillman's death: Investigator quickly learned "friendly fire" killed athlete. *The Washington Post.* Retrieved from http://www.washingtonpost.com

Young, N. (2006). Let's impeach the president. On *Living with war.* [CD]. Burbank, CA: Reprise Records.

SPOTLIGHT ESSAY/MUSIC: *THE DISINTEGRATION LOOPS I-IV,* WILLIAM BASINSKI

The Disintegration Loops I-IV (2003) is a four-disc series produced by classically trained musician and composer William Basinski and released in 2003 on his 2062 (MMLXII) label. The pieces were created when Basinski played back a collection of pastoral tape loops he had recorded in the 1970s and noticed that the magnetic tape was slowly flaking away. Basinski recorded the loops' demise, repeating each until it settled into silence. The ghostly, ethereal recordings are nearly ambient in nature, although close observation reveals the decay of the loops, with the tracks varying from just over 10 minutes to more than an hour in length.

Coincidentally, "Basinski was listening to the playbacks of his transfers as the attacks of September 11 unfolded, and . . . they became a sort of soundtrack to the horror that he and his friends witnessed from his rooftop in New York that day" ("William Basinski," para. 2). Each of the four volumes bears a front cover image of the smoke plume from the World Trade Center towers' collapse drifting over lower Manhattan, the sky turning from day to night. Basinski dedicates the series to the victims of 9/11, and its recording of the loops' death serves as a reminder of the losses endured that day.

There are six individual loops used across the four volumes of the series, with one loop being used three times and another twice for a total of nine tracks. The first loop, entitled simply "1.1," "1.2," and "1.3" in each of its respective appearances, consists of a roughly 30-second horn-and-string melody layered over a subtle clamor of percussive clanking noises. Already endowed with a fuzziness from the beginning of each repetition, the loop becomes increasingly rougher with each turn of the reel, drifting into the distance as the flakes of its melody drift from the tape. Loop 1 appears three times in the series—as "1.1" on volume I, and as "1.2" and "1.3" on volume IV, persisting for 63 minutes at first, then diminishing to just shy of 22 minutes the second time, and 12 the last. The loop suggests a fanfare of sorts, gesturing toward the pageantry of the creation of the World Trade Center towers and their status as symbols of U.S. commerce, although that pageantry is undergirded with an ominous low end and the insistent clamor of the percussive element.

The second loop, entitled "2.1" and "2.2" in its two appearances, consists of another approximately 30-second passage composed of a massive, shimmering electronic pulse beneath which a bass drone and slight horn introjections appear. From the first, the electronic pulse is brittle, crackling with the imprecision of analog equipment, a crackle that becomes more profound with the decay of the analog tape medium. Loop 2 appears twice in the series—as "2.1" on volume I, and as "2.2" on volume II, enduring for a mere 11 minutes at first, then for a hardier 33 minutes the second time. The loop's pulse suggests a Morse code, tapping out the distress signal of 9/11, the siren-like horns and eerie bass drone underlining the surreal nature of the post-collapse moonscape, as well as the gentle rain of debris over lower Manhattan after the towers' disappearance.

The third, fourth, fifth, and sixth loops, entitled "3," "4," "5," and "6," respectively, each appear once in the series. Loop 3 appears on volume II, is 42 minutes in length, and consists of an approximately 10-second segment composed of swooning, rattling, deep strings beneath a keening horn lead. The edges of the loop are ragged with distortion, suggesting the frazzled resurgence of patriotism in the wake of 9/11, an imperfect reassertion of national identity in a time of great crisis.

Loop 4 appears on volume III, is 20 minutes in length, and consists of another 10-second passage made up of a jittery high electronic melody line above a supporting synthetic wash, a distant, slightly distorted string accompaniment, and a percussive clatter much like that of Loop 1. The loop is by far the least stable of any of the loops' first appearances, and its short running time reflects its instability, a fragile fight song riddled with the corrosive effects of doubt.

Loop 5 also appears on volume III, is a robust 53 minutes in length, and consists of a 15-second passage based around an interwoven rise-and-fall horn and counterpoint bass melody, again featuring clanking percussion beneath. The loop's intertwined melodic line suggests the possibility of alliance in the wake of 9/11, though its ramshackle feel points to the failure of the United States to turn global sympathy post-9/11 into anything more truly collaborative than a "coalition of the willing."

Loop 6 appears on volume IV, is just shy of 41 minutes in length, and is made up of a short original segment of approximately 5 seconds with a swift, warbling electronic line and interspersed lower horn accompaniment over what sounds like someone's feet scuffling on an echoing stairwell. The loop's brevity, along with the footstep sound, recalls the limited escape time allotted to those descending the stairwells of the towers, as well as the omnipresence of threat after 9/11, always lurking behind the scenes and hunted by intelligence organizations who were themselves one step behind on 9/11.

William Basinski's *The Disintegration Loops I-IV* traces the trajectory of 9/11, from the heady confidence preceding the event, to the stunned disillusion of its occurrence, and through the ineffectuality of national response. As the loops' impact decays with each repetition, approaching silence, so too does U.S. foreign policy lose its own voice by refusing to listen to (and often silencing) others in favor of unilateral action, becoming less effective in the process.

—*Lloyd Isaac Vayo*

References

Basinski, W. (2003). The disintegration loops I-IV. On *The Disintegration Loops*. [CD]. New York: 2062 MMLXII.

Bio: William Basinski. (n.d.). MMLXII home page. Retrieved July 28, 2008, from http://www.mmlxii.com

William Basinski—*The Disintegration Loops I-IV.* (2004, March 21). Pitchfork Media. Retrieved from http://www.pitchforkmedia.com

SPOTLIGHT ESSAY/MUSIC: "FLY ME TO NEW YORK" BY CASSETTEBOY

"Fly Me to New York" is a song by the tape collage artists of Cassetteboy (Brits Steve Warlin and Michael Bollen) featuring DJ Rubbish that appeared on their 2002 debut album *The Parker Tapes*. Based primarily around tightly edited samples from Frank Sinatra songs, and also featuring excerpts from songs by the Smiths and a number of hip-hop artists, the song narrates the events of 9/11 from the perspective of one of the pilot-hijackers.

Beginning with a spoken word passage from DJ Rubbish concerning the ongoing hostilities in Iraq, and a selection of hip-hop samples arranged to advocate the 9/11 attacks, the song shifts to a middle section composed of Sinatra samples, which are manipulated into the pilot-hijacker's narrative. The samples state "I've got a razor in my pocket ... once I get you up there, I'll be holding my knife deep in the heart of you ... I'm mental and I'm flying the plane ... let's fly into buildings, let's turn to ashes ... and now my skin is melting away" (Cassetteboy, 2002). The song then returns to another selection of hip-hop samples, including DJ Rubbish's suggestion that oil is the real motivation for conflict, and concludes with a Smiths (1984) sample that states "there's no one but yourself to blame." Through the reflexive use of Sinatra's music and the other samples, guilt is placed squarely on the United States.

A brief glance at a handful of the Frank Sinatra samples demonstrates the way in which "Fly Me to New York" functions as a footnoted text, yielding greater critical insight when the sources of the samples are traced and analyzed. The latter half of the razor line is drawn from the Dean Martin song "Money Burns a Hole in My Pocket" (often sung with Sinatra in Rat Pack performances), which also features the lyrics "how I wish I had oil wells in Texas to keep me supplied / with money while I sit by your side" (Sinatra & Martin, n.d.), referencing George W. Bush's past and present relations with Big Oil and their influence on the decision to invade Iraq.

Similarly, the sampled line concerning prior flight is part of "The Best Is Yet to Come" and the phrase "you think you've flown before, but you've never left the ground" (Sinatra, 1964). The song also contains the lyric "I'm gonna teach you to fly" (Sinatra, 1964), referencing the training of pilot-hijackers Mohamed Atta, Marwan al-Shehhi, Ziad Jarrah, and Hani Hanjour (or Nawaf al-Hazmi) at U.S. flight schools.

Further, the first half of the line concerning the pilot-hijacker's mental state comes from "I Won't Dance," and is part of the verse containing the lines "when you dance, you're charming and you're gentle / 'specially when you do the Continental" (Sinatra, 1957). This verse recalls the seemingly gentlemanly hijackers, as well as the airline-as-point of vulnerability (Continental being another carrier in the United States).

Additionally, the second half of the line concerning the pilot-hijacker's target and flaming demise is drawn from "What Now, My Love?" and the line "watching my dreams turn to ashes" (Sinatra, 1966). The song also contains the line "there's the sky, where the sea should be" (Sinatra, 1966), aptly describing the topsy-turvy feelings in the wake of the towers' collapse.

Finally, the middle portion of the line concerning the pilot-hijacker's melting skin comes from "I've Got You under My Skin," as part of the verse containing the lines "I've got you deep in the heart of me / so deep in my heart, that you're really a part of me" (Sinatra, 1955), referencing the hijackers' presence within the United States before the attacks and within the national psyche thereafter. Another verse states "I'd sacrifice anything come what might / . . . don't you know you fool, you can never win" (Sinatra, 1955), drawing attention to the hijackers' suicidal devotion and the difficulties of waging a "War on Terror."

Other samples are drawn from "Fly Me to the Moon," "Theme from New York, New York," "Come Fly with Me," "Leaving on a Jet Plane," and "My Way," illustrating Cassetteboy's mining of Sinatra's broad catalog and use of songs both immediately recognizable and slightly obscure. The choice of Sinatra as sample centerpiece is not accidental, and reflects his noteworthy place within American popular song, making his work an ideal jumping off point for the reflexive critique of U.S. guilt in relation to 9/11 embodied by "Fly Me to New York."

—Lloyd Isaac Vayo

References

Cassetteboy. (2002). Fly me to New York. On *The Parker Tapes* [CD]. Barry's Bootlegs.
Sinatra, F. (1955). I've got you under my skin. On *The Complete Reprise Studio Recordings* [CD]. New York: Warner Brothers (1995).
Sinatra, F. (1957). I won't dance. On *The Complete Reprise Studio Recordings* [CD]. New York: Warner Brothers (1995).
Sinatra, F. (1964). The best is yet to come. On *The Complete Reprise Studio Recordings* [CD]. New York: Warner Brothers (1995).
Sinatra, F. (1966). What now, my love? On *The Complete Reprise Studio Recordings* [CD]. New York: Warner Brothers (1995).
Sinatra, F., & Martin, D. (n.d.). Money burns a hole in my pocket. On *Together: Frank Sinatra and Dean Martin* [CD]. Greenville, SC: Horizon (2006, April 7).
The Smiths. (1984). Accept yourself. On *Hatful of Hollow* [CD]. New York: Sire.

SPOTLIGHT ESSAY/MUSIC: GREEN DAY

Unlike many bands that glorify sex, popularity, glamour, and affluence, Green Day's music centers on the political frustration of a band with working class roots. In fact, an article in *Rolling Stone* heralded the band for being "Working Class Heroes" (Colapinto, 2005). The primary themes that emerged from Green Day's post-9/11 music include a frustration with the limited economic choices that men from a working-class background face and anger with the Bush administration's military response to the 9/11 terrorist attacks. These themes are enacted in two of Green Day's music videos inspired by the album *American Idiot*, released September 21, 2004.

The release of *American Idiot* six weeks before the 2004 presidential election notified the group's audience that Green Day had changed its focus. Traditionally, Green Day was known for its neurotic, goof-punk rock. However, 9/11 changed both Green Day and the United States. Consequently, *American Idiot* had a serious tone and took the form of a protest. The album was unique in its use of a narrative form. It was called the world's first punk-rock opera. The plot centers on a teenage drug abuser, "Jesus," who leaves the decaying suburbs to move to the city. After a brief love affair with a woman, "Whatsername," he returns to the decaying suburbs, conforms, and gets a job.

The band members' backgrounds are instrumental in the band's transformation. Billie Joe Armstrong is the child of a waitress mother and a truck driver father. His father died leaving Armstrong's mother to raise her five children alone. Mike Dirnt was born to a heroine-addicted, teenage mother who gave Dirnt up for adoption. Dirnt's adoptive parents divorced leaving him to be raised by a single mother (Colapinto, 2005).

Cinematographer Samuel Bayer and Green Day collaborated on the videos for "Wake Me up When September Ends" (2004b) and "Holiday" (2004a). The videos do not retell *American Idiot*'s rock opera story line. Instead, each video provides its own story line and a different type of protest of the government's response to the 9/11 terrorist attacks.

The "Holiday" video serves as a punk masculine/aggressive protest of the government's more traditional masculine/aggressive response to the 9/11 attacks. Throughout, Armstrong asserts his masculinity and frustration with the government by shouting at the viewer with aggressive posturing, recklessly riding atop his careening car, and jumping off his car to sing with the dancers as if he is the dictator of his own micro-universe. The video is taken from a low position to enhance Armstrong's powerful masculine image. The punk-influenced lyrics contain antiauthority ironies that are called-out such as "Kill all the fags that don't agree," "To a hymn called faith and misery," and "Can I get another amen?" As Armstrong sings these refrains, he is not singing his opinion but those of an imagined government he protests.

The "Holiday" video demonstrates Green Day's punk influences and antiestablishment criticism of the military, priests, and police by contrasting the notions of apparent freedom. What is a holiday and who is on holiday? Holiday freedom is a disregard for responsibility—something that would apparently be in tune with a punk attitude and a break from traditional masculinity—but is altered in the context of the group's belief that the U.S. government acts as if it is on holiday. The use of the word "Holiday" suggests an ironic condition—what appears good is actually bad. The government is on holiday and divorced from reality.

The "Wake Me up When September Ends" video starts with a dialogue between actors Jamie Bell and Evan Rachel Wood, as older teenagers in love. The teenagers are isolated in a field that seems to represent a pre-9/11 innocence. Bell tells Wood about his fear of circumstances preventing them from being together. In the next scene, Wood pays for their meals after Bell can't find any money in his pockets. As Wood provides the money, Bell hunches in humiliation. Wood reassuringly pats Bell on the arm as they leave. Bell is emasculated because he lacks the economic power needed to provide for Wood. The symbolic castration is completed through Wood's economic means and Bell's lack thereof.

Soon afterward, the scene changes to a birthday celebration. The cake is decorated with "18" symbolizing adulthood. Wood shoves the cake into Bell's face enacting a wedding tradition and reinforcing the idea that Bell needs to become a man. Manhood is being thrust upon Bell because of his age and the symbolic marriage rite. Wood's actions bring Bell's masculinity into question once again because she takes a dominant role by pushing Bell into a less "boyish" role.

To regain his masculinity, and to Wood's dismay, Bell joins the armed forces. At times the camera shoots upward at Bell making him appear larger and more masculine. The lyrics enhance the sorrowful mood with the refrain, "The innocent can never last." By joining the military, Bell regains some of his masculinity because he regains power in his soldier role and economic means from his military paycheck.

Although they have different structures, both music videos and the *American Idiot* album relate antiwar messages reflecting the emergence of a post-9/11 masculinity. The masculine/aggressiveness of "Holiday" contrasts the practical realism forced upon young men by 9/11 in "Wake Me up When September Ends." 9/11 is not explicitly discussed in the videos because it becomes ever-present—it is a condition of existence rather than an event.

—*Elizabeth Crisp Crawford and Timothy R. Gleason*

References

Armstrong, B. J. (n.d.). *Green Day authority*. Retrieved November 29, 2005, from http:// www.greendayauthority.com/TheBand/bjprofile.php

Colapinto, J. (2005, November 3). Working class heroes: On the road with Green Day, the nation's most passionate punk-rock protest singers. *Rolling Stone*, Retrieved from http://www.rollingstone.com

Green Day (Producer). (2004a). Holiday [Music video]. Retrieved from http://www .youtube.com

Green Day (Producer). (2004b). Wake me up when September ends [Music video]. Retrieved from http://www.youtube.com

SPOTLIGHT ESSAY/MUSIC: MUSICAL RESPONSES TO 9/11

Americans responded to the events of 9/11 with both personal and public displays of grief and anger. Popular American artists also contributed a variety of songs that reacted to and interpreted those painful events. The very different approaches of that musical interpretation demonstrated a dichotomous approach that pervaded American culture. Artists such as Bruce Springsteen in "The Rising" (2002) and Steve Earle in "Jerusalem" (2002) evoked soulful, introspective examination of personal loss and U.S. policies that some say led to the attacks. Other artists, such as Alan Jackson, who released a song "Where Were You When the World Stopped Turning?" (2001) and Toby Keith, who wrote and released two songs, "Courtesy of the Red, White and Blue" (2002) and "The Taliban Song" (2003), embraced an aggressive, confrontational approach to those events. These different interpretative approaches to the events of 9/11 represented the conflicted ideas about the resulting post-9/11 culture.

Springsteen's soulful ballad "The Rising," from the album of the same title, tells of a man coming out "through the darkness" much like those citizens appearing out from the cloud of dust caused by the collapse of the Twin Towers. But Springsteen's ballad calls for a response of introspection where the cloud of events remains unclear. "Sky of love, sky of tears . . . sky of mercy, sky of fears," he sings, calling for patience and love until the skies clear. Springsteen wants us to think rather than react, to pause to console one another, and to begin to heal. In "Into the Fire," he sings of the horrors unfolding as one disappeared into the dust "up the stairs into the fire." But instead of retribution for the deaths of the hundreds of firefighters caught in the collapse, the refrain pleads "May your strength give us strength, may your hope give us hope, may your love give us love." That intensely personal loss acts as a means to reaffirm the values of faith, hope and love.

Steve Earle took the events of 9/11 as an opportunity to expand the personal to the political in his biting, evocative album *Jerusalem*. The title cut, which he placed at the end of the album, tells the story of a man who wakes up to a television screen showing tanks rolling "'cross the ground where Jesus stood." Faced with that stark contrast, he must choose to believe there was no hope for peace from the reality of the events, or to find a different future. "I believe that one fine day," Earle concludes, "all the children of Abraham will lay down their swords forever in Jerusalem." The image of Abraham, the father of Judaism, Christianity, and Islam is particularly significant, as is Earle's optimistic and hopeful outlook on the intractable political problem of Middle East peace.

Conversely, country music star Alan Jackson wrote and sang "Where Were You (When the World Stopped Turning)" in direct response to the event of 9/11. He asks Americans to recall that day from their individual perspectives by posing questions to the listener. But Jackson connected with the larger questions Americans asked about the events of that day by admitting that, like many Americans he was "not a political man" who watched CNN but could not tell the difference in "Iraq and Iran." For many in America, the events of 9/11 were difficult to explain, much less understand. Like Springsteen, Jackson recoils from politics when he sings of the foundations of his faith. Less overtly patriotic than most would assume, Jackson wanted Americans to remember the events from their own individual perspectives, but to avoid, not answer, the "Why do they hate us?" question, focusing instead on country, family and faith.

Toby Keith took a dramatically different approach in his post-9/11 music. In two songs, "Courtesy of the Red, White and Blue" and "The Taliban Song" released in live performance format, Keith sheds the nuance of personal loss and reminds Americans that the events of 9/11 should be seen as an attack on freedom. "This nation that I love has fallen under attack," he sings. But there is no cautious retrospection in Keith's music. America aroused by the events of 9/11 should not sit back and wonder why, but instead should respond, promising that you will be sorry you messed with the U S of A. And how will we follow up? Keith answers, to the delight of his concert crowds, "We'll put a boot in your ass, it's the American way."

But it is with Keith's lesser known satirical balled, "The Taliban Song," which he tells his audience is a "patriotic love song," where he makes his strongest case for American retribution. Sung from the perspective of a "middle-eastern camel-herdin' man" with a two bedroom cave in "North Afghanistan" the complaints are not about poverty but about how the neighborhood has gone to "hell" since the Taliban came. Written after the invasion of Afghanistan, Keith sings to a live audience about retaliation to the attack on New York to the raucous cheers of the crowd.

The different song themes arising from the events of 9/11 are no surprise. In some ways, they mimic differences in the attitudes of Americans that were made evident in the red state-blue state split during the 2000 election. Popular music in the aftermath of 9/11 reflected those conflicted attitudes about the proper approach to foreign policy in the post-Cold War era. That Americans could make popular these disparate songs interpreting the events 9/11 says as much about the lack of a consensus approach to the rise of new threats to peace as it does about the rich variety of popular song writing. But it poses a more significant concern. Failing to arrive at a popular consensus on what the events of 9/11 meant, makes a unified approach, necessary when engaged in war, impossible. Recognizing that music reflects popular opinion might offer the nation's leadership a refrain from the partisan fights and an opportunity to get all Americans singing from the same hymnbook.

—*Kurt Hohenstein*

References

Earle, S. (2002). Jerusalem. On *Jerusalem* [CD] Artemis Records.
Jackson, A. (2001) Where were you when the world stopped turning (Do you remember?). On *Drive* [CD]. Arista (2002).
Keith, T. (2002) Courtesy of the red, white and blue. On *Unleashed*. [CD]. Nashville: Dreamworks.
Keith, T. (2003). The Taliban song. On *Shock 'n Y'all* [CD]. Nashville: Dreamworks.
Springsteen, B. (2002a). The rising. On *The Rising* [CD]. New York City: Sony.
Springsteen, B. (2002b). Into the fire. On *The Rising* [CD]. Sony.

SPOTLIGHT ESSAY/MUSIC: "ON THE TRANSMIGRATION OF SOULS" BY JOHN ADAMS

On September 19, 2002, John Adams and the New York Philharmonic Orchestra premiered Adams's composition, "On the Transmigration of Souls," a piece that the New York Philharmonic and Lincoln Center's Great Performers commissioned Adams to create to commemorate the first anniversary of the terrorist attacks of September 11, 2001. Performances of the work followed in other cities throughout the United States. The piece was awarded the 2003 Pulitzer Prize in music and was released on a Nonesuch Records CD in 2004.

In creating "On the Transmigration of Souls" Adams wanted his work to center on those left behind after the attacks. To this end, he included textual excerpts in his 25-minute composition, some of these sung, others spoken. The text comes from three main sources: the missing person signs that were posted in lower Manhattan after the attacks, personal reminiscences taken mainly from the *New York Times* "Portraits of Grief" series, and a random list of victims ("Interview with John Adams," 2002). For example, phrases such as "missing Jennifer de Jesus" and "Louis Anthony Williams. One World Trade Center. Port Authority, 66th Floor. We love you, Louis. Come home" are two of many lines taken directly from missing persons flyers posted around the World Trade Center site in September and October of 2001. Other incorporated text such as "The lover says: Tomorrow will be three months, yet it feels like yesterday since I saw your beautiful face, saying, 'Love you to the moon and back, forever'" origi-nate from a *New York Times* "Portraits of Grief" profile ("Texts for 'On the Transmigra-tion of Souls' by John Adams," 2002). In addition to the textual additions to the music, taped city sounds are interwoven throughout the piece. An adult chorus and children's choir are also prevalent.

In interviews about this piece and the process Adams engaged in while creating it, Adams reflected that engaging in such a project forced him to think through his own emotions and feelings of uncertainty he had after the terrorist attacks ("Interview with John Adams," 2002). In addition, Adams hoped that he would be able to use his music as a way of speaking to people's emotions and hopefully giving something—by way of this composition—to them (Child, 2002). However, Adams is clear that he did not intend for "On the Transmigration of Souls" to fill roles such as assisting with the healing process or that of a musical memorial. Instead, he prefers to call his work a "memory space," explained here in an interview with the New York Philharmonic:

> I want to avoid words like "requiem" or "memorial" when describing this piece because they too easily suggest conventions that this piece doesn't share. If pressed, I'd probably call the piece a "memory space." It's a place where you can go and be alone with your thoughts and emotions. The link to a particular historical event—in this case to 9/11— is there if you want to contemplate it. But I hope that the piece will summon human experience that goes beyond this particular event. "Transmigration" means "the move-ment from one place to another" or "the transition from one state of being to another." It could apply to populations of people, to migrations of species, to changes of chemical composition, or to the passage of cells through a membrane. But in this case I mean it to imply the movement of the soul from one state to another. And I don't just mean the transition from living to dead, but also the change that takes place within the souls of those that stay behind, of those who suffer pain and loss and then themselves come away from that experience transformed. ("Interview with John Adams," para. 5)

Responses to "On the Transmigration of Souls" were positive, noting the ways Adams used musical language to evoke emotion among listeners ("On the Transmi-gration," n.d.). *Atlantic Monthly* writer David Schiff points out that the piece integrates music and sound in ways that are common in film but less so in classical music, but the elements Adams combines are done so with "imagination" and "technical skill" (para. 10). Schiff also enthusiastically points out the value of such innovation within the classical music genre and says about "On the Transmigration of Souls": "Terrifying and heartrending, it offers reassuring proof that contemporary classical music—too often dismissed out of hand as obscure and unpleasant—has something unique to say to a wide public" (para. 2). The *New York Times*, the *Los Angeles Times*, and the *Guardian* reviews are similar in their praise for Adams and his ability to meet the goals of such a challenging commissioned work.

—*Amy M. Damico*

References

Child, F. (2002, September). *Performance today: "On the Transmigration of Souls."* NPR. Retrieved from http://www.npr.org

Interview with John Adams. (2002). Retrieved from http://www.earbox.com/ W-transmigration.html

On the Transmigration of Souls, for children's chorus, chorus, orchestra & tape. (n.d). *All Music Guide*. Retrieved September 6, 2009, from http://www.dilettantemusic.com/ work/531550

Schiff, D. (2003, April). Memory spaces. John Adams's "On the Transmigration of Souls" finds redemption in September 11, and should bring contemporary classical music to a new audience. *The Atlantic Monthly*. Retrieved from http://www.theatlantic.com

Texts for "On the Transmigration of Souls" by John Adams. (2002). Retrieved from http:// www.earbox.com/W-soulstext.html

SPOTLIGHT ESSAY/MUSIC: RADIOHEAD

Radiohead is an experimental rock band hailing from Oxford, England. Formed in the late 1980s, the band has released seven full-length albums to date, and has evolved from a traditional rock outfit to incorporate classical and electronic flourishes into their music. As one of the preeminent bands of the past decade, Radiohead's influence looms large and resonates deeply within popular culture, doing so particularly with audiences in their native Britain and in the United States. Beginning with 1997's *OK Computer*, Radiohead assumed a position of cultural criticism—that album's meditation on millennial technology manifesting itself in songs that demonstrate a profound discomfort with a postmodern life marked by alienation. Fatigued by touring and weary of the direction of their music, the band retreated into the studio in 1999 and early 2000 to produce a new batch of songs, emerging in October 2000 with *Kid A*, which was swiftly followed by its companion piece, *Amnesiac*, in June 2001 (recorded during the same sessions). The two albums constituted a sea change in Radiohead's sound, a shift from more guitar-driven forms to abstract electronica informed by the Warp Records label. After another bout of touring, *Hail to the Thief* emerged in June 2003, and was marked by a similar distaste with the current state of affairs in the world.

Given Radiohead's cultural engagement, the clustering of these albums in the period just prior to and shortly after 9/11 points to the ways in which *Kid A* and *Amnesiac* address the pre-9/11 climate of fear and impending doom and *Hail to the Thief* addresses the post-9/11 environment of constant and multiple threats. Accordingly, the artwork, promotional materials, and lyrics of each album relate to the impending or recent events of 9/11. *Kid A*, released less than a year prior to 9/11, offers a consistently bleak outlook on the cultural landscape prior to the event, as seen in the foreboding artwork depicting snow-covered mountains and fields in crude digital renderings, environments stalked by genetically mutated bears. In a foreshadowing of 9/11, one of the promotional "blips," 30-second commercial spots aired on music networks such as MTV prior to the album's release, shows onlookers staring in horror as a flock of bears flies past the surrounding skyscrapers and is accompanied by a fragment of the song "In Limbo," calling to mind the terrifying uncertainty of the appearance of the hijacked planes above the streets of Manhattan. Fear, death, and renewal mark the album, as seen in the lyrics of "Kid A," "The National Anthem," "Idioteque," and "Motion Picture Soundtrack." Although the threat is vague and undefined, a sense of building terror is evident in *Kid A*, and is developed further in *Amnesiac*.

Amnesiac, released just months prior to 9/11, continues the less than rosy approach of *Kid A*, with its artwork more directly foreshadowing the events to come through the inclusion of several images of paired skyscrapers, in one case engulfed in flames. Where the previous album is jittery with fear, *Amnesiac* is nearly resigned to its fate, too close to the event to affect any change, although it will not go down without a fight. This mixture of resignation and resistance is apparent in the lyrics of "Pulk/Pull Revolving Doors," "Knives Out," "Like Spinning Plates," "You and Whose Army?" and "Dollars and Cents." The album concludes with "Life in a Glasshouse," which offers counsel to figures of power although the events of 9/11 suggest that this advice fell on deaf ears.

Hail to the Thief, released nearly two years after 9/11, is preoccupied with the post-9/11 landscape more generally and the abuses of the Bush administration more specifically, as evidenced by the title's accusation of electoral shenanigans in 2000. If *Kid A* and *Amnesiac* carve a trajectory from fear to resignation, then *Hail to the Thief* demonstrates the anger on the far side of the event, and the artwork follows suit, constructing aerial maps composed of buzz words, including "God . . . armed . . . prosecuted . . . security . . . sirens . . . good cop/bad cop . . . decay . . . [and] survival" that spur reflection on political and cultural discussions after 9/11. The anger that comes from a world in which 9/11 can happen and in which the response is a War on Terror is evident in the lyrics for "2 + 2 = 5," "Go to Sleep," "The Gloaming," "I Will," and "A Wolf at the Door." In their commentary on the run-up to and fallout from 9/11, Radiohead offers a critical evaluation of culture that yields valuable insights into the event and its aftermath.

—*Lloyd Isaac Vayo*

References

Radiohead. (2000). *Kid A* [CD]. Capitol Records, Los Angeles, CA.
Radiohead. (2001). *Amnesiac* [CD]. Capitol Records, Los Angeles, CA.
Radiohead. (2003). *Hail to the thief* [CD]. Capitol Records, Los Angeles, CA.

SPOTLIGHT ESSAY/MUSIC: *THE RISING* BY BRUCE SPRINGSTEEN

Bruce Springsteen's music has been perceived and embraced by fans and some critics as joyful rock-and-roll sound reminiscent of the music he grew up with in New Jersey. The sound is bombastic and carefree; however, that sound has often belied the lyrical content that Springsteen explored. Springsteen, who lives in New Jersey not far from New York City, tells the story of how in the aftermath of the 9/11 attacks, a man stopped his car and yelled to Springsteen, "We need ya" (Binelli, 2002; Wenner, 2004). Through reading the obituaries of the 9/11 victims appearing in the *New York Times*, Springsteen discovered that many were fans of his music. In response, he called the relatives of several victims to better understand their stories (Tyrangiel, 2002). Then Springsteen, who always claimed that rock and roll saved his life and often preached of its healing effects from the stage, set out to create *The Rising* (2002). This album expresses the confusion and pain associated with the nation's healing process, which began in the days after 9/11. To complete the album, Springsteen also reunited with the E Street band for the first time since 1984's *Born in the USA*.

The reviews of the album ranged from stellar—"a singular triumph" (Loder, 2002, para. 10) to tepid—"disturbingly generic" (*Austin Chronicle*, 2002). Although "about Sept. 11, and . . . the first significant piece of pop art to respond to the events of that day" (Tyrangiel, 2002, p. 53), the album still sounds like a typical Bruce Springsteen and the E Street Band album. Lyrically it reads like an apolitical Springsteen album, albeit one tempered by a national tragedy. Many of the songs on the album, including "Waitin' on a Sunny Day," "Let's Be Friends," "Further on (up the Road)," "Mary's Place," and even "My City of Ruins," were actually written years earlier and are about Springsteen's Asbury Park, although some see a relationship between them and the events surrounding 9/11. Some of the songs that explicitly tackle 9/11, "Lonesome Day" and "The Rising," are similar to "Born in the USA" in their composition—carefree sounds that contrast with weightier lyrical themes. Other September 11-oriented songs musically express the seriousness of the event such as multiple viewpoints on suicide bombers expressed in "Paradise" and "Into the Fire," a song revering the rescue workers of September 11.

Many of the songs on *The Rising* address generic themes of loss and hope in the face of adversity. Even those songs that are explicitly about 9/11, such as "Into the Fire," "Countin' on a Miracle," and "The Rising," can be interpreted generally as songs about loss and hope. In addition, numerous songs on the album have Springsteen looking for some type of salvation in the midst of the suffering. Songs such as

"Lonesome Day," "Into the Fire," "Waitin' on a Sunny Day," and even the title song "The Rising," show the desire to survive and make sense of all that has occurred. Together, the songs on the album suggest that processing the event through music can be part of a larger healing process.

The Rising is unquestioningly one of Springsteen's most popular albums, and one of the most interesting comments about the connection between 9/11 and *The Rising* may be from a caustic review in the *Village Voice:* "He sounds as genuinely hurt and confused as any of us, but if he's gained any insight into that hurt or confusion, he's not about to express it" (Harris, 2002, para. 10). Maybe that confused hurt is what made *The Rising* so popular and effective. Springsteen, like many Americans, simply could not understand the attacks of 9/11 and like them, Springsteen was simply "trying to make sense of everything that had happened" (DeCurtis, 2002, para. 18).

—*Robert Bell*

References

Binelli, M. (2002, August 20). Bruce Springsteen's American gospel. *Rolling Stone, 903*, 62–64.

Columbia Radio Hour Interview, Part 1. (n.d.). Retrieved March 6, 2008, from http://frankenschulz.de/bruce/columbia.html (originally posted on http://www.monmouth.com)

DeCurtis, A. (2002, December 12). Bruce Springsteen. *Rolling Stone, 911*, 83–84.

Harris, K. (2002, August 6). Lift every voice. *Village Voice.* Retrieved from www.villagevoice.com

Loder, K. (1984, December 6). The *Rolling Stone* interview: Bruce Springsteen. *Rolling Stone.* Retrieved from http://www.rollingstone.com

Loder, K. (2002, July 30). [Review of the album *The Rising*]. *Rolling Stone.* Retrieved March 20, 2008, from http://www.rollingstone.com

Oko, D. (2002, August 23). [Review of the album *The Rising*]. *Austin Chronicle.* Retrieved March 20, 2008, from http://www.austinchronicle.com

Springsteen, B. (2002). *The rising* [CD]. New York: Sony.

Tyrangiel, J. (2002, August 5). Bruce Springsteen. *Time, 160*(6), 52–59.

Wenner, J. (2004, October 14). Voices for change: "We've been misled"—Bruce Springsteen talks about his conscience, and the nature of an artist and his audience. *Rolling Stone, 959*, 73–74, 76.

SPOTLIGHT ESSAY/MUSIC: *SELF EVIDENT* BY ANI DIFRANCO

There is a strong history linking music, politics, and social change. One only need think of songs as powerful and well known as the civil rights standards "We Shall Overcome" and "If You Miss Me from the Back of the Bus," to see the place that music has had in social and political protest. This includes, most recently, those songs used to critique U.S. foreign policy after 9/11. Taking a stand on political issues is not without potential significant cost to the artist. Although some artists who have used their music and celebrity status to push for social and political change (such as Bob Geldof for

Band Aid, Bono for the [RED] campaign, and Chris Martin for Oxfam's Make Trade Fair) have been rewarded with media and public adulation, others have not been so fortunate. Sinead O'Connor's protest against child abuse in the church on *Saturday Night Live*—which involved her tearing up a picture of the Pope—sounded a death knell to her career in the United States, and the (previously apolitical) Dixie Chicks were on the receiving end of radio boycotts, public burnings of their CDs by Republican former fans, and even death threats after singer Natalie Maines, on the eve of war against Iraq, said that she was ashamed to share the same home state as George Bush. There is always the potential for a "shut up and sing" response to an artist's political statements, whether these are made in song or not.

At more than nine minutes long, and more spoken than sung, DiFranco's "Self Evident," which explored 9/11, its context and aftermath, was never going to be a radio hit or be considered for a TV performance. The only recorded versions of "Self Evident" are from live performances, and this underscores the urgency and immediacy of the song, as well as the need for an audience to provide an "us" in the call to action DiFranco presents. DiFranco situates the events of 9/11 by describing the way she felt about the World Trade Center. In the song, she also references the bombing of the World Trade Center (WTC) in 1993, and remembers joking with her flat mate about the fact that a change in the New York skyline would also mean having to change all the takeaway coffee cups that use it in their design. Her throwaway joke in 1993 turned out to be a prophetic description of what would follow eight years later. The "tallness" of the WTC refers not just to its height, but also its significance as an emblem of the United States. Although "pride goes before a fall" would be a simplification of DiFranco's analysis of 9/11, she makes it clear that she believes that the king-of-the-castle attitude that led to the construction of the WTC, also led to its downfall.

The events of 9/11 are described in the piece as deeply shocking, even (perhaps especially) for a country so used to seeing New York spectacularly dismantled by special effects in any number of Hollywood movies: "every borough looked up when it heard the first blast / and then every dumb action movie was summarily surpassed." Not only is there the immediate terror of the events that are happening, but there is also the expressed fear of what will follow these events. The expressed fear is accompanied by DiFranco's perspectives on the current government officials and existing foreign policy.

DiFranco likens the immediate call for retribution after 9/11, by then President George W. Bush, politicians, security officials, and the media, to the very attitude of the United States toward the "other" that she sees as having caused 9/11 in the first place. She rejects this approach and uses her song to express her feelings about the Bush administration. Bush comes under her fire as a president who stole the election. She specifically references the disenfranchising of African American Florida voters as being a deliberate ploy by Jeb Bush, Florida's governor, to get his brother reelected as president.

Although DiFranco's compassion for those who died or were traumatized on 9/11 is apparent in the song, she also brings the listener's attention to others who have died or are suffering in different, and yet related, ways. She begins this section by referencing those countries most affected in recent years by U.S. interventionist foreign policy, in her view Palestine, Afghanistan, and Iraq. However, she then mentions two other places, El Salvador and the Pine Ridge Reservation. Both places have histories of violence and extreme poverty, which DiFranco links to results of U.S. domestic policy.

It is clear from the diverse references DiFranco makes throughout the entire song that she holds the voice of someone who died in 9/11 in equal—but not higher—standing to the voices of women without access to abortion, those on death row waiting to be executed, and those living with poverty and war. All these voices are "poems" telling the audience things are very wrong and desperately in need of change. DiFranco criticizes U.S. greed (especially for oil), sense of entitlement, and lack of understanding of the dire situations of others. She describes those who died on 9/11 as "3000 some poems disguised as people" and calls for citizen action to ensure that they didn't die in vain.

The title of the piece, "Self Evident," comes from the American Declaration of Independence. Authored by Thomas Jefferson, the preamble begins: "We hold these truths to be self evident, that all men are created equal, that they are endowed by their Creator with certain unalienable Rights, that among these are Life, Liberty and the pursuit of Happiness." By using the Declaration of Independence as the basis for her song, DiFranco situates her feminist critique of Bush and of U.S. foreign and domestic policy not as the ranting of a fringe militant or an unrealistic idealist, but firmly within the context of U.S. citizenship and civic duty. Only by protesting and fighting against those policies that preceded and followed 9/11, as well as any others that maintain or create the marginalization of one group over another, DiFranco argues, can we do our job to honor the voices of the dead.

—*Deborah Finding*

Reference

DiFranco, A. (2001). Self evident. On *So much shouting, so much laughter* [Live]. [CD]. Buffalo, NY: Righteous babe records. (September 10, 2002)

SPOTLIGHT ESSAY/MUSIC: *YANKEE HOTEL FOXTROT* BY WILCO

Yankee Hotel Foxtrot is the fourth album by Chicago-based band Wilco, released on April 23, 2002. *Yankee Hotel Foxtrot* resonates with 9/11 in two specific areas: album packaging (including the album title) and lyrical content. The front cover image depicts two tall buildings against a monochromatic background (available in varying colors), the mixed residential/commercial Marina City complex in Chicago, referencing the World Trade Center towers as they appeared against the stark blue sky of 9/11. Further images of skyscrapers appear in the lyric booklet, along with a long shot of a city skyline seen from across a body of water, referencing Manhattan and the skyline transformed by the events of September 11. The album title, drawn from a fragment taken from *The Conet Project: Recordings of Shortwave Numbers Stations*, track "Phonetic Alphabet NATO," in which a female voice intones "yankee . . . hotel . . . foxtrot . . ." (the phonetic symbols for Y, H, and F) and included in the song "Poor Places," references the import of radio communication to 9/11, be it air-traffic-control communications, cell-phone communications from the planes to family members, or fire and police communications in the towers (Gupta, 2008). In the pairing of the band's name and the phonetic symbols, the very same ones used for communication with spies during the Cold War, those symbols are greeted with Wilco, short for "will comply," pointing to the album's rendering of hidden emotions in the wake of 9/11. Additionally, the album's relation to *The Conet Project* foreshadows the militarization of language after 9/11, including wiretapping and online surveillance under the Foreign Intelligence Surveillance Act (FISA).

In regards to lyrical content, three songs in particular bear an eerie relevance to 9/11, despite the fact that Tweedy had written the lyrics well in advance of the event. The songs, "War on War" (Wilco, 2002a), "Jesus, Etc." (Wilco, 2002b), and "Ashes of American Flags" (Wilco, 2002c) are the third, fourth, and fifth tracks, composing the core of the 11-track album. "War on War" suggests the post-9/11 "War on Terror" that would follow, while also pointing to the futility of the exercise. The song alludes to the fate of the United States in the event of the impending conflict and references the adrenaline rush of survival. Additionally, the song includes the phrases "let's watch the miles flying by," referring to air travel, and "you are not my typewriter / but you could be my demon / moving forward through flaming doors," calling to mind in the post-9/11 mentality the fireballs that scorched through the elevator shafts and into the lobby of the towers immediately after the planes' impact.

Similarly, "Jesus, Etc." and "Ashes of American Flags" contain lyrics, that although written prior to the attacks, resonate with post-9/11 imagery the country was immersed in. "Jesus, Etc." suggests a turning to faith in the wake of a fundamentalist-perpetrated event, and contains the chorus "tall buildings shake / voices escape singing sad sad songs" calling to mind the impacts of Flights 11 and 175 into the North and South Towers and the sorrow and perspective shifts that they motivate in onlookers. The song also contains an equally suggestive bridge section, which can be interpreted as referencing the towers' collapse and the limited time left to those trapped inside. "Ashes of American Flags" can be understood as addressing the impossibility of going on in the wake of 9/11, saying "speaking of tomorrow / how will it ever come," and concluding with an acknowledgment of the torn nation. To this end, *Yankee Hotel Foxtrot* exists as an unintentional monument to an unforeseen event, and its resonance with the events of 9/11 contributes to its continued relevance six years after its release.

—*Lloyd Isaac Vayo*

References

Gupta, J. (2008, July 27). Wilco settle lawsuit. *Filter Magazine*. Retrieved from http://www.filter-mag.com

Wilco. (2002a). War on war. On *Yankee Hotel Foxtrot*. [CD]. Nonesuch, Los Angeles, CA.

Wilco. (2002b). Jesus, etc. On *Yankee Hotel Foxtrot*. [CD]. Nonesuch, Los Angeles, CA.

Wilco. (2002c). Ashes of American flags. On *Yankee Hotel Foxtrot*. [CD]. Nonesuch, Los Angeles, CA.

Chapter 7

VISUAL CULTURE

INTRODUCTION: VISUAL CULTURE AND SEPTEMBER 11, 2001

September 11 was, in many ways, a visual event. Images of the planes flying into the Twin Towers, the wreckage at the Pentagon, and the smoldering field in Shanksville, Pennsylvania, appeared on television programs and Web sites, magazine covers, and newspapers. Photographs taken by amateurs and professionals alike captured the events as they were unfolding, recording in still photo shots the excruciating moments of the day. Among the many images that have come to evoke the 9/11 attacks, those focused on the Twin Towers are perhaps the most familiar. In part a result of their presence in Hollywood movies and popular TV shows, the Towers were recognizable to people around the world. At 110 stories and more than 1,000 feet in height, they shaped the New York skyline. Prior to 9/11, the Twin Towers "represented the strength and fortitude of the American public. They represented growth, and commerce, and power in the global arena. The images of the Twin Towers standing tall above the New York skyline easily helped the world envision these characteristics as being unique to American culture" (Hatfield, 2008, p. 67). On September 11, the familiar image of the Twin Towers became even more significant because it was no longer there.

Visual culture of all kinds responded to that absence—as well as to the events of 9/11 more generally. Movies, television shows, and other elements of popular culture removed images of the Towers from their future releases. Spontaneous memorials made of flowers, photos, prayer cards, and letters were created at all of the crash sites. Drawings of the attacks made by children registered that even the young were not immune to the changed landscape. Photographers captured and made public a wide array of 9/11-related images within moments of the attacks. Artists painted, sculpted, performed, and drew new works of art in an effort to reflect on, and process, the significance of the events. Eventually, more official visual responses emerged, from exhibits and collections to online historical documentation, thereby making the visual aspects of September 11 part of the nation's official memory.

IMAGES OF THE TWIN TOWERS IN *SEX AND THE CITY*

Since the show's first season in 1998, the opening credits of HBO's *Sex and the City* featured time-lapse images of iconic aspects of New York life: traffic on a street, the Brooklyn Bridge, the Chrysler Building, and the Twin Towers. Each image was associated with one of the show's four female stars, and their names rushed across the screen against the backdrop of their respective icon. The name of the leading actress, Sarah Jessica Parker, appeared against the background image of the Twin Towers, suggesting that her character, Carrie, was as central to *Sex and the City* as the Towers were to New York. The summer before September 11, 2001, *Sex and the City* (*SATC*) had already filmed six new episodes, set to air January 6, 2002. After the attacks, the only change made to these episodes was the removal of the image of the Towers from both the opening titles and specific scenes. In the post-9/11 credits, beginning with the episode "The Good Fight," which aired on January 6, 2002, Parker's name appears over the Empire State Building, instead of the Towers. The skyline shots, taken from a different angle, do not include the buildings.

Andreas Huyssen (2003) explains that "for a New Yorker . . . the image of the twin towers simply represented home on the metropolis [as opposed to global capitalism]. . . . Unwieldy and ugly as they were, they anchored the island's skyline" (p. 160). Although not quirky like the character of Carrie, the towers represented her as the lynchpin of the show. They were potent visual symbols in the show before 9/11, but afterwards the Towers were inextricably linked with the terrorist attacks, a symbol more powerful than any created within the New York of *SATC* (Schneider, 2004, p. 34).

The Twin Towers do appear in one episode of the 2002 season, "All That Glitters," in a snow globe in Carrie's window. The episode begins with the four women deciding that they "have to shake things up," and the snow globe becomes symbolic of this. The snow globe with the Twin Towers represents the fabulous life of single New Yorkers, which may perhaps have to be shelved as Carrie considers getting married. The Towers' appearance in a snow globe, just the kind of souvenirs tourists were buying at Ground Zero after the attacks, evokes a sense of nostalgia after 9/11 that fits well with Carrie's longing for the single life in the episode. Carrie looks at the snow globe again in a melancholic scene at the end of the episode, a look that becomes even more poignant through the presence of the Twin Towers memorialized in a snow globe.

—*Victoria Pass*

References

Huyssen, A. (2003). Twin memories: Afterimages of nine/eleven. In A. Huyssen (Ed.), *Present pasts: Urban palimpsests and the politics of memory* (pp. 158–163). Stanford, CA: Stanford University Press.

Schneider, S. J. (2004). Architectural nostalgia and the New York City skyline on film. In W. D. Wheeler (Ed.), *Film and television after 9/11* (pp. 29–41). Carbondale: Southern Illinois University.

Missing Posters, Spontaneous Memorials, and Other Initial Responses

Some of the first items of visual culture to appear after the attacks were posters of the missing. Posters generally displayed the names and faces of someone who had not returned home after September 11, as well as personal information and messages of love, hope, and desperation. Hung by family members and friends around the city, and especially at Ground Zero, the posters reflected the emotions felt by those whose greatest wish was that there would be survivors of 9/11 who would eventually find their way home. The posters' presence in the city of New York recorded the widespread impact of the attacks and became visual memorials for those who were unaccounted for in the hours, days, and weeks that followed. The images from the posters were so moving that they were reprinted in the *New York Times* in a special section titled "Portraits of Grief." In 2002, the entire Portraits of Grief series was collected in a single volume, published as *Portraits 9/11/01: The Collected "Portraits of Grief."*

In contrast to the missing posters, memorials and shrines registered a mournful recognition of what had happened. The loss of life at all three crash sites was profound and final, yet communities across the country needed ways to pause, reflect, and mourn for those who had died. Spontaneous memorials sprung up at each of the locations that had been attacked, as well as in towns and cities across the country and even around the world. Consisting of objects like candles, flowers, flags, and personal messages, these visual markers of loss helped people to process the events of September 11, as well as look inward and remember those who were gone. When words were included, they ranged from expressions of wrath, vengeance, and retribution to deep sorrow, mourning, and loss.

Other visual images and objects appeared at the spontaneous memorial sites so prevalent after September 11. Children's drawings of the attacks or of the rescue workers were especially poignant, while banners from states across the nation celebrated the United States and its rescue workers. Groups and individuals around the world also sent visual reminders that the United States was not alone, including posters and cards with heartening words. Japanese schoolchildren made cascades of colorful origami cranes and sent them to Ground Zero as an expression of their sorrow and care (Sanderson, 2004).

As time went by, some of the most popular memorial sites overflowed with objects and had to be contained and organized. While the process was different at each of the major crash sites, in general the objects left at the memorials were collected into specific areas that became the new destination for mourners. In New York City, for example, St. Paul's Chapel became the major repository of the flowers, drawings, flags, letters, candles, notes, and other items left in memory of those who had died. As Kristen Sanderson (2004) has documented in *Light at Ground Zero*, the church itself became a living memorial to those who died on September 11. Other crash sites also began to organize spontaneous memorials into more formal visitor sites.

Grassroots exhibits of visual responses made by ordinary people emerged within weeks of the attacks. *Here Is New York*, an exhibition opened in a SoHo storefront on September 25, just two weeks after 9/11, gave people the chance to share their personal photographs of September 11. Similarly, on October 13, *The September 11 Photo Project* gathered more than 3,000 photos and personal reflections from anyone who was interested in sharing their images or words. In November 2001, Exit Art, a New York arts organization, sent an invitation to anyone interested in submitting their personal representations of how September 11 changed their lives. The only requirement was that the submissions had to be made on pieces of paper measuring 8-1/2 by 11 inches—there were 2,500 submissions. Children were also invited to respond to the attacks in visual form. A partnership between the Museum of the City of New York and the New York University Child Study Center resulted in a 2002 exhibit of children's art about September 11 titled *The Day Our World Changed*. The 9-11 Sculpture Project aimed to "build, tour and permanently locate a sculpture created from World Trade Center steel" and invited anyone who want to contribute to do so by writing thoughts, poems, and prayers on 8 by 12-inch bronze metal pages that were to be part of the sculpture (www.9-11sculptureproject.org). Around the world, ceramic studios also joined efforts and gave people the chance to paint tiles that reflected their emotions after 9/11. Thousands of tiles were created with images ranging from the Twin Towers to firefighters to poems and flags. Known as *Tiles for America*, collections of tiles were hung on chain link fences around the city of New York, including at the Tribute WTC Center (http://tilesforamerica.com/#preload). These grassroots exhibits reflected an awareness that September 11 impacted people everywhere, not just at the crash sites, and that visual images were one way to help people both individually and collectively express the emotional impact of the events.

As the *Reactions* and *September 11 Photo Project* exhibits suggest, photography was one of the most frequent mediums used to capture the events surrounding 9/11. From ordinary people to professional photographers, photographs of the attacks and the recovery effort proliferated. In addition, photography was used in the aftermath to create visual expressions of mourning those who were lost and of honoring those who performed acts of bravery during the crisis.

From the plethora of photographs taken on and after September 11, several images have become closely associated with day. While no single photograph of the Twin Towers has become more popular than any other, those featured on the covers of *People, Time,* and *Newsweek* directly after the attacks have become the most widely recognized. What these images have in common is that they include, from various perspectives, photographs of the second plane as it is about to crash—or is in the act of crashing—into the North Tower. This moment—the exact moment of impact—has come to stand for all of the shock, horror, and sadness associated with the day, regardless of where the attack took place (Hatfield, 2008).

One specific photo that has become closely associated with 9/11 is Richard Drew's snapshot of a man falling from the North Tower. Known simply as "Falling Man," (2001) the photo was raised to iconic status when Tom Junod published his 2003 article, "The Falling Man," in *Esquire* magazine. The photo was first widely circulated on the Internet and in news programs, only to be quietly removed from view because of the controversial nature of the image.

REACTIONS AT EXIT ART, NEW YORK

In November 2001, Exit Art, a nonprofit cultural center and exhibition in New York City, sent out 10,000 worldwide invitations to participate in a project called *Reactions*: "We want to know how the events of September 11 have altered your behavior—toward others, your city, your daily life—how the events changed your perception of reality and the world around you" ("Reactions," 2001, para. 2). Remarkably, even this radical organization regarded the attacks on the World Trade Center as inevitably global and metaphysical: "The essence of life has changed. The world's psyche has been irrevocably altered" ("Reactions," 2001, para. 1). Organizers thought of Exit Art as a "vessel of people's feelings" and the *Reactions* exhibition as "a work of art, a way of mourning together" (Urschel, 2002, para. 6). For Exit Art cofounder Jeanette Ingberman it filled a necessary void: "We don't really have national rituals to deal with death" (Cheng, 2002, p. F14).

To preserve a democratic process, one in which everyone who was interested had the chance to submit their work, participants had to stay within set criteria: Submissions had to be made on a flat 8½ × 11-inch sheet of paper in any format. All submissions were to be retained and exhibited, leading Exit Art to display 2,443 pieces by people from 2 to 81 years old, from 27 countries. Most of the artwork was hung edge to edge, in alphabetical order by participant, on densely packed rows of suspended metal bars across the width of the front gallery. Further works were displayed in notebooks on the gallery walls. The submissions included drawings, paintings, photographs, poems, collages, diary entries, musical scores, letters, digital prints, and graphic designs. On the opening day there were 3,000 visitors with the exhibition running from January 26 to April 20, 2002. For Holland Cotter, of the *New York Times*, there was an "attitudinal mix, which reveals an undercurrent of dissident, antiestablishment political anger that found little public voice in the we-are-united, zero-tolerance atmosphere following the terrorist attacks" (p. 33).

After *Reactions* was exhibited in New York and Pasadena, the Library of Congress's Prints and Photographs Division acquired it all at cost and included a selection in its exhibition *Witness and Response: September 11 Acquisitions* at the Library of Congress, which ran from September 7 to November 2, 2002. As a process of mourning, a national ritual of remembrance, *Reactions* was enshrined in the central archive of the United States.

—*Francis Frascina*

References

Cheng, S. (2002, June 20). On the town: Three exhibitions coming to Los Angeles sketch a stoic and sensitive portrait of Ground Zero after the Sept. 11 attack. *Los Angeles Times*, p. F14.

Cotter, H. (2002, February 1). Amid the ashes, creativity. *The New York Times*, sect. E, pt. 2, p. 33.

Reactions. (2001, November). Invitation. *Exit Art*.

Urschel, D. (2002, December). Response to horror. *The Library of Congress Information Bulletin*. Retrieved from http://www.loc.gov

Thomas E. Franklin's (2001) photograph of firefighters raising the U.S. flag over the debris of the fallen Towers also became well known, reinforcing the ideas of pride and resilience in American life. Reminiscent of Joe Rosenthal's photo of soldiers raising the U.S. flag at Iwo Jima during World War II, the image equated the 9/11 firefighters with war heroes. A commemorative U.S. postal stamp based on the image was also issued.

In the years following September 11, 2001, Web sites have been created to house collections of photographs related to the attacks. Among these are *New York* magazine's *Days of Terror: A Photo Gallery* (http://nymag.com/news/articles/wtc/gallery/), *Time* magazine's "Shattered" (http://www.time.com/time/photoessays/shattered/), and the Library of Congress's *The September 11 Digital Archive* (http://911digitalarchive.org/). Such sites document the photographic images of September 11, creating archives that can be viewed and researched online. Some professional photographers, and the organizations for which they worked, also collected their photos into books, all released in 2002. These include David Halberstam's *New York September 11*, released

---

THE HEROES U.S. POSTAL STAMP AND THE "PHOTO SEEN AROUND THE WORLD"

Many images have become associated with September 11, but one has had a particularly lasting impact on American culture. The Thomas E. Franklin photograph of firefighters raising the U.S. flag over the debris of the fallen towers quickly became known as "The Photo Seen 'Round the World" (Mielke, 2002). Reminiscent of Joe Rosenthal's photo of soldiers raising the U.S. flag at Iwo Jima during World War II, the image equated the 9/11 firefighters with war heroes. It was reproduced in magazines, newspapers, and Web sites. In addition, firefighters "with flags began to appear in paintings and drawings, and on pins, buttons, T-shirts, hats and Christmas ornaments. Taverns, hair salons and offices hung the picture. Phoenix, Arizona, firefighters reenacted the scene before the start of Game 1 of the World Series featuring the Diamondbacks and New York Yankees" (Mielke, 2002, para. 27).

In 2002, the U.S. Postal Service issued a Heroes 2001 stamp based on Franklin's photographic image. Meant to commemorate emergency workers who were killed in connection with September 11, the stamp was dedicated by Postmaster General John E. Potter who asked "every American to use the Heroes of 2001 stamp on every letter and package they send. Because by doing this, we are also sending a message to our friends and a stark reminder to our enemies: We are Americans. We do not shirk our duty. We do not flee from danger. And we do not forget our heroes" ("New Fundraising Stamp," 2002, para. 3). Proceeds from the sale of the stamp were donated to families of relief works killed or injured while assisting in the rescue and recovery efforts of September 11.

—Sara E. Quay

References

Mielke, V. (2002). Icons: The photo seen round the world. *9/11: Pop culture and remembrance*. Retrieved from http://septterror.tripod.com/index.html

New Fundraising Stamp Honoring Heroes of 9/11 Issued Today in New York City. (2002, June 7). *Philatelic News*. Retrieved from http://www.usps.com/news

by Magnum Photographers; *September 11, 2001: A Record of Tragedy, Heroism and Hope*, by the editors of New York Magazine; and *September 11: A Testimony*, by the staff of Reuters.

Artists Respond to 9/11: Honoring, Remembering, and Healing

In the immediate aftermath of the attacks, photographers, painters, sculptors, and other visual artists began to create works of art. Some focused on the role firefighters, police officers, and others played in the rescue and recovery effort. *Life* magazine photographer Joe McNally's "Faces of Ground Zero" (2001), for example, featured life-sized images of 85 family members of the victims, Ground Zero rescue workers, and 9/11 survivors. Martha Cooper's online piece entitled "Missing" (2002), focuses on the spontaneous memorials and other words of support offered to rescue workers after the attacks, while Sarah Yuster painted "Firefighters' Commemorative" (2002), a portrait of a firefighter against a backdrop of the New York skyline without the Twin Towers. Gary Suson's "September.eleven.net" documented the recovery effort at Ground Zero. Known as the official photographer at Ground Zero, Suson had unprecedented access to the people working in "the Pit." In September of 2003, the New York Historical Society hosted an exhibit of Suson's photographs, entitled *9/11: Loss and Remembrance.* The show was primarily focused on portraits he had done of a group of men at Ground Zero known as the "Band of Dads," mostly of retired New York City Fire Department (FDNY) firefighters, who persistently dug at Ground Zero for their missing firefighter sons, dads, and brothers. Suson eventually opened his own museum dedicated to September 11, the Ground Zero Museum Workshop (www.groundzeromuseumworkshop.com).

Finding ways to visually represent and remember the victims of the attacks was also important to some artists. Kevin Ryan's virtual exhibit, *49 of 2870—A Memory of September 11* (2002), did so by creating a mosaic from images of 49 September 11 victims.

9/11 PORTRAITURE EXHIBITS

Missing—An Installation by Barbara Siegel, CUNY—Lehman College Art Gallery, September 3–October 26, 2002

A Life Lost, a Spirit Preserved: The Art and Photography of James Potorti, Municipal Art Society, September 11–October 10, 2002

A Community of Many Worlds: Arab Americans in New York City, Museum of the City of New York, March 2–September 1, 2002

Stronger Than Ever: NYPD Responds to 9/11, New York City Police Museum, September 6–January 5, 2003

Pilgrimage: Looking at Ground Zero, Arts Atrium Gallery, Union College, Schenectady, New York, February–March 2002

Faces of Ground Zero, Grand Central Terminal's Vanderbilt Hall, January 9–20, 2002

The images used in the piece were from the missing posters left around New York City after the attacks. Cheryl Sorg's "A Missing Piece" (2002) also tried to respond to the loss of life on September 11. The work "has the handmade look of a quilt, but with little squares of paper held together by tape, instead of stitched patches of fabric. When backlit, the image reveals 3,062 tiny candles: one for each person who died in the September 11 attacks" ("9/11 in Art and Culture," 2001, para. 14).

Another common subject of 9/11 art was the Twin Towers. "Grace" (2002), by Pietro Costa, for example, used a "tower of light, made of concentric neon circles with 3,000 pieces of paper at its base, bearing the names of those killed in the attacks. Interspersed with those names are blank pieces of paper, representing the unknown number of homeless and the undocumented victims of September 11" ("9/11 in Art and Culture," 2001, para. 3). Along similar lines, Hans Haacke's "Poster Project" (2002) used the negative space in white posters to create the form of the Twin Towers. These shapes "were placed throughout the city so that the walls or posters behind Haacke's work would fill the negative spaces, showing that New York is now seen only after being filtered through the memory of September 11 . . . An online site has a downloadable version, where the negative space is filled by the contents of the user's desktop" ("9/11 in Art and Culture," 2001, para. 4). Jean Holabird (2001) continued a watercolor series of lower Manhattan she had started in January 2001, recording the absence of the Towers where before she had painted their presence.

Joan Waters's "Drawn Together" (2002), invited participants to collaboratively create a chalk-drawn, life-sized image of the World Trade Center (WTC), evoking a crime scene in which the missing victim appears only in outline. People around the country drew the images in parking lots and other venues, thereby provoking conversation and thought about the significance of the attacks. Hope Gangloff and Jason Search created "Forever Tall" (2004), a huge mural of the New York skyline that included an outline of the Twin Towers set against a floral background. Offering a different perspective, Bruno Surdo's 35-foot mural, "September 11, 2001: 'Tragedy, Honor and Memory'" (2002) was first displayed at Chicago's Daley Plaza. The mural "incorporates debris, such as business cards and letterhead and concrete dust, in the painting which depicts World Trade Center, victims, survivors, rescuers and somber Americans" (9/11 in Arts & Culture, 2005, para 10). Finally, honoring the artists who had used studio space in Tower One, one of whom died in the attacks, "Microviews: Artists' Documentation of the World Trade Center" (2002), incorporated a range of mediums to reflect the artists' inside perspective on what the World Trade Center had signified ("9/11 in Art and Culture," 2001).

Other visual responses to the tragedy included "9.11.01" (2001), by Flux Factory, which focused on how people responded emotionally to September 11 by incorporating images and written testimonies in an online format. In 2002, at the Brooklyn Working Artists Coalition, a show opened featuring at least 30 sculptors from around the world whose art focused directly or indirectly on September 11. At the American Craft Museum, *September 11: Artists Respond* (2002) featured artists from around the country who had created more than 60 nine-by-nine-inch panels marking the lives lost in the attacks. Michelle Pred's "In Memory: Exploring the Repercussions" (2002), "includes a painted airplane wing, dedicated to the passengers of the San Francisco bound United Flight 93, one of the hijacked planes, and sculptures created from objects confiscated at airport security checkpoints" ("9/11 in Art and Culture," 2001, para. 28). James Gilroy's exhibit, "Before and after 9/11" (2001), featured a series of paintings Gilroy had completed prior to the attacks as well as some he painted in response to the events. Looking much like the occurrences Gilroy witnessed firsthand on 9/11, the paintings he completed prior to September 11 have a strange foreshadowing about them. The "before" images are abstracted, yet recognizable figures; the "after" works consist of columns encrusted with what could be vegetation, ash, or some other element that is left to the viewer to determine ("9/11 in Art and Culture," 2001).

Visual projects were not just focused on, or drawn from, the United States. "In Memoriam: September 11, 2001" (2002), by Moshe Gershuni, incorporated words from the Jewish prayer devoted to personal loss, while "In Memory: The Art of After-ward" (2002), by the Legacy Project, a work examining "themes of loss and remem-brance," included art from 16 countries around the globe. "Unity Canvas" (2002), at the Williamsburg Art and Historical Center, exhibited 200 works of art from artists around the globe in a shared response to the attacks.

Performance artists and dancers also responded to September 11 by creating a range of artistic performances. On the first anniversary of 9/11 "Complacency: A Renegade Action by Kat Skabra," was danced and performed by 34 different artists for four consecutive hours. Skabra described the work as "intended to cite U.S. complacency and political militaristic interventions abroad as one of the many reasons for the September 11 attacks" ("9/11 in Art and Culture," 2001, para. 5). That same evening, at the Evening Stars Music and Dance Festival held in Battery Park, the internationally acclaimed Merce Cunningham Dance Company offered a performance to honor the anniversary of the attacks.

In 2002, Susan McKeever of the Williamsburg Dance Company, created a patriotic performance called "United We Fall" in response to 9/11, while Valeri Norman cho-reographed "Out of Place," a dance in honor of those individuals who were displaced from their homes as a result of the attacks. Laurie Anderson's "Happiness" offered a more personal work by a performance artist who had experienced the attacks firsthand. A group project, "Even the Birds Were on Fire" (2001) by the Brooklyn Artists Alliance, incorporated multiple mediums into the performance, including collage, photographs of missing persons, sound from the attacks—including jets, planes, and helicopters—as well as writings of Amiri Baraka and Noam Chomsky. Taken together, the performance aimed at relentlessly creating an atmosphere of anxiety reminiscent of 9/11. The work, which has been performed throughout the country, attempts to evoke the emotional atmosphere of the bombing of the World Trade Center and its after-math. Visitors to the installation are invited to leave memorial objects or write their commentaries about 9/11, the ongoing war, and the exhibition itself onto a paper wall. These offerings will be incorporated into the exhibit and the performance ("9/11 in Art and Culture," 2001, para. 24).

Not all artists found a welcoming culture in which to create their work after September 11, however. Increased security limited art that could be performed or hung in public locations, while the USA Patriot Act caused concern among some artists that their freedom of expression might be contained if they produced art that was critical of the U.S. government. Some artists encountered such problems, including Steven Kurtz, who in 2004 was arrested while creating an exhibit at the Massachusetts Institute of Technology using genetically modified food. The film *Strange Culture* was produced based on his experience. In 2005, filmmaker Rakesh Sharma was arrested while taking images of New York taxi cabs, and in 2006 Arun Wiita was arrested for taking photos in a New York subway. In 2005, an entire conference—What Comes After: Cities, Art and Recovery—focused on the impact the Patriot Act was having on the post-9/11 art community (James, 2005; Rothenberg & Kornblum, 2005).

As time passed, more permanent 9/11 exhibits opened in museums and historical societies around the country, including the Library of Congress's *Witness and Response: September 11 Acquisitions at the Library of Congress*, the *Wall of Prayer* at the Museum of the City of New York, and the Smithsonian Institution's *September 11: Bearing Witness to History.*

Memorials and Museums

One of the most challenging questions to arise after September 11 was how the nation as a whole, as opposed to individuals or smaller communities, would remember the events of the day and those who had been lost. In general, public memorials are created with this purpose in mind—to offer official sites and symbols by which to remember an event.

Some 9/11 memorials were objects, such as the statue called *Double Check* and the sculpture titled *The Sphere*, which survived the attacks and were rededicated as official commemorations of the event. New objects were also created to remember those who were lost in the attacks, including a bronze relief at the New York Firehouse, Engine 10, known as the FDNY Memorial Wall (2006) and Eric Fischl's controversial bronze statue, *Tumbling Woman* (2001). Souvenirs containing images related to the attacks, sold at museums or in areas around Ground Zero, gave everyone the chance to bring home their own personal 9/11 memorial.

In addition to dedicated memorial objects, the attacks were also documented by numerous organizations and institutions dedicated to visually recording—through Web sites or physical locations—the legacy of September 11. The Library of Congress, for example, together with the Internet Archive, tapped into the wealth of online material that was posted on Web sites within hours of the attacks, including names, images, and information about the events. This information has been gathered into an official 9/11 resource center—http://september11.archive.org—that continues to grow. Similarly, blogs and personal Web sites recorded images and sounds taken with cell phones and first-person accounts of the day. The September 11 Digital Archive (http://911digitalarchive.org/) collected and lists personal Web sites about September 11.

Sounds of September 11 were also collected by groups such as the Library of Congress's American Folklife Center, Columbia University's Oral History Research Office, and National Public Radio's Sonic Memorial Project. Primarily oral histories

DOUBLE CHECK AND THE SPHERE

Among the remnants and debris cleared from Ground Zero after the September 11 attacks, two works of art were found damaged, but salvageable: *Double Check*, the bronze statue of a business man created in 1982 by sculptor J. Seward Johnson, and *The Sphere*, Fritz Koenig's metallic orb-shaped work. *Double Check* still sits in Liberty Plaza Park, adjacent to the Twin Towers, where it has been since 1982. The statue was uncovered from the rubble of the Twin Towers and served as a temporary memorial during the rescue and recovery process. Rescue workers placed a hard hat on the statue's head, a fire hose coil by his side, left flowers in his arms, and taped notes to loved ones on his body.

After it was removed from Ground Zero, the statue was refurbished by Johnson who left the dents and markings made by the falling debris as a reminder of what had happened. The statue was returned to Liberty Plaza, and an identical one was created and placed in Liberty State Park, Jersey City, looking across the water at Ground Zero. This twin *Double Check* stands as a memorial to 9/11 and includes the hard hat and coil that became so significant during the recovery effort ("Damaged Downtown," 2005).

Similar to *Double Check*, prior to September 11 Koenig's *The Sphere* (1971) was located near the World Trade Center, specifically in Austin Tobin Plaza between the North and South Towers. The sculpture gained notoriety after the attacks in part because it was recovered from the debris at Ground Zero, having survived the collapse of the towers with only minor damage. In addition, a documentary made by Percy Adlon five weeks after September 11, featured Koenig in the plaza talking about the sculpture. As one of the surviving physical remains of the Twin Towers site, *The Sphere* was relocated to Battery Park where it was rededicated on the six-month anniversary of the attacks, at 8:46 a.m., the time when the first place crashed into the North Tower. It now stands, alongside an eternal flame, as a memorial to the victims of 9/11 and will be moved back to the site when the National September 11 Memorial is completed ("Tribute in Light," 2002).

Both *Double Check* and *The Sphere* survived the attacks and have become symbols and attractions for visitors to Ground Zero. The recovery of these artworks is especially poignant for it is estimated that more than $100 million worth of art in and around the World Trade Center site was destroyed in the September 11 attacks (Knox, 2001; Marks & Vogel, 2001).

—*Sara E. Quay and Dena Gilby*

References

Cotter, H. (2002, February 1). Amid the ashes, creativity. *The New York Times*, pp. B33, 35.

Damaged Downtown Statue Restored to Honor 9/11 Victims. (2005, June 17–23). *Lowermanhattan.info*. Retrieved from http://www.lowermanhattan.info

Knox, N. (2001, September 27). Art lies under the rubble. *USA Today*, p. 2B.

Marks, P., & Vogel, C. (2001, September 17). Arts groups at a tragedy's center try to assess where to begin. *The New York Times*, p. E1.

Tribute in Light to New York Victims. (2002, March 6). *BBC News*. Retrieved from http://news.bbc.co.uk

of those who survived the attacks or helped in the recovery, the sounds of September 11 also include phone calls made by victims as well as recordings of sounds from the World Trade Center's history—sounds of weddings that had once been held there, sounds of the Twin Towers' elevators and doors, sounds of the piano playing at Windows on the World restaurant (Kirshenblatt-Gimblett, 2003).

In the years since September 11, 2001, memorials and museums have been erected across the country to give visitors places to remember and learn about the events that occurred that day. Each of the three crash sites has its own memorial that is open to visitors. The Pentagon completed its official memorial in 2005. The area outside Shanksville, Pennsylvania, has encountered challenges to building a visitors site to replace the less formal—but no less moving—current memorial. Ground Zero itself has become a memorial site, with the Firefighters Memorial, the WTC Tribute Visitors Center, and St. Paul's Chapel standing as the major places at which visitors can learn about, and remember, the events that occurred that day. The Ground Zero Museum Workshop, which opened in 2005 not far from Ground Zero, also gives visitors to lower Manhattan a place to focus their attention on remembering September 11.

ERIC FISCHL'S *TUMBLING WOMAN*

Tumbling Woman is a sculpture produced in 2001 by Eric Fischl, a visual artist from New York City. The sculpture depicts the contorted form of a woman falling through space. Protests surrounded the fall 2002 initial installation of the piece in Rockefeller Center because the statue evoked some of the most horrifying images of September 11— the people who literally tumbled to their deaths from the upper floors of the Twin Towers. Such interpretations led to the sculpture's removal: "[T]he emotional impact of seeing a woman in freefall, twisting and turning in space, was too much for people and the monument was removed from the corporate lobby" only a few days into a planned two week display (Vallen, 2006, para. 3).

In response to these accusations, Fischl maintained that although "[o]ne might see a moment of impact in a kind of way that implies brain splattering, a graphic moment there . . . [t]he thing is that if you look at the piece itself, it feels like a dream in which somebody is floating. There's no weight there that is sending the crushing, rippling current back through the body as it hits a solid mass" (Rakoff, 2002, para. 10). *Tumbling Woman* is a powerful piece that brings attention to one of the most painful specters of 9/11, eliciting strong reactions from viewers still traumatized by the sight of falling bodies.

—Lloyd Isaac Vayo

References

Rakoff, D. (2002, October 27). An interview with the artist—Eric Fischl. *New York Art World*. Retrieved from http://www.newyorkartworld.com

Vallen, M. (2006, April 20). Mark Vallen's "art for a change." *Art for a Change*. Retrieved from http://art-for-a-change.com

THE GROUND ZERO MUSEUM WORKSHOP

The Ground Zero Museum Workshop is a small museum located in Chelsea, a few miles from the World Trade Center site. It was founded and assembled by Gary Suson, who was appointed as the official photographer for the Uniformed Firefighter Association a few weeks after September 11. According to Suson, the association approached him to fulfill this role after seeing a compilation of photographs he had assembled and posted on the Web site, september11.net (http://september11.net/). Three weeks after September 11, Mayor Giuliani closed the site to the public, and Suson was the only photographer given access. According to the Ground Zero Museum Workshop materials, this job came with some rules: His role as the photographer would be unpaid, he could not release images until given permission to do so, and a portion of any profits he made from the eventual sale of his photographs had to be donated to a 9/11 charity. Suson worked on the site for six months and in May 2002 was given permission to release his photographs to the viewing public.

In 2005, Suson opened the not-for-profit Ground Zero Museum Workshop with the goal of sharing his images and artifacts collected at the World Trade Center site during the recovery efforts. Given Suson's appointment as the FDNY photographer, the Workshop's main imagery and narrative centers around the New York City (NYC) firefighters and the culture they were immersed in during the recovery effort. Through this, stories perhaps not previously known to the general public are told. For example, the Workshop has an example of a cross and a Star of David, chiseled from the steel beams of the World Trade Center towers, and given to families who lost loved ones. The Workshop also houses glass collected at the WTC site, a rare find given most of the glass windows were vaporized. Another case contains German beer cans from the 1970s, believed to have been wedged by workers into the infrastructure of the towers when they were being built.

The Workshop's tone is also set by some choices regarding the room's atmosphere and presentation. For example, the walls have a border text that wraps around the room. The words "recovery," "dig," "prayer," "freedom," "heal," "remembrance," and "love" are all given short definitions and are followed by a quote that reads "Two bullets went into the World Trade Center but only LOVE came out.—FDNY Chaplain Chris Keenan" and the following death tolls: "Civilian 2749, FDNY 343, PAPD [Port Authority Police Department] 37, NYPD [New York Police Department] 23, Fire Patrol 1, EMS [emergency medical service] 10."

Celtic background music is played during part of the presentation and self tour, which contributes to the tone of the Workshop. Tissue boxes are placed throughout, and complimentary chocolate, described by the guide as "a natural anti depressant" is available in a restroom that also contains collections of seemingly peaceful items such as seashells and hero-themed folk art on the walls. Finally, contributing to the atmosphere is the small number of visitors permitted in the space at one time; it allows for easy movement throughout the space.

—Amy M. Damico

Reference

Ground Zero Museum Workshop. (n.d.). [Web site]. Available at http://www.groundzero museumworkshop.com/

NAMING THE VICTIMS

Memorials built to honor the victims of September 11 faced the challenge of remembering the victims of the attacks while not celebrating the events themselves. The common solution to the challenge was to create memorials that represent each of the people who died in the attacks. Some memorials list the names of the victims, while others represent the victims symbolically through the shape and form of the memorial.

The memorial at Boston's Logan airport, for example, *The Place of Remembrance*, is a square, glass structure with an open ceiling through which visitors walk into the space. Two flat, glass panels stand at opposite entrances, one for each of the planes that took off from Boston that day, American Airlines Flight 11 and United Airlines Flight 175. On the side of the plaques facing outward, the time the flights took off—7:59 and 8:14 a.m.—respectively, are inscribed. On the other side of each, facing each other in the center of the memorial, are listed the names of the passengers who died on the planes. Visitors enter the memorial on one of two walkways, each of which follows the flight path of each of the planes.

In Shanksville, Pennsylvania, the current memorial recognizes the 40 passengers who died on United 93 in two ways. A collection of 40 slate angels, each with the name of a passenger written on it, lines the fence that looks toward the crash site. Memorial benches, also inscribed with passengers' names, stand looking out over the field. The future memorial will also recognize each person who died in Shanksville on September 11. *A Tower of Voices* will be visible from the highway and will include 40 wind chimes. Along a wall next to the sacred ground will be the names of each of the victims.

—*Sara E. Quay*

Other sites across the country found their own ways to remember the men and women who died in the attacks (Dunlap, 2006; "Tribute in Light," 2002). For example, in Providence, Rhode Island, Project Hope has displayed hundreds of painted 9/11-memorial tiles in a tunnel near Water Park. In 2003, Staten Island, which lost 270 residents in the attacks, completed a memorial overlooking New York Harbor, the Statue of Liberty, and lower Manhattan where the Twin Towers once stood. In 2008, Logan Airport, where American Airlines Flight 11 and United Flight 175 departed from on the morning of September 11, opened its 9/11 memorial to the public.

Conclusion

The 9/11 attacks were themselves visual events, targeted at buildings recognized around the world as symbols of U.S. life, and captured live by television cameras and photographers. Visual images played an important role in the days, months, and years after September 11. Most immediately, they served as visible expressions of the wide range of emotions surrounding the attacks, as evidenced in the outpouring of spontaneous and makeshift memorials and shrines. Photography played a major role in the initial documenting and processing of the day's events.

As the shock of 9/11 wore off, new forms of visual culture appeared. Exhibits and collections began to give shape to the events surrounding the day and formed narratives about what had taken place. More recently, the establishment of official museums and memorials commemorating September 11 suggest that the attacks have become part of U.S. history and will be stored in the nation's memory for generations to come.

—*Sara E. Quay*

References

Damaged Downtown Statue Restored to Honor 9/11 Victims. (2005, June 17–23). *Lowermanhattan.info*. Retrieved from http://www.lowermanhattan.info

Dunlap, D. W. (2006, June 11). A hands-on tribute to the pain and valor of 9/11. *The New York Times*. Retrieved from http://www.nytimes.com

Hatfield, K. L. (2008, Summer). Communication research: Falling towers, emerging iconography: A rhetorical analysis of Twin Tower images after 9/11. *Texas Speech Communication Journal, (33)*1, 62–73.

James, C. (2005, September 12). Beyond comforting afflicted. *New York Times*. Retrieved from http://www.nytimes.com

Kirshenblatt-Gimblett, B. (2003). Kodak moments, flashbulb memories: Reflections on 9/11. *The Drama Review, 47*(1), 11–48.

Knox, N. (2001, September 27). Art lies under the rubble. *USA Today*, p. 2B.

Lakoff, G. (2001, September 16). Metaphors of terror. *The days after*. Retrieved from http://www.press.uchicago.edu

Mandell, J. (2001, November 18). History is impatient to embrace Sept. 11. *The New York Times*, sec. 2, col. 1.

Mandell, J. (2005, September 8). Inappropriate art. *Gotham Gazette*. Retrieved from http://www.gothamgazette.com

Marks, P., & Vogel, C. (2001, September 17). Arts groups at a tragedy's center try to assess where to begin. *New York Times*, p. E1.

9/11 in Art and Culture. (2001). Rebuilding NYC. *Gotham Gazette*. Retrieved from http://www.gothamgazette.com/rebuilding_nyc/topics/culture/art.shtml

Rothenberg, J., & Kornblum, W. (2005). New York's visual art world after 9/11. In N. Foner (Ed.), *Wounded city: The social impact of 9/11* (pp. 242–262). New York: Russell Sage Foundation.

Sanderson, K. (2004). *Light at Ground Zero: St. Paul's Chapel after 9/11* (2nd ed.) Baltimore: Square Halo Books.

Senie, H. (2006). Mourning in protest: Spontaneous memorials and the sacralization of public space. In J. Santino (Ed.), *Spontaneous shrines and the public memorialization of death* (pp. 41–56). New York: Palgrave Macmillan.

Tribute in Light to New York Victims. (2002, March 6). *BBC News*. Retrieved from http://news.bbc.co.uk

Yocom, M. (2006). We'll watch out for Liza and the kids: Spontaneous memorials and personal response at the Pentagon, 2001. In J. Santino (Ed.), *Spontaneous shrines and the public memorialization of death* (pp. 57–98). New York: Palgrave Macmillan.

SPOTLIGHT ESSAY/VISUAL CULTURE: 9/11 EXHIBITS

According to the *Gotham Gazette*'s Web site (www.gothamgazette.com) on the eve of the first anniversary of September 11 more than 150 museums across the country presented exhibitions of amateur or mixed amateur and professional works relating to the attacks. Some of the exhibits helped viewers remember 9/11 and those who had been lost, while others began to make sense of the events by creating a narrative of what had occurred.

Many of the exhibits used objects to stand in for that which is absent—the World Trade Center towers and the people who worked in them, as well as those who died at all three crash sites. Given these common themes, the museums and exhibition spaces usually contain the following exhibit setup: a photograph wall, objects from the site, children's art, and a room where visitors can respond to the exhibitions or simply sit and reflect (Cotter, 2002; Coulter-Smith & Owen, 2005; Gardner, 2002). An example is Barbara Siegel's installation "Missing" that was held September through October 26, 2002, at the Lehman College Art Gallery. One can see the overlap, furthermore, between this and the World Trade Center Memorial and Museum that contains photographic walls that re-create the earlier missing posters and makeshift memorials (see www.lehman.edu/vpadvance/artgallery/gallery/ for an encapsulation of the exhibition that includes an artist's statement in the Exhibitions Archive section of the site).

On September 7, 2002, the Library of Congress opened an exhibit called *Witness and Response: September 11 Acquisitions at the Library of Congress*, which included materials collected immediately after, and since, the 9/11 attacks. Running until October 26, 2002, the exhibit is now available online (www.loc.gov/exhibits/911/ 911-overview.html) and includes digital images of posters, photographs, newspaper pages, drawings, as well as writings, music, and other artifacts related to 9/11.

Artifacts from the World Trade Center were collected and eventually placed in museum exhibits and special collections. Fliers of the missing, for example, were collected and exhibited in *Missing: Last Seen at the World Trade Center, September 11, 2001* and *Missing: Streetscape of a City in Mourning*. A *Wall of Prayer* was erected at the Museum of the City of New York, while the Smithsonian Institution curated the *September 11: Bearing Witness to History*, an exhibit featuring photographs and artifacts related to the World Trade Center attacks and their aftermath.

Still other anniversary exhibits, for example, the Doll and Toy Museum of New York City's Doll Making workshop held on September 11, 2002, explicitly sought to help participants to continue to heal from the trauma of the day. Indeed, the event advertised itself as "A session of doll-making to help children and adults heal after September 11." A similar exhibit, *Help/Fear*, a quilt by Barbara Pucci of Brooklyn, was displayed in *America from the Heart: Quilters Remember September 11, 2001* and later published in book form. Pucci describes her process in a way that clearly delineates how the quilt making was therapy for her when she states: "I forced myself to start working on a new piece—this piece—in an attempt to unlock myself and find movement again . . . I began trying to print a scroll, a kind of prayer shawl, to speak for those of us that are getting caught in the crossfire" (Bresenhan, 2002, p. 106).

The result is a rectangular quilt measuring 26 by 39 and a half inches that contains a border with Arabic, English, and Hebrew text surrounding three panels. The center panel contains what appears to be a brick wall. Flanking this wall are two similar side panels that have wavy, gray and white pieces. These are, perhaps, abstractions of the pieces of paper, paper that was used by people now lost or missing, and that Pucci describes as seeing falling from the sky on the day of the attack. Like many of the early visual responses to the attacks, which used materials and imagery as symbols of those people, objects, buildings that were lost, the paper that Pucci simulates in her quilt becomes a metaphor for people lost in the attacks. In this way Pucci used her quilt not only to commemorate, but also to express her values and to demonstrate that art is a model for how to deal with trauma, and to allow the viewers to examine their own feelings about the attacks.

What all of these works have in common is their evocation of the human and the fragility of life. Some do this through words spoken, others through gesture and poses of sitters and, in the case of Gilroy's exhibition through the way in which the human figure is completely (or nearly totally) erased in the after images.

Since the first anniversary of September 11, there have been periodic exhibitions and their emphasis has been less on 9/11 as an event and more on abstract ideas. Museums have turned their attention to historicizing the attacks by carefully arranging a few objects and interweaving them with explanatory text. *The Art of 9/11*, for example, was on view at Apex Art September 7 through October 15, 2005. Curated by art critic and philosopher Arthur Danto, this show developed another fundamental value of the United States—that of the individualism and aesthetic response to 9/11. The artists assembled by Danto are all fixtures of contemporary art; indeed, by and large these artists are the "old masters" of the contemporary. Indicative of the works is Cindy Sherman's *Untitled* (2004, color photograph, 55-1/2 by 56-1/2 inches) that represents Sherman as a clown against a vibrantly colored, striped background. The viewer can interpret this in multiple manners: Sherman feels like a clown, performing and making light of difficult times; she perhaps asks the viewer to identify with her character as the masks people wear to cover their insecurity; the background may reflect the sense that the world is chaotic and indiscernible. These are but a few of the notions arising from this work, and, one could posit, of the show as a whole. Danto's accompanying text attempts to place the events of 9/11 into the context of Western world history in that he links the works of this show to Wittgenstein and Schubert.

Jeff Mermelstein's photograph of Johnson's *Double Check* sculpture was part of the *Here Is New York* exhibition, but more recently was shown as part of a 25-year survey of Mermelstein's work in his one-person show at the Steven Kasher gallery (May 11–June 10, 2006). In placing this work—itself part of a series called Ground Zero, September 11, 2001—alongside his "Sidewalk" and "No Title Here" series Mermelstein historicizes the photograph; that is, sets it outside of its time and place of manufacture and into the history of his own body of work as responding less to a singular event and more to ideas, themes, and concepts in the history of photography.

The most recent New York City gallery show to overtly deal with 9/11 ran at the White Box gallery from October 29 to November 23, 2008, and was called *Sedition*. The exhibition was curated by artist-activists Dread Scott, Kyle Goen, and Hajarah Abdus-Sabur and expressly questioned the aftereffects of 9/11 in terms of freedom of speech and, thus, can be viewed as manifestation of the long-term ramifications of 9/11 on art and artists in New York City in addition to being expressions of democratic values.

—*Dena Gilby*

References

Bresenhan, K. (2002). *America from the heart: Quilters remember September 11, 2001*. Lafayette, CA: C & T.

Cotter, H. (2002, February 1). Amid the ashes, creativity. *The New York Times*, pp. B33, 35.

Coulter-Smith, G., & Owen, M. (Eds.). (2005). *Art in the age of terrorism*. London: Paul Holberton.

Danto, A. (2005). The art of 911. *Apex Art*. Retrieved from http://www.apexart.org

Gardner, J. (2002, March/April). Collecting a national tragedy. *Museum News*, pp. 42–45; 66–67.

George, A., Peress, G., Shulan, M., & Traub, C. (2002). *Here is New York: A democracy of photographs*. New York: Scalo.

Kifner, J., & Saulny, S. (2001, September 14). Posting handbills as votive offerings. *New York Times*, p. A9.

Kimmelman, M. (2001, December 30). Offering beauty, and then proof that life goes on. *New York Times*, p. AR35.

Kirshenblatt-Gimblett, B. (2003). Kodak moments, flashbulb memories: Reflections on 9/11. *Drama Review, 47*(1), 11–48.

Marks, P., & Vogel, C. (2001, September 17). Arts groups at a tragedy's center try to assess where to begin. *The New York Times*, p. E1.

9/11 in Art and Culture. (2001). Rebuilding NYC. *Gotham Gazette*. Retrieved from http://www.gothamgazette.com/rebuilding_nyc/topics/culture/art.shtml

Rothenberg, J., & Kornblum, W. (2005). New York's visual art world after 9/11. In N. Foner (Ed.), *Wounded city: The social impact of 9/11* (pp. 242–262). New York: Russell Sage Foundation.

Weena, P. (2008, Nov/Dec). Too young and vibrant for ruins: Ground zero photography and the problem of contemporary ruin. *Afterimage*. Retrieved from http://www.entrepreneur.com

Zeitlin, S. (2006). Oh did you see the ashes come thickly falling down? Poems posted in the wake of September 11. In J. Santino (Ed.), *Spontaneous shrines and the public memorialization of death* (pp. 99–118). New York: Palgrave Macmillan.

SPOTLIGHT ESSAY/VISUAL CULTURE: ART AND THE WORLD TRADE CENTER

Prior to September 11, the World Trade Center complex—which included but was not limited to the Twin Towers—housed significant and varied works of art in the offices and lobbies of the buildings. David Ebony (2002) claimed that at least $10 million worth of public art was destroyed in the attacks. Among the most notable losses were Joan Miro's 1974 "Tapestry," one of only two tapestries he created; Louise Nevelson's sculpture *Sky Gate, New York* at 1 World Trade Center; Roy Lichtenstein's series *Entablature* at 7 World Trade Center; and Elyn Zimmerman's memorial commemorating those killed or wounded in the 1993 World Trade Center attack (Ebony, 2002; Koplos, 2002; Reger, 2002; Zimmerman, 2002). Also lost was James Rosati's *Ideogram*, a stainless steel sculpture that sat between the Twin Towers. Commissioned in 1969 by the Port Authority Art Committee, the sculpture may have survived the attacks. However, its material was indistinguishable from the rubble at Ground Zero and, therefore, the work was not recovered (Ebony, 2002; Knox, 2001; Koplos, 2002).

Artworks owned by corporate and private collections housed in the World Trade Center tower offices were also lost. In this regard, it is estimated that as much as $100 million worth of art was destroyed, including more than 300 works by the French artist, Rodin, that were in the collection of the accounting firm Cantor Fitzgerald (Ebony, 2002; Koplos, 2002). In a special issue of the *IFAR Journal*, Suzanne Lemakis (2002) reported on extensive losses incurred by the Citigroup Corporation at 7 World Trade Center; 1,113 objects were destroyed, many of them prints by renowned American artists, such as George Caleb Bingham and Jacob Lawrence.

Aside from direct losses in the attacks itself, there were a number of works that initially survived, but for a variety of reasons did not endure the recovery efforts or were damaged beyond repair. Masayuki Nagare's 1975 *Cloud Fortress*, which stood at the Church street entrance to the central plaza of the World Trade Center, withstood the attacks but not the recovery process. Alexander Calder's *Bent Propeller*, a 1970 red stabile located outside of 7 World Trade Center, was found in the rubble, but the damage was too extensive for the artwork to be saved.

Some World Trade Center art did survive the September 11 attacks, however. Nomura Securities, a Japanese bank, had more than 110 works that were damaged but eventually restored, as were 289 works by an artist with a studio nearby (Smith, 2002). *Modern Head*, by Roy Lichtenstein, which originally stood in Battery Park, also survived. In August 2008, just weeks before the seventh anniversary of September 11, the work was donated by its owner, Florida Marlins owner Jeffrey Loria, to the Smithsonian American Art Museum, which placed it at southwest exterior corner of their building in Washington, D.C. (Smith, 2002). Ned Smyth's *The Upper Room*, created between 1984 and 1987 was also in Battery Park when the attacks took place but was undamaged on 9/11 and remains in its original spot. Finally, the George Gustav Heye Center, Smithsonian National Museum of the American Indian, was housed just four blocks from Ground Zero in the old United States Custom House. When the attacks occurred, the building was quickly secured from infiltration of airborne debris. The interior of the museum suffered, but the collections and exhibitions were essentially unharmed. A massive cleanup was eventually completed on the interior space, particularly the rotunda and collector's office (Haworth, 2002).

Aside from housing works of art, the World Trade Center had connections to the broader New York art community. The Lower Manhattan Cultural Council (LMCC), for example, whose offices were in the World Trade Center, sponsored a Worldviews studio program that provided space in the Twin Towers, along with funding, for artists working on projects that related to New York City. Not only were the offices and studios with all of the artists' work destroyed, but one of the artists, the emerging sculptor Michael Richards, was killed in the attack. LMCC became highly involved in efforts to keep the arts alive in lower Manhattan after 9/11, hosting a periodic summit named "What Comes After: Cities, Art + Recovery" as well as temporary exhibitions. In September 2005, the international summit was held, and throughout the month of September associated events were sponsored: for example, the LMCC ran *Return to the Land of Wonders* by the Iraqi filmmaker Maysoon Pachachi, as well as the exhibitions *After Effects*; *A Knock at the Door . . .*,; *Focus Sphere, 2005*; and *Greetings without Flowers*.

—Dena Gilby

References

Ebony, D. (2002, January). World Trade Center art works destroyed. *Art in America*, *90*(1), 27.

Haworth, J. (2002, February 28). The downtown institutional impact. The 9/11 double issue. *IFAR Journal*, *4*(4) and *5*(1). Retrieved from http://www.ifar.org

Koplos, J. (2002, September). WTC sculpture: Lost or destroyed? *Art in America*. Retrieved from http://findarticles.com

Lemakis, S. (2002, February 28). Art lost by Citigroup. The 9/11 double issue. *IFAR Journal*, *4*(4) and *5*(1). Retrieved from http://www.ifar.org

Reger, L. (2002, February 28). The heritage emergency national task force. The 9/11 double Issue. *IFAR Journal*, *4*(4) and *5*(1). Retrieved from http://www.ifar.org

Smith, G. (2002, February 28). Art damaged on 911: The insurance adjusters role. The 9/11 double issue. *IFAR Journal*, *4*(4) and *5*(1). Retrieved from http://www.ifar.org

Zimmerman, E. (2002, February 28). The World Trade Center memorial, 1993. The 9/11 double issue. *IFAR Journal*, *4*(4) and *5*(1). Retrieved from http://www.ifar.org

SPOTLIGHT ESSAY/VISUAL CULTURE: *FALLING MAN* BY RICHARD DREW AND RELATED IMAGES

Questions about representing the horror at the World Trade Center on September 11 developed almost as soon as the attacks commenced. After the first plane's impact, the sight of individuals jumping from the highest floors of the North Tower to certain death terrified office workers in the South Tower into evacuating, despite the presumed relative safety of their own building (Flynn & Dwyer, 2004, p. B8). However, for newsrooms, the plight of these figures raised different concerns. Although live coverage of the towers aflame continued until they collapsed, and footage of the attacked, damaged, and fallen buildings persisted in relentless replay in subsequent days and months, images of those jumping to their deaths quickly disappeared from U.S. television (Junod, 2003, p. 180). Photographs of these victims appeared fleetingly even in print (Cauchon & Moore, 2002, p. 5A). As publications such as *USA Today*, *The New York Times*, and *Esquire* have suggested, this most visible evidence of mortal human suffering provoked deep unsettlement among the living, whether bereaved relatives or unrelated witnesses (Cauchon & Moore, 2002, p. 5A; Flynn & Dwyer, 2004, pp. A1, B8; Junod, 2003).

Tom Junod's *Esquire* article "The Falling Man" (2003) dwells on the haunting effects of a particular photograph—published widely before vanishing almost entirely—that portrays an unidentified man's descent from the North Tower. Associated Press (AP) photographer Richard Drew had captured an impossible moment on film, when in a single frame the solitary figure appears almost gracefully posed, in aesthetic alignment with both towers serving as backdrop (p. 177). The picture—by permanently capturing a single moment—shows a man in eternal flight, as if the viewer could say "No!" and stop him from falling. Yet Junod acknowledges that this image is misleading, a happenstance of a fluke photo (p. 180). In reality, the falling man, "in his life outside the frame [of the photo] . . . drops and keeps dropping" in uncontrolled free fall (p. 177). Time does not stand still, and it does not move in reverse: The planes collide into the buildings, the towers collapse, and people die. What is happening in the photo has happened, has passed, is past—fated deaths, once set in motion, that victims could not avoid and witnesses could not avert. Junod argues that "we have somehow taken it upon ourselves to deem their deaths unworthy of witness" (p. 181). But he also argues that in spite—indeed, because—of this, we must witness them (p. 199).

Junod's inquiry addresses without fully answering the question of how to witness such events. In the documentary *9/11: The Falling Man*, which traces the story behind Junod's *Esquire* article, footage of individuals jumping out of the towers is included, and their doom is reflected in the horrified stares of bystanders, eyes open wide, hands covering mouths, tears sliding down cheeks. Relatives of the deceased from the towers struggle to accept that their own trapped loved ones might have faced, and made, the choice to die in this way. In the format of a documentary, such reactions purport to evidence a fraught reality rather than narrowly construe its meaning. Such a journalistic approach poses one possibility for public acknowledgment of these public deaths.

However, other approaches have proven more problematic. In 2005, photographer Kerry Skarbakka performed multiple jumps, while wearing a body harness, from Chicago's Museum of Contemporary Art (Marlan, 2005, pp. 1, 28–29). He did so to showcase his sense that the act of falling is about human vulnerability (Skarbakka, 2008). His Chicago performance generated objections from New Yorkers who, according to the *Daily News*, regarded his jumps as callous exploitations of those who had jumped on September 11 (Lisberg, June 16, 2005, p. 5; Lisberg, June 17, 2005, p. 7). The *Daily News* quoted then New York Governor George Pataki as saying, "It's an utter disgrace that someone would try to turn horrible human suffering and tragedy into an act" (Lisberg, June 17, 2005, p. 7).

The image of the falling person also appears in Don DeLillo's novel *Falling Man* (2007), in which an artist performing such jumps in a business suit throughout New York City provokes similar objections (p. 33). A main character in the book,

Lianne, perceives "something awful about the stylized pose . . . But the worst of it was the stillness itself and her nearness to the man" (p. 68). While the performance repels her, her proximity to the artist's suspension of fate proves the most troubling. It is as if the performance not only conjures the past, but prolongs it. It is, perhaps, as if the public, visual process by which people died on September 11 feels too personal and intimate, making viewers feel vulnerable even as they observe the horror of the fall.

—*Christine Muller*

References

Cauchon, D., & Moore, M. (2002, September 2). Desperation forced a horrific decision. *USA Today*, p. 5A.

DeLillo, D. (2007). *Falling man*. New York: Scribner.

Flynn, K., & Dwyer, J. (2004, September 10). Falling bodies: A 9/11 image etched in pain. *The New York Times*, pp. A1, B8.

Junod, T. (2003, Sept.) The falling man. *Esquire*, 177–183.

Lisberg, A. (2005, June 16). Go jump in a lake, pal! 9-11 families rage at phtog's fake plunges. *Daily News*, p. 5.

Lisberg, A. (2005, June 17). "Artist" sorry for stunt. *Daily News*, p. 7.

Marlan, T. (2005, June 10). To leap without faith. *Chicago Reader*, p. 1, 28–29.

Skarbakka, K. (2008). Artist statement. Retrieved from http://www.skarbakka.com/

SPOTLIGHT ESSAY/VISUAL CULTURE: FEAR AND THE VISUAL ARTIST IN POST-9/11 UNITED STATES

New York, a historical gateway to immigrants, would appear to be the most democratic and welcoming of U.S. cities. The subject of books, films, comics, and television shows, New York City has been romanticized in its many visual renderings from Woody Allen to Robert Frank. It is not a stretch to say that New York City remains the most photographed city in the world.

But for how long? In the aftermath of September 11 and the implementation of the USA Patriot Act, the city of New York became wary of photographers, both amateur and professional. Capturing the city's public spaces on film, without the proper permit or insurance, is now subject to a fine or arrest in post-9/11 New York City. The Mayor's Office of Film, Theater and Broadcasting (MOFTB), prohibits filmmakers from shooting without a permit and a $1 million insurance policy. These restrictions place particular constraints on the practice of street photography, the art of documenting people or objects, and their relationship or interaction with public spaces. Such spontaneous art has been replaced by a fear of how photographs of subways, train stations, and public byways might be used for malicious purposes.

Because photography is an art form that comes closer than any other to depicting reality, it can also be construed as an artistic form that needs to be controlled. Yet, photography cannot be wholly contained by government restriction or regulation. Instead, the MOFTB's fear of the unknown may be the only reason such rules exist, since their reasons for these restrictions are articulated merely as "safety from terrorism." This murky, vague language is echoed in the USA Patriot Act, the legislation that informs the MOFTB, which defines domestic terrorism in part in part as: "activities that-(B) *appear to be intended:* [emphasis added] (i) to intimidate or coerce a civilian population; (ii) to influence the policy of a government by intimidation or coercion" (Layoun, 2006, p. 48)

As Mary Layoun (2006) writes in *Visions of Security,* "if intention is ascribed to appearance, then the distinction rests on the interpretive abilities of whoever decides what intention is indicated by what appearance" (p. 49). Thus the rules are vaguely spelled out, allowing room for those who enforce them to misinterpret and potentially misuse such parameters. Layoun expands her argument by noting "most particularly, characterizing intention on the basis of appearance at least implicitly offers a chilling invitation to potentially virulent discrimination against any outsiders, strangers, and foreigners whose appearance is notable" (p. 49).

In such a paranoid climate, consider the plight of three contemporary visual artists. Rakesh Sharma, an award-winning documentary filmmaker from Mumbai, India, visited New York City in 2005 to screen his film *The Final Solution.* Taking advantage of his New York City location, Sharma decided to shoot footage of taxicabs as they were leaving Madison Square Garden. While white tourists continued to snap away, Sharma was arrested and searched without a warrant. Sharma's case is ironic, as his photographic goal was part of a larger project to document changes in the lives of taxi drivers and ordinary New York citizens in the wake of September 11.

Equally disturbing is the racial profiling that occurred when Arun Wiita, a graduate student at Columbia University, photographed a subway station in 2006. As he explained to the officer that handcuffed and detained him, his photographs were not part of a terrorist plot, but part of a project to "document how the subway is an integral part of the fabric of life in the city" (Carlson, 2007, p. 1). Yet, his project was illegal according to city guidelines.

For more than 20 years, film essayist Jem Cohen has been collecting footage for his portraits of people and places, crafting such films as *Benjamin Smoke, Lost Book Found,* and *Chain.* These films would not exist if not for Cohen's extensive and obsessive use of street footage: countless shots of city streets, structures, passersby, bridges, abandoned industrial parks, alleys, and forgotten byways. Often, Cohen captures such imagery from the window of a moving Amtrak train—a practice that was halted by police one day in January 2005.

In the everyday acts of their creative lives, Cohen, Sharma, and Wiita were collectively harassed, arrested, and detained while cameras and film were damaged or seized by New York City police. Their crime? Capturing the city's public spaces on film. For Sharma and Wiita, their crime also appears to be the color of their skin, where both "intention" and "appearance" have been misidentified. Both of Indian descent, each cites racial profiling as the reason they were singled out amidst other photographers on the streets. Both have filed and won lawsuits against the NYPD. As for Cohen, his experience has led him not to file suit but to rally for artists' rights, creating a Web site and organization called "Picture New York" (subtitled, appropriately, "without pictures of New York") (Goodman & Gonzalez, 2007).

Ironically, many of history's celebrated (and often government-supported) street photographers—from Walker Evans to Robert Frank—snapped their photos in secret, hiding their cameras from their subjects in order to reveal the spontaneous human gesture, expression, or event. In contrast, Cohen, Sharma, and Wiita were out in the open with their equipment (as well as their intentions) on streets and in public spaces, capturing buildings and cars, and walkways and other inanimate objects, trying to capture the fabric of New York City in a way that only photography can.

In a 2007 interview at Democracy Now, Jem Cohen makes the case for street artists like himself:

> I would just like people to think back about the tradition of New York street photography. It's a tradition that's very much integral to the city . . . a tradition based on spontaneity. That spontaneity is not really separable from the art form itself. And these regulations, in attempting to form a framework that isn't really about public safety, would really be endangering an art form that is so much a part of New York. (Goodman & Gonzalez, 2007, para. 53)

These new rules threatened to lead to the extinction of street photography in New York, an art form that serves to communicate the city visual identity to the rest of the world.

Effective on August 13, 2008, the MOFTB modified their rules to ease restrictions on street photographers and documentary filmmakers. Now, "standing on a street, walkway of a bridge, sidewalk, or other pedestrian passageway while using a handheld device and not otherwise asserting exclusive use by any means, including physical or verbal, is not activity that requires a permit" (www.nyc.gov). Such news is a crucial victory for the visual artist, thanks in part to Cohen and his fellow New York City photography activists.

—*Rachel Thibault*

References

Carlson, J. (2007, December 10). Columbia grad student sues NYPD. Retrieved from http://gothamist.com

Goodman, A., & Gonzalez, J. (2007, August 2). Independent artists lead fight against proposed New York City regulations limiting filming, photography in public places. *Democracy now!* Retrieved from http://www.democracynow.org/

Layoun, M. (2006). Visions of security. In A. Martin & P. Patrice (Eds.), *Rethinking global security: Media pop culture, and the war on terror*. New Brunswick, NJ: Rutgers University Press.

Mayor's Office of Film, Theatre, and Broadcasting Adopts Permit Rules. (2008, July 14). Retrieved from http://www.nyc.gov

SPOTLIGHT ESSAY/VISUAL CULTURE: *HERE IS NEW YORK* AND *THE SEPTEMBER 11 PHOTO PROJECT*

In the midst of media-saturated representations of September 11, alternative visual responses to the attacks appeared in New York City, ranging from ad hoc shrines and vigils to public exhibitions of thousands of photographs taken by ordinary people. For many participants, the exhibits *Here Is New York* and *The September 11 Photo Project* were a "democracy of photographs" because the constantly changing displays in temporary spaces arose from community or grass-root demand and organization. The demand, in large part, was a result of a process: Cameras became tools with which the hands and eyes of beholders were able to record, represent, and enter into dialogue about the trauma of events.

Here Is New York opened in a vacant storefront at 116 Prince Street, SoHo, on September 25, 2001. There were four initial organizers: Michael Shulan, one of the joint owners of the building on Prince Street; Gilles Peress, photographer for the *New Yorker;* Alice Rose George, a photo editor and independent curator; Charles Traub, photographer and chair of the MFA Department of Photography, Video and Related Media at New York's School of Visual Arts. Photographers without imposed definitions of "professional" or "amateur" brought in their photographs to be scanned and saved as digital files, printed at a standard size on ink jet printers, and clipped to wires hung across walls and across the ceiling.

This was a free public exhibition, and anyone who wished to pay a flat fee of $25 per image, irrespective of the name or status of the photographer, could order an ink-jet print of their chosen "photograph." Resultant funds went to the Children's Aid Society, a charity for children of the victims of the attacks, such as illegal immigrants and restaurant workers. Large numbers of visitors caused the original closure date of October 15 to be abandoned and eventually extended to December 25. To accommodate the display of images, the exhibition expanded into the vacant storefront next door. By the end of 2001, more than 30,000 prints had been sold with more than 5,000 images submitted by some 3,000 photographers. A crowd outside the doors forced *Here Is New York* to reopen on January 2, 2002.

The exhibition space on Prince Street evoked alternative exhibition strategies, often in temporary storefronts, of activist art groups from the late 1970s and early 1980s. In 2001, *Here Is New York* was an alternative to mainstream galleries, museums, and publishing media empires producing images in newspapers and magazines. A Web site (www.hereisnewyork.org) and book version (George et al., 2002) constituted an "archive" for the project and its radical strategy. The temporary project also became an official exhibition traveling to galleries and museums, and there were unofficial displays in schools and libraries. The emphases on anonymity, digital standardized reproduction, unframed, and unconventional display, flat-fee purchase, and a choice of personal and Internet ordering, contributed to the exhibit's radical significance. However, corporate sponsorship of the official traveling exhibitions with their advertising logos on www.hereisnewyork.org compromised some of the claims for a true "democracy of photographs."

The September 11 Photo Project was cofounded by Michael Feldschuh, a Wall Street professional and amateur photographer, and James Murray, an artist and New York City firefighter. Feldschuh experienced shock, helplessness, and a compulsion to photograph,which was a common response by crowds watching the WTC towers fall. He also witnessed the spontaneous and unofficial vigils and shrines in public squares and outside firehouses throughout the city. Many of these were transitory, ephemeral, and subject to the vagaries of weather, unsympathetic removal, and, eventually, to the City Authority's decision to clear the shrines in places like Union Square. Feldschuh wished to preserve the culture of community response and site, and he aimed to do so in a space safe for display and viewing. He found a partially demolished gallery at 26 Wooster Street in SoHo, which was made ready in three weeks with construction workers donating time and materials. The *September 11 Photo Project*, which opened on October 13, 2001, with approximately 200 photos and six volunteers, aimed to "display, without exception, every set of photographs and words participants submitted" and to "welcome all who wished to see them" (Feldschuh, 2002, p. vii.).

Flyers encouraged people to submit photographs and any text, which were hung together as submitted, by a simple clip from a "T" pin sunk into the wall, to preserve a personal rather than thematic or chronological emphasis. The presentation of the art was informal, consisting primarily of changing displays dependent upon submissions, as well as loosely placing one group of photos and texts next to another. The evidence of accompanying texts reveals that the images had complex and diverse functions including the need to document, to confirm the "reality" of the "unbelievable" experience, and to share in communal mourning and reparation through image making. Neither the exhibits nor copies were for sale and, unless already signed, displayed anonymously.

More than 40,000 people visited *The September 11 Photo Project*, which closed on January 8, 2002, with the exhibition subsequently travelling to other venues in the United States. More than 4,000 items had been submitted by the closure increasing to more than 5,500 photographs and statements as the exhibition toured and attracted in excess of 200,000 visitors in its first few months. *The September 11 Photo Project* is now a permanent part of the Miriam and Ira D. Wallach Collection of the New York Public Library and has a presence as a Web site (http://www.sep11photo .org/html/home.html).

These two photographic projects were in contrast to the co-optation of 9/11 images by media and the "selling of 9/11" as a "commodity" (Heller, 2005). Images by photographers, ranging in age from younger than 10 to older than 80 years, offered alternatives to the consumer market in postcards, clothes, shop displays, advertising posters, and publications that mushroomed almost immediately (Sturken, 2007) after the attacks. Amongst diverse reasons for *Here Is New York* and *The September 11 Photo Project* (including mourning, loss, trauma, reparation, and the desire for community rebelonging), there is also evidence that they constituted attempts by participants to produce a cultural remembrance resistant to official versions of the events that focused on unquestioned patriotism.

—*Francis Frascina*

References

Feldschuh, M. (Ed.). (2002). *The September 11 photo project*. New York: Regan Books.

George, A. R., Peress, G., Shulan, M., & Traub, C. (2002). *Here is New York: A democracy of photographs*. New York: Scalo.

Heller, D. (Ed.). (2005). *The selling of 9/11: How a national tragedy became a commodity*. New York: Palgrave Macmillan.

Sturken, M. (2007). *Tourists of history: Memory, kitsch, and consumerism from Oklahoma City to ground zero*. Durham, NC: Duke University Press.

SPOTLIGHT ESSAY/VISUAL CULTURE: MADAME TUSSAUDS WAX MEMORIAL OF 9/11

On September 4, 2002, Madame Tussauds wax museum in New York City opened an exhibit entitled *Hope: Humanity and Heroism*, subtitled *Images of American Resolve, Strength and Unity*. This exhibit, unlike other portraits in the museum that focused on specific people, captured a specific moment in time—5:02 p.m., September 11, 2001. The *Hope* exhibit was not included in the Madame Tussauds formal brochure at the time, although it did have its own separate brochure at the entrance to the exhibit. Essentially a diorama, the exhibit featured the wax portraits of three firefighters, unnamed in the brochure, erecting a flag amongst the rubble at Ground Zero. At the doorway to the exhibit was an enormous sign, bedecked in an U.S. flag, with a placard directing uninterested visitors to an alternate exit. Next to the sign was a staircase that overlooked the exhibit space, where visitors could hear iconic patriotic music playing, such as "Proud to Be an American." The staircase led down to the floor, where several benches, reminiscent of pews, were set up for people to sit and look at the exhibit. Unlike any other room in the museum, the exhibit itself was raised several feet off the floor and was the only display in the room, aside from several photographs that lined the hallway toward the exit. The entire room was dark, while the exhibit was spotlit from several angles.

In the late-nineteenth century, wax museums like the Musée Grévin in Paris and Madame Tussauds London were popular because they gave visitors the unusual experience of seeing "familiar events, people and stories in exacting detail at a time when photographs were not easily reproduced and had yet to accompany newspaper reports" (Boyer, 1996, p. 14). The contemporary experience of Madame Tussauds is more often quite the opposite in that visitors see celebrities and scenarios they have seen dozens of times on television and in photographs. These wax figures are no longer proxies for media coverage, but rather validate and are validated by media coverage.

Although part of Tussauds mission has always been to record history, perhaps the most problematic aspect of the 9/11 exhibit was described in the *Hope* brochure: "HOPE captures our emotions in a compelling visual display centered around a lifelike wax portrait of the three firefighters raising the flag at Ground Zero. Visitors will stand with the firefighters as they stood at 5:02 on September 11, 2001." The suggestion that visitors could and would insert themselves into such a moment suggests that it is possible to understand the monumental event of 9/11, which was extremely diffi-cult for many people to comprehend. Also of concern was the fact that this oppor-tunity to understand or experience 9/11 was housed in a Museum that calls itself an "attraction," a term that implies a kind of fun or entertainment. Madame Tussauds, a museum dedicated to giving people the opportunity to take photos with pop stars and celebrities, all within the larger context of the corporatized, consumption-driven, cartoonish excess of Times Square, was an unlikely fit for the serious nature of the *Hope* exhibit. Indeed, because the mood in the room was reverent and mournful, rather than exuberant and entertaining as other rooms in the museum were, *Hope* was counterproductive to the museum's goal of being an attraction. According the *Hope* (2002) brochure,

> For 200 years, Madame Tussauds has chronicled history and current events by creating and exhibiting portraits of influential individuals and significant moments in time. Madame Tussauds New York decided to represent September 11 by focusing on the increased sense of patriotism and resolve of the American people. This exhibition is our way of thanking and honoring all those who devoted themselves to the recovery of our city and our nation.

Relying on this statement from Tussauds, the choice to represent this moment seems logical and even reasonable. However, there are plenty of "significant moments in time" that have never been addressed by the museum because, as seen throughout the rest of museum, it focuses on individuals, not "moments" that can be depicted in dioramas. Emotionally resonant with 9/11, Iwo Jima is an appropriate example of a historical moment, captured in a photograph by Joe Rosenthal and then recreated as a bronze monument located in Washington, D.C. Many people believed that the 9/11 photograph upon which the wax firefighters were based, a photograph taken by Thomas Franklin of New Jersey's *The Record*, was actually reminiscent of Iwo Jima. In other words, in creating the *Hope* exhibit Madame Tussauds had essentially created its own Iwo Jima-type monument out of the moment captured in the photograph at Ground Zero. Despite the potential to strike a chord with visitors, the uncanny wax figures unveiled near the one-year anniversary of 9/11—within the context of New York's Times Square—arguably fell short of the enduring significance of the Iwo Jima monument in Washington, D.C. The formal exhibit was closed within a year, and the three firefighter portraits were moved to another room in the museum, the Gallery, to share the spotlight with political leaders and religious figures.

Madame Tussauds *Hope* exhibit embodied a trio of interesting paradoxes as an attraction. The frame of the work, complete with U.S. flag and music, provokes a nationalism within a museum that prides itself on the universal appeal of its subjects. The form of the *Hope* exhibit deliberately provokes nostalgia (as did the source photo-graph) by hearkening back to an image from World War II within the context of an event barely a year old. Finally, the curators at Madame Tussauds placed a memorial-style exhibit within a museum that exists primarily for immersion and entertainment, in that this museum is situated in the sanitized realm of Times Square, the Giuliani-era centerpiece of a revitalized, strong, and most importantly, fun New York City. The result of these paradoxes is that the *Hope* exhibit created, however briefly, a memorial of mourning in the carnivalesque heart of the city; a scenario strongly out of step with its environs.

—*Lián Amaris*

References

Benjamin, W. (1968). *Illuminations* (Harry Zohn, Trans.). New York: Harcourt, Brace & World.

Boyer, M. C. (1996). *The New York panorama: A paradoxical view*. In Patricia Phillips (Ed.), *City speculations* (pp. 11–19). Queens, New York: Queens Museum of Art.

Madame Tussauds New York. (2002). *Hope: Humanity and heroism: Images of American Resolve, Strength and Unity* [Brochure].

SPOTLIGHT ESSAY/VISUAL CULTURE: MEMORIALS AT GROUND ZERO

The most complex 9/11 memorial site to be undertaken was in and around Ground Zero, the location most symbolically associated with the attacks. The earliest memorials were unveiled on the six-month anniversary. The first, known as "Tribute in Light," consisted of two beams of light shining straight into the night sky over Lower Manhattan. The beams, which were created by searchlights, evoked the presence of the Twin Towers, which had once soared above the city. Tribute in Light appeared on the New York skyline every night beginning at dusk between March 11 and April 14, 2002, and reappeared on each anniversary of the attacks through 2008. The other memorial, *The Sphere*, a bronze and steel sculpture that once stood between the Twin Towers and was recovered from the wreckage at Ground Zero, was installed in Battery Park with an eternal flame beneath it. A similar object, known as *Double Check*, was also reinstalled in its original space near Ground Zero.

A firefighter memorial, known simply as the FDNY Memorial Wall, was among the first permanent memorials at Ground Zero. Unveiled in June 2006, the mural is a bronze relief installed on the side of Ten House, the fire station adjacent to where the Twin Towers stood. The images on the relief tell the story of the station's 343 firefighters who fought to save victims of the attacks and died doing so. The name of each firefighter lost as a result of September 11 is listed on the memorial, which is a popular site among visitors to Ground Zero (Dunlap, 2006).

St. Paul's Chapel—originally a refuge for rescue and recovery workers in the days and weeks after September 11 as well as a site of spontaneous memorials for over a year—gradually returned to its original function as a place of worship. Its connection with 9/11, however, changed the church's role in Lower Manhattan. The pews on which firefighters rested and prayed—leaving their boot marks on the wooden planks—were removed and replaced with chairs that could be easily moved for different purposes. Most of the objects left by visitors on the fence outside the church were slowly removed and saved to be given to museums, while a select number were kept and displayed in the chapel itself to serve the needs and interest of visitors who made pilgrimages to Ground Zero (Wilson, 2002). In her book *Light at Ground Zero*, Kristen Sanderson (2004) documents the role St. Paul's played during the recovery effort and its gradual shift in the church's identity to include being one of the memorials at Ground Zero.

The development of a permanent memorial at Ground Zero was more complex. The site itself—the space where the Twin Towers had once stood—became a memorial almost immediately, drawing mourners from around the world. Visitors left flowers, messages, flags, and other tokens on the fence that had been erected around the site creating a shrine around the perimeter. In an effort to both contain and assist visitors in viewing Ground Zero, the city built viewing platforms in December 2001. At the same time that the platforms—set 13 feet above the ground and giving a clear view at the site—were being constructed to meet the immediate needs of mourners, long-term plans for the reconstruction of Ground Zero were being debated. In the first year, 13 exhibitions directly addressed the issue of what to do with the space. With the exception of a few architectural drawings, almost all of these proposals were photographic exhibitions detailing the events, people, and efforts at the site. ("Briefing: The Void at Ground Zero," 2008; Muschamp, 2001).

After much debate and discussion, plans for an official memorial and museum at Ground Zero were released. A design competition in which 13,683 participants from 63 nations submitted 5,201 proposals resulted in the winning plans for Ground Zero created by Michael Arad and Peter Walker. Entitled "Reflecting Absence," the design selected and being brought to life at the former location of the Twin Towers was selected for its ability to make "the voids left by the destruction the primary symbols of our loss. It is a memorial that expresses both the incalculable loss of life and its consoling renewal, a place where all of us come together to remember from generation to generation" (www.national911memorial.org).

Known as the National September 11 Memorial and Museum at the World Trade Center, this complex site includes both a memorial site—meant to recognize the site as sacred ground—and a museum—meant to educate and inform visitors of the events. The memorial is being built in the footprint of the Twin Towers, consisting of two massive pools of water and man-made waterfalls. Names of all those who died in the 9/11 attacks, as well as those who perished in the 1993 World Trade Center bombing, will be inscribed around the pool and a Memorial Plaza will surround the pools with trees and grass.

The mission of the museum is to honor the memory of those who died at the World Trade Center, to illustrate the toll terrorism takes on individuals' lives, and to reaffirm the importance of human dignity. At the museum, visitors will

> descend along a graduated ramp toward the core exhibitions at . . . the archaeological heart of the World Trade Center site. On display will be *in situ* features, including what remains of the structural columns that outline the space where the Twin Towers stood

and a section of the original slurry wall that held back the Hudson River on 9/11—a symbol of strength and resilience. On the final leg of the journey to bedrock, visitors will descend alongside the "Survivors' Stairs," the last standing vestige of the original World Trade Center complex near Vesey Street, which provided an escape route for many on 9/11. In the context of the post-9/11 world, the Stairs will remind visitors that, in some sense, everyone is a survivor of September 11. (www.national911memorial.org)

In the meantime, visitors to Ground Zero can explore the Tribute WTC Visitor Center, located next to the FDNY Firehouse 10. Opened with the support of the September 11th Families' Association, the Tribute WTC Visitor Center "creates a central place for information about 9/11 at the WTC site. Visitors learn factual information about the events on September 11, the identity of 2,973 people killed in the attacks, the unprecedented rescue and recovery operations, and the tremendous spirit of support and generosity that arose after the attacks" ("About Us," 2007, para. 2).

—*Sara E. Quay*

References

About Us. (2007). Tribute WTC visitor center. Retrieved from http://www.tributewtc.org

Briefing: The Void at Ground Zero. (2008, August). *The Week, 8*(374), 13.

Dunlap, D. W. (2006, September 14). No home yet for 9/11's "'Survivors' Stairway." *The New York Times*. Retrieved from http://www.nytimes.com

Dunlap, D. W. (2006, June 11). A hands-on tribute to the pain and valor of 9/11. *The New York Times*. Retrieved from http://www.nytimes.com

Muschamp, H. (2001, December 22). With viewing platforms, a dignified approach to Ground Zero. *The New York Times*. Retrieved from http://www.nytimes.com

Museum: Overview. (2008). National September 11 Memorial & Museum at the World Trade Center. Retrieved from www.national911memorial.org

Tribute in Light to New York Victims. (2002, March 6). *BBC News*. Retrieved from http://news.bbc.co.uk

Wilson, M. (2002, November 8). St. Paul's chapel near Ground Zero slowly dismantles 9/11 memorial. Retrieved from http://www.nytimes.com

SPOTLIGHT ESSAY/VISUAL CULTURE: NATHAN LYONS'S PHOTOGRAPHS

In the days following 9/11, residents of and visitors to New York left their mark on the city by creating and posting expressions of their emotions. Evidence of this can be found in the photographs of Nathan Lyons, who roamed the city's streets photographing, in black and white, drawings, writings, and signs that were hung around Manhattan in the aftermath of the attacks. The resulting body of work, *After 9/11* (Lyons, 2003), has been exhibited and published as a book of photographs under the same name. *After 9/11* contains 152 photographs that serve as a testament to the urge people felt to express themselves in a society that had been dramatically disrupted.

A number of Lyons's photographs include words and phrases people wrote in response to the attacks. These images show handwritten messages in formal or informal settings. For example, one photo captures a drawing of an eagle against a background of the stripes of a flag (Lyons, 2003, p. 39). The eyes of the eagle appear sad, suggesting the suffering that the bird (a symbol for the United States itself) experienced after the attacks. On top of the drawing, people have written their names and/or messages, including phrases like "GOD BLESS AMERICA" and "New Horizon." In a similar photo, Lyons focuses on a white sheet of fabric covered with messages, including, once again, the frequently repeated phrase "God Bless America," as well as the more aggressive message "God forgives the USA does NOT!!" (p. 110). These personal, public expressions of emotion reflect the widespread need on the part of ordinary Americans to convey their feelings—from anger to grief—after the attacks.

In addition to handwritten drawing and messages, Lyons also photographed signs that were hung or posted around the city. In one photo, Lyons captures the images of two different side-by-side signs (Lyons, 2003, p. 31). One sign is a request for donations to For Their Children, an organization established after September 11 to help children whose parents died in the attacks. The sign appears as light gray with dark sans serif text. There is nothing extraordinary about it at all, but it stands in sharp contrast to the other sign in the photo, which is for *Maxim* magazine's third annual real swimsuit issue. Taken together, the two signs suggest the competing needs of the city, indeed the nation, after the attacks. On the one hand, there was a desire to remain focused on what had happened on 9/11 and a need to care for those who were most impacted by the event. On the other hand, there was a longing to return to normal—even if normal meant *Maxim*'s third annual swimsuit contest.

Another theme present in Lyons's images is the theme of commerce. For example, a photo on page 35 depicts a building with seven signs on and next to it. Slightly above the center of the photo are images of the U.S. flag and the words "GOD BLESS AMERICA." Below these is a large sign reading, "PEEPWORLD," advertising DVDs, videos, and books. Other nearby signs advertise for a men's club, male room, books, and photography processing. Despite the patriotic somewhat Christian message reflected in "GOD BLESS AMERICA," it is PEEPWORLD—the world of shopping, buying, spending money—that visually overwhelms the other message. This tension is seen elsewhere, such as in the photograph of a poster reading "SUPPORT NEW YORK/ SHOP NEW YORK" over an image of the Statue of Liberty.

A further theme in Lyons's photographs is war. While the United States was not at war when the photos were taken, Americans knew that war might be the country's response. As such, issues of a future war emerge in additional photographs, such as in an image of an American call for war on a small poster in a window. Here, an illustration of Uncle Sam sticking his middle finger out is accompanied by the words, "To Those Responsible We're Coming for You" (p. 28). In contrast, a simple but direct antiwar example is present in a photo of a sticker stuck on an Airborne Express drop box that reads, "ATTACK IRAQ? NO!" (p. 163). The fact that images dealing with war appeared so soon after the attacks indicates the brewing debate about whether or not to go to war. Such images reveal that some Americans were ready to stop grieving and take vengeful action, while others—as captured in the photo of a sticker that reads "OUR GRIEF IS NOT A CRY FOR WAR!" (p. 42)—were dedicated to restraint.

Nathan Lyons's book of photographs, *After 9/11*, visually captures the spontaneous expressions of emotions experienced in New York after the September 11 attacks. By photographing the images and words posted by ordinary people adjacent to other signs that appeared in the city, Lyons has provided a record of the range of responses, the call for normalcy, and the early debate about going to war. The last photograph in the book suggests that these first responses would be played out in larger ways as the days and months went by. The photo is of a sign comprised of photographs of sheep and a quote from the infamous Nazi Hermann Goering about convincing people to go to war: "All you have to do is tell them they are being attacked, and denounce the pacifists for lack of patriotism and exposing the country to danger. It works the same in every country" (p. 167). The location of this photograph, as the last, seems prescient in retrospect as the implications of the country's response to 9/11 continue to unfold.

—*Timothy R. Gleason*

Reference

Lyons, N. (2003). *After 9/11*. New Haven, CT: Yale University Art Gallery.

SPOTLIGHT ESSAY/VISUAL CULTURE: *OUT OF THE RUINS* AND *THE DAY OUR WORLD CHANGED*

Artist Jean Holabird's *Out of the Ruins: A New York Record, Lower Manhattan, Autumn 2001* (2002), and *The Day Our World Changed: Children's Art of 9/11* (2002), by Robin Goodman and Andrea Fahnestock, provide two different examples of early visual responses to September 11. Holabird, a professional artist who was displaced from her home by the attacks, collected watercolors she had painted of lower Manhattan before and after 9/11 into her book. Goodman and Fahnestock, conversely, collected and exhibited the art made by New York City school children from ages 5 to 18 years. *The Day Our World Changed* is the book version of that exhibit.

In January 2001, nine months before the September 11 attacks, Jean Holabird began painting, in watercolors, what she called "A Window a Day," a project in which she painted images of New York through different windows "because they [windows] form a natural frame within which to compose" (p. 137). In the first pages of *Out of the Ruins*, Holabird includes some of her paintings that have the Twin Towers and World Trade Center in them. Forming a literal break in the paintings' timeline, on page 13 the pre-9/11 paintings stop, and a statement by the artist describes what she experienced on September 11. Displaced from her home four blocks from the World Trade Center, Holabird writes that as "an instinctive coping device, I drew. To me the buildings were still there, horribly changed, true, but as intrinsically part of my daily life as they had been intact" (p. 13).

The rest of the book focuses on Holabird's post-9/11 watercolors which, although similar to the "A Window a Day" format she used before the attacks, had some important differences. "After September 11," she wrote, "the scaffolding throughout the neighborhood provided 'frames' or 'windows' from which to capture the constantly changing vistas" (p.137). Interspersed with quotations from poets and writers, the watercolors focus on the changes at Ground Zero as the site was torn down and the ruins cleared. "When the last vestiges of the North Tower were dismantled," Holabird states, "my need to draw the site ended" (p. 13). The result is a collection of paintings—more than one completed a day—that chronicle the dismantling of Ground Zero.

The paintings suggest, in part, that while the act of destruction did not end with the attacks—months of demolition followed as Ground Zero, the Pentagon, and the land outside of Shanksville were cleared of the wreckage—out of this destruction would come new creation. The last image in Holabird's book gives visual voice to this very idea. A depiction of Park Place and Greenwich, made on December 14, 2001, the painting is made only of monochromatic gray tones. Yet this does not make the work somber or dark; rather, Holabird's representation is quite hopeful. In the background is a mass of wreckage that at first glance looks like a stand of trees in a forest, its volume emphasized by the graphic way in which Holabird has treated this painting; that is, it is a deep gray mass. Under and to the viewer's right is a bright, white, irregular circle from which emanate shafts of light gray. Like the structure, these shafts are simple, geometric forms. The whole then becomes a mass that radiates light suggesting that from the wreckage comes light and life. As Holabird herself states, "When the last vestiges of the North Tower were dismantled, my need to draw the site ended. What had begun as a chronicle of destruction became, at last, an odyssey toward acceptance" (p. 13).

In contrast to *Out of the Ruins*, which focuses on the work of a single, professional artist, *The Day Our World Changed* is a compendium of art by children from 53 New York City schools. The exhibit, which featured art selected by a panel of professionals, parents, and children, was displayed at the Museum of the City of New York on the first anniversary of the attacks. A result of a partnership between the Museum of the City of New York and the New York University Child Study Center, the exhibit—and its resulting publication—emphasized children's visual representations of September 11, as well as professional perspectives on how children witness violence and history. The book categorizes the images into segments—"The Attack"; "The City Mourns"; "Heroes & Helpers"; "Memories & Tributes"; and "Hope & Renewal"—suggesting a narrative of September 11 and its aftermath that children and adults might understand.

The artworks included in *The Day Our World Changed* are quite diverse. Some focus specifically on the event, but others are more concerned with people and emotions. Eight-year-old Sandra O'Hare's *An Unhappy Day in N.Y. City* is typical of those works in the section called "The Attack" (p. 52). The piece centers on a little girl foreground, with two other figures behind her. Between the three figures are swatches and splashes of color representing ground, smoke, and fire. In "The City Mourns" many of the artworks include faces with tears or sad faces. Meghan Hall Plunkett, the 16-year-old daughter of a firefighter, for example, created a flat mask-like face in which the open eyes contain not pupil and iris but stars and stripes, reflecting the U.S. flag (p. 66). Five tears fall from these eyes, and in each one is a different image related to September 11—the Twin Towers, a firefighter's hat with FDNY 220 on it, 10 faces, a police badge, and what seems to be an emergency services tent. The book concludes with a section meant to reflect the resilience of children; the closing image by Katie Profusek, *Squeezing of America*, ends *The Day Our World Changed* on a high note. In her own words, the 17-year-old writes: "My drawing is of a hand gripping America. This expresses the U.S.A.'s strength and ability to shine (even [after] the circumstances of the WTC)" (Goodman & Fahnestock, 2002, p. 124).

Both *Out of the Ruins* and *The Day Our World Changed* record immediate visual responses to the September 11 attacks. In doing so they offer not only narratives of the path from devastation to recovery, but perspectives on the literal and figurative changes 9/11 made to the nation's people and places.

—*Dena Gilby and Sara E. Quay*

References

Goodman, R., & Fahnestock A. (2002). *The day our world changed: Children's art of 9/11*. New York: Harry Abrams.

Holabird, J. (2002). *Out of the ruins: A New York record, lower Manhattan, autumn 2001*. Corte Madera, CA: Gingko Press.

SPOTLIGHT ESSAY/VISUAL CULTURE: POSTCARDS

Postcards with images associated with September 11 appeared on newsstands and stores quickly after the attacks. They disappeared just as quickly, replaced by standardized images and phrases that have come to be widely associated with the attacks. The presence of these early postcards documents some of the first reactions to 9/11. The fact that they were available for purchase for only a short amount of time suggests that the function they served in the aftermath of September was temporary, but significant.

The images on 9/11 postcards varied greatly, reflecting the chaos that ensued in American life before a standardized story of the events had been constructed. One card, for example, reads "We Will Never Forget" beneath a montage of images that include: Yankee Stadium crowded for a memorial service; Oprah Winfrey, Rudolph Giuliani, Hillary and Bill Clinton and others clasping hands and singing; a pile of World Trade Center rubble within which lays a large piece of wood containing the phrase "God Bless FDNY & NYPD" in bright orange spray-paint; three military officers carrying a casket draped with the U.S. flag; and a confused looking child standing before the flowers of a makeshift memorial as a maternal figure rests her chin on her hands while exuding a pensive facial expression. This hodgepodge of images registers how difficult it was, at first, to know what to focus on. What were the primary images that were associated with 9/11? Celebrities and politicians? The military? Rescue workers? While gradually some images would surface as the most acceptable, even official, in this early postcard what that image would be remains unclear.

This lack of focus is reflected in other 9/11 postcards such as those of the Statue of Liberty. A symbol of American values, Lady Liberty is often altered in some way on these early cards. In one card, for example, she sports medieval armor, holding a sword and shield. In another card, she sheds a tear before the smoking towers. Still other 9/11 postcards focus on the forgotten ephemera that adorned the city. The image of the exploding World Trade Center is one of the most potent images in the 9/11 archive, and it appears on some of the postcards. The apparent randomness of such images reflects the still unfolding story that the nation, with the help of the media, would gradually begin to tell itself about the events of September 11. Eventually, postcards related to 9/11 would include only images that were optimistic (as in those that depict the future World Trade Center site), or nostalgic (the New York City skyline with the Twin Towers in faded silhouette like a memory), or proud (the Statue of Liberty waving a flag). After the attacks, however, it was unclear what would happen and the variety of images appearing on 9/11 postcards reflected this uncertainty.

Phrases on 9/11 postcards were also unique to the historical moment. There were expressions that over time became closely associated with September 11, such as "We Will Never Forget" or "God Bless America." There were also statements that have faded from popular use, including "Gone but Not Forgotten," "We Will Be Stronger," or "America's Darkest Moment." Such phrases may have fallen out of use for good reason. Acknowledging that victims were "gone" was eventually replaced with the idea that we must celebrate heroes and remember those who were lost. Saying the country will be "stronger," suggests that it had been weak, an idea that runs counter to America's image of itself as a global leader. Claiming that 9/11 was the nation's "darkest" event sets it into competition with other grave moments, including World War II and Vietnam.

While some of the phrases found on 9/11 postcards are no longer widely used to describe the day, their presence in the immediate aftermath is a reminder of how devastating the attacks were to the national psyche. In the days and weeks after September 11, it truly did feel like the darkest moment in American history to many people on the streets. With the pentagon on fire and clouds of ash floating over lower Manhattan, America's vulnerability was revealed in shocking terms. People were suddenly aware that friends and family were gone from their lives. They clung to the memories as they deleted useless numbers in their cell phones. The phrases and imagery on early 9/11 postcards capture this intense pathos that historical distance erodes and time heals.

The 9/11 postcards point to the fact that, as soon as any event happens, a process occurs by which the media agrees upon the standard linguistic terms and visual images to refer to that event. It is a process of trial and error as words and images can be quickly embraced only to be later discarded as more acceptable ones came into use. The 24-hour news cycle has accelerated this process to an almost instantaneous agreement. The image of the plane hitting the World Trade Center, the subsequent orange explosion, and the terms "September 11" and "We will Never Forget" swiftly emerged as standard fixtures. Yet other words and images—used early on after an event takes place—capture those unmediated sentiments and therefore are an important part of understanding what occurred.

The 9/11 postcards' strange and unconventional representations of September 11 allude to this other narrative, one that perhaps only New Yorkers and Washingtonians experienced by virtue of their proximity to the destruction. It is a story of suspended subway lines, a thick layer of ash covering the city like a volcanic eruption, the deaths of friends, family, and colleagues, and survivors who grew grateful for the innocuous situations that flared on that fateful morning and prevented them from reaching work fatally on time.

Over time, postcards with 9/11 images disappeared from gift shops and news-stands, replaced by optimistic, nostalgic, or patriotic images and words. The cards' demotion to the clearance rack and inevitable disappearance tangibly marked the organization and simplification of September 11 images and words.

—Daniel Larkin

References

Adorno, T. (1991). Freudian theory and the pattern of fascist propaganda. In Bernstein, J. (Ed.), *The culture industry: Selected essays on mass culture* (pp. 114–135). London: Routledge.

Baudrillard, J. (2005). *The intelligence of evil or the lucidity pact.* (C. Turner, Trans.). Oxford and New York: Berg.

Eco, U. (1986). *Travels in hyperreality and other essays.* (W. Weaver, Trans.). San Diego, New York and London: Harcourt Brace Jovanovich.

SPOTLIGHT ESSAY/VISUAL CULTURE: SMITHSONIAN'S NATIONAL MUSEUM OF AMERICAN HISTORY

Museums faced a curious question in the days after 9/11. The attacks were clearly "historic," curators agreed. But no one yet had an understanding of the ways in which these events were or would be "history." Should they begin to collect objects as the events of the day, that is, fire at the destruction sites, search for victims, and so on, unfolded? If so, what constituted the important, significant components to document? What would future groups want and need to know?

A number of museums, both inside and outside of New York City, tackled these questions head-on. In doing so, historians found themselves in a rather unprecedented predicament: collecting, and even exhibiting, 9/11 objects at a time when most agreed that interpreting the meaning of the attacks was impossible. A look at the path charted by one of the museums quickest to the disaster sites—the Smithsonian's National Museum of American History (NMAH)—documents the challenges of this approach, the unique narratives of 9/11 that emerged through it, and a new museum practice born by the attacks—history that aims to be less historical (Greenspan, 2006).

As early as two days after 9/11, directors at NMAH began a series of museum-wide discussions about their options—namely, collecting now, or waiting. Collecting now promised opportunities to acquire critical, fleeting objects. But it also required historians to operate without the customary distance from the past that their work typically afforded. And this struck some as unique. Many were aware of the lack of emotional distance they felt. Not only did they see the Towers' complete destruction on television, but many lived around Washington D.C., and were, thus, even more intimately affected by the attack on the Pentagon. Further, most, if not all, of NMAH's collectors and curators believed that interpreting 9/11—that is, situating it within larger temporal and geographic frameworks and explaining why it happened—was impossible so soon after the attacks. Interpretations could only be partial and subjective—the opposite of their professional mandate.

Within a few weeks, museums decided that the opportunity to collect was too great to pass up. NMAH historians were at the Pentagon, the WTC site, and the field in Shanksville, Pennsylvania, by early October 2001. But the challenges of "collecting immediately" remained, and pushed historians to draw a subtle line: They would *collect* objects without *interpreting* them. To do this, the three historians kept the collection criteria narrow. They collected objects around "the event, rescue, and recovery"—acquiring objects that documented the scale of the destruction (twisted steel, broken telephones) and the unique recovery operations that followed (crushed ambulances, patches from FDNY). Historians explained that narrow, standardized collection criteria ensured objective collections in the present—and analytic histories in the future.

Untangling "collection" from "interpretation" was not as easy as it sounded, however. Indeed, challenges appeared in highest relief when NMAH shared its early collections with the public. Their exhibit—for the first-year anniversary—revealed that no matter how specific the criteria, specific histories emerge through collecting (while others do not). In this case, objects told of the incredible power of the destruction, and of the heroism, personal and national, that day. Further, the exhibit showed that, while a noninterpretive approach avoids linear narratives, it does indeed generate a particular sort of historical understanding—one that, in the case of 9/11, happened to compliment the politics of the day.

Because no one believed that typical, interpretive museum fare was possible, NMAH curators imagined something new—something "closer to an art show," as one put. Simply put, the exhibit would be commemorative, not historical. The museum explicitly avoided considerations of 9/11 as part of world events, which curators said that they, and the public, were not ready to consider. Instead, the exhibit, titled *September 11: Bearing Witness to History*, cohered around the different ways in which Americans witnessed the events—in person and on television. Curators showcased three types of witnesses: photographers who rushed to the scene; rescue and recovery workers; and the media. Select objects and images illustrated each of the three "witness" categories, with each category filling one exhibit room. The greatest departure was the presentation of the objects. Curators decided to present objects—including crushed phones and a photographer's camera from that morning—on plain pedestals inside glass boxes. Only the labels identifying them joined the pieces together, as did additional panels containing first-person narratives. Curators said that this display allowed the objects to be symbols rather than part of a linear narrative, and enabled visitors to interpret for themselves the objects' significance.

But, by sidestepping the bigger, political questions that made them expectedly uneasy, and by focusing primarily on heroic witnesses like rescue workers and the media, historians unwittingly generated a number of understandings of 9/11. First and foremost, the exhibit framed the attacks in particularly empowering, national terms. In this exhibit, personal and national strength triumphed over concurrent fears, vulnerabilities, and sadness. In addition, it gently corroborated the dominant, political understandings of the attacks. The exhibit's title, combined with an absent world context, defined "history" in a particular way—it became phenomena that actively unfold in front of people and for which few, if any, are responsible. For 9/11, this understanding of history had particular resonance. After the attacks, government officials largely avoided questions about why and how 9/11 occurred and instead suggested that the events were unimaginable and unexplainable (understandings that would falter with the publication of the Senate's *9/11 Commission Report* a year later). 9/11 became more like a natural disaster—something that just happened and that brings people together—rather than one with political underpinnings and consequences.

The efforts of museum curators and collectors to present an "uninterpreted 9/11," then and now, are understandable. Few seem willing to ask difficult, uncomfortable questions about why 9/11 occurred. And in many ways the exhibit was a great success. It received record crowds, prompting curators to extend the initial run for months. A travelling exhibit soon followed. But this approach *did* tell a particular, and political, story of the attacks. And, in doing so, it raises questions for museums. Public historians would likely readily acknowledge the roles that they play in shaping knowledge about the past. But, as 9/11 revealed, collecting and exhibiting history "literally as it happens" depends on historians de-emphasizing these roles and/or projecting them onto a future date. What kind of history emerges when museums actively avoid history-making?

—*Elizabeth Greenspan*

Reference

Greenspan, E. (2006). Scaling tragedy: Memorialization and globalization at the world trade center site. *Proquest, Dissertations and Theses database*. (AAT 3211076).

SPOTLIGHT ESSAY/VISUAL CULTURE: SNAPSHOT PHOTOGRAPHS

In the days following September 11, family photographs proliferated in public spaces and via the media, underscoring how Americans saw themselves before the attacks. Much has been written about the television and newspaper images of the Twin Towers, as well as the snapshot portraits of loved ones pasted around Manhattan. Photographs explicitly served as an emblem, and at times as a mirror, of an unprecedented national trauma. As Hirsch (2003) reflects on the photographs memorializing the New York victims of September 11:

> The familiar family pictures engage us in the "affiliative looking" that characterizes ordinary family photographs. We all have pictures like these in our own albums, and thus we invest them with a form of looking that is broadly shared across our culture. In this way, precisely, they become markers of loss: the loss of our children's childhood, the loss of a time before, the imagined loss of a mother, or father, or friend. They mark the ordinariness, the familiarity, the domesticity that for so many was interrupted by the attacks. (p. 75)

The haunting images of the attacks became affixed to the nation's photographic album and are now permanently lodged in American cultural memory. Nikki Stern, former executive director of the Families of September 11, stated: "Those pictures [of September 11] assaulted us. They still do. You're never free of it" (as cited in Friend, 2006, p. 73). According to Friend (2006), the photos were so powerful that the Families of September 11 organization created a Web site to "solicit snapshots for an online 'Resiliency Album' that would depict surviving parents and children enjoying positive occasions and rites of passage" (p. 70). The instinctive approach to share and collectively appreciate these family snapshots suggests a more positive form of remembering and a visual substitute for the harrowing images of the attacks. Snapshot collectors echo this approach in their search for "found" photographs from the twentieth century, gathering up everything from black-and-white prints to color Polaroids. Acquiring and presenting images of unfamiliar fellow Americans can foster a transition from inward to outward, as a photo that originally was rooted to a personal story becomes part of a cultural narrative.

Nearly a decade later, collecting and exhibiting the photographs of strangers invokes parallel psychological and sociological impulses to rediscover, understand, and preserve the America that Americans thought America was—to recoup what was considered specifically American about American culture before the 9/11 attacks. In the months and years since 2001, the function of vernacular photographs in everyday life remains unchanged. A photograph—whether kept, lost, or given away—can still serve as an artifact, heirloom, keepsake, memento, relic, souvenir, token, totem, or talisman. Rather than recovering the complete history surrounding each image, cultivating an a collection of anonymous photographs is an act of transformation, where each image is appropriated and recontextualized.

The immeasurable wounds of September 11 and its associated images demanded to be assuaged, and the movement to gather pictures of the America that existed before the attacks suggests a widespread cultural response. Preserving such snapshots offers an alternative visual archive in the wake of absence and national trauma. Within the space of photographic representation and recognition, collectors circulate and protect countless photographs that, so many decades later, can become cathartic, entertaining, and empowering.

—*Kelly Xintaris*

References

Friend, D. (2006). *Watching the world change: The stories behind the images of 9/11*. New York: Farrar, Straus, and Giroux.

Hirsch, M. (2003). I took pictures: September 2001 and beyond. In J. Greenberg (Ed.), *Trauma at home: After 9/11* (pp. 69–86). Lincoln: University of Nebraska Press.

SPOTLIGHT ESSAY/VISUAL CULTURE: SPONTANEOUS MEMORIALS

In the aftermath of 9/11, Ground Zero was noteworthy for a number of reasons. It was a surreal zone of spectacular devastation. It was the unintended burial ground of thousands. It was an historic site of international terrorism and the icon of the burgeoning War on Terror. It was a bizarre, at times vulgar, tourist destination. And it was a thriving, grassroots memorial and public space. Within days, city residents, families of victims, and tourists covered downtown's landscape with an endless supply of banners, teddy bears, and flowers. Structures intended to keep people out—from boards sealing entrances of office buildings to wobbly emergency railings—became foundations for first reactions and testimonies. It was as if thousands upon thousands of personal memorials could absorb, possibly overpower, the death and destruction marked there.

The aftermath of 9/11 was by no means the first time that individuals employed practices of spontaneous memorialization to respond to large-scale violence. But it marked one of, if not the, most cohesive and widespread expressions to date, and gave a newfound legitimacy to these practices. Since 9/11, we expect individuals to commemorate violence at sites of destruction through impromptu vigils and homemade objects—and thereby initiate processes of remembering faster than ever before.

The first instance of "spontaneous memorialization" dates to 1995 in the aftermath of the Oklahoma City bombing. In the weeks following the bombing, individuals throughout the country travelled to the area and hung homemade memorials on the fence surrounding the destruction site, including homemade banners and U.S. flags. Before this, such expressions were limited to clusters of flowers at the sites of car crashes and objects left at the Vietnam Veteran's Memorial. In the intervening six years, such memorializations assumed a central role in the aftermath of sudden violence. The death of Princess Diana in 1997 and the Columbine School shooting in 1999 generated similarly immediate outpourings at the sites of death. Since 9/11, such practices have marked the 2003 Madrid train bombing, the Virginia Tech Shooting in 2007, and the 2008 earthquake in Sichuan province, China, among others.

These expressions were not identical; objects reflected the varying nature of the violence, from terrorist attack to sudden environmental disaster. But in each of these instances, memorializations enabled a broader group—including, but not limited to, those who lost loved ones—to express sympathy and reflect upon the meanings of the violence. Handwritten commentaries—that it should not happen again, that justice will be achieved—entwined with condolences. Through these expressions, individuals joined and gave definition to a broader collective, and began to forge shared understandings of violence out of individual experiences (Haney et al., 1997).

The response to 9/11 at Ground Zero was similar. Within weeks, thousands of objects dotted multiple spots on its periphery; they would continue to proliferate through the summer of 2002. But they were unique in one significant regard: They included expressions from individuals both within and outside of the United States. Memorials—whether spontaneous or official—tend to define violence as belonging to local and national groups. But here, the displays reflected, and facilitated, conversations about 9/11 occurring across national boundaries.

Take for example, two objects that hung on the St. Paul Chapel fence—the largest memorial at the site—in June. One corner displayed a large U.S. flag. It read: "Made on 9-15-01 in Pleasant Hill, CA; Hung on SF Bay area freeway overpasses; flown here to NYC on 6-9-02 to share with all; God Bless America, we will never forget." Mirroring it on the opposite corner of the fence was a large Italian flag. Inside the three stripes of green, white, and red, an inscription read: "We'll *never* forget 9-11; a huge and warm hug by your Italian friends. Uniti insiemi per la pace [united together for peace]. Proud to be friend of America." Signatures from individuals from throughout Italy filled the flag.

Each flag tells its own story. The U.S. flag narrates its movement through time and space, linking individuals on one side of the country to those on the other. The Italian flag professes support to the United States, connecting individuals across two nations. But together, they tell a third story—of unexpected symmetry. The anthropologist Miles Richardson once described spontaneous shrines left at sites of violence as "gifts of presence;" through such shrines, individuals materially marked their sympathies and sadness as well as their physical attendance at a place of death (Richardson, 2001). No matter when you visited a place like Ground Zero, you would never actually see the full complement of thousands who had also walked the same path. But you would see their memorials. You would see the cities and nations for which they spoke. Countless others—origami cranes from Japanese school children, a series of flowers assembled by a family from Scotland, handwritten comments in Russian, Spanish, French, and Chinese—hung alongside U.S. flags, marking responses that transcended any one national context.

Of course, Ground Zero displayed memorials from select groups—individuals who both wanted to be in NYC and had the financial means to make the trip. Furthermore, many visited out of a desire to honor and memorialize. But even memorials highlighting select connections served as a reminder of connections in the broader sense—how remembering, like violence, crisscrosses people and places.

Indeed, Ground Zero's memorials were part of a broader conversation. By September 12, 2001, the doorways outside the embassies in Moscow, Berlin, and Beijing, among others, overflowed with flowers, burning candles, and notes of support. At 10 a.m. on the morning of September 14, 43 cities across Europe held a coordinated moment of silence. Thousands gathered in Uhuru Park in Nairobi that afternoon for a memorial. On September 15, the 60,000 fans and players that filled Tehran's main stadium observed a one-minute moment of silence in advance of the World Cup qualifying match between Iran and Bahrain. On September 16, individuals congregated in Amman, Jordan, for a candle-lit vigil in commemoration of the victims.

It is difficult to know exactly why so many, located so far from the violence, responded to 9/11 so immediately—both in hometowns and at Ground Zero. But one of the most unique aspects of such memorializations is that they gave "presence" to such individuals and collectives as much as they remembered 9/11. Spontaneous memorializations of 9/11, and the understandings they facilitate, reflect the increasingly interconnected relationships and policies of our times—indeed, much more so than many of the permanent memorials, museums, and monuments that have replaced them.

—*Elizabeth Greenspan*

References

Greenspan, E. (2006). Scaling tragedy: Memorialization and globalization at the world trade center site. *Proquest, Dissertations and Theses database.* (AAT 3211076)

Haney, C., Leimer C., Lowery J. (1997). Spontaneous memorialization: Violent death and emerging mourning ritual. *Omega, 35*(2), 159–171.

Richardson, M. (2001). The gift of presence: The act of leaving artifacts at shrines, memorials and other tragedies. In P. C. Adams, S. D. Hoelscher, & K. E. Till (Eds.), *Textures of place: Exploring humanist geographies* (pp. 257–272). Minneapolis: University of Minnesota Press.

SPOTLIGHT ESSAY/VISUAL CULTURE: THE TWIN TOWERS AS VISUAL ICONS

Even before the Twin Towers came into existence the idea of tall, looming buildings were part of the American psychic landscape through their imagined forms on the covers of pulp magazines such as *Amazing Stories* and *Wonder Science Stories*. They had been seen by millions of Americans in early science fiction films like Fritz Lang's dystopian *Metropolis* (1926) as well as the world's first science fiction musical film *Just Imagine* (1930). The future, it seemed, would be dominated by these constructions of American power and grace.

Huge, lanky, inspiring buildings have been part of U.S. twentieth-century history in ways it is difficult to remember. When Superman arrived on planet Earth in the late 1930s his ability to "leap tall buildings in a single bound" was what set him apart from other heroes. This ability was also the perfect metaphor to show that the power of this particular immigrant far exceeded the concrete, steel, and glass exhibitionism of the American empire.

The skyscraper has rivalled the cowboy and the Hollywood star as the most seen, most associated image of America. When Franz Kafka wrote *America* (published in 1927, but written much earlier) he had never set foot on American soil. Instead, he imagined his version of America entirely from pictures he had seen of American life in leaflets and postcards, and in consequence, the novel was dominated by images of luxurious tall buildings and a view of the sky constantly ringed by rooftops forming stone circles hundreds of feet above.

For many Americans, standing on the top floor of these buildings was the highest point above the ground that they had ever been. Staring down into the sprawling spaces revealed a previously unknown order in their cities. The sense of power in American achievement flowed both ways; look upwards to technological greatness or downwards to the avenues and streets below to see order imposed on chaos.

In the 1960s, New York was ready for a new statement of purpose, a project to literally dwarf the achievements of landmarks such as the Empire State Building and the Chrysler Building. After overcoming resistance from the commercial sector, who feared the sudden addition of thousands of new offices in a slowing economy, in 1972 and 1973 the Twin Towers were erected in lower Manhattan. The buildings quickly proved their iconic value as potent symbols of American culture, including the country's financial power (Caputi, 2005; Hatfield, 2008). Materials advertising the Twin Towers emphasized their nearly impossible height. As a 1984 brochure claimed, the Twin Towers were "[t]he closest some of us will ever get to heaven" ("Unfortunate World Trade Center Ads," 2008). Filmmakers adopted their image as instant shorthand for New York and, in 1976, they became "New York," widely as a result of the poster artwork for the remake of *King Kong*. In the film, Kong leaps from one tower to the other. The poster, however, depicted Kong astride the Towers as the beast challenged the civilized. Similarly, the blockbuster catastrophe movie, *The Towering Inferno*, may have been set in another city and in another building, but the ghostly outline of the Twin Towers was not hard to spot. It was clear to viewers which buildings the producers really meant.

By the second half of the twentieth century, pictures of the Twin Towers permeated popular culture. The buildings were seen in hundreds of movies and television shows. They served as the backdrop for the opening credits to of TV shows such as *Diff'rent Strokes, Barney Miller, Friends, Sex and the City*, and *Law and Order: Special Victims Unit*. They appeared on the cover of comic books like *The Uncanny X-Men #189, Damage Control*, and regularly framed the Manhattan skyline on news and magazines covers and graced music video for songs like the Spice Girls "2 Become 1" and Madonna's "Like a Virgin" and "Papa Don't Preach." Their bland grey blocky expanses reflected more than just the desire for more office space or the dream to reach ever higher. The image of Twin Towers had come to symbolize American political and commercial power (Hatfield, 2008). They stood for confidence and American exceptionalism. Rooted in their position as a center of moneyed power—the top floor of the South Tower even had a permanent exhibition on the history of money and commerce—the towers also became something else. They became targets.

The images that have become representative of the September 11 attacks focus almost entirely on the Twin Towers. Regardless of the perspective from which the Towers are viewed, images of the second plane flying into the North Tower, as well as smoke and fire billowing from both buildings, have become icons in American culture. Those images represent not just the real horror of the day, but "the vulnerability of the American public and the magnitude of the destruction caused by terror" (Hatfield, p. 63).

In the aftermath of September 11, America found it hard to see images of the Towers. The Twin Towers episode of *The Simpsons* wasn't "banned" as such; stations instinctively knew that it should not play. Even after the image of the Twin Towers was removed from the *Spider-Man* movie poster, movie-goers were warned that the film contained images of the Twin Towers. There was even a long debate as to the title of *The Two Towers*, the *Lords of the Rings* sequel. As the country adjusted to the new Manhattan skyline, images of the Twin Towers returned, especially in tourist sites like Battery Park, near Ground Zero, and souvenir shops across the city. Here tourists from around the world could see, and purchase, photographs of the Twin Towers prior to September 11 taken at all times of day, from different vantage points, and in a range of colors: black and white, sepia tones, or full color. Images of the Tribute in Light display, which lit up the space where the Towers had stood with two beams of light, are also available. Museums like the Tribute WTC Visitor Center, located near Ground Zero, sell postcards, including holiday cards, which sport the Twin Tower image with red, green, or blue backgrounds, in panoramic or regular views. The Towers also appear on commemorative coins, magnets, bookmarks, and posters (http://www.tributewtcstore.org).

Even in their absence the Twin Towers continue to be visual icons in American culture. The power, glory, and greatness of the American dream were temporarily tarnished as millions of Americans grappled with the implications behind "the hole in the sky." The phrase "Ground Zero" lost its reference to atomic bombs and instead came to stand for the place where the Towers could once be seen. The Towers had become symbols not of construction but destruction. Instead of acting as proud fingers pointing skywards and toward a prosperous future, they reminded us of our vulnerability. The twisted wreckage of the outer walls took on the vestige of a bombed cathedral shell. The Towers had already begun their transformation into the sacred.

The Twin Towers were once so tall that under the right atmospheric conditions, snow and rain could be seen falling upwards. Just as confusing, rain would sometimes appear blood red. Blood falling from the sky may be, for those thousands who have witnessed it, the most powerful iconic image of the Twin Towers.

—Brian M. Clarke

References

Caputi, J. (2005, November 1). Guest editors introduction: Of towers and twins, synchronicities and shadows: Archetypal meanings in the imagery of 9/11. *Journal of American Culture, 28*(1), 1–10.

Hatfield, K. L. (2008, Summer). Communication research: Falling towers, emerging iconography: A rhetorical analysis of Twin Tower images after 9/11. *Texas Speech Communication Journal, 33*(1), 62–73.

Unfortunate World Trade Center Ads. (2008, September 11). *Oddee.* Retrieved from http://www.oddee.com/

Selected 9/11 Books, TV Shows, Films, Music, and Visual Arts

9/11 WEBSITES

Flight 93 National Memorial (U.S. National Park Service): http://www.nps.gov/flni/index.htm
Here is New York: http://hereisnewyork.org
National September 11 Memorial & Museum: www.national911memorial.org
New York magazine's "Days of Terror: A Photo Gallery": http://nymag.com/news/articles/wtc/gallery/
Pentagon Memorial Fund: www.pentagonmemorial.net
September 11: Bearing Witness to History: http://americanhistory.si.edu/september11/
September 11 Digital Archive: http://911digitalarchive.org/
September 11 News Archives: http://www.september11news.com/
September 11 Photo Project: http://www.sep11photo.org/html/home.html
September 11: Screenshot Archive of Online New Sites: http://www.interactivepublishing.net/september/
September 11 Web Archive: http://september11.archive.org/
Sonic Memorial Project: www.sonicmemorial.org
Time magazine's "Shattered": http://www.time.com/time/photoessays/shattered/
Tragedy: A musical gallery: http://www.kalvos.org/tragedy.html
Unwavering Spirit: Hope and Healing at Ground Zero: http://www.trinitywallstreet.org/congregation/spc/

ALBUMS

The Rising (2002), Bruce Springsteen
Halos and Horns (2002), Dolly Parton
Vigil (2002), Greenwich Village Songwriters Exchange
Walking Scarlett (2002), Tori Amos
One Beat (2002), Sleater-Kinney
Detours (2008), Sheryl Crow

ARTWORKS

"Faces of Ground Zero" (2001), Joe McNally
"Even the Birds were on Fire" (2001), Brooklyn Artists Alliance
Before and After 9/11 (2001), James Gilroy
Double Check (rededicated 2002), J. Seward Johnson
The Sphere (rededicated 2002), Fritz Koenig
Tumbling Woman (2002), Eric Fischl
Drawn Together (2002), Joan Waters
Poster Project (2002), Hans Haacke
Grace (2002), Pietro Costa
Missing (2002), Barbara Siegel
Forever Tall (2004), Hope Gangloff and Jason Search
FDNY Memorial Wall (2006), Viggo Rambusch

ART EXHIBITS

Here is New York (2001)
The September 11 Photo Project (2001)
Reactions at Exit Art (2001)
The Day Our World Changed (2002)
Tiles for America (2002)
The 9-11 Sculpture Project (2002)
Witness and Response: September 11 Acquisitions at the Library of Congress (2002)
September 11: Bearing Witness to History, Smithsonian Institution (2002)
Missing: Last Seen at the World Trade Center, September 11, 2001 (2002)
The Art of 9/11 (2005)

DOCUMENTARY FILMS

Underground Zero (2001)
9/11 (2002)
7 Days in September (2002)
September 11 (2002)
The First 24 Hours (2002)
Collateral Damages (2004)
Fahrenheit 9/11 (2004)
Saint of 9/11: The True Story of Father Mychal Judge (2006)
Strange Culture (2007)
Brothers Lost: Stories of 9/11 (2007)
Vito After: A 9/11 Responder Copes in the Aftermath (2008)

FICTION

The Guys (2001), Anne Nelson
On That Day: A Book of Hope for Children (2001), Andrea Patel
Poetry after 9/11: An Anthology of New York Poets (2002), Dennis Loy Johnson
September 12th: We Knew Everything Would be All Right (2002), Scholastic
The Amazing Spider-Man, #36 (2002), J. Michael Straczynski, John Romita, Jr.,
     and Scott Hanna
110 Stories: New York Writes after September 11 (2002), Ulirch Baer
The Little Chapel That Stood (2003), A. B. Curtiss
The Man Who Walked Between the Towers (2003), Mordicai Gerstein
One Tuesday Morning (2003), Karen Kingsbury
The Insistence of Beauty (2004), Stephen Dunn
Windows on the World (2004), Frédéric Beigbeder
In the Shadow of No Towers (2004), Art Spiegelman
September Roses (2004), Jeanette Winter
T. Bear's Tale: Hugs Across America (2004), Susan Lucarelli
Extremely Loud and Incredibly Close (2005), Jonathan Safran Foer
The Days of Awe (2005), Hugh Nissenson
The Emperor's Children (2006), Claire Messud
A Disorder Peculiar to the Country (2006), Ken Kalfus
Falling Man (2007), Don DeLillo
The Terror Dream: Fear and Fantasy in Post-9/11 America (2007), Susan Faludi
American Widow (2008), Alissa Torres
In the Garden of Last Days (2008), Andre Dubus
Netherland (2008), Joseph O'Neill

FILMS

The Guys (2002)
United 93 (2006)
World Trade Center (2006)

NONFICTION

New York September 11 (2001), David Halberstam
"In the Ruins of the Future" (2001), Don DeLillo
One Nation: America Remembers September 11 (2001), Life Magazine
September 11, 2001: A Record of Tragedy, Heroism, and Hope (2001), the Editors of *New York
     Magazine*
September 11: A Testimony (2001), Staff of Reuters
America's Heroes (2001), Sports Publishing, Inc.

A New World Trade Center: Design Proposals from the World's Leading Architects (2002), Max Protetch

September 11, 2001: American Writers Respond (2002), William Heyen

September 11: An Oral History (2002), Dean Murphy

What We Saw: The Events of September 11, 2001, in Words, Pictures, and Video and Report from Ground Zero (2002), Dan Rather and Susan Ellingwood

The Day America Cried (2002), Terri J. Schwartz

Here Is New York: A Democracy of Photographs (2002), Gilles Peress, Michael Shulan, Charles Traub, and Alice Rose George

Longitudes and Attitudes: Exploring the World after September 11 (2002), Thomas Friedman

Men of Steel: The Story of the Family That Built the World Trade Center (2002), Karl Koch III and Richard Firstman

Never Forget: An Oral History of September 11, 2001 (2002), Mitchell Fink

Out of the Blue: The Narrative of September 11, 2001 (2002), Richard Bernstein and *The New York Times*

Portraits 9/11/01: The Collected "Portraits of Grief" from the New York Times (2003), *The New York Times*

The 9/11 Commission Report: Final Report of the National Commission on Terrorist Acts upon the United States (2004), National Commission on Terrorist Acts upon the United States.

Wake-Up Call: The Political Education of a 9/11 Widow (2006), Kristen Breitweiser

The 9/11 Report: A Graphic Adaptation (2006), Sid Jacobson and Ernie Colon

Touching History: The Untold Story of the Drama That Unfolded in the Skies over America on 9/11 (2008), Lynn Spencer

SINGLE TRACKS

"Freedom" (2001), Paul McCartney

"Self Evident" (2001), Ani Difranco

"Let's Roll" (2001), Neil Young

"What More Can I Give" (2001), Michael Jackson and friends

"Where Were You When The World Stopped Turning/Do You Remember " (2001), Alan Jackson

"Rules" (2002), Wu-Tang Clan

"Undivided" (2002), Bon Jovi

"Skylines and Turnstiles" (2002), My Chemical Romance

"911 for Peace" (2002), Anti-Flag

"Courtesy of the Red, White and Blue" (2002), Toby Keith

"Firehouse" (2002), Christine Lavin

"The Bravest" (2003), Tom Paxton

"One Last Time" (2003), Dusty Drake

"Have You Forgotten? " (2003), Darryl Worley

"When the Eagle Cries" (2003), Iced Earth

"What Would You Do? " (2003), Paris

"Bomb the World" (2003), Michael Franti and Spearhead

"An Open Letter to NYC" (2004), Beastie Boys

"Sacrificed Sons" (2005), Dream Theater
"On That Day" (2006), Leonard Cohen
"If This Is Goodbye" (2006), Mark Knopfler
"The Evil Has Landed " (2008), Testament

TV/VIDEO DOCUMENTARIES

World Trade Center—In Memoriam (2001), A&E Home Video
America 9/11: We Will Never Forget (2001), Media Vision Entertainment Group
First Response (2001), The History Channel
The 11th of September, Bill Moyers in Conversation (2001), New Video Group
ABC News Primetime 63 Reasons to Hope: The Babies of 9/11 (2001; DVD 2007), ABC News
Tales from Ground Zero (2001), Animal Planet
In Memoriam—New York City 9/11/01 (2002), HBO Home Video
America Rebuilds (2002), PBS
Heroes of Ground Zero (2002), PBS
The Day the Towers Fell (2002), The History Channel
Portraits of Grief (2002), Discovery Channel
Frontline: Faith and Doubt at Ground Zero (2002), PBS
Clear the Skies—9/11 Air Defense (2002), BBC Warner
Telling Nicholas (2002), HBO
New York Firefighters: The Brotherhood of 9/11 (2002), Discovery Channel
CNN Tribute: America Remembers (2002), Warner Brothers
War on Terror: A Year in Review (2002), The History Channel
Portrait of a Terrorist: Mohamed Atta (2002), A&E Home Video
Terror Tech: Defending the High Rise (2003), The History Channel
Suicide Bombers (2003), A&E Home Video
CNN Tribute: America Remembers Commemorative Edition (2003), Warner Brothers
Fireboats of 9/11 (The History Channel, 2003; DVD 2008), A&E Home Video
The War against Al Qaeda (2004), The History Channel
The 9/11 Commission Report (2004), The History Channel/A&E Home Video
Trapped in the Towers: The Elevators of 9/11 (2005), A&E Home Video
The Pentagon (2005), The History Channel
Man Who Predicted 9/11 (2005), The History Channel
The Road to 9/11 (2006), PBS
CBS Evening News: Special Edition (September 11, 2001; DVD 2006), CBS News
ABC News Specials: September 11, 2002: One Year Anniversary (2002; two-DVD set, 2006),
       ABC News
ABC News: Where Things Stand 9/11/06 (2006; DVD 2007), ABC News
ABC News Primetime 9/11 Babies: 5 Year Anniversary (2006; DVD 2007), ABC News
Inside 9/11 (2006), National Geographic
Miracle of Stairway B (2006), The History Channel
What Really Happened: Inside the Twin Towers (2006), Discovery Channel
Nova: Building on Ground Zero (2006), PBS
Metal of Honor (2006), Spike TV
Deadly Dust (2007), A&E Home Video

Ground Zero Search and Recovery (2007), The History Channel
102 Minutes That Changed America (2008), A&E Television Networks
Grounded on 9/11 (2008), History Channel/A&E Television Networks
A Nation Remembers: The Story of the Pentagon 9/11 Memorial (2008), 45 North Productions
The World Trade Center: The Rise and Fall of an American Icon (2008), History Channel/A&E

TELEVISION PROGRAMS

Third Watch, "In Their Own Words," "September 10," and "After Time" (2001), NBC
The West Wing, "Isaac and Ishmael" (2001), NBC
DC 9/11: Time of Crisis (2003), Showtime
Rudy: The Rudy Giuliani Story (2003), USA Network
The Hamburg Cell (2004), A&E
The Flight That Fought Back (2005), Discovery Channel
Flight 93 (2006), A&E
The Path to 9/11 (2006), ABC

Further Reading

Anker, E. (2005). Villains, victims, and heroes: Melodrama, media, and September 11. *Journal of Communication, 55*(1), 22–37.

Atkins, S. (Ed.). (2008). *The 9/11 encyclopedia.* Westport, CT: Greenwood Press.

Breitweiser, K. (2006). *Wake-up call: The political education of a 9/11 widow.* Boston: Grand Central.

Chermak, S., Bailey, F., & Brown, M. (2003). *Media representations of September 11.* Westport, CT: Greenwood.

DeLillo, D. (2001, December). In the ruins of the future. *Harper's Magazine, 303,* 33–40.

Dixon, W. (Ed.) (2004) *Film and television after 9/11.* Carbondale: Southern Illinois University Press.

Dunbar, D., & Reagan B. (2005). *Debunking 9/11 myths: Why conspiracy theories can't stand up to the facts.* New York: Hearst.

Faludi, S. (2007). *The terror dream: Fear and fantasy in post 9/11 America.* New York: Metropolitan Books.

Feldschuh, M. (Ed.). (2002). *The September 11 photo project.* New York: Regan Books.

Friend, D. (2006). *Watching the world change: The stories behind the images of 9/11.* New York: Farrar, Straus, and Giroux.

Gengaro, C. L. (2009). Requiems for a city: Popular music's response to 9/11. *Popular Music and Society, 32*(1), 25–36.

Heller, D. (Ed.). (2005). *The selling of 9/11: How a national tragedy became a commodity.* New York: Palgrave Macmillan.

Holabird, J. (2002). *Out of the ruins: A New York record, lower manhattan, Autumn 2001.* Corte Madera, CA: Gingko Press.

Jacobson, S., & Colón, E. (2006). *The 9/11 report: A graphic adaptation.* New York: Hill & Wang.

Johnson, D. L., & Merians, V. (2002). *Poetry after 9/11: An anthology of New York poets.* Hoboken, NJ: Melville House.

Jones, R., & Dionisopoulos, G. (2004). Scripting a tragedy: The "Isaac and Ishmael" episode of *The West Wing* as parable. *Popular Communication, 2*(1), 21–40.

Junod, T. (2003, September). The falling man. *Esquire,* 177–183.

Keniston, A., & Quinn, J. F. (Eds.). (2008). *Literature after 9/11*. New York: Routledge.

Kirshenblatt-Gimblett, B. (2003). Kodak moments, flashbulb memories: Reflections on 9/11. *The Drama Review, 47*(1), 11–48.

Lampert, J. (2009). *Children's fiction about 9/11*. New York: Routledge.

McParland, R. (2009). Music in the post 9/11 world. *Popular Music and Society, 32*(2), 297–300.

Melnick, J. (2009). *9/11 culture*. Hoboken, NJ: Wiley-Blackwell.

National Commission on Terrorist Acts Upon the United States. (2004). *The 9/11 commission report: Final report of the national commission on terrorist acts upon the United States.* New York: W. W. Norton.

Norris, P., Kern, M., & Just, M. (Eds.) (2003). *Framing terrorism: The news media, the government, and the public.* London: Routledge.

Portraits 9/11/01: The collected "Portraits of Grief" from the New York Times (2003). New York: Henry Holt.

Project for Excellence in Journalism. (2002). Return to normalcy? How the media have covered the war on terrorism. New York. Retrieved from http://www.journalism.org

Project for Excellence in Journalism. (2006). How 9–11 changed the evening news: PEJ analysis. New York. Retrieved from http://www.journalism.org

Ritter, J., & Daughtry, J. M. (Eds.). (2007). *Music in the post 9/11 world*. New York: Routledge.

Sanderson, K. (2004). *Light at ground zero: St. Paul's Chapel after 9/11*. Baltimore: Square Halo Books.

Simpson, D. (2006). *9/11: The culture of commemoration*. Chicago: University of Chicago Press.

Spigel, L. (2004). Entertainment wars: Television culture after 9/11. *American Quarterly, 56*(2), 235–270.

Zelizer, B., & Allen, S. (Eds.). (2002). *Journalism after September 11*. London: Routledge.

Index

About the Editors and Contributors

The Editors

SARA E. QUAY, PhD, is dean of the School of Education and coordinator of the Endicott Scholars honors program at Endicott College. She is the author of several books, including two published by Greenwood—*American Popular Culture through History: Westward Expansion* (2003) and *The Cultural History of Reading: American Literature* (2008)—as well as articles on a range of topics such as pedagogy, leadership, student learning, and cultural studies.

AMY M. DAMICO, PhD, is an associate professor in the School of Communication at Endicott College and is the faculty advisor to the Endicott Scholars honors program. Her previous publications include articles on media literacy and health, children's media, and teaching and learning. She has developed an upper-level course on 9/11 and popular culture and integrates components of this subject in many of her classes.

The Contributors

REBECCA A. ADELMAN is an assistant professor of media and communication studies at the University of Maryland, Baltimore County. In June 2009, she earned her PhD in comparative studies from the Ohio State University (Columbus), where her dissertation research focused on intersections of visuality, terror, and citizenship in contemporary American culture. Her interdisciplinary teaching and research interests include visual culture, media studies, cultural studies of war and militarization, trauma studies, gender and sexuality studies, and political philosophy.

HEATHER MARIE AKOU is an assistant professor of dress studies and member of the Islamic Studies Program at Indiana University (Bloomington). Her current research focuses on contemporary Islamic fashion, particularly concerning the role of the Internet and other new media.

AMARNATH AMARASINGAM is a doctoral candidate in the Laurier-Waterloo doctoral program in religious studies. He is the editor of *Religion and the New Atheism: A Critical Appraisal*, forthcoming with Brill Academic Publishers. He has also published articles in the *Journal of Contemporary Religion*, the *Journal of Religion and Film*, as well as *Mental Health, Religion and Culture*.

LIÁN AMARIS is a performance artist and scholar currently living in New York City. Amaris has Master's degrees from New York University in performance studies and interactive telecommunications, and a bachelor of arts degree in theater from the University of Massachusetts Amherst. She has published on performance art, the avant-garde, gaming, and online culture.

ROBIN ANDERSON is a doctoral student in the Department of Communication at the University of Massachusetts Amherst. Her current research interests involve the role of immigrant labor in the food economy of the United States and its affect on culture. Other interests include the feasibility of photography as a tool for social and political change and the limits and possibilities of fair trade in building community.

GEORGIANA BANITA is visiting assistant professor in American studies at the University of Paderborn, Germany. After studying for a doctoral degree at Yale University and the University of Konstanz, she completed her PhD in Konstanz in 2009 with a thesis entitled *Literature and Ethical Spectatorship after 9/11*. She has published widely in the field of literature and visual culture and is currently at work on a second book project on the transnational contexts of American literature in the twenty-first century.

ROBERT BELL teaches in the Department of English and is the director of Writing Across the Curriculum at Loyola University New Orleans. His interests include popular music, twentieth-century literature, and writing. He has been known to play with a guitar.

ELIZABETH BENACKA completed her PhD in communication studies with a concentration in rhetoric from Northwestern University in 2007. She currently works as a lecturer at Lake Forest College, hopefully helping a new generation of students to analyze and appreciate the rhetorical nature of humor.

LORI BINDIG earned her doctorate in communication at the University of Massachusetts Amherst, where she was awarded the title of University Fellow in 2004. She is the author of *Dawson's Creek: A Critical Understanding*.

ELIZABETH BOJSZA is a dramaturg, director, and teacher. She has worked professionally in New York City, Long Island, and in community-based theater. Elizabeth currently teaches theater at Stony Brook University, where she earned her MFA in dramaturgy in 2004, and is the literary manager for Young Playwrights Inc, a theater company dedicated to fostering the development of playwrights 18 years of age and younger (www.youngplaywrights.org).

Ms. M. BOSAU uses her education and expertise in marketing communication to work for the greater good. As a nonprofit executive and development professional, she has raised more than $20 million for community-based nonprofit organizations.

BRIAN M. CLARKE is currently working on a study of history and politics as presented in the graphic novel. He has a masters degree in intelligence and international relations and a masters with distinction in scriptwriting for television and radio. He has worked as a professional writer and editor for more than 20 years.

AARON COOLEY holds undergraduate and graduate degrees from the University of North Carolina at Chapel Hill. He has mentored, tutored, and taught students in a range of diverse educational settings and previously worked at the North Carolina General Assembly. His writing has appeared in *Educational Studies*, the *International Journal of Philosophical Studies*, the *Journal of Popular Culture*, the *Political Studies Review*, and the *Southern California Interdisciplinary Law Journal*.

DAVID COON is an assistant professor at the University of Washington Tacoma. His research interests include gender and sexuality, cities and suburbs on screen, and the work practices of media professionals.

ELIZABETH CRISP CRAWFORD (PhD, University of Tennessee) is an assistant professor in the Department of Communication at North Dakota State University. Her research interests include advertising message strategy, advertising education, and mass communication and society.

LANCE EATON currently teaches at several colleges and universities in Massachusetts on topics such as comics, monsters, and popular culture. In addition to this, he has been a regular contributor to *Publisher's Weekly*, the *Library Journal*, and *Audiofile Magazine*. He has a masters degree in public administration and American studies from Suffolk University and University of Massachusetts, respectively.

ANNEKA ESCH-VAN KAN has studied theater in Frankfurt on the Main, Giessen (Germany) and at Stony Brook University (MA, Theater Arts). She is currently affiliated with the Graduate School for the Study of Culture at Justus-Liebig University Giessen (Germany), where she has been working on her doctoral thesis on political theater in the United States since 2001.

DEBORAH FINDING is a researcher at the Gender Institute of the London School of Economics and Political Science (LSE Gender Institute). Her work is concerned with narratives of sexual violence in popular music and draws on both trauma theory and feminist cultural studies, as well as several years of nongovernmental organization (NGO) work with abused women. She is also a freelance journalist, writing more widely on popular culture, with publications including *The Guardian* and *DIVA Magazine*.

FRANCIS FRASCINA's publications include *Art, Politics and Dissent: Aspects of the Art Left in Sixties America* (Manchester University Press, 1999) and *Modern Art Culture: A Reader* (Routledge, 2009). His essays on September 11 and visual culture can be found in a range of journals and in *The Selling of 9/11: How a National Tragedy Became a Commodity*, edited by Dana Heller (Palgrave Macmillan, 2005).

DANIEL R. FREDRICK is an assistant professor in the Writing Studies Department at the American University of Sharjah in the United Arab Emirates. He teaches courses that emphasize rhetoric, writing, speaking, and delivery. His research interests include rhetorical analyses, classical rhetoric, Cicero, and the teaching of writing.

TAMAR GABLINGER is a postgraduate at the Institute for Social Sciences at the Humboldt University, Berlin, and specializes in sociology of religion. She is currently an area chair for conspiracy theories at the Popular Culture Association.

TIM S. GAUTHIER is director of the Department of Interdisciplinary Studies at University of Nevada, Las Vegas. His work focuses on contemporary fiction. He is the author of *Narrative Desire and Historical Reparations: Byatt, McEwan, Rushdie* (Routledge, 2005) and is currently at work on a study of literary responses to 9/11.

SANJUKTA GHOSH is a professor of communication and of women and gender studies at Castleton State College. Her areas of research are South Asian representations in U.S. media and representations of nonmediated forms of South Asian popular culture such as food and clothing. Race, class, and sexuality are other important vectors that inform her teaching, research, and community activism.

DENA GILBY is a professor of art history at Endicott College in Beverly, Massachusetts. She possesses master's and doctoral degrees in art history from the University of Wisconsin and a bachelor's degree in English literature and classical humanities from St. Louis University. Her main areas of research include women, identity, and art in antiquity, early Modernism, and ancient culture, and the use of ancient art in contemporary film and advertising.

TIMOTHY R. GLEASON is an associate professor of journalism at the University of Wisconsin-Oshkosh. He holds a PhD in communication studies from Bowling Green State University.

LEE ANN GLOWZENSKI is a doctoral candidate at Duquesne University in Pittsburgh, Pennsylvania. Her dissertation focuses on the use of physics concepts in 9/11 novels.

ELIZABETH GREENSPAN teaches in the Harvard College Writing Program. She completed her PhD in anthropology and urban studies at the University of Pennsylvania. For her doctoral research, she investigated memorialization at Ground Zero during the first years after the attacks.

STARR HOFFMAN is the librarian for digital collections at the University of North Texas Libraries in the Government Documents Department. Starr holds a MS in library science and MA in art history and is currently pursuing a PhD in higher education, in which her research interests include distance learning, digital collections, academic libraries, and institutional use of graphic novels. Her position at University of North Texas supports her education and her lifelong position as a popular culture junkie, although she is more commonly referred to as a "geek."

KURT HOHENSTEIN is an associate professor of history. He has written extensively on U.S. political and legal history and recently published *Coining Corruption: The Making of the American Campaign Finance System*. He is currently working on a narrative nonfiction book about the event of September 11.

DAVID HOLLOWAY is a senior lecturer in American studies at the University of Derby, in England. He is author of *9/11 and the War on Terror* (Edinburgh University Press, 2008) and *The Late Modernism of Cormac McCarthy* (Greenwood Publishing Group, 2002), and coeditor of *American Visual Cultures* (Continuum, 2005). He has contributed widely to edited book collections on American cultural and intellectual history and has written for journals including the *Southern Quarterly, Comparative Literature Studies*, and *PUBLIC: Art, Culture, Ideas*.

STEFANIE HOTH studied English and American literature and culture, history and political sciences at Giessen, Germany, and Coventry, United Kingdom. In 2007, she received a PhD from the University of Giessen for a thesis on fictional media representations of 9/11. From 2004 to 2007, she was part of the research training group Transnational Media Events from Early Modern Times until the Present. At present she works as a teacher in Wiesbaden.

KEVIN HOWLEY is associate professor of media studies at DePauw University. Dr. Howley's research and teaching interests include the political economy of communication, cultural politics, and the relationship between media and social movements. His work has appeared in the *Journal of Radio Studies, Journalism: Theory, Practice, and Criticism, Television and New Media*, the *International Journal of Cultural Studies*, and *Social Movement Studies*. He is author of *Community Media: People, Places, and*

Communication Technologies (Cambridge, 2005) and editor of the new volume, *Understanding Community Media* (Sage, 2009).

A. A. HUTIRA teaches English at Youngstown State University. Among her favorite topics to write about are urban legends, popular culture, and Colonial America, especially the Salem witch trials.

LEE H. IGEL, PhD, is an assistant professor in the School of Continuing and Professional Studies at New York University. He is the author of a string of articles about sports management and its relationship to business, politics, and society.

LEE JARVIS is a lecturer in politics and international relations at Swansea University. His recent publications include *Times of Terror: Discourse, Temporality and the War on Terror* (Palgrave Macmillan, 2009) and articles in *Security Dialogue* and *Critical Studies on Terrorism*.

JULIA KAZIEWICZ is a PhD student at the College of William and Mary. She is interested in twentieth-century American literature and visual culture. Her current work focuses on the rise of postmodernism during the early Cold War.

ANTHONY J. KOLENIC researches the intersection of popular culture studies, disaster studies, and performance studies. His work has appeared in a number of scholarly journals.

SCOTT LADERMAN is an assistant professor of history at the University of Minnesota, Duluth. He is the author of *Tours of Vietnam: War, Travel Guides, and Memory* (Duke University Press, 2009).

DANIEL LARKIN writes about visual art for various online magazines in New York City. He lives in Harlem.

JUSTINE LUTZEL earned her MA in English from the University of Rhode Island and is working toward her PhD in American culture studies at Bowling Green State University. Her dissertation investigates the presence of madness in fictional texts as well as the quest for social justice for the mentally ill.

RYAN MALPHURS is a doctoral candidate at Texas A&M where he studies legal and political rhetoric.

CHRIS MCINTYRE has a PhD in political science from the University of North Texas. He has taught classes in American popular culture as well music and politics. His research focuses on public opinion and public policy.

MITCHELL MCNAYLOR (JD, University of Florida Levin College of Law, 2007; MA, The Ohio State University, 1998; BA, Louisiana State University, 1996) is a writer currently on an extended visit to northern Alabama.

ORA C. MCWILLIAMS is currently a PhD student in American studies at the University of Kansas. He has his MA in popular culture from Bowling Green State University.

JOE MOFFETT is associate professor of English at Kentucky Wesleyan College, where he teaches courses in writing and literature. He is the author of *Understanding Charles Wright* (University of South Carolina Press, 2008) and *The Search for Origins in the Twentieth-Century Long Poem* (West Virginia University Press, 2007), among essays and book reviews in a number of journals.

CHRISTINE MULLER is a PhD candidate in American studies at the University of Maryland, College Park. She explores her primary interest in cultural trauma through life writing, popular culture, and literature texts relating to September 11.

MARK NIMKOFF is a PhD graduate of the Institute of Communications Research, University of Illinois at Urbana-Champaign. Dr. Nimkoff's work examines museum depictions of media history, analyzing cultural dynamics that encourage and shape materialization of media historical narrative within museum space.

KATHRYN PALMER is a doctoral candidate in the Department of Communication Arts at the University of Wisconsin-Madison, specializing in rhetoric. Her dissertation addresses how September 11 is portrayed in film and television in ways that reflect and shape public sentiment and memory. Her broader research interests include examining culture as a political and historical force and interpreting the persuasive power of visual images.

VICTORIA PASS is a doctoral candidate in visual and cultural studies at the University of Rochester. She is writing her dissertation on the interaction between surrealism, fashion, and shopping culture in the years between World War I and World War II. She received her MA in art history from the Art Institute of Chicago, and her BA in art history from Boston University.

ENRICA PICARELLI is a doctoral candidate in cultural studies of the Anglophone world. He has a background in postcolonial studies. He has been working extensively on the topics of television and science fiction.

DAVIDA PINES is an associate professor of rhetoric at Boston University's College of General Studies. She is currently working on a book about comics and catastrophe.

STEPHANIE C. PLUMMER holds two degrees, a BA in art history from the University of Nebraska at Omaha, and a master's degree in popular culture from Ohio's Bowling Green State University. Her academic interests include museology, foodways, art, and children's culture; and her passions include art and cultural preservation, conversation, and community.

YVONNE D. SIMS is the author of *Women of Blaxploitation: How the Black Action Heroine Changed American Popular Culture* (McFarland, 2006). Her research interests focus on the intersections of race, ethnicity, and gender in popular culture particularly film. She is an assistant professor of American and ethnic studies at The Pennsylvania State University-Harrisburg.

ELIZABETH SPIES is a doctoral candidate at the University of California, Riverside. She is currently completing her dissertation on Cold War poetry and advertising propaganda.

SHARON SUTHERLAND is assistant professor at the University of British Columbia Faculty of Law. She teaches mediation, tort law, and law and theatre, and practices as a child protection mediator. Sharon's current research examines applications of drama and theater to conflict resolution pedagogy and practice.

SARAH SWAN is an LLM candidate at Columbia University. Her current research interests include torts, law and popular culture, and law and the humanities. She has written on a variety of topics related to law and popular culture, including the portrayal of female attorneys on television, issues of morality in post 9/11 works, and dystopic elements in popular texts.

MARGARET J. TALLY is a professor in the graduate studies Social Policy Program at the State University of New York, Empire State College. She has written in the area of gender and media, and looked at the ways in which female audiences respond to Hollywood representations of older women. Her most recent work is looking at how the abortion debate and unplanned pregnancies are being framed in contemporary Hollywood film and television programs for women.

RACHEL THIBAULT is a PhD student at the University of Massachusetts Amherst. Her research interests include activist documentary practices, film and censorship, and online film and fan culture.

ALISSA TORRES lives in New York City with her family.

BRYONI TREZISE, PhD is a lecturer in performance studies at the University of New South Wales, Sydney Australia. Her research investigates the performance of cultural memory in a range of social, political, and theatrical contexts. Her work has appeared in *Performance Paradigm* and *Performance Research*.

LLOYD ISAAC VAYO is a doctoral candidate in American culture studies at Bowling Green State University. His research is focused on 9/11 and sound, particularly ideas of the spectral voice.

GABRIELLE WATLING is an associate professor of English at Endicott College. She received her PhD from James Cook University in Townsville, Australia, and she works in the fields of post-Colonialism, literary theory, and British literature.

KATHLEEN WILLIAMS is a PhD student in the Journalism and Media Research Centre at the University of New South Wales, Australia. She is currently researching film trailers, YouTube, and online spaces.

ROB WILLIAMS, PhD (www.robwilliamsmedia.com) is a Vermont-based musician, historian, consultant, and media educator/maker who teaches face-to-face and online history and media studies courses at Champlain College and Sacred Heart University, acts as editor and publisher of *Vermont Commons: Voices of Independence* news journal, and serves as board copresident of the Action Coalition for Media Education (ACME at www.acmecoalition.org). When he is not raising yaks at his yak farm and playing with his two children, he roams the countryside with his guitar and laptop, singing and delivering multimedia keynotes and workshops on a wide variety of media-related topics.

KELLY XINTARIS is a graduate of the MFA in Writing program at the School of the Art Institute of Chicago. Her previous publications include poems in the 2008 annual issue of *Sojourn: A Journal of the Arts* and essays in the *Encyclopedia of Twentieth-Century Photography* (Routledge, 2006).

NICHOLAS YANES is currently a PhD student in the University of Iowa's Department of American Studies.

SHAWN DAVID YOUNG is a doctoral candidate in the American Studies program at Michigan State University. He holds the MA in American Culture Studies from Washington University, St. Louis, and the BS in Music Industry Studies from Appalachian State University, Boone, North Carolina. His primary areas of research include religion and American culture, popular music studies, counterculture theory, and post-World War II political history. He also contributes as a news editor to *Religion Compass Exchanges*, an online news source from Wiley-Blackwell.